A Commentary on the Didache
and on 1–2 Clement

Classic Studies on the Apostolic Fathers

Edited by Jeremiah Bailey, George Kalantzis, and Jacob N. Cerone

Volume 2

Classic Studies on the Apostolic Fathers serves two primary purposes. First, it would bring back into print important studies on the Apostolic Fathers. Many of these books can be difficult to find, prohibitively expensive, and often only available in poor condition. Second, it would provide translations of seminal works which have not yet appeared in English. Works would be chosen for the series based on the following factors: 1) Influence. This would include both works of continuing significance and works which shaped the flow of the scholarly conversation but whose theses may have fallen out of favor at the moment. The latter sort of book is often neglected despite the illumination it can provide on the nature of the current consensus. 2) Availability. The series would target books which continue to be frequently cited in modern scholarship, but which have limited availability outside of libraries. Out of print works written between the 1920s and 1980s are still frequently cited and can be hard for even libraries to acquire. 3) Cost of Production. The series would target, at least initially, those works which could be reproduced most easily including works in the public domain which are costly to acquire in printed form and translation projects of a shorter length. Each chosen title would appear in the series with a foreword written by one of the editors or a suitable contributor explaining the importance and significance of the work.

A Commentary on the Didache and on 1–2 Clement

Rudolf Knopf

EDITED AND TRANSLATED BY
Jacob N. Cerone

WITH A FOREWORD BY
Andreas Lindemann

PICKWICK *Publications* · Eugene, Oregon

A COMMENTARY ON THE DIDACHE AND ON 1–2 CLEMENT

Classic Studies on the Apostolic Fathers 2

Copyright © 2023 Jacob N. Cerone. All rights reserved. Except for brief quotations in critical publications or reviews, no part of this book may be reproduced in any manner without prior written permission from the publisher. Write: Permissions, Wipf and Stock Publishers, 199 W. 8th Ave., Suite 3, Eugene, OR 97401.

Pickwick Publications
An Imprint of Wipf and Stock Publishers
199 W. 8th Ave., Suite 3
Eugene, OR 97401

www.wipfandstock.com

PAPERBACK ISBN: 978-1-6667-4773-7
HARDCOVER ISBN: 978-1-6667-4774-4
EBOOK ISBN: 978-1-6667-4775-1

Cataloguing-in-Publication data:

Names: Knopf, Rudolf, author. | Cerone, Jacob N., editor and translator. | Lindemann, Andreas, foreword.

Title: A commentary on the Didache and on 1–2 Clement / by Rudolf Knopf ; edited and translated by Jacob N. Cerone ; foreword by Andreas Lindemann.

Description: Eugene, OR: Pickwick Publications, 2023 | Series: Classic Studies on the Apostolic Fathers 2 | Includes bibliographical references and index.

Identifiers: ISBN 978-1-6667-4773-7 (paperback) | ISBN 978-1-6667-4774-4 (hardcover) | ISBN 978-1-6667-4775-1 (ebook)

Subjects: LCSH: Didache—Commentaries. | Clement I, Pope. First epistle of Clement to the Corinthians—Commentaries. | Second epistle of Clement to the Corinthians—Commentaries.

Classification: BR60.A62 K567 2023 (print) | BR60.A62 (ebook)

01/23/23

For students of the Apostolic Fathers

Contents

Series Foreword
Classic Studies on the
Apostolic Fathers

THE LATE SCHOLAR OF early Christianity Larry Hurtado described the second century as "the Cinderella century," because it occupies the liminal space between the apostolic period of the New Testament and the world of the apologists at the end of the second century and beginning of the third. The post-apostolic era was a vibrant period of development as early Christians struggled to narrate their beliefs about the person of Jesus, decide the structure of their assemblies, find their place in the vastness that was the Roman Empire, and tackle the social issues that arose when a Jewish sect took on a massive influx of gentiles.

Some of the earliest voices of this period are found in the grouping of texts that is commonly called "The Apostolic Fathers." These texts are a record of early Christian self-expression composed without the limits of later creeds and bear witness to the hard work of identifying one's own theological boundaries or rejecting the boundaries that others have created. The presentation of these texts as a collection, however, is an artificial construct of scholarship, which is reflected in the variety of genres found within: the corpus includes epistolary material (both corporate and individual; both pseudepigraphic and genuine), a sermon, an apology, and an apocalypse. In many respects, it is precisely this variety that makes the Apostolic Fathers an excellent entry point to the broader second century.

Even though in the last few decades there has been an increase in interest in the *Apostolic Fathers*, the volume of scholarship remains small. There are likely many causes for this neglect, but two seem particularly prominent. First is the inherent difficulty of any transitional period to fit comfortably within the delineations of historical scholarship. To those who were trained in New Testament studies, the boundaries of that corpus have more recently tended to exclude the post-apostolic writings, while those trained in Patristics or Late Antiquity sometimes gloss over the second century in favor of the action-packed third and fourth centuries. Hurtado argued (and we agree), however, that the study of the second century makes the scholars working on either side of that century better. When we skip over these texts, we erase important strata of early Christian theological development.

Another significant cause of this neglect is access to scholarship. The student who wishes to study these texts closely is already faced with the challenge of greatly expanding their Koine vocabulary and, if they desire to engage in textual criticism, acquiring Latin, Coptic, and Syriac. Having accomplished these things, the would-be student of the Apostolic Fathers is then confronted by the reality that most of the secondary literature is in German, French, or Italian. In addition, much of the important English language scholarship is out-of-print and/or prohibitively expensive to acquire. Studying these texts beyond a surface level might, therefore, seem quite daunting.

The goal of *Classic Studies on the Apostolic Fathers* is to bridge this gap by bringing back to print some of the most important but hard-to-find resources in English and by providing translations of important works of scholarship on the Apostolic Fathers into English for the very first time. It is our hope that *Classic Studies on the Apostolic Fathers* will allow students and scholars to see for themselves the promise of these texts and engage this vital period anew.

—Jeremiah Bailey,
George Kalantzis, and
Jacob Cerone

Preface

JACOB N. CERONE

RUDOLPH KNOPF'S COMMENTARY ON the Didache and 1–2 Clement first appeared in 1920 within the handbook series titled *Handbuch zum Neuen Testament. Ergänzungs-Band* under the title *Die Lehre der Zwölf Apostel. Die zwei Clemensbriefe*. This volume, being one of the first comprehensive, verse-by-verse commentaries on a non-canonical text, marked a significant development in the German-speaking world of New Testament studies. Knopf's commentary, along with the rest of the supplementary volumes to the series, helps set the stage for future commentaries on texts commonly designated *The Apostolic Fathers*. Though certainly dated, Knopf's commentary on the Didache and 1–2 Clement remains an important work in the field, as Andreas Lindemann demonstrates in his foreword to this volume.

In the English version of this work, I have made many translation and editorial decisions that should be mentioned here. First, I have attempted to provide a translation that is clear and easy to read, despite the concise and often unclear original. This required the expansion of incomplete, abbreviated constructions or the division of lengthy constructions into multiple sentences. Second, where there was ambiguity in the German original, I have provided Translator's Notes (TN) in the footnotes. These notes include alternative translations or explanations for the translation provided. Third, when either Knopf or Lindemann cited German texts, I have chosen to translate these citations into English.

In addition to these small, rather mundane matters, I have made major editorial changes to the original format of Knopf's commentary. The German typesetter rarely used headings, line breaks, or paragraph indentations to guide the reader. For instance, in the introduction to each of the respective works (i.e., Didache, 1–2 Clement), new headings were demarcated solely with the use of Small Caps, making it difficult to see when a section ends and a new one begins. This has been updated to modern typesetting conventions. Furthermore, Knopf's fresh translations of the Didache and 1–2 Clement are presented in a unique but unfortunate manner. The translation appeared in the main body of the page and the running commentary in the footer. Line breaks were not used in the running commentary to segment the material. Instead, Knopf used Roman numerals and small caps in a somewhat convoluted, though consistent, way to indicate new sections and their relationship to one another. The result is wall after wall of text with little to no markers to aid readers as to how they should process the material.

In order to make the commentary easier to use, significant revisions to the format have been made. In this vein, the outlines Knopf provides for each ancient text is used to restructure the respective headings for the commentary. Introductions to each section have been taken from the commentary and relocated to the beginning of its respective section. Following this material is Knopf's translation of the text and then his commentary on it. Since Knopf did not consistently provide introductions to the main divisions he commented upon, I and the series editors felt it necessary to write brief introductions where they were lacking. This additional material was supplied by me, but in accordance with the views Knopf expresses throughout the work. Translator's notes appear in all instances where I have added such material.

Our hope is that these translation decisions and editorial revisions have made Knopf's valuable commentary more accessible and will not be viewed as a corruption of his historical work.

Foreword

ANDREAS LINDEMANN

1. Introduction

THE COMMENTARY BY RUDOLF Knopf, presented here for the first time in English, appeared in 1920 as a contribution to the series "Handbuch zum Neuen Testament" (HNT).[1] This commentary series was conceived at the beginning of the twentieth century by the church historian Hans Lietzmann. Lietzmann, who taught in Jena, consciously strived for the series to be a concise, strictly historical-critical interpretation of the writings of the New Testament.[2] Accordingly, the authors within this series came from the environment of the "History of Religions School" and "liberal theology." In the "Ergänzungsbänden" (Supplementary Volumes) authors also interpreted the writings of the Apostolic Fathers, not unlike the writings of the New Testament, but without further explanation of the designation "Apostolic Fathers."[3]

---

1. Otto Merk, "Knopf," 215 says of Knopf's commentary on the Didache and the letters of Clement that it remains "unsurpassed even up to this day."

2. On the concept of the HNT, cf. Hammann, *Paul Siebeck*, 170: The commentary series was designed to explain the writings of the NT "with philological precision and understanding for the history of religions context of early Christianity." On this, see the programmatic and detailed preface to the third volume: Lietzmann, *Die Briefe des Apostels Paulus*, v–x.

3. In addition to the commentaries published between 1906 and 1920, monographs on the history of early Christianity and its contemporary environment, along with a grammar, appeared within the series as "Ergänzungsbände" (Supplementary Volumes).

2. The Apostolic Fathers

The epithet "Apostolic Fathers" is often traced back to Jean-Baptiste Cotelier (1629–86), who in 1672 edited the non-New Testament texts from the time before the church fathers (*SS. Patrum qui temporibus apostolicis floruerunt*). However, presumably it was William Wake (*Genuine Epistles of the Apostolic Fathers*) who first explicitly used the term "Apostolic Fathers."[4] The writings collected under this heading were often received in the early church though without attaining canonical status. The assumption was that the authors named within this collection or later attributed to them had some associa- tion with the apostles.[5] Wake sees them as "the contemporaries of the Holy Apostles; some of them bred up under our Saviour Christ himself, and the rest instructed by those great men whom he commissioned to go forth and preach to all the world." He continues by saying, "we cannot doubt but that what they deliver to us, must be, without controverse, the pure doctrine of the Gospel; what Christ and his Apostles taught, and what they had themselves received from their own mouths."[6] However, the question of whether this title refers only to a temporal proximity to the apostolic writings or a proximity to them with respect to theological content can be answered differently. The Did., which was discovered in 1883, was shortly thereafter also attributed to the Apostolic Fathers. This means that the collection consists of writings from the time between 90 CE and 150 CE, which are not canonical, but which also do not give the impression that they were of "apostolic" origin by means of pseudonymous attribution.[7] And thus the statement by J. B. Lightfoot re- mains valid: "The term itself . . . is sufficiently elastic."[8]

4. De Jonge, "Origin," 503–5. Cf. also Rothschild, "Invention," 7–33.

5. The letter from the church in Rome to the church in Corinth was connected with the Κλήμης Paul mentioned in Phil 4:3. In the Muratorian Canon, the author of the extensive work "The Shepherd" is identified with the Ἑρμᾶς mentioned in Rom 16:14. The anonymous letter entitled "Barnabas" is attributed to the Barnabas mentioned sev- eral times in Acts and by Paul. Ignatius and Polycarp were considered to be disciples of John the Evangelist.

6. Wake, *Genuine Epistles*, 157 (cited according to de Jonge, "Origin," 504–5).

7. A controversial discussion in the literature is about whether it would be better to include the letter to Diognetus—which can be dated only with uncertainty—among the Apologists instead of the Apostolic Fathers.

8. Lightfoot, *Apostolic Fathers* 1.1, 3. His work entitled *A Revised Text of Clement of Rome: The Two Epistles to the Corinthians—With Introductions and Notes*, published in Cambridge in 1869, was a watershed in that Lightfoot comprehensively discussed the introductory questions, edited the Greek text, offered a translation, and provided a historical investigation and theological interpretation of 1–2 Clem. Lightfoot cited approvingly the thesis that the Apostolic Fathers were "not great writers, but great characters" (p. 7). Lightfoot deplored the modest interest in these writings, especially

3. Apostolic Fathers in the HNT

Although there have been numerous editions of the writings of the Apostolic Fathers since the seventeenth century,[9] these texts were hardly perceived to be theological works in the true sense of the word. They were rarely commented on in detail. Apparently, as "late" writings, they were not a topic for New Testament scholarship. For research on church history, they were possibly too "early" and perceived to be of lesser value than the Apologists or the church fathers. In any case, the decision to include their interpretation in the HNT was unusual.[10] "The fact that Lietzmann included the Apostolic Fathers in the handbook and had them annotated in the same way as the canonical New Testament was in accordance with the state of affairs—they were written largely at the same time as its later components—and was only consistent: when the environment of the New Testament was treated in special supplementary volumes (by Wendland and Bousset), it was impossible to leave the Apostolic Fathers aside."[11] According to Kurt Aland's judgment, the commentaries published from 1920 to 1923 were written "by outstanding experts."[12]

Commentary on the writings of the Apostolic Fathers within the HNT had a prehistory. In 1904 two extensive books edited by Edgar Hennecke were published: *Neutestamentliche Apokryphen in deutscher Übersetzung und mit Einleitungen* as well as *Handbuch zu den neutestamentlichen*

---

in the ancient church of the West, as seen in the paltry number of translations into Latin. "The Reformation brought a great change. The exigencies of the crisis turned the attention of both the contending parties to questions of Church order and polity; and the first appeal was naturally to those writers who lived on the confines of the Apostolic age" (p. 12). He detected, however, a growing interest in these texts within the nineteenth century when the authenticity and early dating of some of the canonical writings were questioned.

9. Bibliographical data can be found in von Gebhardt et al., *Patrum Aposticorum Opera* 1.1, xvii–xix. On the early history of reception, see Ulrich, "Apostolischen Väter," 256–67.

10. Kümmel, *Das Neue Testament*, 558n354: According to the archives of J. C. B. Mohr (Paul Siebeck), the original title of the "Handbuch zum Neuen Testament" was planned to be "Handbuch zu den Schriften des Neuen Testaments und seinen Aprokryphen."

11. Aland, *Glanz*, 32. Aland writes (in 1979!): "To this day, the Apostolic Fathers lead a marginal existence in the consciouness of even New Testament scholars (much to the detriment of many monographs and essays; the interest in them has been correspondingly low)" (32).

12. Aland, *Glanz*, 32. The interpreter of the epistles of Ignatius was Walter Bauer; the commentary on the epistle of Barnabas was written by Hans Windisch; and the commentary on the Shepherd of Hermas was written by Martin Dibelius.

Apokryphen, which included concise explanations and comments.[13] In the edited translation of the Greek text, the term "Apocrypha" is explained. What is meant is "historical sources from the oldest form of Christianity" that are "equal to the New Testament books as the oldest apologetic, gnostic, and martyrological works of the second century." Furthermore, it is stated that "in this sense there is no boundary between the New Testament canon and the extra-canonical (apocryphal) literature published here."[14] The designation "Apostolic Fathers" is not encountered in either volume. First Clement, Ignatius, Polycarp, and the epistle to the Laodiceans are found under the heading "Epistles." Clement and Polycarp are "disciples of the apostles" and Ignatius is considered to be a "faithful successor."[15] In contrast, however, in the second edition of the translation of the Greek text published in 1924,[16] in the chapter titled "Stimmen der Kirche" (Voices of the Church), 1 Clem., Barnabas, Ignatius, and Polycarp, as well as "the presbyter of Irenaeus" are explicitly compiled under the heading "Apostolic Fathers," and this is placed under the understanding "that those in question belonged as apostolic disciples or otherwise men of repute among the apostles, more precisely in the post-apostolic era."[17] The whole edition shows the strong interest in this special, in a certain way quite "open" era of church and theological history.

4. Life and Works

Rudolf Knopf, born 1874 in Biala (Galicia, at that time part of the Habsburg monarchy), studied Protestant theology in Vienna and received his doctorate in 1898 in Berlin. In 1899 he received his habilitation in Marburg in New Testament studies. He became an independent professor (i.e., less than full professor) in 1907 in Vienna, and later in 1909 became a full professor there. In the summer semester of 1914, he began teaching in Bonn, where he died on January 19, 1920, after a short battle with illness. Knopf "sought to combine the concerns of liberal theology with the research in the history of religions of his time and saw himself as a representative of that 'history of religions school.'"[18] He was especially in-

---

13. Like the HNT, both of these volumes were published by J. C. B. Mohr (Paul Siebeck).

14. Hennecke, *Apokryphen*, vi.

15. Hennecke, *Apokryphen*, 80.

16. Unlike the comprehensive edition of the translations of the Apocrypha, which continues to be used to this day, the "Handbook" has not been reprinted.

17. Hennecke, *Apokryphen*, 2nd ed., 480.

18. Merk, "Knopf," 215.

terested in the New Testament "in its transition to the patristic literature" and wrote commentaries on 1–2 Pet, Jude, and Acts.[19]

In 1899 Knopf wrote a monograph on 1 Clem.[20] The presentation of the manuscript tradition is followed by Knopf's own edition of the text.[21] Knopf then describes the "literary character" of 1 Clem.[22] He emphasizes "that we must not presuppose in Clement an exact and detailed knowledge of the Corinthian church-relations." We do not learn what the dispute was about in Corinth, "it was perhaps not so easy to describe briefly." The statements in 1 Clem. 4–38 are designed "to be a homiletic-paraenetic congregational address." In Clement's argumentation from the Bible (OT), one notices that the author has all the evidence "at hand, [and he] does not have to search for it while writing." Thus, 1 Clem. is not an "occasional letter," but rather "one clearly sees that the letter is intended to be read publicly for the edification of the congregation." The future fate of the letter shows that this intention was realized, as the reference to Dionysius demonstrates (Eusebius, *Hist. eccl.* 4.23.11). Finally, Knopf emphasizes the direct relationship between 1 Clem. and Paul's 1 Cor.

In the aforementioned edition of the text of the Apocrypha by E. Hennecke, Knopf was responsible for the introduction and translation of 1 Clem.[23] In the accompanying *Handbuch*,[24] he discussed the references to the OT, which occupy "such a wide space like that of no other ancient Christian writing." The author, familiar with the LXX, was presumably born a pagan, but was "probably a member of a Christian community for decades" and was among those who, according to the picture sketched in 1 Clem. 63:3, "walked among us without fault from youth to old age." Knopf's statement—"Beside the word of God in the OT, there is not yet a written NT text that serves as a second, equal authority, but rather 'the

---

19. In 1909, Knopf published his 123-page volume *Paulus* in the series Wissenschaft und Bildung, which was supplemented to some extent in 1913 (*Probleme der Paulusforschugn*). His volume *Ausgewählte Märtyrerakten* was reprinted several times with an extensive list of secondary literature.

20. Knopf, *Clemensbrief.* In the preface, Knopf writes, "The present work, in all its parts, owes its origin to the suggestions of my highly respected teacher, Prof. Adolf Harnack."

21. Knopf, *Clemensbrief,* 94–148.

22. Knopf, *Clemensbrief,* 156–94. The following citations are taken from this section.

23. Hennecke, *Apokryphen,* 84–112. The church historian Hans von Schubert was responsible for 2 Clem.; Paul Drews, professor of practical theology in Jena, was responsible for the Did.

24. Hennecke, *Handbuch,* 173–90. The following citations come from pp. 173–76 of this work.

Lord,' i.e., Christ"—however, is not supported by the evidence he cites.[25] The NT did not exist at this time, yet the corresponding writings were "for the most part already available and known to the author of our letter." Knopf takes the knowledge of 1 Cor and Rom as "certain," whereas references to other Pauline letters "must be presupposed more than they can be proved." It is "very doubtful" that Clement had knowledge of Col, Eph, and the Pastoral Epistles. It is, however, "very likely" that he had knowledge of 1 Pet. In 1 Clem. 36, Heb is "quoted literally, even if silently." Acquaintance with the other NT writings "cannot be proved," which is in a certain tension with the remark quoted at the beginning. Concerning 1 Clem. 1:3, Knopf writes under the heading "Gliederung in der Gemeinde" (Divisions in the Congregation): "The two strata of the older and the younger in the congregation stand opposite one another. From the number of the older ones, partly by election, partly by emergence of the individual as a result of charismatic gifting, a group of 'leaders' is formed, the ἡγούμενοι (or προηγούμενοι). The elected ones among this group are the ministers, the episcopes (and deacons), for whom the title 'presbyters,' 'elders,' according to their specific sense, is appropriate."

In what is probably his most important work, *Das Nachapostolische Zeitalter*, Knopf describes the historical development of the church and goes into detail about the writings written after the death of Paul up to "around 140 CE."[26] At the beginning of the chapter "Gemeindeverfassung" (Constitution of the Church), he emphasizes that the Didache shows "the closest relationship to the constitutional conditions of the apostolic age"; the "ministers" do not yet appear "as the guardians and keepers of pure doctrine in the face of a degenerated prophethood and teaching," and "the examination of the apostles, prophets, and teachers is carried out [*sic* unchanged] by the church itself." The church, however, became more cautious toward the pneumatics, and thus their number became "sparser."[27] In 1 Clem., which is presumably older than the Did., the data on the constitution of the church were "much more confused and ambiguous"; the theory of the church office

25. The words of Jesus cited in 13:2 and in 46:8 were "just as holy" as "the words of God from the OT"; Knopf noted at the same time, however, that the use of Jesus' words here is "rather loose."

26. The book follows the publication of Weizsäcker, *Das apostolische Zeitalter*. This "incision" separates "primitive Christianity from the early Catholic Church" (Knopf, *Das nachapostolische Zeitalter*, v). The book "was given 'high praise' by none other than Adolf Harnack" (Plümacher, "Knopf," 165–66). According to the judgment of Martin Hengel and Anna Maria Schwemer, *Geschichte des frühen Christentums*, 10, the book is a "work that has not been outdated even after about a hundred years."

27. Knopf, *Das nachapostolische Zeitalter*, 152–59. In the Did., there exists "an extraordinarily strong continuity with the conditions of the apostolic age" (159).

was "measured in contrast to the Did., a significantly more advanced one."[28] First Clement develops a theory of the origin of the apostleship and the consequent origin of the church offices, which, however, "is by no means to be regarded as historically grounded in any way."

In 1919 Knopf's comprehensive volume *Einführung in das Neue Testament* was published.[29] As the title already indicates, it differs considerably from the books of the genre "Einleitung in das NT" (Introduction to the NT), in which the historical conditions of the composition of the New Testament writings are presented. In Knopf's book, however, "in 388 pages . . . a tremendous amount of material is covered, and it must be said that the book gives a good overview of the whole field of knowledge in a compact and easily readable form."[30] In §19, Knopf presents the early Christian literature and he explains the term "Apostolic Fathers": "Their authors are thus to be designated as ecclesiastical writers ('fathers') of the earliest times who still had direct contact with the apostles, were their disciples, which in truth is admittedly hardly true for any of them (most likely still true for the author of 1 Clem.)."[31] In the chapter "Briefliteratur" (Epistolary Literature),[32] Knopf says of 1 Clem.: "The extensive letter of 1 Clement, full of character, is of special value to us because of the fact that, in contrast to so many early Christian writings, its origin and destination (Rome to Corinth) as well as its time of composition can be determined with a reliability that is nowhere

28. Knopf, *Das nachapostolische Zeitalter*, 160–72; citation comes from p. 160.

29. Knopf et al., *Einführung*. The following citations come from this edition. On later editions, see below.

30. This was R. Bultmann's view in his review of the book in *DLZ* 42 (1921). Knopf did not indicate the special shape of the book since there is no foreword or something similar. Bultmann writes, "I welcome the book as an introduction and hope that in this sense, i.e., precisely as an *introduction*, it will have a good effect" (254; emphasis in original). As a "classic" work from the same period, we can mention the work of Adolf Jülicher, entitled *Einleitung in das Neue Testament*. In this work, Jülicher addresses the writings of the Apostolic Fathers only in so far as they refer to statements that were regarded as "canonical authorities from ca. 70 to ca. 140 CE" (§35, [pp. 425–32]). The differences even in more recent times are seen by a comparison between Werner Georg Kümmel's *Einleitung in das Neue Testament* and Philipp Vielhauer's *Geschichte der urchristlichen Literatur*. Whereas Kümmel orients his work on the New Testament canon, Vielhauer uses the subtitle "Einleitung in das Neue Testament, die Apokryphen und die Apostolischen Väter" (Introduction to the New Testament, the Apocrypha, and the Apostolic Fathers) for his work.

31. Knopf, *Einführung*, 67.

32. Knopf, *Einführung*, 69–95. The Pauline epistles are treated first, then the post-Pauline letters within the NT, and then the letters among the Apostolic Fathers (1 Clem., the epistles of Ignatius, the epistle of Polycarp, and the epistle of Barnabas).

else attainable."[33] One can conclude on the basis of the information about the death of the apostles and the ministers appointed by them that the letter was written toward the end of the second generation, and the information about the recent persecution refers to the end of Domitian's reign or the beginning of Nerva's (95/96 CE). The author's name is already testified to by Dionysius of Corinth (Eusebius, *Hist. eccl.* 4.23.11): "The church commissioned a single, outstanding man from its midst to write on its behalf." His name may have been Clement, but "unfortunately nothing more is known about Clement, to whose name a famous corpus of pseudepigraphal literature . . . later attached itself." [34] In any case, "beyond the needs of the moment, he has delivered a literary work of art, which in many places completely abandons the form of occasional writing, and in broad homiletical lines of thought and exposition, which were familiar to the author from his other activities in the church, draws the ideal of the right way to life as a Christian."[35]

In the chapter "Kirchenordnung und Predigt" (Church Order and Preaching), Knopf says of the "Doctrine of the Twelve Apostles" (Didache) that it is "one of the most important and most curious writings of all early Christian literature."[36] It has "a very ancient character," "the church office, the bishops and deacons, is still very much in the background next to the charismatics"; this and "the sparse use of Christian writings, the instructions about the cult, the un-Pauline type of the Lord's Supper, as well as the absence of polemics against heresies" speak for "possibly a very early setting for the writing" which shows "still quite little of the 'Catholic' development of ancient Christianity."[37] The Did. should likely be dated to the period from about 90 to 150 CE. Rome is excluded as the place of origin for the text, as well as Asia "with its rapidly developing urban Christianity." Against Egypt as a place of origin is the statement in 9:4: "Grain that grows on hills does not exist in Egypt." Thus, the Did. may have originated "in remote areas of Syria, in circles of Christians who practice agriculture and animal husbandry and who still had close contact with the Judaism of Syria," as the Jewish echoes in the prayers at the Lord's Supper indicate.[38]

Knopf presents 2 Clem. in the same chapter.[39] This writing "of relatively little importance" is a sermon which "was delivered originally in

33. Knopf, *Einführung*, 89.
34. Knopf, *Einführung*, 89.
35. Knopf, *Einführung*, 90.
36. Knopf, *Einführung*, 134.
37. Knopf, *Einführung*, 135.
38. Knopf, *Einführung*, 136.
39. Knopf, *Einführung*, 136–37 (the following citations come from these pages;

a congregation during a Sunday worship service, probably following a scriptural (OT) reading." Knopf writes, "The *content* is rather meager," being mostly exhortations to repentance and turning away from the world. Second Clement "must have originated at a time before 150 CE," as the use of apocryphal gospels shows and the "often repeated reference to the imminent end, which is the mainstay of the paraenesis, along with the still quite undeveloped, strongly mythological speculation." Corinth is possible as the provenance of the composition, but Rome is more likely. In the congregation where the "Shepherd of Hermas, with his exhortation to repentance and his eschatological paraenesis was written, our homily, which is strongly related to the Shepherd in stimulus and thought, may have been written around the same time."

In 1923, the second edition of Knopf's introduction to the NT appeared, "carefully revised and expanded," with the assistance of Hans Lietzmann and "edited by Professor Dr. Heinrich Weinel."[40] The publication of the fourth edition in 1934—one year after Hitler's rise to power—was, as Weinel explains in the preface, "a sign that the book has proven itself to be an excellent, concise, clear and prudently judicious textbook even in a greatly changed theological situation."[41] The introduction "Der Theolog und das NT" (The Theologian and the NT)[42] was completely new, wherein now it was stated explicitly: "*The theologian stands in the succession of the apostles and is heir to their office as God's interpreters.*"[43] The theological importance of the always unfinished work on the New Testament is emphasized.[44]

In his HNT commentary,[45] Knopf naturally takes over many statements from his previous works on the Did. and 1 Clem.,[46] but now places

---

emphasis in original).

40. R. Bultmann offered a detailed review in *Theologische Literaturzeitung (TLZ)* 48 (1923) 394–96: "The new edition has essentially left the book in its old form; in detail, some things have been supplemented and improved" (394). "The book has proved itself and will continue to prove itself" (396). Subsequent editions appeared as Knopf, Lietzmann, and Weinel in 1930 and 1934, and it was reprinted without revision in 1949.

41. Knopf et al., *Einführung*, 4th ed., v.

42. Knopf et al., *Einführung*, 4th ed., 1–5. This section goes back to Lietzmann (cf. the letter from Lietzmann to Weinel on September 22, 1932 [Aland, *Glanz*, 712: "I even enjoy this."]).

43. Knopf et al., *Einführung*, 4th ed., 4.

44. Knopf et al., *Einführung*, 4th ed., 4 (emphasis mine).

45. Knopf, *Die Apostolischen Väter I. Die Lehre der zwölf Apostel. Die zwei Clemensbriefe*, Handbuch zum Neuen Testament Ergänzungsband (Tübingen: Mohr [Siebeck], 1920), which is the volume published here as a translation.

46. The introductory questions for the Didache are discussed briefly on pp. 1–6 in this volume, and those for 1 Clement are discussed on pp. 58–62.

them in service of complete interpretations of these texts. In the introduction to 2 Clem.,[47] a text on which he had not previously published an
independent work, Knopf states that despite the early attestation of this
writing as the second letter of Clement, it is "excluded that 1 and 2 Clement
are written by the same author."[48] Second Clement "is the oldest Christian
homily we have."[49] The author remains unknown, but one can conclude
"that he belongs to the leaders of the congregation, that is to the clergy, the
presbyters, who are responsible for exhorting the congregation."[50] As to the
provenance of the letter, the "early connection" with 1 Clem. "provides a
hint. The congregation in which the sermon was preached may be Rome or
Corinth."[51] The reference in 7:1 to the sea voyage (καταπλεῖν) and to sport-
ing competitions speak in favor of Corinth; 2 Clem.'s proximity to Hermas,
however, speaks in favor of Rome and Knopf emphasizes this point.[52]

5. Contemporary Research

5.1 Contemporary Research and
the Term Apostolic Fathers

The term "Apostolic Fathers" has been criticized in scholarly literature because these texts "do not represent a unified group of writings according to
literary-historical categories."[53] It is noticeable, however, that the large reference work *Religion in Geschichte und Gegenwart* (*RGG*) does not contain
an article on the Apostolic Fathers until the fourth edition.[54] In the series
"Schriften des Urchristentums" (Writings of Early Christianity), which
began in 1956, Part 1 bore the title *Die Apostolischen Väter*[55] and with it
meant "such authors of the early Christian era . . . who, according to the
present state of research, can be credibly identified personally as disciples
or hearers of the apostles, including Paul, and who, at the same time or
even without personal acquaintance with these apostles, are nevertheless
to be addressed in their entire teaching to a high degree as bearers and

47. See pp. 204–7 in this volume.
48. See p. 204 in this volume.
49. See p. 204 in this volume.
50. See p. 205 in this volume.
51. See p. 205 in this volume.
52. See pp. 205–206 in this volume.
53. Thus Drobner, *Lehrbuch*, 38.
54. Lindemann, "Apostolische Väter," 652–53.
55. Fischer, *Die Apostolischen Väter*.

proclaimers of the apostolic tradition, but are not to be counted among the New Testament authors."[56] In the two volumes of the series published later, the designation "Apostolic Fathers" was avoided.[57] A bilingual edition published in 1992 retains the traditional designation.[58] Wilhelm Pratscher[59] emphasizes that historically the Apostolic Fathers are writings from the period "from the end of the 1st to the end of the 2nd centuries," and theologically they are *documents that correspond to the standard of the broader church* (which emerged in the 2nd cent.)"; as a result, the writings "understood to be heretical" are excluded.[60]

5.2 Contemporary Research on the Didache

After a long interruption, new editions of the commentaries on Ignatius and Polycarp, as well as 1–2 Clem. (see below) appeared in the HNT. In 1989 the series *Kommentar zu den Aposolischen Vätern*, which has been completed in the meantime, began as a supplement to the commentary series KEK on the NT.

A new edition of the Did. commentary in the HNT is still lacking. In the edition by A. Lindemann and H. Paulsen, the traditional positions concerning the "introductory questions" have been adopted: The "regulations

56. Fischer, *Die Apostolischen Väter*, ix–xv, here x. The volume includes 1 Clem., the letters of Ignatius and Polycarp, as well as the Quadratus Fragment, whereas the writings otherwise counted among the Apostolic Fathers are excluded—the writing to Diognetus not least because it could not be assigned to any known author (271).

57. The second part, published in 1984 by Klaus Wengst, contains the Did., Barn., and 2 Clem. with its own reconstruction of the text and detailed, valuable introductions, as well as Diognetus, although this writing cannot be dated more precisely than after the end of the second century and before Constantine (cf. Wengst, *Die Apostolischen Väter*, 308f). Part 3, edited by Ulrich H. J. Körtner and Martin Leutzsch in 1998, contains the Papias Fragments and Hermas and is commented upon and explained at length. Heinrich Kraft compiled the Concordance on the writings of the Apostolic Fathers, entitled *Clavis Patrum Apostolicum*, published in 1963 in Darmstadt. It was compiled on the basis of the critical editions of the texts which had been published up to that point (excluding Diognetus).

58. *Die Apostolischen Väter*, Greek-German parallel edition based on the edition of F. X. Funk, K. Bihlmeyer, and M. Whittacker, with translations by M. Dibelius and D.-A. Koch, newly translated and edited by A. Lindemann and H. Paulsen (Tübingen: Mohr, 1992), with concise introductions on the printed writings, including the Papias Fragments and the Quadratus Fragment.

59. Pratscher, "Corpus," 15–16.

60. Pratscher, "Corpus," 15–16. Cf. also Ulrich, "Die Apostolischen Väter," 267–70: The topics discussed in these writings and also the answers given to the current problems (of that time) can be relevant in the ecclesiastical present of the twenty-first century.

pertaining to the election" of ἐπίσκοποι and the διάκονοι do not support the idea of the "monarchial episcopate," but the codification of such regulations probably points to the second century. In addition to the teaching of the Two Ways in Did. 1–6, there are other pieces of tradition of different origin, such that the provenance derived from Did. 7–10 (Syria) is saying nothing at all of the stage of redaction.[61] For Georg Schöllgen, the Did. "is only concerned with the external forms of life in already established communities"; theological problems "play no role explicitly."[62] The interest is "to remedy grievances and to establish new regulations for changed circumstances—often against resistance."[63] For Bruno Steimer, Did. is "not a pseudepigraphal church order" because it does not claim any foreign authority.[64]

Kurt Niederwimmer[65] notes in his comprehensive commentary: "The Didache is not a 'theological' work, but rather provides regulations for ecclesiastical praxis, a handbook for ecclesiastical morals, ecclesiastical rituals, and ecclesiastical discipline.[66] In 1:1—6:1 there is "a superficially Christianized, originally Jewish writing *de duabus viis*";[67] in 7:1—10:7(8) there is "an archaic liturgical tradition (written or oral) about baptism and the celebration of a meal,"[68] as well as a tradition "about the reception of wandering charismatics" (11:1—15:4);[69] finally, there is a short apocalyptic depiction of end-time events (Did. 16).[70] The redactor ("Didachist"), who not only put these traditions together but also edited them,[71] had "no direct literary model" for them. The Did. does not claim to want to "regulate church-wide conditions," rather "obviously [only] local conditions are in view."[72] But in that the Did. "preserved archaic traditions of a particular area [which are]

61. Lindemann and Paulsen, *Die Apostolischen Väter*, 1–2.

62. *Didache. Zwölf-Apostel-Lehre*, translated and introduced by Georg Schöllgen. The same volume also contains the *Traditio Apostolica. Apostolische Überlieferung*, edited by Wilhelm Geerlings.

63. Schöllgen, *Didache*.

64. Steimer, *Vertex Traditionis*, 339: "The author of the Didache is a personality authorized by the congregation, whose orders reflect authentically real congregational relations"; the anonymity is just "the adequate expression to insinuate the orthonymity of the composition, namely the authorship by the congregation as a whole."

65. Niederwimmer, *Didache*.

66. Niederwimmer, *Didache*, 13.

67. Niederwimmer, *Didache*, 67.

68. Cf. also Lindemann, "Zur frühchristlichen Taufpraxis"; Koch, "Eucharistievollzug."

69. Niederwimmer, *Didache*, 67.

70. Niederwimmer, *Didache*, 67. Cf. Lindemann, "Die Endzeitrede."

71. Niederwimmer, *Didache*, 271. Cf. Niederwimmer, "Der Didachist."

72. Niederwimmer, *Didache*, 13.

of great importance."[73] With regard to the dating of the Did., there are "no compelling reasons" to deviate from the "setting of ca. 100 or 120 CE."[74] Niederwimmer concludes that while the author "nowhere assumes the apostolic or episcopal, or charismatic *potestas*," one would "hardly err in imagining him as a respected and influential bishop."[75] The Did. does not have a theology in the proper sense, and "what he says rests on tradition."[76]

The essays on the transmission of the text and on the redaction traditions in the Didache within Clayton N. Jefford's edited volume *The Didache in Context* are of great value.[77]

The contribution on the Did. in the volume edited by W. Pratscher[78] is by Jonathan A. Draper.[79] He assumes that the final version of this writing was written "when the Gospels were still transmitted orally and in a relatively unconsolidated form" since "only such passages from Matt and Luke are available that are not found in Mark."[80] The proximity to the Jesus tradition found in the Logia source Q and in the Gospel of Matthew speaks for the fact that the text of the Did. was written within the environment of the Gospel of Matthew.[81] The fact that the Did. refers to a congregation "in which there is no mention of the forgiveness of sins through incorporation into Christ at baptism,"[82] and in which the words of the institution of the Lord's Supper are not mentioned, speaks for a very early dating.[83] Contrary to the tendency of Niederwimmer, Draper shows that the Did. has a clearly constructed "theological profile."[84]

73. Niederwimmer, *Didache*, 15.

74. Niederwimmer. *Didache*, 79.

75. Niederwimmer, *Didache*, 271.

76. Niederwimmer, *Didache*, 272.

77. Jefford, *Didache in Context*.

78. Pratscher, *Die Apostolischen Väter*.

79. Draper, "Didache."

80. Draper, "Didache," 20.

81. Cf. Lindemann, "Die Endzeitrede."

82. Draper, "Didache," 20.

83. Draper, "Didache." However, this need only mean that the Didache is not directly influenced by Pauline theology.

84. Draper, "Didache," 24–34. As theological topics, he mentions talk of God as Father, Christology (admittedly limited to the aspect that Jesus is ὁ παῖς θεοῦ), talk of the Spirit, as well as eschatology and ecclesiology.

First Clement in Contemporary Research

One of the central topics of research on 1 Clem. is the question of whether the Roman ἐκκλησία claimed for itself "primacy" according to the contemporary political model when it intervenes in the Corinthian's affairs.[85] Furthermore, researchers search for the motives behind the "political" (στάσις) deposition of the Corinthian πρεσβύτεροι.[86] Clare K. Rothschild sees the formal similarities between 1 Clem. and Paul and concludes: "1 Clement adopts Paul's position as a primary (but not its only) rhetorical strategy."[87] She calls the Roman letter to Corinth virtually a "pseudepigraphon."

The controversial theological question often discussed about the extent to which the description of "apostolic succession" in 1 Clem. 44:1–6 can be regarded as historically reliable and the extent to which the "primacy of Rome" can be regarded as an indication of "early Catholicism" has played a minor role in more recent scholarship. Lindemann, whose commentary appeared in 1992 as Knopf's "successor" in the HNT,[88] questions the unusually precise dating (95/96 CE) supported often from 1 Clem. 1:1, since news of a persecution of Roman Christians at the time of Domitian is uncertain. But the fact that 1 Clem. speaks of ἐπίσκοποι, not of a mono-episcopate, speaks in favor of a dating "before 100 CE." The author of 1 Clem. was not a "Jewish-Christian," but rather "closely acquainted with Jewish or Jewish-Christian tradition,"[89] as shown especially by the numerous scriptural quotations. Lindemann regards this letter as particularly important if only because it "obviously reflects the average state of Christianity within the Roman congregation at the end of the 1st century,"[90] which includes the intensive use of the LXX and also "the impartiality with which Stoic or generally non-Christian or non-Jewish tradition and terminology is taken up."[91] Lindemann considers that the statement in 63:2 that the present letter is a "petition (ἔντευξις) for peace and concord" may be meant juristically, which would fit the political function of the terms στάσις and ὁμόνοια used to characterize the Corinthian situation.[92] Lindemann also argues that,

85. Cf. Lindemann, "Der 'Erste Clemensbrief.'"

86. Influential was the study by Mikat, *Die Bedeutung der Begriffe*. A similar question was posed by Schmitt, *Paroikie und Oikoumene*.

87. Rothschild, "1 Clement as Pseudepigraphon," 67.

88. Lindemann, *Die Clemensbriefe*. Lindemann is also the author of the essay on 1 Clem. in Pratscher's edited volume *Die Apostolischen Väter*.

89. Lindemann, *Die Clemensbriefe*, 13.

90. Lindemann, *Die Clemensbriefe*, 20.

91. Lindemann, *Die Clemensbriefe*, 20.

92. Lindemann, *Die Clemensbriefe*, 12, 13.

with respect to the vague structure of 1 Clem., the repeatedly encountered doxologies should be understood as signals which structure the letter.[93] On the question of the relationship between the NT and 1 Clem. beyond that of 1 Cor, which is cited in 1 Clem. 47, Lindemann states that a literary relationship between 1 Clem. 36:2–5 with Heb 1 is "probable" without necessitating that Hebrews as a whole was known in Rome.[94] Lindemann rejects the thesis that 1 Clem. "teaches a version of Christianity understood merely in terms of morality"[95] because 1 Clem. understands "humans as creatures capable of responding with μετάνοια."[96] Lindemann's commentary offers a larger excursus on the tradition of the "phoenix" from which the plausibility of the hope for the resurrection is derived in 1 Clem. 25.[97]

In his comprehensive commentary on 1 Clem., published in 1998, Horacio E. Lona observes that the letter, which seems to be only loosely arranged, nevertheless possesses a unity in form and content "toward the achievement of the rhetorical goal that is directly related to the situation in Corinth: the restoration of peace and harmony."[98] The demands made from the Roman church actually require a claim to legitimacy, but this is apparently presupposed without question.[99] The Corinthian conflict was due to the refusal of some members of the congregation "to accept all the consequences of an institutionalization of the ministry without contradiction."[100] Why Rome felt compelled to intervene is not explained, but possibly "something" of the "idea of Rome" and Rome's special role with respect to Corinth was also "alive in the Christians within the capital."[101] The fact that, despite its high reputation, 1 Clem. "did not play a significant role in the process of the formation of the canon" may be due to the fact that the letter was "all too obviously connected with an ecclesiastical conflict [that] lacked the character of the 'original.'"[102] The very unusual prescript "may also have

93. Lindemann, *Die Clemensbriefe*, 13–16.

94. Lindemann, *Die Clemensbriefe*, 18–20.

95. Lindemann, *Die Clemensbriefe*, 22.

96. Lindemann, *Die Clemensbriefe*, 23.

97. Lindemann, *Die Clemensbriefe*, 88–89, 263–77. Cf. the excursus by Knopf on pp. 122–125 in this volume.

98. Lona, *Der erste Clemensbrief*, 24.

99. Lona, *Der erste Clemensbrief*, 30. On the date of 1 Clem., Lona opts for the last decade of the first century; see pp. 77–78.

100. Lona, *Der erste Clemensbrief*, 81.

101. Lona, *Der erste Clemensbrief*, 88.

102. Lona, *Der erste Clemensbrief*, 110.

contributed" to the fact that 1 Clem. "was so rarely included in the list of canonical or paracanonical books."[103]

5.4 Second Clement in Contemporary Research

Regarding 2 Clem., Rüdiger Warns held the view that this writing is in conflict with an already developed Valentinian Christology in Egypt and therefore could have been written only around 160 CE.[104] In the proemium (2 Clem. 1:1–8), the preacher of 2 Clem. asks "the programmatic question: 'What payment shall we give God in exchange for what he has given us?'" (1:3, 5),[105] followed by the first answer in 2 Clem. 2–7 (confession, connected with good works) and the second answer in 8–14 (repentance, abstinence). In 2 Clem. 15–18, there is an eschatological conclusion, and 2 Clem. 19 and 20 probably originate from a different author.[106]

Andreas Lindemann, like Warns, assumes that "there was a gnostic Christianity in the circle of 2 Clement," but in light of the lack of direct polemics, "a targeted confrontation with gnosis" cannot be proven.[107] In retrospect, Lindemann notes about the "theological character" of 2 Clem. that in research "an overall negative judgment" prevails with respect to 2 Clem.'s theology.[108] It should be noted, however, "that it is a sermon concentrated on a topic and not a carefully elaborated letter or even a theological treatise in the strict sense of the word."[109] Rather, the statements on Christology and on soteriology should be taken "seriously in the same way as the admonitions, the number of which naturally predominates within a συμβουλία/ ἔντευξις."[110] On 19:1—20:4, Lindemann suggests that this section was "originally formulated to create a transition between the reading of Scripture and the subsequent reading of the written sermon contained in 2 Clem. 1–18,"[111]

103. Lona, *Der erste Clemensbrief*, 110.

104. Warns, "Untersuchungen." On this, see Lindemann, *Die Clemensbriefe*, 195: A more precise dating to the "middle of the 2nd cent." is hardly likely.

105. Rothschild, "'Belittling,'" 122–23 analyzes 2 Clem. 1:1–2 according to the question of how the phrase μικρὰ φρονεῖν should be translated. Since 2 Clem. presupposes the ancient relationship of patronage as a model for one's relationship to Christ, it can be assumed that the author urges the addressees not to "underestimate" ("we must not undervalue our salvation") the salvation (σωτηρία) given by Christ.

106. Warns, "Untersuchungen," 108.

107. Lindemann, *Die Clemensbriefe*, 192.

108. Lindemann, *Die Clemensbriefe*, 195–96.

109. Lindemann, *Die Clemensbriefe*, 196.

110. Lindemann, *Die Clemensbriefe*, 196.

111. Lindemann, *Die Clemensbriefe*, 255.

and so it is more of an overture than an epilogue. It was only through the connection with 1 Clem. that this section of the text moved to the end so that the doxology in 20:5 "now forms the conclusion of the corpus of both of 'Clement's' letters," which is quite in keeping with the style.[112]

William Pratscher understands 2 Clem. as a whole to be paraenesis, which is motivated first by Christology (2 Clem. 1–3) and then by eschatology (2 Clem. 4–18).[113] All in all, 2 Clem. is a "symbouleutic speech."[114] It is not about theological reflection, but "about proper conduct, that is, not about ethics as a theoretical reflection of the practice of faith, but about practice itself."[115] Regarding the "question of the opponent," Pratscher notes that a "direct polemic against the Gnostic opponents" is "nowhere present, but always only implicit"; nevertheless, it is a deliberate confrontation with gnosis.[116] Pratscher also emphasizes that the "negative judgment" of the theology of 2 Clem. does not apply on the whole, but "neither should the impression arise that the preacher has the theological reflectiveness of, for example, one like Paul."[117] Second Clement is "an interesting document from the east, perhaps from Egyptian, gentile Christianity, toward the middle of the 2nd century."[118]

Christopher Tuckett notes, "Commentaries on 2 Clement are not that numerous!"[119] He then offers a comprehensive introduction (pp. 1–82), a new edition of the text along with an English translation (pp. 83–123), and a comprehensive commentary (pp. 125–303). The question of authorship cannot be answered ("perhaps of his somewhat self-effacing modesty"); the author was "not a Jew before becoming a Christian."[120] Second Clement is not a homily and is not a work of "missionary preaching" but is rather addressed to "a group of Christians gathered for some kind of liturgical worship."[121] The change of address in 19:1—20:4 suggests that it is a later addition.[122] On the citations found in 2 Clem., Tuckett notes that it is hard to say whether

---

112. Lindemann, *Die Clemensbriefe*, 255–56.

113. Pratscher, "Der zweite Clemensbrief." Pratscher is also the author of the essay on 2 Clem. in his edited volume *Die Apostolische Väter*.

114. Pratscher, *Der zweite Clemensbrief*, 24, 26.

115. Pratscher, *Der zweite Clemensbrief*, 43–44.

116. Pratscher, *Der zweite Clemensbrief*, 54: "That it is mostly only a distancing, not a more detailed theological arguing [*sic.* argument] is another matter."

117. Pratscher, *Der zweite Clemensbrief*, 237.

118. Pratscher, *Der zweite Clemensbrief*, 238.

119. Tuckett, *2 Clement*, v.

120. Tuckett, *2 Clement*, 17.

121. Tuckett, *2 Clement*, 23, 25.

122. Tuckett, *2 Clement*, 33.

the author knew books that later became "New Testament." Old Testament
texts[123] are cited frequently.[124] On the question of the "opponents,"[125] Tuckett
notes "the false teachers" were not gnostics, but that it is "more appropriate to see the relationship between 2 Clement and (incipient) Gnosticism
as rather more fluid and less clear-cut than has sometimes been the case
in the past."[126] The question of the provenance and date of 2 Clem. is "ultimately unanswerable, at least with any certainty (or even a degree of high
probability)."[127] Its provenance is probably Rome around the middle of the
second century, "but one cannot say more."[128] Tuckett provides a system-
atic overview of the theological topics in 2 Clem. On "Jews and Judaism,"
he notes that the author "is living in a context where non-Christian Jewish
neighbours are virtually non-existent" and thus it is likely, "apparently without any challenge, that Jewish traditions are to be used for (predominantly
Gentile) Christians."[129] In this extremely rich, very detailed commentary,
Tuckett offers an in-depth exegesis of each verse.

Knopf and Current Scholarship: An Assessment

A comparison between the commentary by Knopf, written about a hundred
years ago, and the works on the Did. and on 1–2 Clem. that have appeared
since then shows that exegetical and historical questions of detail are still
often discussed and answered in a very similar way. This makes Knopf's
commentary valuable even to this day, and not only as a document valuable
within the history of interpretation. The fact that the question of the theological statements discernible in these writings plays a comparatively minor
role in Knopf's work corresponds to the original, fundamental approach
of the Handbuch zum Neuen Testament. This approach was modified in
various ways in the volumes within this series published after 1945. In the
commentaries, some of which are considerably more extensive, a significant
amount of space is given to the theological positions expressed within the
writings of the Apostolic Fathers.[130]

123. Tuckett, 2 Clement, 38, calls these "Jewish scripture."

124. For 2 Clem., the OT Scriptures were probably not "Jewish" but a part of his
own tradition.

125. Cf. Tuckett, 2 Clement, 47–57.

126. Tuckett, 2 Clement, 54.

127. Tuckett, 2 Clement, 58.

128. Tuckett, 2 Clement, 64.

129. Tuckett, 2 Clement, 74–75.

130. Hans Lietzmann's letters indicate his demand to the staff of the HNT that it

The question of how to deal with the early Christian writings that later became a part of the "New Testament," which were not yet ἡ γραφή or αἱ γραφαί in the proper sense in the second century, was and still is intensively investigated.[131] A virtually groundbreaking achievement was the work *The New Testament in the Apostolic Fathers*, prepared in 1905 by seven scholars as "Committee of the Oxford Society of Historical Theology," with precise graded analyses of what can be classified as quotations without reasonable doubt or possible or probable allusions within the Apostolic Fathers.[132] Exactly one hundred years later, under the same title, a two-volume work was published that followed on from this work, but was methodologically modernized in several respects.[133] However, restraint is necessary investigating the question of possible citations. An undoubtedly clear reference to the New Testament writing 1 Cor is present in 1 Clem. 47.[134] In Did. 8:2, the Lord's Prayer is quoted with wording that is almost identical to Matt 6:9–13, but it cannot be said whether the Didachist was already familiar with the Gospel of Matthew as a literary work. In 2 Clem., there are several statements that go back to the Jesus tradition (connected with the phrase λέγει), but no textual relationship can be demonstrated.

Another topic is the role of the ecclesiastical offices described or presupposed in the texts and the authority associated with them. First Clement offers an early form of the idea of "apostolic succession," not as a "new" demand, but with reference to tradition which was also to be recognized in Corinth. The question of whether Ignatius, who introduces himself to the addressees of his letters as ἐπίσκοπος of Antioch, had held a "monarchical" episcopal office before his arrest or whether he merely thinks he can claim such an office is controversial.

The early Christian writings compiled under the undoubtedly inaccurate collection called the "Apostolic Fathers" are of considerable importance for the history of the church and theology. They can be read as historical sources, insofar as they reveal at least individual aspects of the development of the church for the period between 90 and 150 CE, that is, between the late pseudepigraphal writings, which became canonical in connection with the original Christian writings written orthonymously

---

"give up its purely philological-historical attitude in its exclusivity and move to a stronger treatment of the theological problems as well" (letter to H. W. Beyer on January 21, 1935, in Aland, *Glanz*, 803).

131. Pratscher, "Die Rezeption." Cf. Lindemann, "Paul"; Lindemann, "Paulus."

132. Oxford Society of Historical Theology, *New Testament in the Apostolic Fathers*; cf. pp. iii–v.

133. Gregory and Tuckett, *Reception*; Gregory and Tuckett, *Trajectories*.

134. Cf. Rothschild, "Reception."

or anonymously in the first century CE, and the early apologists, whose works were written around the middle of the second century. Contrary to the collective name attributed to them, the "Apostolic Fathers" did not claim to be in direct connection with the apostles or to possess a historically justified, prominent authority. Precisely for this reason, however, these writings should also be understood as independent theological texts and as early Christian testimonies of faith. It is a special merit of Rudolf Knopf that he has worked this out in his commentary.

Didache

Introduction

Outline

Superscription

Editions and Literature

The first edition of the Did., which includes a valuable commentary, is P. Bry-ennios, Διδαχὴ τῶν δώδεκα ἀποστόλων (Constantinopolis, 1883). — A. von Harnack, *Lehre der zwölf Apostel: Nebst Untersuchungen zur ältesten Geschich-te der Kirchenverfassung und des Kirchenrechts*, Texte und Untersuchungen zur Geschichte der altchristlichen Literatur (Leipzig: Hinrichs, 1884; Ana-statischer Neudruck 1893), 1f. — A. von Harnack, *Die Apostellehre und die jüdischen beiden Wege*, 2nd ed. (Leipzig: Hinrichs, 1895). — A. von Harnack, "Apostellehre," in *Realenzyklopädie*, ed. A. Hauck, 3rd ed. (Stuttgart: Metzler, 1893), 1:711–30. The last two mentioned publications include a rich bibliog-raphy of ancient literature. — P. Sabatier, *La Didachè ou l'Enseignement des douze apôtres* (Paris: Fischbacher, 1885). — J. R. Harris, *The Teaching of the Apostles* (London: Clay, 1887). This work contains beautiful facsimiles of the entire manuscript. — P. Schaff, *The Teaching of the Twelve Apostles* (New York: Funk & Wagnalls, 1889). — C. Taylor, *The Teaching of the Twelve Apostles with Illustrations from the Talmud (Lectures)* (Cambridge: Bell, 1886). — The manual volume by G. Rauschen, *Florilegium Patristicum I: Monumenta aevi apostolici* (Bonn: Hanstein, 1904). — F. X. Funk, *Patres Apostolici I*, 2nd ed. (Tübingen: Laupp, 1901). — An edition of the Did. that includes a critical apparatus as well as an Old Latin translation can be found in H. Lietzmann, *Die Didache, mit kritischem Apparat*, 3rd ed., Kleine Texte 2 (Bonn: Marcus und Weber, 1912). — J. Schlecht, *Doctrina XII Apostolorum: Die Apostellehre in der Liturgie der katholischen Kirche* (Freiburg im Breisgau: Herder, 1901). — P. Drews, "Die Kirchenordnungen," in *Neutestamentliche Apokryphen*, ed.

E. Hennecke (Tübingen: Mohr, 1904), 182–94, as well as P. Drews, "Apostlelehre (Didache)," in *Handbuch zu den neutestamentlichen Apokryphen*, ed. Hennecke (Tübingen: Mohr, 1904), 256–83. — P. Drews, "Untersuchungen zur Didache," *Zeitschrift für die neutestamentliche Wissenschaft und die Kunde des Urchristentums* 5 (1904), 53–79. — T. Schermann, *Eine Elfapostelmoral oder die X-Rezension der "Beiden Wege"* (München: Lentner, 1903). — A. Seeberg, *Der Katechismus der Urchristenheit* (Leipzig: Deichert, 1903). — A. Seeberg, *Das Evangelium Christi* (Leipzig: Deichert, 1905). — A. Seeberg, *Die beiden Wege und das Aposteldekret* (Leipzig: Deichert, 1906). — A. Seeberg, *Die Didache des Judentums und der Urchristenheit* (Leipzig: Deichert, 1908). — G. Klein, *Der älteste christliche Katechismus und die jüdische Propaganda-Literatur* (Berlin: Reimer, 1909). — L. Wohleb, *Die lateinische Uebersetzung der Didache kritisch und sprachlich untersucht mit einer Wiederherstellung der griechischen Vorlage und einem Anhang ueber das Verbum "altare" und seine Komposita*, Studien zur Geschichte und Kultur des Altertums 7.1 (Paderborn: Schoeningh, 1913). For a larger selection from the extensive literature, see O. Bardenhewer, *Geschichte der altchristlichen Literatur*, 2nd ed. (Freiburg: Herdersche Verlagshandlung, 1913), 102f.

Transmission

The text of the Did., which was broadly disseminated and often mentioned in ancient Christendom, was edited by Bryennios in 1883 from an eleventh-century manuscript which is now located in the Library of the Patriarch in Jerusalem (in what follows, the abbreviation for this manuscript will be H).[1] This manuscript is by far the most important witness to the text. The first part of the Teaching, namely the Two Ways (1:1—6:1), is also preserved within a Latin translation (L). The main witness for this translation is a manuscript in Munich. A fragment of L (1:1—2:5) is also preserved in a Melker codex. The letter of Barnabas can be considered (see below) a secondary witness for certain parts of the text. Additionally, some writings from the later ecclesiastical antiquity are of help: For example, Book VII of the Apostolic Constitutions (A) originating from the fourth century and the Apostolic Church Ordinance (K). Von Harnack prints the possible fragments of both texts in his edition of the Didache (Did. 178–92, 225–37 ab), as well as certain parts of the Life of Archimandrite Shenouda (Shenoute of Atripe), which Iselin edited in *Texte und Untersuchungen* (S). Little comes

---

1. TN: Knopf originally used the abbreviation M (i.e., "Manuskript") for this manuscript. However, the abbreviation H (short for Codex Hierosolymitanus) is used throughout this translation, in conformity with the contemporary literature.

from the use of the Didache in the syntagma of Athanasius and in the pseudoathanasian *Fides Nicaena* (Batiffol, *Studia Patristica*, 2:121).

Points of Contact and Witnesses

The first part of the Did., the Two Ways, shows close points of contact with Barn. 18–20 (see comments), and also there are points of contact between Barn. 4:9f and Did. 16:2. Unfortunately, however, it cannot be said that the two texts are directly dependent upon one another. The similarities between the texts go back instead to a common source, the Two Ways. Overall, Barnabas seems to have retained its more original form. Even contact between Hermas, *Mand.* II.4–6 and Did. 1:5 (cf. comments on this verse) does not give way to a sure conclusion. The other witnesses to the text are mostly late, and there are not many of them. The most important are Clem. Alex. *Strom.* 1.20.100.4, Euseb. *Hist. eccl.* 3.25.4, the 39th Festal Letter of Athanasius, the stichometry of Nicephorus, and the list of 60 canonical books (the last three texts printed by Preuschen, *Analecta*, 2:42–52, 62–64, 68–70).

Sources

It can be considered a certainty that Did. 1–6 was originally a Jewish text which dealt with the "Two Ways." It is also likely that the form of this proselyte catechism, which was available to the author of the Did., contained the largest part of ch. 16, the concluding apocalyptic portrait (Did. 16:3–7). Perhaps Did. 16:2 was also a part of the Jewish text, since a clear parallel to this passage can again be found in Barnabas (4:9f). The Jewish text has been taken over by the Did. without significant alterations. Only what is written in Did. 1:3–6 is a Christian revision of the Jewish *Vorlage*: The words of the Lord are brought in only here, in connection with the Two Ways. Yet these words of the Lord are missing in the form of the Two Ways presented in Barnabas.

Date and Provenance

At first glance, it is clear that the work is very old. It still bears witness to the old Pneumatics, beside whom the official ministerial office plays only a minor role. The authorities of the past, besides the OT, are the Lord in the Gospel and the Twelve Apostles. Non-gospel portions of the NT are not taken into consideration. The cult is still very free, and the prayers of the Lord's Supper have a completely non-Pauline form. The longing for the end is tense and is substantial. The Did. could not have been composed later than 150 CE. But other observations show that the date should not be placed too early either: the idea of giving the Lord's teaching to the gentiles through the Twelve Apostles (cf. Acts and Matt 28:19f), the decline of the old Pneumatics (11:3–12), the church scattered throughout the world (9:4; 10:5), and the number of congregations (11:6) all point clearly and with certainty beyond the apostolic age. Unfortunately, it is difficult to date the text more precisely, leaving a broad range of dates between 90–150 CE. If the author knows Matthew and possibly even Luke, as he presumably does, then it is not necessary to depart far from a post 100 CE date as the earliest possible option. Not much can be deduced from the obvious relationship between the Did. and Barnabas, since this relationship is judged to be indirect. This is similarly true of the Did.'s relationship with Hermas. The earliest author who explicitly refers to the Did. is Clement of Alexandria (see above). Therefore, unfortunately, the date of the origin of this extremely significant work must be left rather indefinite.

The question of the provenance of the Did. is not as problematic. It could not have originated in the West; only the East is possible, though certainly not Asia Minor. Either Egypt or Syria or Palestine are options. Contact with Barnabas, which probably originated in Egypt, the most ancient reception of the Did. in Clement of Alexandria, and the strange form of the doxology in the Lord's Prayer in 8:2 (see the discussion there) causes one to think of Egypt as the provenance for the Did. Contrary to this assumption, however, is the reference to "bread on the hills" in Did. 9:4 (see discussion there), which would have been an impossible concept for the inhabitants of the Nile valley as well as those of the Delta. Standing behind the two-part doxology (of course βασιλεία and δόξα; omit καὶ ἡ δύναμις) is Matt 6:13 as well as Tatian and cur. (vac. syr. sin.).[2] The scarcity of water mentioned in Did. 7:2f, fits poorly in the context of the rich supply in Egypt. The Did. does not evidence any knowledge of presbyters and therefore hardly could have been written in Egypt (see Hauschildt, "πρεσβύτεροι"). The strange close connection the Christian congregations share with Judaism (see Did. 8–10), whose customs and traditions still influence the Christian congregations, suggests that Syria and Palestine are much more likely to have been the provenance of the work than Egypt. Admittedly, the adoption of the Two Ways could take place anywhere within the diaspora. — Because of the circumstances presupposed in Did. 13, one

---

2. TN: cur. = Curetonian Syriac; vac. = is missing; syr. sin. = Sinaitic Syriac. Thank you to both Stephen Carlson and James Dowden for their clarification on the meaning of these abbreviations.

must assume that the Did. did not originate in a clearly urban community, but in more remote, rural or small-town circles. From Did. 11:6 (see the discussion of this passage), it can be concluded that the Christians and Christian congregations are not spread out too thinly.

The Superscription

Of the two superscriptions that H offers, the second, fuller one is likely the original one, whereas the first, abbreviated form comes from the scribe of the manuscript. A teaching based on the words of the Lord (1:3–5; 4:13; 8:2; 11:3; 15:3f) will be presented. διδαχή is conceived here very anciently as practical instruction about moral commandments and congregational ordinances; see Barn. 16:9; 18:1 and the διδάγματα τοῦ Χριστοῦ in Justin, *1 Apol.* 14.4. The apostles are the mediators of the moral teaching and the church order, not in the sense that the author wanted his booklet to be thought of as written by them, but in such a way that the apostles, and specifically the Twelve, as is often the case, appear in the post-apostolic age as mediators and guarantors of all teaching, tradition, and institutions; see the general view of the Acts of the Apostles; see further Matt 28:19; Luke 24:47; Acts 1:8; 1 Clem. 44:1–3; Rev 21:14; etc. "The teaching" comes from the Lord and is vouched for and passed on by the Twelve apostles. The addition of τοῖς ἔθνεσιν recalls Matt 28:19, but does not need to have originated from there; on the matter, see still Justin, *1 Apol.* 39.3: ἀπὸ γὰρ Ἰερουσαλήμ ἄνδρες δεκαδύο τὸν ἀριθμὸν ἐξῆλθον εἰς τὸν κόσμον . . . διὰ δὲ θεοῦ δυνάμεως ἐμήνυσαν παντὶ γένει ἀνθρώπων ὡς ἀπεστάλησαν ὑπὸ τοῦ Χριστοῦ διδάξαι πάντας τὸν τοῦ θεοῦ λόγον. The abbreviated title διδ. τ. δωδ. ἀποστ. is offered in all places of the early church literature where the Did. is mentioned, except in H; see Eusebius, *Hist. eccl.* III 25.4: τῶν ἀποστόλων αἱ λεγόμεναι διδαχαί, Athanasius in his 39th Festal Letter: διδαχὴ καλουμένη τῶν ἀποστόλων, stichometry of Nicephorus: διδαχὴ ἀποστόλων, list of the 60 canonical books: διδαχαὶ τῶν ἀποστόλων (see the Preuschen, *Analecta II*, 49f, 64, 69); also the Latin church called the writing: *doctrina apostolorum*, see the superscription: *De doctrina apostolorum* in the Munich manuscript and Ps. Cyprian, *Adv. aleat.* 4. The reason the original, fuller title was abbreviated to διδαχὴ τῶν [δώδεκα] ἀποστόλων and not to διδαχὴ κυρίου is because the second abbreviation was too broad and indefinite and did not distinguish the text sufficiently from the Gospel literature.

I. The Two Ways: The Baptismal Catechism (1:1—6:2)

The majority of the exhortations preserved here comes from a Jewish proselyte catechism, which was simply adopted and prepared for congregational
use (cf. the introduction). The very general content of this Jewish work,
which stayed away from everything that had to do with Jewish ceremonial
and cultic laws, made it easy to adopt the writing. We view the revised and
Christian transmitted text as a Christian phenomenon, but take into account the Jewish parallels. As can also be observed elsewhere, the Jewish
diaspora prepared the Christian proclamation. On the surface at least, it
was a great advantage in this case, since one did not need a new version of
a moral teaching but could follow older, proven wisdom. The proverbial
literature of the LXX was gladly and often used by Christians.

A. There Are Two Ways (1:1)

Translation

$^{1:1}$ There are two ways, one which leads to life and one to death;
but there is a great difference between the two ways.

Textual Notes

1:1 The image of the two ways or of pairs (God and mankind; the righteous
and the unrighteous; of justice and injustice) occurs extraordinarily often
within the LXX. The number exceeds the hundreds; see the concordance
under the term ὁδός. Furthermore, the construction "the way of life and
death" is found in Jer 21:8; see then Prov 12:28 and Ps 1:1f (the entire
psalm is a variation on the theme of the two ways); T. Ash. 1; as well as
Matt 7:13f and 2 Pet 2:15. It is also often used in the rabbinic literature;
see, for example, Pirqe 'Abot 2:1 (Fiebig, *Mischnatraktate*, 2:5f): "Rabbi
(here meaning R. Judah HaQadosh) said, 'what is the right way which a
person should choose'" (see additional examples in Klein, *Katechismus*,
159ff and 185f). Furthermore, the comprehensive designation "halakah"
for the parts of the Jewish tradition regulating the way of life belongs here;
see also ἡ ὁδός in 1 Cor 4:17; Acts 9:2; 19:9, 23; 22:4; 24:14, 22 = Christianity. The image of the two ways also appears throughout the literature of the
world in both religious and ethical instruction. For Greece, see primarily
the fable of Prodicus about Heracles at the crossroads in Xenophon, *Mem-
orab.* II 1.21–33 or Hesiod, *Works and Days* 287–92: τὴν μέν τοι κακότητα

καὶ ἰλαδὸν ἔστιν ἑλέσθαι. Ῥηιδίως· λείη μὲν ὁδός, μάλα δ' ἐγγύθι ναίει· Τῆς δ' ἀρετῆς ἱδρῶτα θεοὶ προπάροιθεν ἔθηκαν Ἀθάνατοι· μακρὸς δὲ καὶ ὄρθιος οἶμος ἐς αὐτήν. Καὶ τρηχὺς τὸ πρῶτον· ἐπὴν δ' εἰς ἄκρον ἵκηται, Ῥηιδίη δὴ ἔπειτα πέλει, χαλεπή περ ἐοῦσα. Theognis 911f: Ἐν τριόδῳ δ' ἔστηκα. δύ' εἰσὶν πρόσθεν ὁδοί μοι· Φροντίζω τούτων ἤντιν' ἴω προτέρην. See further Vergil, *Aen.* VI 540–43; Plutarch, *Dem.* 26 and especially *St.* (Lactanz, *Instit.* VI 3 said of the two ways: *quas et poetae in carminibus et philosophi in disputationibus suis induxerunt*). The Fatiha, the first Quranic Surah, reads: "Praise be to God, the Lord of the world, the merciful beneficent one, the king of day and night. We serve you and we implore you to lead us on the straight way, the way of those upon whom you are gracious and not the path of those with whom you are angry and who go astray." In the religious literature of India, the image recurs frequently; see the title of the famous Buddhist collection of proverbs *Dhammapada*, which means something like "The Way of Truth," or the foundational sermon of the Buddha in Benares on "the middle way, the four noble truths, and the noble eight-part path" (Mahāvagga I 6.17ff, text in, for example, Bertholet and Grube, *Lesebuch*, 219f or Oldenberg, *Buddha*, 147ff). Buddha thought of himself as a teacher of a "path," that is, practical behavior which leads to knowledge and salvation. The "path" is for him the quintessence of the "norm" (Beckh, *Buddhismus*, has worked this out everywhere rather beautifully). And so much more could be quoted from all times and from many peoples. — In any case, the text of the beginning of the Did. offered in L is: *viae duae sunt in saeculo, vitae et mortis, lucis et tenebrarum. in his constituti sunt angeli duo, unus aequitatis, alter iniquitatis.* How old this form must be, which belongs to a parallel recension, is seen in Barn. 18:1; see also Herm. *Mand.* VI 2.1 and immediately before the two ways.

B. Description of the Way of Life (1:2—4:14)

1. Basic and General Description (1:2)

TRANSLATION

1:2 Now the way to life is this: "First, love God, who created you; second, love your neighbor as yourself." And whatever you do not want done to you, do not do to another.

TEXTUAL NOTES

The way of life is described in such a way that first the great general and comprehensive commandment is given, the observance of which determines the way of life (1:2). The author uses a transitional formula (1:3 at the beginning) to connect this general command with a long series of ethical commandments (originally 2:2—4:14). When the Jewish catechism was revised by Christians (cf. above), a series of words of the Lord were inserted: 1:3 (from εὐλογεῖτε) to 1:6. The introduction of a transitional formula in 2:1 denotes the resumption of the ancient, Jewish thread.

1:2 See Barn. 19:1, 2, 5. The way of life is fundamentally and generally characterized by the "sum of the law" (the highest commandment) and by the attached "golden rule" in its negative expression. The recognition of Deut 6:4, 5 (the beginning of the scheme) and Lev 19:18 as the core of the law was already attainable in Judaism; see the probably original version of Luke 10:25–28 (from Q, counterpart Mark 12:28–34), where the scribes and not Jesus himself answer the question about the greatest commandment. But admittedly, the connection is nowhere attested in this form within Judaism, and the use of πρῶτον and δεύτερον is very reminiscent of Mark 12:29, 31 (Matt 22:38, 39). On the form (τὸν θεὸν τὸν ποιήσαντά σε), see Did. 5:2 as well as Sir 7:30: ἐν ὅλῃ δυνάμει ἀγάπησον τὸν ποιήσαντά σε, which has certainly served as a model, and then Barn. 19:2 and the form in which Justin, 1 Apol. 16.6 has cited the word of Mark 12:28. The third part of the main commandment is the golden rule, which is cited in the negative form, and thus different from Matt 7:12 and Luke 6:31. (Admittedly, the beginning is strongly reminiscent of Matt 7:12: πάντα δὲ ὅσα ἐὰν θελήσῃς.) It is known within Judaism in this form; see primarily Tob 4:15: ὃ μισεῖς, μηδενὶ ποιήσῃς and also the narrative in b. Šabb. 31a (Goldschmidt, *Der babylonische Talmud*, 1:388): "A gentile came to Shammai and declared that he was ready to become a proselyte of Judaism if he could be taught the law in the time it takes him to stand on one foot. Shammai chased him away. Then he went to Hillel and brought with him the same request. Hillel answered him immediately, '*Whatever you hate, do not do that to your neighbor. This is the entire law. Everything else is an explanation of it. Go and learn that.*'"
— A similar conversion story is said about Aqiva in 'Abot de R. Nathan (see Klein, *Katechismus*, 85f). There are a large number of parallels, both from non-Christian and non-Jewish tradition in Resch, *Aposteldekret*, 132–41; see further, with small expansions, at Seeberg, *Aposteldekret*, 7; Funk on this

passage[3] and Funk, *Doctrina*, 4f (the golden rule in the negative form, as here, is also found in the western text of the apostles' decree in Acts 15).

2. Love, Forgiveness, and Giving (1:3–6)

TRANSLATION

[1:3] The teaching that is contained in these words is this: "Bless those who curse you and pray for your enemies," and fast "for those who persecute you." For what grace (will be given to you) if you "love those who love you? Do not the gentiles also do the same?" Instead, you shall "love those who hate you," and you will have no enemy. [4] Abstain from carnal and fleshly desires. "If anyone hits you on the right cheek, let him hit you on the other, and you will be perfect." "If anyone compels you to go a mile, go two miles with him." "If anyone takes your coat, also give him your shirt." "If anyone takes what is yours, do not demand to have it back," for you will not be able to. [5] "To everyone who asks of you, give and do not demand it back," for the Father wants all to be given from his own gifts of grace. Praise be to the one who gives according to the commandment, for he is blameless. Woe to the one who takes. Of course, if anyone is in need and takes, he is blameless. But whoever is not in need will be called to account for why he took and for what purpose. He will be imprisoned and interrogated about what he has done, and "he will not come out from there until he has paid the last penny." [6] Clearly this word has been spoken about this matter: "Let your charitable gifts sweat in your hands until you know to whom you should give them."

TEXTUAL NOTES

1:3 On the procedure of the redactor, see what has been said above. Von Harnack disagrees, ascribing a deeper plan to the redactor: what is written in 1:3–6 is supposed to be an exposition of the first part of the double commandment, an explanation of the love of God, while the love of neighbor is unfolded from 2:1 on (cf. von Harnack, *Prolegomena*, 93). However, the content of the Christian interpolation, wherein 1:3f deals with the behavior against the enemy and 1:5f deals with proper giving,

---

3. TN: It is not clear which source Knopf references here. It could be any among those listed in the bibliography.

does not speak in favor of von Harnack's view. — The insertion in 1:3–5 employs the material from Matt 5:39–48 and Luke 6:27–36 in such a way that it follows neither text exclusively; see, for example, Did. 1:4 with Matt 5:39–41, but ἐὰν ἄρῃ τις τὸ ἱμάτιόν σου with Luke 6:29; Did. 1:4 end and 1:5 beginning are much more reminiscent of Luke 6:30 than Matt 5:42. The redactor either proceeds from both gospels freely and from memory or he follows a tradition of the words of the Lord unknown to us. The words of the Lord, not necessarily specific written gospels, move next to the OT texts as sacred authority; on the use of Jesus' words, see also 1 Clem. 13; many passages in 2 Clem.; Justin, 1 Apol. 15–17.

1:3 The precepts of loving one's enemies that appear here differ strikingly from the parallels in Matt 5:44, 46 and Luke 6:27f, 32, and again differently in Justin, 1 Apol. 15.9: εἰ ἀγαπᾶτε τοὺς ἀγαπῶντας ὑμᾶς, τί καινὸν ποιεῖτε; καὶ γὰρ οἱ πόρνοι τοῦτο ποιοῦσιν. ἐγὼ δὲ ὑμῖν λέγω· εὔχεσθε ὑπὲρ τῶν ἐχθρῶν ὑμῶν καὶ ἀγαπᾶτε τοὺς μισοῦντας ὑμᾶς καὶ εὐλογεῖτε τοὺς καταρωμένους ὑμῖν καὶ εὔχεσθε ὑπὲρ τῶν ἐπηρεαζόντων ὑμᾶς. For an explanation of the sense of the Did., see the explanations of the gospels. Nevertheless, there are two peculiarities within the Did.: (1) νηστεύετε δὲ ὑπὲρ τῶν διωκόντων ὑμᾶς. The "persecutors" here (as in general the "enemies" throughout the entire context) are personal enemies, those who desire evil, and evildoers, who oppress Christians. But, of course, the hatred of the circumstances can be "for the sake of the name." Fasting is to be performed for the persecutors. The explanation of the rule is to be sought either in the fact that fasting is a good work which supports prayer in the most powerful way, is as often found in ancient texts. Prayer and fasting become one. The parallels are then the long explanations in the *Didaskalia* 21 (Flemming, *Didaskalia*), where it is commanded to perform the regular weekly fast and the great fast at Easter for the benefit of unbelieving Jews (105.24; 108.2): "Therefore, when you fast, pray and beg for the lost . . . . But you shall fast continually on these days, always, and especially those who are of the (gentile) nations. For because the people (of the Jews) did not obey, I have freed them (the gentiles) from the blindness and from the error of idols, and have received them, that through your (the apostles') fasting and the fasting of those who are from the gentile nations, and through your service in these days, asking and praying because of the error and the ruin of the people, your prayer and your petition may be accepted before my Father in heaven . . . and forgive them (the Jews) for all that they have done to me. For this reason, I also said to you previously in the gospels, 'Pray for your enemies,' pray well for those who mourn the ruin of unbelievers. Therefore, know, brothers, that you must keep our fast, which we observe at the Passover, because the brothers have not obeyed." The second way of explaining νηστεύειν is that the savings one makes while

fasting are to be used to help the persecutors; on this, see Herm. *Sim.* V
3.7f, see further Origen, *Hom. Lev.* X, end (Lommatzsch, *Origenis Opera*,
9:372): *invenimus enim in quodam libello ab apostolis dictum: beatus est, qui
etiam ieiunat pro eo, ut alat pauperem*; Aristides, *Apol.* 15.9 (Goodspeed,
Apologeten, 21): "And if someone among you is poor or in need and you
do not have any excess food, then fast for two or three days to provide the
necessary food for the needy"; finally *Didaskalia* 21, end (114.4ff): "Rejoice
. . . and break your fast (namely in the Easter vigil) and offer the profit of
your six-day fast to the Lord God. You, who have worldly possessions in
abundance, help the poor and needy and refresh them diligently, so that
the reward of your fasting may be received." (2) The other peculiarity is: καὶ
οὐχ ἕξετε ἐχθρόν. The future tense expresses the consequence of the previous imperative such that the possible translation "and you shall have no
enemy" is excluded. The word is mentioned in *Didaskalia* 1 (3.9) in such a
way that it appears connected with other instructions of the Sermon on the
Mount such as the word of the Lord: "And again he says in the gospel, 'Love
those who hate you and pray for those who curse you, and you shall have
no enemies.'" Perhaps the saying originates from a lost gospel tradition.
The instruction can be explained either as follows: the enemy whom one
loves cannot in truth be an enemy, since one does not perceive him as such:
the perfect one has no enemy, only brothers and sisters. (Stoic parallels in
Epictetus, *Ench.* 1: ἐὰν δὲ τὸ σὸν μόνον οἰηθῇς σὸν εἶναι, τὸ δὲ ἀλλότριον, ὥσπερ
ἐστίν, ἀλλότριον, οὐδείς σε ἀναγκάσει οὐδέποτε, οὐδείς σε κωλύσει . . . ἐχθρὸν
οὐχ ἕξεις, οὐδὲ γὰρ βλαβερόν τι πείσῃ, see *Ench.* 30: σὲ γὰρ ἄλλος οὐ βλάψει,
ἂν μὴ σὺ θέλῃς· τότε δὲ ἔσῃ βεβλαμμένος, ὅταν ὑπολάβῃς βλάπτεσθαι, related
is also *Diatr.* III 22.100). Or else, good confidence is expressed that one can
change the enemy's mind through friendly behavior; see 1 Pet 2:15; Justin,
1 Apol. 14.3 (of the Christians): ὑπὲρ τῶν ἐχθρῶν εὐχόμενοι καὶ τοὺς ἀδίκως
μισοῦντας πείθειν πειρώμενοι. Clement of Alexandria, *Strom.* 2.19.102.4: καί
μοι δοκεῖ τὸν πιστὸν προμαντευόμενος Ὅμηρος εἰρηκέναι· δὸς φίλῳ. <φίλῳ μὲν
κοινωνητέον, ἵν᾽ ἔτι καὶ μᾶλλον περιμένῃ φίλος>, ἐχθρῷ δὲ ἐπικουρητέον, ἵνα
μὴ μείνῃ ἐχθρός· ἐπικουρίᾳ γὰρ εὔνοια μὲν συνδεῖται, λύεται δὲ ἔχθρα. Clement
of Alexandria, *Strom.* 7.12.69.4: τίς δ᾽ ἂν καὶ ἐχθρὸς εὐλόγως γένοιτο ἀνδρὸς
οὐδεμίαν οὐδαμῶς παρέχοντος αἰτίαν ἔχθρας;

1:4 The introductory admonition is very strange. It sounds as if it introduces a warning against sexual sins. The particularly striking σωματικῶν
has already been changed by Bryennios to κοσμικῶν (cf. Titus 2:12; 2 Clem.
17:3; Apost. Const. VII.1), but surely too quickly. For the author, according
to the context, anger, vindictiveness, and insistence on one's own right are
desires that are connected with the earthly-fleshly nature of man and with his
bodily construction. Similarly, the σαρκικαὶ ἐπιθυμίαι of 1 Pet 2:11 are to be

understood in the broadest sense. Post-Pauline Christianity can speak easily of desire which resides in the σάρξ. On σωματικαὶ ἐπιθυμίαι, see 4 Macc 1:32: τῶν ἐπιθυμιῶν αἱ μέν εἰσιν ψυχικαί, αἱ δὲ σωματικαί, καὶ τούτων ἀμφοτέρων ὁ λογισμὸς ἐπικρατεῖν φαίνεται, where a trichotomy of the human being is present (reason, soul, body). The root of the view of σωματικαὶ ἐπιθυμίαι is to be sought in Greek literature, namely in Plato. The most ancient expression of Christianity does not speak so contemptuously of the body, which after all is given by God and is worthy of resurrection. For Plato, see clearly *Phaidon* 11, p. 66Bf: ἕως ἂν τὸ σῶμα ἔχωμεν . . . καὶ συμπεφυρμένη ᾖ ὑμῶν ἡ ψυχὴ μετὰ τοιούτου κακοῦ, οὐ μὴ ποτε κτησώμεθα ἱκανῶς οὗ ἐπιθυμοῦμεν . . . ἐρώτων δὲ καὶ ἐπιθυμιῶν καὶ φόβων καὶ εἰδώλων παντοδαπῶν καὶ φλυαρίας ἐμπίμπλησιν ἡμᾶς πολλῆς . . . καὶ γὰρ πολέμους καὶ στάσεις καὶ μάχας οὐδὲν ἄλλο παρέχει ἢ τὸ σῶμα καὶ αἱ τούτου ἐπιθυμίαι. The younger Stoics, under Platonic influence, also speak contemptuously of the body; see Seneca, *Ep.* 65.16: *nam corpus hoc animi pondus ac poena est; premente illo urgetur, in vinclis est, nisi accessit philosophia et illum respirare rerum naturae spectaculo iussit et a terrenis ad divina dimisit.* Seneca, *Helv.* 11.7: *corpusculum hoc, custodia et vinculum animi, huc atque illuc iactatur; in hoc supplicia, in hoc latrocinia, in hoc morbi exercentur: animus quidem ipse sacer et aeternus est et cui non possit inici manus.* Epictetus, *Diatr.* I 9.11: . . . οἳ ἐπιγνόντες τὴν πρὸ τοὺς θεοὺς συγγένειαν καὶ ὅτι δεσμά τινα ταῦτα προσηρτήμεθα τὸ σῶμα καὶ τὴν κτῆσιν αὐτοῦ καὶ ὅσα τούτων ἕνεκα ἀναγκαῖα ἡμῖν γίνεται εἰς οἰκονομίαν καὶ ἀναστροφὴν τὴν ἐν τῷ βίῳ, ὡς βάρη τινὰ καὶ ἀνιαρὰ καὶ ἄχρηστα ἀπορρίψαι θέλωσι καὶ ἀπελθεῖν πρὸς τοὺς συγγενεῖς, I 3.3: . . . δύο ταῦτα ἐν τῇ γενέσει ἡμῶν ἐγκαταμέμικται, τὸ σῶμα μὲν κοινὸν προς τὰ ζῷα, ὁ λόγος δὲ καὶ ἡ γνώμη κοινὸν πρὸς τοὺς θεούς . . . . Epictetus also speaks often of the σωμάτιον or the σωμάτιον κτησείδιον; see the index in Schenkl's edition *Quaestiones Epictetae*; on the Stoic contempt of the body, see Bonhöffer, *Epictet und die Stoa*, 33–40. On the series of the words of the Lord, see Matt 5:39–41; Luke 6:29f; Justin, *1 Apol.* 16; and above all as very noteworthy with respect to the order of the words and in the version of the last saying in agreement with Tatian in the Diatessaron: "*Qui percutit maxillam tuam, porrige ei et alteram partem . . . .* And whoever compels you to go with him one mile, go with him two. And whoever wants to take your tunic, give him your cloak as well. If anyone takes your possessions away, do not demand them back" (Zahn, *Tatians Diatessaron*, 133f). The promise: καὶ ἔσῃ τέλειος is reminiscent of Matt 5:48; see, however, the comments at Did. 6:2. The addition of a curious justification—οὐδὲ γὰρ δύνασαι—contains the very flat reminder that the poor Christian, belonging to the lower classes, will not be able to recover what was stolen by the more powerful, violent pagan. But there was no mention of poor Christians and miserable pagans before, but only of personal enemies; and could such a hard truth simply be put forward as general experience in the Roman legal state? We see from many papyri the fury of the provincials, also their countless appeals against the lower authorities to the higher ones. Thus, the justification must be understood from the inner compulsion of the "perfect": it is inwardly impossible for him to take back what is his by countervailing force or by legal means. Von Harnack suggested καίπερ δυνάμενος as the original text, which then had been altered into the weaker οὐδὲ γὰρ δύνασαι for the catechumens.

1:5–6 The second group of intercalated exhortations is about giving. The closest parallel is Hermas, *Mand.* II 4–6, which must come from the same source as Did. 1:5f and offers the exhortation in a partly more original form (thus the weakening of Did. 1:6); see further *Didaskalia* 17 and Apost. Const. IV 3. — On the beginning of v. 5, see Luke 6:30; Matt 5:42; Justin, *1 Apol.* 15.10. On πᾶσι γὰρ κτλ., see Luke 6:36 and, for even closer parallels, see Sib. Or. II 88f: πλοῦτον ἔχων σὴν χεῖρα πενητεύουσιν ὄρεξον, Ὧν σοι ἔδωκε θεός, τούτων χρήζοντι παράσχου (and almost exactly thus in Carmen, *Phocylideum* 28f). The χαρίσματα here are earthly, worldly gifts (Hermas has ἐκ τῶν ἰδίων δωρημάτων); the subject embedded in ἰδίων can be God (thus, the gifts he has given) or man (thus, the gifts each has received). The second version is the better one; divine grace is denoted by χαρισμάτων. The ἐντολή is probably a word of the Lord, which was just now (beginning of v. 5) alluded to. ἀθῷος here and immediately afterward has the final judgment in view. — The unrestricted commandment simply to give necessarily led to serious abuses in the ancient Christian congregations, as everywhere else. They are to be countered here (1) by sharpening the conscience of the alms receiver by severe threats and (2) by limiting the unconditional commandment by a rule of prudence recommended to the almsgiver. The generosity of the Christians among themselves and the abuse that could be committed with it has been noticed even by a superficial, though sharp-sighted observer like Lucian in *Pereg.* 13. — εἰ μὲν γὰρ χρείαν κτλ. The γάρ introduces the entirety of the following thought for this reason, for the οὐαὶ τῷ λαμβάνοντι is first explained by the ὁ δὲ μὴ χρείαν ἔχων κτλ. The author alludes to Matt 5:25f (Luke 12:58f), however it is no longer an earthly but a heavenly judge. The ἐξετασθήσεται is the embarrassing questioning in the sense of Matt 18:34, which may also be implied here. The popular meaning is: wrongfully acquired property accompanies the one who receives, up to the heavenly seat of judgment.

1:6 The provision cancels the general commandment at the beginning of v. 5. The origin of the saying, which is introduced with a grand citation formula (cf. 16:7), cannot be determined. It is often repeated in later ecclesiastical literature from Augustine on into the Middle Ages (passages in Resch, *Agrapha*, 91f; also in Funk and Drews). On the content, see Sir 12:1:

ἐὰν εὖ ποιῇς, γνῶθι τίνι ποιεῖς and especially Sib. Or. II 79: ἱδρώσῃ σταχύων χειρὶ χρῄζοντι παράσχου. In Christian ethics, apart from Did. 1:6, only from the end of the second century onward is the warning against giving too quickly issued; see Clement of Alexandria in *Anastasius Sinaites Quaest.* 14 (Stählin, *Clemens Alexandrinus III*, 225): ἐλεημοσύνας δεῖ ποιεῖν, ὁ λόγος φησίν, ἀλλὰ μετὰ κρίσεως καὶ τοῖς ἀξίοις. ὥσπερ γὰρ ὁ γεωργὸς σπείρει οὐκ εἰς ἅπασαν γῆν ἀλλ᾽ εἰς τὴν ἀγαθήν, ἵνα αὐτῷ καρποφορήσῃ, οὕτω δεῖ σπείρειν τὴν εὐποιΐαν εἰς εὐλαβεῖς καὶ πνευματικούς, ἵνα τῆς ἀπ᾽ αὐτῶν εὐκαρπίας διὰ τῶν εὐχῶν ἐπιτύχῃς (what follows is a reference to Sir 12:2).

3. A Catalog of Vices of the Sins of Action (2:1–7)

TRANSLATION

[2:1] Now the second commandment of the teaching: [2] "Do not murder," "do not commit adultery," do not molest boys, do not fornicate, "do not steal," do not practice sorcery, do not mix poison, do not abort a fetus or kill the newborn, "do not covet your neighbor's property." [3] "Do not commit perjury," "do not bear false witness," do not insult others, do not bear grudges for evil (which you have suffered). [4] Do not be doubleminded or duplicitous, for duplicity is a snare of death. [5] Your word is not to be a lie or empty, but instead characterized by action. [6] Do not be covetous or a robber or a hypocrite or mischievous or proud. Do not plot against your neighbor. [7] Do not hate anyone, but admonish some, pray for others, and love some more than your own soul.

TEXTUAL NOTES

2:1 On the traditional formula δευτέρα δὲ κτλ. inserted by the Christian redactor, see the comments above at 1:3. In the original "ways," 2:2 is immediately connected with 1:3.

  2:2 See Barn. 19:4–6. First, in ch. 2, a catalog of vices follows, which warns against a number of crude sins of action. On ancient Christian vice catalogs, see Lietzmann's excursus on Rom 1:31; also see Resch, *Aposteldekret*, 110ff; Seeberg, *Katechismus*, 25ff; Seeberg, *Evangelium*, 123. In Resch and Seeberg see also the studies on the types and relationships of the Jewish-Christian catalogs. In the vice catalog here—as well as in the related catalogs of the following chapters—we see clearly Jewish, Old Testament influence not only in general by the fact that sins of action are enumerated, but even more precisely by the fact that the Decalogue has had an influence on the sins mentioned; see Lev 20:13–17 (Deut 5:17–21): οὐ φονεύσεις, οὐ μοιχεύσεις, οὐ κλέψεις (in this order in AF, cf. also Matt 19:18), οὐ ψευδομαρτυρήσεις . . . οὐκ ἐπιθυμήσεις . . . ὅσα τῷ πλησίον σού ἐστιν. The enumeration in Did. 2:1–3 expands the list in the Decalogue, mostly by inserting related sins in each case. Note also the rhetoric, the tone of the passage: first general forms with -εύσεις and then more specific forms such as -ήσεις. See then the series in 5:1, which is related to 2:1–8. — παιδοφθορήσεις πορνεύσεις is easily related to μοιχεύσεις; see, for example, Carmen, *Phocylideum* 3: μήτε γαμοκλοπέειν, μήτ᾽ ἄρσενα κύπριν ὀρίνειν. In the urgent warning against sexual sins, Hellenistic Jewish ethics can probably also be recognized. παιδοφθορεῖν is a Hellenistic word; see Barn. 10:6; Justin, *Dial.* 95.1; Tatian, *Diat.* 8.1. Murder, fornication, theft, sorcery, and the mixing of poison are fittingly added, since their practice was mostly aimed at the life and property of the other and at the arousal of love and hatred. Magic is immensely widespread in the Hellenistic era; some material can be found in Wendland, *Kultur*, 133f; Friedländer, *Sittengeschichte*, 1:514ff; see further Dieterich, *Abraxas*; Cumont, *Religionen*, ch. 7; for texts, see Acts 8:9–11; 13:6, 8; 19:16; Carmen, *Phocylideum* 149: φάρμακα μὴ τεύχειν· μαγικῶν βίβλων ἀπέχεσθαι, Wünsch, *Antike Fluchtafeln*; Wünsch, *Zauberpapyrus*; in the literature, see Theocritus, *Id.* II; Horace, *Epod.* 5; *Sat.* I 8; Lucian, *Dial. meretr.* 4; Apuleius, *Metam.* I; III 19–25; etc. — φαρμακεύειν does not just have to do with the preparation of deadly poison, but also the preparation of magical potions or food through which, for example, hatred and love are aroused, the tongue of an opponent in court is bound, the limbs of a fighter are strengthened or paralyzed, dreams are sent, and so on. The deep abhorrence which Jews and Christians are supposed to have of all these things is due to their connection with paganism and its idols (cf. Did. 3:4). φθορά = the more classical ἀποφθορά, premature birth or miscarriage, the *abortus*, and φθόριον is the abortifacient. — Abortion of the foetus is here because it follows murder, fornication, and magic potions; the same covens certainly made poisonous potions and love potions and mixed them with abortifacients or interfered with the womb of pregnant women (cf. *Qui abortionis aut amatorium poculum dant . . . relegantur*: a decision of Severus or Caracalla in the *Corpus juris: Digesta* XLVIII 19; 39.5; a survey of the means of contemporary medicine, with a lot of ancient magic along with it, is given in Soranus, Περὶ γυναικείων, 19). The abandonment of the newborn follows after abortion (cf. also 5:2). On the abandonment of children, which was widespread at the time, see Oxyrhynchus Papyri I 37 and 38 IV 744 (the three pieces reprinted in Lietzmann, *Griechische Papyri*, numbers 5, 18, 19); Justin, *1 Apol.* 27.1; 29.1; Minucius Felix Octavius

30.2: *vos enim video et vixdum procreatos filios nunc feris et avibus exponere, nunc adstrangulatos misero mortis genere elidere*; Apuleius, *Metam*. X 23: *maritum habuit, cuius pater peregre proficiscens, mandavit uxori suae, matri eiusdem invenis—quod enim sarcina praegnationis oneratam eam reinquebat—ut, si sexus sequioris* (= feminine) *edididisset fetum, protinus quod esset editum, necaretur*. On the moral and legal side of the question, see Marquardt, *Privatleben*, 1:82 and Mitteis, *Reichsrecht*, 361.

2:3 See Barn. 19:4. οὐκ ἐπιθυμήσεις . . . οὐ ψευδομαρτυρήσεις comes from the Decalogue (see above). The period is better after ἀποκτενεῖς (thus Bryennios). Already purely formulaic (-ήσεις, cf. above) οὐκ ἐπιθυμήσεις belongs together with what follows, but also in terms of content, inasmuch as ἐπιορκήσεις and ψευδομαρτυρήσεις after all usually take place in court, in negotiations about what is mine and what is yours, where the property of one's neighbor is desired. On the content, see Sib. Or. II 64, 68f: Μήδ' ἐπιορκήσῃς μητ' ἀγνὼς μήτε ἑκόντι· Ψεύδορκον στυγέει θεός, ὅττι κεν ἄν τις ὁμόσσῃ and almost in agreement verbatim in Carmen, *Phocylideum* 12 and 16f. The Did. prohibits perjury, though not oaths in general (unlike Jas 5:12). κακολογήσεις and μνησικακήσεις again connect easily with what precedes; for parallels, see Prov 20:20 and 1 Clem. 2:5; 62:2; Barn. 2:8.

2:4–5 Sins of hypocrisy with the tongue and the mind are a good transition from the preceding; on the exhortation, see (other than Barn. 19:7) the woe in Sib. Or. III 36ff: αἳ γένος αἱμοχαρὲς δόλιον κακὸν ἀσεβέων τε, Ψευδῶν διγλώσσων ἀνθρώπων καὶ κακοηθῶν, Λεκτροκλόπων εἰδωλολατρῶν δόλια φρονεόντων. — δίγλωσσος and the rare διγνώμων belong to the later language; for δίγλωσσος, see Prov 11:13; Sir 5:9, 14; 16:1; 28:13; Sib. Or. III 37 (just cited). On διγνώμων, which is not yet attested, see the parallel formation εὐγνώμων as well as δίγνωμος (e.g., Hippolytus, *Haer*. V 26.1; X 15.2: δίγνωμος, δίσωμος. *Etymologicon Magnum*, ed. Gaisford, under ἀλλοπρόσαλλος: δίγνωμος, διπρόσωπος . . .). παγὶς θανάτου is taken over from the LXX; see Ps 17:6; Prov 14:27; 21:6; as well as 13:14; Tob 14:10; and see in general the frequent use of παγίς in Psalms and the wisdom books. The expression here can mean: deadly snare or snare with which death catches a person. On the idea, see Prov 6:2: παγὶς γὰρ ἰσχυρὰ ἀνδρὶ τὰ ἴδια χείλη, also 11:9: ἐν στόματι ἀσεβῶν παγὶς πολίταις, see further the philippic against the tongue in Sir 28:13–26; Jas 3:1–12. — The λόγος is ψευδής when it is mendacious· κενός when it is vain, boastful. The words ἀλλὰ μεμεστωμένος πράξει stand out among the whole of the negative admonitions, have no parallel in Barnabas, and are absent in L; they are present in KAS and therefore must probably be judged as additions. Truthful speech must prove itself by deed; see Poimandres XVI 2 (Reitzenstein, *Poimandres*, 349): Ἕλληνες γάρ, ὦ βασιλεῦ, λόγους ἔχουσι κενοὺς οὐδὲ ἀποδείξεων ἐνεργητικούς . . . ἡμεῖς δὲ οὐ λόγοις χρώμεθα, ἀλλὰ φωναῖς μεσταῖς τῶν ἔργων. On the thought, see 1 Clem. 38:2; Ign. *Eph.* 15:1f; Jas 1:22; 1 John 3:18; Justin, *1 Apol.* 14.5: οὐ γὰρ σοφιστὴς ὑπῆρχεν ἀλλὰ δύναμις θεοῦ ὁ λόγος αὐτοῦ ἦν. Justin, *1 Apol.* 16.8: οὐ γὰρ τοὺς μόνον λέγοντας ἀλλὰ τοὺς καὶ τὰ ἔργα πράττοντας σωθήσεσθαι ἔφη, but also the Greek wisdom, Theognis 979: μη μοι ἀνὴρ εἴη γλώσσῃ φίλος, ἀλλὰ καὶ ἔργῳ.

2:6 See Barn. 19:3, 6. The warning against lying and boasting (2:4f) is followed by the warning against greed (πλεονέκτης) and robbery (ἅρπαξ), hypocrisy (ὑποκριτής), malice (κακοήθης), arrogance (ὑπερήφανος) and the evil desire that turns into acts of deceitfulness (οὐ λήψῃ βουλὴν πονηράν); the series contains related items and also connects well with the preceding (2:3–5). On the secondary order πλεονέκτης and ἅρπαξ, see also 1 Cor 5:10f. "Robbery" is of course not highway robbery, but the violent act of the strong against the weak, of the cunning against the harmless, keeping with the forms of civil order.

2:7 See Barn. 19:11, 5. First of all, the text with ἀλλά is questionable. H has three components: οὓς μὲν ἐλέγξεις, περὶ δὲ ὧν προσεύξῃ, οὓς δὲ ἀγαπήσεις ὑπὲρ τὴν ψυχήν σου; K has four components through the insertion of οὓς δὲ ἐλεήσεις after ἐλέγξεις (from Jude 23); on the other hand, A omits everything from περί on, and L also has only one component, the last one: *quosdam amabis super animam tuam.* In H, on which we base the translation and explanation, people are divided into three groups. The first includes those who still can be saved, even if they are afflicted by sins; they may be found inside or outside of the church. The earnest, convicting repentance is to be attributed to them; whether ἐλέγχειν as in 1 Cor 14:24f is still connected with the spiritual gift of reading the mind (cf. Weinel, *Wirkungen*, 183ff) cannot be said, though probably not; see the use of the word in Did. 4:3; 15:3. The second kind of people are those who are lost according to human insight, the inaccessible; they can only be commended to God in prayer. Finally, the third kind are the full-fledged brothers within the church. Jude 22f is apparently in some kind of relationship with Did. 2:7. Love of the enemy, which Jesus demands, is shrunk to praying for the unbelievers that they might be converted: the heart belongs only to the brothers in the church. A noteworthy parallel to the threefold division of people presented here is found in the legend of the Buddha, *Lalita vistara* 25: the completely perfect, who in any case come to the knowledge of the truth; the completely perverse, who can never understand the teaching; and finally those for whom everything depends on having the teaching preached to them (Beckh, *Buddhismius,* 1:65).

4. A Catalog of the Sins of the Mind (3:1–6)

TRANSLATION

³:¹ My child, flee from all evil and from everything which looks like it. ² Do not be angry, for anger leads to murder, nor jealous, nor quarrelsome, nor hot-tempered, for murder comes from all these things. ³ My child, do not be full of lust, for lust leads to fornication; nor be foul-mouthed or have wandering eye, for adultery comes from these things. ⁴ My child, do not be a birdwatcher,⁴ for this leads to idolatry; nor be a conjurer, nor a stargazer, nor a sorcerer, nor desire to look at or listen to these things. For idolatry comes from all these things. ⁵ My child, do not be a liar, for lying leads to theft; nor greedy, nor vain, for stealing comes from all these things. ⁶ My child, do not be a grumbler, for this leads to blasphemy; nor insolent, nor ill-minded, for blasphemy comes from all these things.

TEXTUAL NOTES

A carefully elaborated catalog of vices follows, which begins with the general warning (3:1), and then lists five great sins in five pairs: murder, fornication (adultery), idolatry, theft, and blasphemy. In each of these great sins, it is demonstrated how a relatively small matter, a thought or a minor deed, leads to something greater. On the structure, note still the introductory τέχνον repeated five times. — As parallels to the way in which the admonition against the lesser sins is made forceful by reference to the greater ones arising from them or connected with them, see in addition to the antitheses of the Sermon on the Mount, which can also be mentioned here, the great Stoic catalogs of vice in Diogenes Laertius, *Lives* VII 110–14 (supplement 1 to Lietzmann, *Römer*); Cicero, *Tusc.* IV 5–13, 30; the similar Stoic diatribe in 4 Macc 1:13—3:18; additionally T. Jud. 14–19; among other passages. Wherever a finer ethical understanding shows itself and where higher moral instruction and education set in, there also the superior sins and virtues will be sought after in order to derive the lesser ones from them, and there also the origin of the greater, actual sin will be searched for within the mind. — The salutation τέχνον is, like υἱέ, typical in the style of Jewish wisdom literature; see Proverbs as well as Wisdom of Solomon and Sirach. However, the salutation also recurs often in the religious language of Hellenism; the one to be initiated is the spiritual child of the mystagogue

---

4. TN: Birdwatching within this context means "watching for omens."

who delivers the teachings to him; see Poimandres IV, V, VIII, X, XII, XIII, etc.; the "fathers" and "brothers" in the Mysteries of Mithros (cf. Cumont, *Mysterien des Mithras*, 115f), at the beginning of the Mithras liturgy (μόνῳ τέκνῳ), or at the beginning of the Leiden book of gnostic papyri, VIII Moses: ἀπέχεις τὴν ἱεράν, ὦ τέκνον, . . . βίβλον . . . ἔρρωσο, ὦ τέκνον (Dieterich, *Abraxas*, 155); also in the Greek Thiasoi the honorable designation "fathers" is used often for the leaders, to which then τέκνα and υἱοί must have corresponded. The salutation fits Did. 3 particularly well because it concerns the instruction of catechumen (proselytes).

3:1 The general exhortation, from which the others are derived, stands at the forefront. L and Life of Shenouda conceive of πονηροῦ as masculine, unquestionably incorrectly. As parallels, see b. Ḥul. 44b (Goldschmidt, *Der babylonische Talmud*, 8:936): "Flee from the ugly and from that which is like it." The relatedness of the two phrases should probably be assumed, although the admonition here is φεῦγε ἀπὸ παντὸς πονηροῦ and the formula "and what is similar to it" are often found in corresponding ethical instructions; see, for example, Chrysippus in Stobaeus, *Ecl.* II 70.21 (von Arnim, *Stoicorum veterum fragmenta*, 3:#104): . . . οἷον τὴν φθονερίαν, τὴν ἐπιλυπίαν καὶ τὰ ὅμοια καὶ ἔτι τὰ νοσήματα καὶ τὰ ἀρρωστήματα, οἷον φιλαργυρίαν, οἰνοφλυγίαν καὶ τὰ παραπλήσια. Cicero, *Tusc.* IV 7.16: *ira, excandescentia, odium, inimicitia, discordia, indigentia, desiderium et cetera eius modi*; 11.26: *avaritia, ambitio, mulierositas, . . . cuppedia et si qua similia*; see also Gal 5:21; 3 Bar. 4; Justin, *Dial.* 93.1; etc.

3:2 On the thought see Matt 5:21f, but in our passage it is admittedly more easily and more self-evidently said that anger etc. leads to bloodshed, not that, upon deeper consideration, it is fundamentally equal to murder. ὀργή is the general concept; θυμός is rage (*ira nascens et modo existens, quae θύμωσις Graece dicitur*, Cicero, *Tusc.* IV 9.21). First Clement deals extensively with the ruinousness of ζῆλος (cf. especially 1 Clem. 3:4—6:4). In the ancient congregations, jealousy, envy, and partisanship (περὶ πρωτείων καὶ δόξης τινός, Herm. *Sim.* VIII 7.4) were often very disruptive. ἐριστικός is the quarrelsome one who always takes pleasure in quarreling. τούτων ἁπάντων here and in the following neuter plural in loose design.

3:3 ἐπιθυμία in this context, as often in Jewish and Christian edifying language, means sexual desire, not desire in the broader sense, as it is the case, for instance, with λύπη, φόβος, ἡδονή together with the Stoics, one of the four γένη τῶν παθῶν. ὑψηλόφθαλμος does not occur anywhere else; A has replaced it with ῥιψόφθαλμος = one who casts lustful glances and thus ὑψηλόφθαλμος must also be explained in this way. But can it really mean that? There is probably a textual corruption here. Instead of μοιχεῖαι, we would expect πορνεῖαι; it is the only instance in the five pairs where the main term is alternated within the series.

3:4 On superstition, see the remarks at Did. 2:2. It is inseparable from the pagan gods and therefore leads to idolatry. Fearful timidity speaks from the exhortation, not the consciousness of superior enlightenment. On the belief in bird augury, which is ancient in the east and also widespread among the Greeks and Romans, see for example the many signs from birds in Suetonius' biographies, namely concerning the birth and death of emperors; see further Epictetus, *Diatr.* II 7: Πῶς μαντευτέον and Artemidorus (time of Antonine), *Onir.* II 69, where, in addition to dream interpretation, only divination from stars, sacrifices, birds, and intestines are recognized. People ask the bird diviners about death, danger, disease, business, lawsuits, inheritance, and much more. ἐπαοιδός, the Ionic form (cf. ἐπαοιδή, *Od.* 19.457) has become dominant in Koine Greek; the Attic form is ἐπῳδός. What is meant is the *incantatio*, the spells of healing and of injury by means of magic formulas and rites, especially popular with illnesses. μαθηματικός is the astrologist, the "Chaldean"; astrology is the preferred science of the time, as well as the most popular form of telling the future (see above at Did. 2:1). περικαθαίρειν finally leads into the area of the ancient, widespread, multiform cathartics, the purification and expiation ritual: by water, fire, eggs, pungent, corrosive, as well as disgusting substances, by sacrifices and formulaic sayings, cultic or moral "impurity" is removed, healing spells are created. Good parallels to the presupposed activity here can be found at Hippolytus, *Haer.* IX 14.2f: οὗτοι (elk cords) καὶ μαθηματικοῖς καὶ ἀστρολογικοῖς καὶ μαγικοῖς προσέχουσιν ὡς ἀληθέσι, . . . ἐπαοιδάς τε καὶ ἐπιλόγους τινὰς διδάσκουσι προς τε κυνοδήκτους καὶ δαιμονιῶντας καὶ ἑτέραις νόσοις κατεχομένους (15.4–6 brings a ἐπαοιδή against dog bites, etc.); X 29.3: χρῶνται (also elk cords) δὲ ἐπαοιδαῖς καὶ βαπτίσμασιν ἐπὶ τῇ τῶν στοιχείων ὁμολογίᾳ. σεσόβηνται δὲ περὶ ἀστρολογίαν καὶ μαθηματικὴν καὶ μαγικήν. Epist. Hadriani ad Sevianuum (Preuschen, *Analecta*, 1:16f): *nemo illic* (in Egypt) *archisynagogus Judaeorum, nemo Samarites, nemo Christianorum presbyter non mathematicus, non haruspex non aliptes.* Curiosity, mixed with horror, and old habit seduced the catechumens to watch the magic work, in which they otherwise took no further part, but which is also forbidden. L reads *videre nec audire* and is supported by K.

3:5 He who lies steals. It is also easy to understand that greed leads to theft. More difficult is κενόδοξος; but striving to be respected by means of possessions and honors may well seduce one to unlawful enrichment. The first section of v. 5 is cited by Clement of Alexandria as γραφή in *Strom.* 1.20.100.4.

3:6 γόγγυσος is a rare word; see however Prov 16:28 (Theodotion) and the later grammarian Arcadius (Barker, Ἀρκαδίου περι τονων, 78.1ff): τὰ εἰς δύο σσ παραληγόμενα τῷ υ προπαροξύνεται, μέθυσσος, γόγγυσσος, Διόνυσσος. The other formations of the same root, on the other hand, are frequent. What is meant is grumbling against fate, quarreling with God. On this matter, see in addition to Jude 16; Eph 4:31; (Did. 3:10) for example Theophrastus, *Char.* 17.1: ἔστιν ἡ μεμψιμοιρία ἐπιτίμησις παρὰ τὸ προσῆκον τῶν δεδομένων and Epictetus, *Diss.* III 2.14: ἄνθρωπον . . . μεμψίμοιρον, ὀξύθυμον, δειλόν, πάντα μεμφόμενον, πᾶσιν ἐγκαλοῦντα, μηδέποτε ἡσυχίαν ἄγοντα, πέρπερον. Blasphemy also arises from self-important, puffed-up presumption (αὐθάδεια), because the created man forgets his limitations toward the creator (cf. 2 Pet 2:10). More remote, however, is πονηρόφρων, but of course all sorts of things, including blasphemy, can be derived from this rather general epithet. πονηρόφρων occurs only here and in the dependent passage Apost. Const. VII 7. However, ἀγαθόφρων is attested. The compounds πονηρο- are all rare and late. βλασφημίαι should be understood as the express insults and curses of God, which are much more familiar to the ancient southerners than to us.

5. Positive Exhortations toward Kindness and Humility (3:7–10)

TRANSLATION

[7] Instead, be meek, for the meek will "inherit the earth." [8] Be patient, and merciful, and without falsehood, and be calm, and good, and tremble all the time at the words which you have heard. [9] Do not exalt yourself and do not let your soul become arrogant. Your soul should not cleave to the heights; but you should walk with the righteous and the good. [10] Accept as good whatever happens to you, knowing that nothing happens without God.

TEXTUAL NOTES

The catalog of vices is followed by a series of mostly positive exhortations, some of which are repetitions of what has been said before. Their main content is: be meek, kind, and humble! They cohere well as a contrast to what immediately precedes (v. 6; cf. also v. 1).

3:7 See Barn. 19:4. The *Vorlage* is Ps 36:11; Matt 5:5, as is known, may not be original at all, but a later insertion after Ps 36.

3:8 See Barn. 19:4. The exhortation to meekness is followed by the exhortation to patience, mercy, etc. The series shows some deviations in the side references (Barnabas, AKS) also in L, but the text handed down in H cannot be improved thereby. ἀγαθός is very general, but will probably have to be defined more closely according to the other requirements: good in conversation with others, kind, etc.; see Matt 20:15; Rom 5:7; etc.; frequently in Koine; see also Xenophon, *Cyr.* III 3.4: τὸν εὐεργέτην, τὸν ἄνδρα τὸν ἀγαθόν. Also ἄκακος has a similar sense: without falsehood, guileless. The final exhortation (. . . τρέμων) again clearly shows the purpose of the text for the neophyte.

3:9 See Barn. 19:2, 3, 6. The exhortation in its first part is again negative. In the ancient Christian ethic, as already in the Jewish ethic, the arrogant, rich, and powerful are opposed as the wicked, enemies of God; the pious man is not to be like them (Prov 3:34; 19:6, 17; Sir 6:2; Matt 23:12; etc.), is not to associate with them either, and is to adhere to his congregational brothers, the δίκαιοι καὶ ταπεινοί. The proselyte is to break with his former surroundings; the embers of new faith consume bonds of friendship and kinship (abundant examples of this in von Harnack, *Mission,* 1:377ff).

3:10 See Barn. 19:6. The ἐνεργήματα (Koine), according to context, are the hostile or unfriendly experiences that one has with other people, such as the ὑψηλοί.

6. Congregational Obligations (4:1–14)

TRANSLATION

4:1 My child, remember the one who speaks the word of God to you by night and by day, and you are to honor him as the Lord. For wherever the Lord is spoken of, the Lord is there. 2 Seek out the presence of the saints daily so that you might be refreshed by their words. 3 Do not stir up divisions, but rather reconcile both sides; judge righteously; do not show favoritism when you punish transgressions. 4 Do not doubt whether it will happen or not.

4:5 Do not stretch out your hands to take and clench when giving. 6 If you have earned something through the work of your hands, give it as a ransom for your sins. 7 Do not hesitate to give, and when you give, do not grumble. For you know who is the noble reimburser of your reward. 8 Do not refuse the needy, but instead share all things with your brother and do not say that you possess anything of your own; for if you have fellowship with what is immortal, how much more with what is mortal.

⁴:⁹ Do not withdraw your hand from your son or daughter, but instruct them in the fear of God from their youth. ¹⁰ Do not give orders to your slave or maidservant, who hope in the same God, when you are bitter, lest they lose the fear of God who is over (you) both. For he does not come to appoint those who have a high status but those the Spirit has prepared [*or*: but those over whom he has prepared the Spirit]. ¹¹ But you, who are slaves, must submit yourselves in timidity and fear to your masters as to the image of God.

⁴:¹² Hate all hypocrisy and everything which does not please the Lord. ¹³ Do not forsake the commandments of the Lord, but keep what you have received, without adding or taking away from them. ¹⁴ Confess your sins in the church and do not approach your prayer with an evil conscience. This is the way of life.

Textual Notes

Following the warnings against great (v. 2) and subtle (v. 3) sins is an instruction about the duties within the congregation, which is prepared for in 3:9 and 3:8.

4:1 See Barn. 19:9, 10. At the beginning, there is an apt admonition to the neophyte to respect their spiritual leader. Within the Christian congregation these leaders are primarily the prophets and teachers, secondarily the bishops and deacons (15:1). The apostles are excluded because of instruction in 11:3. In Judaism, the recruitment and instruction of proselytes rested primarily with the learned (*chakamim*, later the *sopherim*). The content of the exhortation is very tense; see, however, the teachers' and sages' tremendous awareness of staus in Dan 12:3; Sir 4:11–28; 38:24—39:11; 51:22–29 and the sayings of the rabbis: "(May) the honor of your colleague (be to you) like the honor of your teacher, and the honor of your teacher like the honor of God" (Pirqe 'Abot 4:12; Fiebig, *Ausgewählte Mischnatraktate*, 2:24); "Reverence for the teacher takes precedence over reverence for the father, because both son and father owe reverence to the teacher" (m. Ker. 6:9); etc.; see also Mark 12:39. As a parallel on Greek soil, see for instance the self-awareness of the Cynic itinerant preacher in Epictetus, *Diatr.* III 22 (e.g., v. 23: ἄγγελος ἀπὸ τοῦ Διὸς ἀπέσταλται, v. 69: ἄγγελον καὶ κατάσκοπον καὶ κήρυκα τῶν θεῶν); see finally Gen 6:6; Heb 13:7, 17. Instead of λόγον τοῦ θεοῦ, on account of what follows λόγον τοῦ κυρίου would fit better (cf. Barn. 19:9); but the Christian would think of Christ as the κυρίου. Are the words ὅθεν γὰρ ἡ κυριότης κτλ. a Christian insertion into the original Jewish *Vorlage*? νυκτὸς καὶ ἡμέρας is a well-known Hebrew construction.

4:2 See Barn. 19:10. The meetings are for edification (the catechumen has no access to the eucharistic meal). They often take place, even if only in the form of the conventicle and the house church in very small circles. On ἅγιοι, see Did. 10:6; 16:7. On ἐπαναπαῇς, a strong aorist passive from ἐπαναπαύομαι, see also Luke 10:6 and Blaß-Debrunner, *Grammatik* §76.

4:3 See Barn. 19:4, 11, 12. Narrower religious duties are followed here and later by more general ones. σχίσμα and μαχομένους do not refer to faith and not to the congregational assembly, but to congregational life in general. Any member of the congregation could come into the position of the arbitrator, and indeed also in real questions of law, as soon as the disputants did not want to go before the public courts (cf. already 1 Cor 6:5ff). Instead of ἐλέγξαι, the easier reading would be ἐλέγχων; the infinitive is final and as an aorist is prescriptive of the individual case. On ἐλέγχειν, see Did. 2:7; on the entire exhortation, see Lev 19:15.

4:4 cannot be explained with certainty. The exhortation sounds decidedly eschatological; see Hermas, *Vis.* III 4.3 as well as *Mand.* IX and probably also Barn. 19:5. But what is the point here? A thought such as Matt 7:1f surely had to be expressed more clearly. Others interpret it as doubts when praying (cf. already the text of K: ἐν προσευχῇ σου μὴ διψυχήσῃς); but does this warning fit into this context? Still others interpret this passage as the indecision of the judge who, hesitating, cannot make up his mind to decide this way or that, and therefore postpones his judgment. But πότερον ἔσται ἢ οὔ be interpreted in such a way? The whole passage gives the impression that here there is an original or later abridgement of a clearer thought.

4:5–8 is about giving. Since chapter 2 is an addition, the original "ways" only here comes to the injunction of this great and important congregational duty.

4:5 See Barn. 19:9. The closest parallel to the pithy exhortation is Sir 4:31: μὴ ἔστω ἡ χείρ σου ἐκτεταμένη εἰς τὸ λαβεῖν, καὶ ἐν τῷ ἀποδιδόναι συνεσταλμένη (constricted); see also Sifre Reeh (a Midrash on Deuteronomy) p. 116, where it is commented at Deut 15:17: "some stretch out their hand and pull it together again." See also Acts 20:35f; 1 Clem. 2:1.

4:6 See Barn. 19:10. The text is secured (by K and Barnabas, as well as by A), although L has *si habes per manus tuas redemptionem peccatorum*, which can refer back to what comes before or what follows. The exhortation applies to self-made people, not to capitalists. If this applies to the apodosis, then one can assume that there is a connection with χεῖρας in v. 5: by the proper use of one's hands, one can procure forgiveness of sins. The idea of the sin-remitting power of almsgiving is well known. Note still the alleviating reading in A: δὸς εἰς instead of δώσεις. λύτρωσιν abstract for concrete.

4:7 See Barn. 19:11. On the thought "God loves a cheerful giver," see, for example, Sib. Or. II 78, 80: πτωχοῖς εὐθὺ δίδου μηδ᾽ αὔριον ἐλθέμεν εἴπῃς ... Ὃς δ᾽ ἐλεημοσύνην παρέχει, θεῷ οἶδε δανίζειν. Leviticus Rabbah 5.5.3 (Wünsche, *Wajikra Rabba*, 34): "The poor man is at your door, and God is at his right hand. If you give him your gift, know who is at his right hand; he who will give you the reward. If you refuse him the gift, know who is at his right hand; he who will punish you for it." Testament of Zebulun 7f; etc.

4:8 See Barn. 19:8. Charity is limited to the circle of the congregation. On the beginning of the verse, see Did. 5:2: ἀποστρεφόμενοι τὸν ἐνδεόμενον, as well as Sir 4:4: μὴ ἀποστρέψῃς τὸ πρόσωπόν σου ἀπὸ πτωχοῦ. On ἴδια, see Acts 2:44; 4:32. Finally, on the argument *a maiore ad minus* at the conclusion, see the end of Rom 15:27.

4:9–11 Verses 6–9 form a household code (*Haustafel*); on this form of Hellenistic paraenesis, see the excursus after Col 4:1 in Myer, *Philipper, Kolosser, Philemon* and for examples of Christian household codes (*Haustafeln*) besides the parallel in Barn. 19:5, 7, see Col 3:18—4:1; Eph 5:22—6:9; 1 Pet 2:18—3:6; 1 Clem. 1:3; 21:6–9; Polycarp, *Phil.* 4; from a Jewish-Hellenistic tradition, see Carmen, *Phocylideum* 175–228; from Stoic tradition the popular ethics (Ἠθικῆς στοιχείωσις) of Hierocles (second cent. CE), which dealt with duties with respect to gods, fatherland, parents, siblings, wife and children, relatives, in household and marriage (cf. Praechter, *Hierokles*, 7ff). The household code (*Haustafel*) in this passage is religiously underpinned in the sense of Jewish-Hellenistic halakah with the reference to the φόβος θεοῦ, which recurs in each of the three instructions. The household code (*Haustafel*) fits here because it too pertains to communal obligations, and because one sets an example in the congregation by fulfilling those obligations.

4:9 The duty one has to a child is to provide him with a religious education: ἀρεῖς τὴν χεῖρα receives its meaning by the following positive regulation. On διδάξεις κτλ., see Ps 33:12: φόβον κυρίου διδάξω ὑμᾶς. The φόβος θεοῦ is the underlying sentiment of Jewish piety, and it has the strongest effect on ancient Christianity.

4:10 Note the "ecclesiastical" restriction: τοῖς ἐπὶ τὸν αὐτὸν θεὸν ἐλπίζουσιν. Slaves lose the fear of God when they see how little their master cares for God, treating them uncharitably. οὐ γὰρ κτλ. justified τὸν ἐπ᾽ ἀμφοτέροις θεόν, master and servant are considered equal in judgment. The exhortation is eschatological; ἔρχεσθαι and καλεῖν refer to the coming and calling to glory. ἀλλὰ κτλ. means either ἀλλ᾽ ἔρχεται ἐπὶ τούτους, οὓς τὸ πνεῦμα ἡτοίμασεν or ἀλλὰ καλεῖν τούτους, ἐφ᾽ οὓς τὸ πνεῦμα ἡτοίμασεν.

4:11 It is God who established the masters in their place. For this reason, they are a τύπος θεοῦ, a visible image of God, and they must be obeyed (cf. Eph 6:5; as well as Col 3:22 and 1 Pet 2:18f). On the question of the freeing of slaves, see also Ignatius, *Poly.* 4:3. The men of the nascent church have little understanding for the gravity of slavery and its moral danger, a clear sign that they themselves have not emerged from the circles of the unfree.

4:12-14 consist of general, concluding exhortations.

4:12 See Barn. 19:2. The warning is rather undetermined and broadly constructed. Only ὑπόκρισις stands out; it was not mentioned before, but it shows itself to be destructive in congregational life.

14:13 See Barn. 19:2, 11. The warning fits excellently into a proselyte teaching; the ἐντολαί are those that came before (cf. Deut 4:2; 13:1; Rev 22:18f).

14:14 See Barn. 19:12. By confession of sin, the conscience is cleansed, and prayer then goes up to God uninhibited. The confession of sins (παράπτωμα but milder than ἁμαρτία) is intended as a public confession of the individual, not as a liturgical confession of the congregation as a whole, as is very beautifully present, for example, in 1 Clem. 60:1f. Of such public habitual *exhomologese* we know very little, but within ancient Christianity see in addition to Did. 14:1 also Jas 5:16. The προσευχή is probably the general prayer with the congregation, hardly the individual prayer in the chamber, despite the presence of σου. The words ἐν ἐκκλησίᾳ, by the way, were hardly present in the Jewish Scriptures.

C. The Way of Death (5:1–2)

Translation

5:1 The way of death is this. First of all, it is evil and filled with a curse: murders, adulteries, desire, sexual immoralities, acts of theft, idolatries, acts of magic, sorceries, robberies, false testimonies, hypocrisies, duplicities, cunning, arrogance, malic, insolence, greed, shameful speech, jealousy, impudence, pride, ostentation, boasting. ² (On this path are) the persecutors of the good, haters of truth, friends of lies, those who do not know the reward of righteousness, who do not adhere to good and to righteous judgment, who do not watch for the good but for evil; from whom gentleness and patience are far off, who "love vain things, chasing after reward," have no pity on the poor, bear no sorrow for the oppressed, do not know their maker, murderers of children, destroyers of the image of God in the womb, who reject the needy, afflict the oppressed, who are intercessors for the rich, merciless judges of the poor, burdened with all sins. May you, children, be preserved from all these people.

Textual Notes

The description of the way of death is naturally much shorter than that of the way of life, because its depiction is general and broad. Warnings already took up a large amount of space in the negative explanation of the previous material; see especially Did. 2 (see the excursus there on the catalog of vices) and Did. 3, but also much of ch. 4. Thus here a short summary seemed to suffice. The long catalog of vices is already divided by its external structure into two parts (v. 1 and v. 2), the first (v. 1) of which contains an extensive series of vices, and the second (v. 2) of which contains an identification of the vices (mostly in participles with a more precise description); at the beginning is a general characterization (πρῶτον πάντων πονηρὰ κτλ.), at the end there is a similar one (πανθαμάρτητοι) as well as an exhortation (ῥυσθείητε κτλ.). On the entire chapter, see Barn. 20 and Hermas, *Mand.* VIII 3–5.

5:1 The series comprises 22 parts; see the series of the same number in Hermas, *Mand.* VIII 3–5; see also the 22 verses in the Syrian *Testamentum Domini nostri Jesu Christi* II 7 (an ancient church order; with a Latin translation by Rahmani). In the enumeration itself, a certain order is unmistakable; on murder, adultery and fornication, theft, and sorcery, see 2:2; furthermore, the order in 2:3–6 evidences connections with Did. 5; also, within the series itself, the order of content is clear, which places related things next to each other. On the other hand, strange disruptions are unmistakable: κλοπαί, ἁρπαγαί, πλεονεξία are torn apart; ὑπερηφανία is separated from θρασύτης ὕψος ἀλαζονεία, etc. On the details: ἐπιθυμίαι here are the impure sexual desires (3:3). On the connection of μαγεῖαι φαρμακίαι with εἰδωλολατρίαι, see 3:4; on αἰσχρολογία, see 3:3.

5:2 The statements are partly very general, partly focused on certain content; unmistakable is the strong emphasis on sins against the poor: mercy and justice with respect to the weak is a main ornament of the pious. There is little to be noticed concerning order; also strong repetitions are not missing. On the specifics: μισθὸν δικαιοσύνης is eschatological; κρίσει δικαίᾳ does not refer to God's judgment, but to one's own judgment (cf. the last components of the list as well as 4:3); μάταια are worldly goods, such as wealth, honors, pleasures; ἀνταπόδομα are those who give nothing away for free; on the saying and the whole context, see Jas 1:23. πονοῦντες . . . καταπονουμένῳ is a wordplay. On οὐ γινώσκοντες τὸν ποιήσαντα αὐτούς, see Wis 15:11. φονεῖς . . . φθορεῖς has consonance; on the content, see Did. 2:2 (different is φθορεῖς in 16:3). On ἀποστρεφόμενοι τὸν ἐνδεόμενον, see 4:8. ἐνδεόμενον . . . θλιβόμενον rhyme. πλουσίων παράκλητοι πενήτων ἄνομοι κριταί is a good antithesis; on the thought, see Sib. Or. II 62f (Carm. *Phoc.* 10f): μὴ ῥίψῃς πενίην ἀδίκως, μὴ κρῖνε προσώπῳ· Ἢν σὺ κακῶς δικάσῃς, μετέπειτα θεός σε δικάσσει. In the catalog of vices (as in general in the two ways) note the complete absence of the Jewish ceremonial or cultic law.

D. Concluding Exhortations and Advice (6:1–3)

Translation

6:1 See that no one leads you astray from this way of teaching by teaching you in a way that causes you to be far from God. 2 For if you can bear the whole yoke of the Lord, then you will be perfect. But if you cannot, then do what you are able. 3 Now concerning food, bear what you are able. But be careful of meat sacrificed to idols, for it is the service of dead gods.

Textual Notes

Within this concluding exhortation, only the beginning (v. 1) belongs to the Jewish form of the two ways; from v. 2 on, the Christian reworking begins once again. In the structure (supplement) and in the content, v. 6 reveals the later hand.

6:1 As a parallel expression, see 2 Pet 2:15.

6:2 is not very clear. It certainly has to do with pressing questions within the Christian congregation. Thus, it is possible that only hints at the issue were sufficient. Namely, it has to do with questions pertaining to asceticism. This is evident not only from the phrase βαστάσαι τὸν ζυγὸν τοῦ κυρίου but also v. 3 where the issue pertains to food. Because of this mention of food asceticism in v. 3, sexual asceticism is primarily meant in v. 3. The ideal is to live entirely sexually abstinent: whoever can do this is τέλειος. The technical expression τέλειος, which is widely used in Hellenism, in philosophy as well as especially in religion, and which is capable of a very broad meaning, is applied here to the perfection of the ascetic (different in 1:4). ὃ δύνῃ is conceived of as a temporary and limited asceticism, abstinence from conjugal intercourse during certain periods (cf. already 1 Cor 7:5).

6:3 Correspondingly, ὃ δύνασαι should be explained here as follows: abstinence from certain things (Acts 15:20, 28), also strict fasting from water and bread, but only for a time (Herm. *Sim.* V). The author lets us assume here that there was already a rather developed order pertaining to food and fasting in the congregation, but he only hints at it and does not want to impose it as a compulsion. However, he does not do away with the regular weekly fast, for it is a commandment. By εἰδωλόθυτον it is not a question of participation in the meal sacrificed to idols, but of eating the flesh of sacrificial animals (cf. 1 Cor 10:25). Post-Pauline Christianity generally did not think nearly as freely as Paul on this question: Acts 15:29; Rev 2:14, 20; Justin, *Dial.* 34.8; 35.1ff; however, on the other hand, see Heb 13:9; Titus 1:14f; and 1 Tim 4:4. Why this too is defilement of food with idols has already been demonstrated by 1 Cor 10:20. On νεκοὶ θεοί, see already Ps 113:11–15; Isa 40:19f; 41:7; 44:12–20; Wis 15:17; etc., then see 2 Clem. 1:6; 3:1; the Kerygma Petri in Clement of Alexandria, *Strom.* 6.5.39f (printed in Preuschen, *Antilegomena*, Fragm. 3a and Klostermann, *Apocrypha I*). The rationalistic theory of dead idols, however, does not exclude a lively belief in demons (cf. already 1 Cor 12:2).

II. Cultic Regulations (7:1—10:6)

The instructions in the following are no longer addressed to the proselytes, but immediately expand out and address the whole congregation. Regulations are issued concerning baptism, fasting, prayer, and the Lord's Supper.

A. Baptism (7:1–4)

Translation

⁷:¹ Now, concerning baptism, baptize in this way: having communicated these things beforehand, "baptize in the name of the Father and the Son and the Holy Spirit" in running water. ² But if you do not have running water, baptize in other water; if you cannot baptize in cold water, then baptize in warm water. ³ If you have neither, then pour water on the head three times in the name of the Father, the Son, and the Holy Spirit. ⁴ Before baptism, the one baptizing and the one to be baptized should fast, and if possible, some others as well. Namely, let the person being baptized fast for a day or two beforehand.

Textual Notes

Περὶ δὲ τοῦ βαπτίσματος, the familiar form of the superscription, is ellip-
tical, as also in 9:1; 11:3. On the following instructions, especially Justin,
1 Apol. 61 should be consulted as a parallel (reprinted also in Lietzmann,
Taufe und Messe). ταῦτα πάντα relates to the preceding instruction to the
proselytes. Whether προειπόντες refers to the catechumenal instruction or
to the act of baptism itself (as liturgy) remains unclear. The triadic baptismal
formula is ancient; see Matt 28:19 and then Justin. Older, however, is the
monodic one with Christ in 1 Cor 1:13; Gal 3:27; Acts 8:16; 19:5. Older also
than the triadic formula of Matt 28 and Did. 7 is the trinitarian formula
by Paul: God, Lord, Spirit. Heitmüller has dealt in detail with the meaning of the formula εἰς τὸ ὄνομα (*Im Namen Jesu*). The mention of the three
names over the baptized person hands him over to the three as property and
places him in their protection; the power of God and the Lord, the power
of the Spirit comes over the baptism of the believer further. Unfortunately,
the Did. does not give a closer indication within the chapter about what
thoughts and experiences are sought in baptism (purification, inclusion in
the church, rebirth, spirit, "seals," φωτισμός). ὕδωρ ζῶν means flowing water
(cf. John 4:10ff); Justin also presupposes flowing water. Throughout antiquity the special power of salvation and atonement is ascribed to living water;
see Rohde, *Psyche*, 2:405f; Gruppe, *Griechische Mythologie*, 2:888. From v. 3
it will have to be concluded that immersion occurs three times (for each
name); Tertullian, *Prax.* 26: *nec semel sed ter, ad singula nomina in personas
singulas tinguimur.* The Mandaeans also immerse their baptized three times;
see Euting, *Qolasta*, F. 9.32; Brandt, *Mandäische Religion*, 221.

7:2–3 introduce admitted possibilities. If there is no running water (in
the summer heat, in water-scarce lands of the east), then standing water; in
the case of the sick and weak, warm water (i.e., in a tub).

7:3 If there is neither cold nor warm water, then pour water on the head
three times, the aspersion baptism, which is testified to here for the first time.
Its validity is not questioned: what is essential is the formula that is repeated.
The lack of water considered here would be unthinkable in Egypt, though
Palestine and Syria would be possible. — When, by whom, and before whom
the baptism is performed is unfortunately not specified. βαπτίσατε in v. 1,
however, applies to all. Any Christian can baptize another. This is not the
case, though, in Ign. *Smyrn.* 8:2, which ties baptism to the bishop and his
authorization. On the whole, see Tertullian, *Bapt.* 4: *nulla distinctio est, mari
quis an stagno, flumine an fonte, lacu an alveo diluatur.*

7:4 Fasting is also part of the dignified performance of baptism: the
baptized and the baptizer must fast; others may also fast. On communal

fasting, see again Justin; on the fasting of the baptized, see Tertullian, *Bapt.* 20: *ingressuros baptismum orationibus crebris, ieiuniis et geniculationibus, et pervigillis orare oportet.* The baptismal candidate and fellow fasters need to fast only on the day of baptism itself. Fasting has cleansing and purifying power, breaks the dominion of demons (at the more ancient level of religion, it reconciles the demons and makes them compassionate through voluntary self-abasement), and prepares the body for the reception of the Spirit. Throughout the ancient world, fasting is immensely popular and widespread; for its connection with the initiatory act, see the following parallels: in the very valuable *synthema* of the Eleusinian Mysteries preserved by Clement of Alexandria in *Protr.* II 21.2, the neophyte says: ἐνήστευσα, ἔπιον τὸν κυκεῶνα, ἔλαβον ἐκ κίστης, ἐργασάμενος ἀπεθέμην εἰς κάλαθον καὶ ἐκ καλάθου εἰς κίστην (on the meaning of the words, see Körte, "Eleusinischen Mysterien," 116–26); before admission into the Isis mysteries, a ten-day fasting takes place in Apuleius, *Metam.* XI 23; likewise before the Osiris consecration in Apuleius, *Metam.* XI 28 and 30; the Mithras mystics are said to have lain in the snow for twenty days and to have fasted for fifty days before their admission, see Nonnus Ad Gregor. Nazianz. orationem De sacris luminibus (Migne *PG* 36, 1064).

B. Fasting (8:1)

Translation

8:1 Your "fasts" should "not" be like those of the "hypocrites," for they fast on Mondays and on Thursdays. You, however, should fast on Wednesdays and on Fridays.

Textual Notes

The mention of fasting in 7:4 transfers over. Fasting and praying, good works including almsgiving, already belong closely together within Judaism (cf. the comments at Did. 15:4).

8:1 The hypocrites here and in v. 2 are either the Pharisees (Matt 6:16) or more likely Jews in general. In any case, the passage is harshly anti-Jewish. On the custom of the strictly observant Jews to fast on Monday and Thursday, see Schürer, *Geschichte*, 2:489f. The custom of fasting on the 2nd and the 5th days of the week is expressly attested in Jewish texts only in the Mishnah. That it goes further back, however, is evidenced not only here in the Did., but also in Luke 18:12. The division of the church week highlights Wednesday and Friday as fast days. Why just these days? In later times, it is justified with reference to the Passion. But if two of the seven days of the week were to be selected, excluding Monday, Thursday, Saturday (because of the immediate vicinity to the joyful celebration of the Lord's Day), and finally Sunday, then only three were left, and Friday had to be selected in any case. The text does not mention what ideas are connected with fasting, nor does it mention how it is carried out. On early church fasting, see Herm. *Sim.* V; Tertullian, *De jejunio adversus psychicos*; Clement of Alexandria, *Strom.* 7.12.75; as well as Origen, *Hom. Lev.* X (Lommatzsch, *Origenis Opera*, 9:366ff).

C. Praying (8:2-3)

Translation

² Furthermore, you should "not pray" like the "hypocrites," but as the Lord commanded us in his Gospel, you should pray: "Our Father in heaven, hallowed be your name, your kingdom come, your will be done, on earth as it is in heaven. Give us today our bread for tomorrow, and forgive us our debts as we forgive our debtors, and lead us not into temptation, but deliver us from evil, for yours is the power and the glory forever."
³ Pray this prayer three times a day.

Textual Notes

8:2 For the Did., there are apparently still Christians who make use of Jewish prayers, such as the main synagogal prayer of the Shemoneh Esrei which certainly goes back to pre-Christian times. τὸ εὐαγγέλιον is, of course, not a particular, individual gospel, but, according to known usage, the proclamation of the Lord and the proclamation from the Lord. Yet, as the whole discussion (fasting and praying, the "hypocrites") proves, the author's use of ἐκέλευσεν ὁ κύριος probably has Matt 6 in mind, and it is also true that the text of the Lord's Prayer is essentially that of Matthew. Only in two places are there deviations which do not occur within any of the manuscripts of Matthew: (1) the salutation ἐν τῷ οὐρανῷ and (2) τὴν ὀφειλήν instead of τὰ ὀφειλήματα. The doxology, which is absent from the original Matthean text but is certainly very old within the liturgical use of the Lord's Prayer, appears here in two parts, with the Egyptian translations (*sah faj*) omitting ἡ βασιλεία καί, certainly a striking touch; see, however, the introduction.

8:3 Here we find the oldest testimony to the regular use of the Lord's Prayer and to the three hours of prayer each day. We think of them best as morning, noon (or afternoon), and evening, for the Jewish times for regular prayer are morning, afternoon, and evening; see Schürer, *Geschichte*, 2:293. Only Tertullian testifies (*Orat.* 25; *Jejun.* 10) to the third, sixth, and ninth hours, but he still clearly shows early morning and evening as the time of the *legitimae orationes*. Striking within the entire chapter is the obviously necessary fight against Jewish custom in the congregation; it is, though, very strange that the Lord's Prayer must be prayed with this wording. That there were still many in the congregations reflected in the Did. who held on to Jewish customs is also evidenced in what follows.

D. The Celebration of the Eucharist (9:1 — 10:6)

Translation

9:1 Concerning the Eucharist, give thanks for it in this way. 2 First, concerning the cup: We give thanks to you, our Father, for the holy vine of David, your servant, whom you have made known to us through Jesus your servant. To you be glory forever.

9:3 Furthermore, concerning the bread: We thank you, our Father, for the life and knowledge you have made known to us through Jesus your servant.

4 As this bread was scattered on the mountains and brought together as one, so let your church also be brought from the ends of the earth into your kingdom. For yours is the glory and the power through Jesus Christ forever.

9:5 However, no one may eat or drink of the Eucharist unless they have been baptized in the name of the Lord. For about this the Lord said, "Do not give that which is holy to the dogs."

10:1 Now after you have taken part, give thanks in this way: 2 We thank you, holy Father, for your holy name, which you have made to dwell in our hearts, and for the knowledge and faith and immortality which you have made known to us through Jesus, your servant.

10:3 To you be glory forever and ever. You, Almighty Master, have created all things for your name's sake; you have given food and drink to men to eat, that they might give thanks to you. But to us you have given spiritual food and drink, and eternal life through your Servant.

10:4 Above all, we give you thanks because you are mighty. To you be glory forever and ever.

10:5 Remember your church, O Lord, to save her from all evil, and to perfect her in your love, and lead her from the four winds into a multitude, she who is sanctified, into your kingdom which you have prepared for her.

10:6 For yours is the power and the glory forever. May grace come, and let this world pass away. "Hosanna to the" God "of David." If anyone is holy, let him come near; if anyone is not holy, let him repent. "Maranatha!" Amen!

However, you should allow the prophets to give thanks as much as they wish.

Textual Notes

The correct understanding of the instructions was probably assessed by Drews ("Untersuchungen zur Didache," 54ff). Here it is a celebration in the narrower circle, in which a real meal (10:1) still takes place, whereas ch. 14 only has in view the general congregational celebration on Sunday without the meal, partaking in the mass, as is the case in Justin, *1 Apol.* 67. At the private meals, which cannot be supervised, the Jewish prayers of thanksgiving are used with the cup and the bread, which are now, according to the instructions of the Did., shaped into and replaced by Christian prayers of thanksgiving. The contact with Jewish prayer forms is quite striking.

The celebration is called ΕΥΧΑΡΙΣΤΙΑ; see v. 5 where the sanctified elements are described as such and the wording of the prayers themselves, in which εὐχαριστοῦμεν σοι occurs four times; see also 14:1. The other name κλάσις τοῦ ἄρτου is presupposed in 14:1; not used, however are κυριακὸν δεῖπνον and ἀγάπη. — εὐχαριστία also appears in Ign. *Phld.* 4; *Smyrn.* 7:1; 8:1; Justin, *1 Apol.* 66.1; cf. also *Dial.* 41 and 70.4. The origin of the name lies in the thanksgiving which characterizes the acts of prayer at the meal, especially when the bread and the wine are distributed. In its full development, however, εὐχαριστία means much more than mere thanksgiving: the entire meal, especially the offering of bread and wine, seemed to be a congregational sacrifice, and especially that of a thanksgiving sacrifice. The expression εὐχαριστία certainly acquired this sense rather quickly. This writing (i.e., the Did.) is the oldest testimony to the fact that the Lord's

Supper is felt to be and is designated as a sacrifice (Did. 14:1–3). In light of this conceptualization of the meal, the celebration enters into a tremendously important context of thought with broad ramifications. It enters into the realm of sacrifice, which has been prevalent in humanity from time immemorial and is inseparably connected with ancient religious life. Sacrifices were also sought and found in Christian worship: not only sanctification of life, good works, especially alms, were perceived as and called sacrifices, but above all the prayers of both the individual and those of the community which are offered in the temple of God, that is to say, within the congregation. They are the pleasant fragrance that ascends to God. Among the prayers, those offered at the gathering for the meal stood out: whatever spiritual edification was offered through the word at this gathering was clothed in the form of prayer, and thus, because of the prayers alone, the Eucharist could be called the sacrifice of the congregation.

But the threads that led from the sacrificial conception to the communal meal were much stronger still. For any ancient consciousness, the sacrifice is something palpable, sensuous: dry and liquid sustenance and source of pleasure. The only place in the Christian cult where this concept of sacrifice could be applied was at the communal meal with its food and drink. There, there were the bowls with the food and the cups containing the drink. The gifts were offered from within the congregation, and prayers were said over them. Especially bread and wine were brought before God, accompanied by prayer. Thus, the idea had to arise that our (i.e., Christians) sacrifice and sacrificial meal is the communal meal along with the Eucharist. The Did., along with 1 Clem. 40–44; Ign. Eph. 5:2; Phld. 4; Justin, 1 Apol. 65–67; Dial. 41, 117 are very important witnesses to the conception of the meal as a sacrifice. If the meal, and especially its culmination the Eucharist, was thus felt to be a sacrifice before God, then sentiments of thanksgiving and supplication had to be connected with the celebration. These thoughts were addressed in the prayers accompanying the act (Did. and Justin). And indeed, as the very name εὐχαριστία shows, it is chiefly thanksgiving that is expressed in the celebration. Once thanksgiving is offered for the earthly gifts, for food and drink for the body (10:3; cf. Acts 2:46 as well as Justin, Dial. 41). These are ancient, foundational thoughts of the whole sacrificial custom, when thanks are given to the deity for earthly welfare by sacrifice. — But the Christian sacrifice, of course, could not stop at this level of thanksgiving. In the celebration of the meal, God is thanked above all not for simply earthly but for higher goods. The gathering for the meal is the closest celebration of the congregation; only those who have been baptized may participate in it. Naturally, therefore, the prayers of thanksgiving from the congregational sacrifice would have referred primarily or exclusively to the proper possessions of the congregation. A

glance at the prayers of the Did. and at Justin, *1 Apol.* 65 confirms this. And
the prayer was connected with the thanksgiving; in the Did. it is eschatological, but of course it can be determined differently with respect to content. —
The celebration of the meal takes on a special meaning by the fact that in it,
as in the meetings of the congregation in general, the exalted heavenly Lord is
believed and felt to be present. In the cult, the mystical unification with him
takes place. At this point, of course, the hints from the Did. are sparse, but the
tremendous eschatological excitement, the jubilant greeting, and the maranatha in 10:6 can be explained from the feeling of the invisibly present one,
and 10:3 refers to Christian gifts, spiritual food and drink, and eternal life,
which the servant of God has brought. But how life is linked to the spiritual
food and drink (sacramentally?) cannot be concluded from the few words
provided, and any allusion to the flesh and blood of Christ as well as to death
and communion with that death is completely absent from the prayers, as is
generally the case for the entire text. Another peculiarity of the celebration
according to the Did. is the prefixing of the cup according to Jewish custom,
which also comes through in the Lukan account (Luke 22:11), and finally
the strikingly strong contact with Jewish prayer formulas. It seems that the
Eucharist of the Did., partaken with joy and rejoicing like the meals of Acts
2:46, has preserved a very original, pre-Pauline content of the celebration. On
the other hand, however, there are unmistakable contacts with ideas of the
Johannine circle, which, however, probably come about indirectly through a
common "Hellenism." On the prayers of the Did., see Drews, "Eucharistie,"
563ff; Goltz, *Gebet*, 207–23; Weiß, *Urchistentum*, 45–47; Schermann, "Liturgische Neuerungen," 225ff; Klein, "Didache," 132 ff; Loeschcke in *Zeitschrift
für die Neutestamentliche Wissenschaft* 54, 193ff.

9:2 Passing around the cup and the bread does not take place (because
of 10:1) at the end of the communal meal, but earlier, perhaps at the beginning. It is Jewish custom at Passover and other feasts, also at the Sabbath meal
on Friday evening at the beginning of the meal to bless first the cup, then the
bread (see 1 Cor 10:6, 21; Luke 22:17). At the consumption, however, also
among the Jews, eating precedes drinking, which Did. 9:5; 10:3 presupposes
(cf. 1 Cor 11:2f). The Jewish table prayer over the wine is: בָּרוּךְ אַתָּה יְיָ אֱלֹהֵינוּ
מֶלֶךְ הָעוֹלָם בּוֹרֵא פְּרִי הַגָּפֶן "Blessed are you, O Lord our God, King of the
world, who creates the fruit of the vine"; on this Jewish prayer, see m. Ber.
4:1 (Hebrew ed. in Staerk, *Gebete*, 1; German trans. Fiebig, *Mischnatraktate*,
vol. 3; ed., trans., and explained by Holtzmann, *Berakot* and by Strack, *Berakhoth*. Also the texts in every Jewish prayer book). The Jewish blessing is
transformed in the Did. into a Christian blessing, certainly not for the first
time, but according to pre-existing tradition. Note that also immediately
before in the Lord's Prayer a particularly venerable, traditional prayer text

was communicated. The reference to the Jewish prayer of thanksgiving is unmistakable. πάτερ ἡμῶν, like 8:2; it is, however, already known as an address for God in Jewish prayer. Difficult is the ἁγία ἄμπελος Δαβίδ κτλ. The result of the image is clear: it is directed toward the wine, which would have been just filled into the cup. Of the different interpretations (the church; Christ himself; the blood of Christ; γνῶσις and ζωή as in v. 3), the messianic one is the best, in spite of the tautology that then exists within the relative clause. The fact that figurative language is used therein makes the tautology bearable. The Messiah and the salvation he has brought are conceived of mystically. The Messiah as the holy wine stock is found also in John 15:1f (Isa 11:1; 2 Bar 36f); "wisdom" as the divine wine stock in Sir 24:17–22 (cf. then Gen 49:11; Ps 79:9–20). But the origin of the image is not only to be found in the OT; see the noteworthy parallel, which Justin, 1 Apol. 54.5f and Dial. 69.2 draws with the Dionysius cult. The solemn archaic-sounding expression παῖς θεοῦ has its origin in the OT, in the ebed YHWH of Deutero-Isaiah; it is used in the Did. and elsewhere within the elevated speech of liturgy and prayer; in addition to Did. 9 and 10, see Acts 3:13, 26; 4:27, 30; 1 Clem. 59:2–4 and Bousset, Kyrios Christos, 68.

9:3 Note the exact parallelism with v. 2. The corresponding Jewish berah[h with dot below]ah in the Mishnah is m. Ber. 6:1: בָּרוּךְ אַתָּה יְיָ אֱלֹהֵינוּ מֶלֶךְ הָעוֹלָם הַמּוֹצִיא לֶחֶם מִן הָאָרֶץ "Blessed are you, Lord our good, King of the world, who brings forth bread from the earth." Apart from the blessings over the bread and the wine, the Jewish liturgy still attests to a three-part table prayer after the meal (text in every Jewish prayer book; German also in Klein, Katechismus, 223f): נוֹדֶה לְּךָ . . . עַל תּוֹרָתְךָ שֶׁלִּמַּדְתָּנוּ וְעַל חֻקֶּיךָ שֶׁהוֹדַעְתָּנוּ וְעַל הַיִּים חֵן וָחֶסֶד שֶׁהוֹנַנְתָּנוּ "We give you thanks . . . for your law which you have taught us, and for your commandments which you have made known to us, and for the life, favor, and mercy with which you have shown us grace." — According to Jewish custom, the flat loaves are placed whole and then broken (κλάσμα) with the hand after the blessing is pronounced over them. ζωή and γνῶσις are two genuine Hellenistic expressions: revealed knowledge, especially of God, the true one, as well as of his will and eternal life. Sin is error, based on a lack of knowledge of the truth. He who has attained a proper gnosis, which is based on revelation, will also act appropriately. And ζωή, the benefit of salvation, is individualistic, hangs directly upon gnosis, displaces the longer, more original Christian βασιλεία. Of the many parallels that can be brought to bear here, see γινώσκειν and ζωή in John; see further Clement of Alexandria, Strom. 4.27.2: θέλημα δὲ τοῦ θεοῦ ἐπίγνωσις τοῦ θεοῦ, ἥτις ἐστὶ κοινωνία ἀφθαρσίας. Philo is entirely at home in these ideas, see, for example, Decal. 81 (ed. Mangey, 194): . . . βουλόμενος δὲ (ὁ θεὸς) τὸ γένος τῶν ἀνθρώπων ἀνοδίαις πλαζόμενον εἰς ἀπλανεστάτην ἄγειν ὁδόν, ἵν' ἐπόμενον τῇ φύσει τὸ ἄριστον εὕρηται τέλος, ἐπιστήμην τοῦ ὄντως ὄντος, ὅς ἐστι τὸ πρῶτον ἀγαθὸν καὶ τελεώτατον, Quis rerum divinar. heres 239 (ed. Mangey, 506): ταῦτα (Lev 11:21) δ' ἐστὶ σύμβολα ψυχῶν, ὅσαι τρόπον ἑρπετῶν προσερριζωμέναι τῷ γηίνῳ σώματι καθαρθεῖσαι μετεωροπολεῖν ἰσχύουσιν, οὐρανὸν ἀντικαταλλαξάμεναι γῆς καὶ φθορᾶς ἀθανασίαν. (On the non-Greek, eastern manner of the formula γνῶσις θεοῦ, γινώσκειν θεόν . . . , see Norden, Agnostos Theos, 56–115).

9:4 Within the prayer of thanksgiving, there is another extension, a request. A parallel to this request is a Jewish request found in the Musaf prayer on the Day of Atonement (cf. the prayer book), in a prayer which begins with וְקָרֵב פְּזוּרֵינוּ מִבֵּין הַגּוֹיִם וּנְפוּצוֹתֵינוּ כַּנֵּס מִיַּרְכְּתֵי אֶרֶץ וַהֲבִיאֵנוּ לְצִיּוֹן :יהי רצון עִירְךָ "Unite our dispersed ones from the midst of the nations, and gather our diaspora from the ends of the earth, and lead us back to your city, Zion"; see also the Shemoneh Esreh 10 (the bracketed material belongs to a more recent time; the unbracketed material to an older and earlier form; Hebrew text present in Staerk, Gebete): "Blow the great trumpet for our deliverance and raise a banner to gather our exiles [and bring us together from the four corners of the earth]. Blessed be Yahweh, who gathers the scattered of his people, Israel." — On the idea of the return of the Jewish exiles, see Isa 40; Ps 125; etc. Second Maccabees 1:27: ἐπισυνάγαγε τὴν διασπορὰν ἡμῶν. Tobit 13:3: (συναχθήσονται). In Christian prayer, the memory of the circle gathered for celebration goes out from the present and the near to the far, to the brothers scattered throughout the world. The glorious final state is here: they will gather his elect from the four winds (Matt 24:31). At the same time, the image of the one bread (see also 1 Cor 10:17) consisting of many grains sounds eschatologically deft, though not mystical (1 Cor 10:17; Ign. Eph. 20:2). The bread that grows on the hills fits quite well with a Syrian or Palestinian origin of the composition, but not at all with an Egyptian origin: where the land rises in Egypt, the ardent desert reigns. The ἐκκλησία here and in 10:5 is the entire church (different in 4:14). The prayer cannot be ancient, since it presupposes a globally dispersed church. The doxology is expanded from v. 2 and v. 3, bipartite as in 8:2 (corresponding to 10:5 with respect to 10:2, 3): the end of the prayer is reached in each case.

9:5 On the celebration of the meal the unbaptized were occasionally admitted, which is forbidden here, see Justin, 1 Apol. 66.1: καὶ ἡ τροφὴ αὕτη καλεῖται παρ' ἡμῖν εὐχαριστία, ἧς οὐδενὶ ἄλλῳ μετασχεῖν ἐξόν ἐστιν ἢ τῷ πιστεύοντι . . . καὶ λουσαμένῳ . . . . In later Greek liturgical language, τὸ ἅγιον is precisely the eucharistic food.

10:1 ἐμπλησθῆναι indicates that we are dealing with a real meal, not a sacramental meal. At the end of the meal (agape and the Eucharist), there is a post-meal prayer. Leaving aside v. 6, this final prayer is a tripartite prayer and closely parallels 9:2–4 in both form and content: two parts of giving thanks for spiritual benefits, joined by a petition for the gathering of the scattered church. Because of the exact parallelism of ch. 10 with ch. 9, it is a very good assumption that 10:4 must be rearranged (Goltz, *Gebet*, 219f): Did. 10:4a belongs (approximately in the form εὐχαριστοῦμέν σοι, πάτερ ἅγιε, ὅτι δυνατὸς εἶ) at v. 3; then this portion also begins with εὐχαριστοῦμέν σοι and ends with διὰ τοῦ παιδός σου and the doxology. Tripartite is also the Jewish post-meal prayer *birkath hammason*, already mentioned above at 9:3, with which some connections were already noted in ch. 9. Once again the text sounds Johannian and early Christian (v. 5).

10:2 Here again there is an aspect of belief in the name: the name is a part of the being of God, something mighty and powerful; he is named over the faithful at baptism, has moved into them, and dwells within them (on this phrase, cf. Jer 7:12; 2 Esd 11:9; Ezra 43:7; Ps 73:7; and then John 17:6, 11f; πάτερ ἅγιε also in John 17:11). κατασκηνοῦν is transitive here. On γνῶσις and ἀθανασία, see 9:3; πίστις enters the series: γνῶσις and πίστις belong closely together and have a long history in the Christian church precisely because of their linkage and their opposition. *Gnosis*, the enlightenment which leads to life, is closely connected with πίστις, a personal act of will resting on mysterious personal experience; see again πιστεύειν and γινώσκειν in John 6:69; 17:8; as well as 1 John 4:16; etc. — ἀθανασία (= ζωή; it is, like ἀφθαρσία, a more Greek expression) is made known by Jesus, the πρωτότοκος ἐκ νεκρῶν (Col 1:18; Rom 8:29), the ἀρχηγὸς τῆς ἀφθαρσίας (2 Clem. 20:5); see also John 1:4; etc.

10:3 The omnipotence of God (δέσποτα παντοκράτορ, δυνατός) is seen within the creation. This takes place ἕνεκεν τοῦ ὀνόματός σου: in order that the name of God in the visible image of his being, the world, might be made known and praised. Note again the significance of the "name"; on the whole context, see the first part of the *birkath hammason* (Klein, *Katechismus*, 223): " . . . he gives bread to all flesh, his love is everlasting. We have never lacked in his goodness and will never lack food until the end, for the sake of his great name. For he feeds and provides for all, is charitable to all, prepares food for all his creatures which he has created." — The consideration moves from earthly food to spiritual food and spiritual drink, a transition which is natural, especially in the sacrament; see 1 Cor 10:3f; John 6:27, 33, 53ff; as well as Ignatius, *Romans* 7:3; see further Justin's explanation in *1 Apol.* 66.2. In terms of content, πνευματικὴ (heavenly, supernatural) τροφή and (πνευματικόν) ποτόν = ζωή (hendiadys) or perhaps better still = γνῶσις and ζωή, although ζωὴ αἰώνιος is mentioned again immediately afterward.

10:5 Close parallels can be found at 9:4: here and there the ἐκκλησία is the whole church. On the four winds (= four corners) of the earth, see, for example, Rev 7:1 etc.; on the whole thought, see Matt 24:31 and Zech 2:6 (ἐκ τῶν τεσσάρων ἀνέμων τοῦ οὐρανοῦ συνάζω ὑμᾶς). The church is sanctified, taken from the secular nature of this age even now. For the double structure of the final doxology, see 9:4.

10:6 A special difficulty is posed by the five short components here, not because of their content, but because of their placement. Since they are directly connected to the clear prayer text, even "amen" is at the end, one must first assume that they belong to the prayer. But should the careful structure of the prayer with its exact correspondence to ch. 9 be crowned by these confused blocks? This is very difficult to assume. Therefore, it has been thought that these are, at least in part, the beginnings of hymns (Goltz, *Gebet*, 212f). Tertullian reports about the custom of such spiritual songs at the end of the meal: *post aquam mannalem et lumina, ut quisque de scripturis sanctis vel de proprio ingenio potest, provocatur in medium deo canere* (*Apol.* 39); see also Hippolytus, *Canones* 32 (Achelis, *Kirchenrechtes*, 106): "They may recite psalms before they leave." But, if we are dealing here with songs, must we not expect explicitly a corresponding instruction for singing, and could the author, who has to communicate the prayers and also the Lord's Prayer in the proper wording, rely here on the fact that the congregation will already know the right songs? Thus the whole matter remains obscure, and we may assume that we are dealing here with calls to prayer in which the longing, eschatologically tense mood of the congregation at the end of the meal, their feeling of closeness, even more of the presence of their heavenly Lord, resounds. Who speaks them, when, and how, remains uncertain. — ἐλθέτω χάρις κτλ.: thus the end of the world is explicitly prayed for (different is Tertullian, *Apol.* 39: *oramus pro mora finis*); on the new world, see also ch. 16. ὡσαννὰ τῷ θεῷ Δαβίδ, see Matt 21:9, 15: ὡσαννὰ τῷ υἱῷ Δαυείδ (however, the text should not be improved here); see then Ps 118:25 (Hebrew), but from where then does the hosanna come (the original text, not the LXX, where ὡσάννα does not appear at all). Certainly the shouting out of hosanna, like amen and hallelujah is taken over from the Jewish liturgical custom. — Here, the God of David is Christ; the coming or present one is cheered. μετανοείτω is probably not to be interpreted according to 4:14 or 14:2, but is an invitation to the unbeliever to become a ἅγιος (4:2), to join the congregation. On "μαραναθά (our) Lord is coming, or better (our) Lord, come," see 1 Cor 16:22 and the commentaries; see also Rev 22:20. It is the urgent invitation to the Lord Christ to come.

10:7 The prophets who take part in meals, for example, are not to be bound by either the wording or the length of the prayers communicated: the Spirit provides them with the words to speak (cf. also 11:7).

III. Rules for Congregational Life (11:1—15:4)

Didache 11:1—15:4 turns its attention to a number of topics that affect congregational life. Topics include how to care for and assess wandering charismatics (11:1-12) and unostentatious Christians (12:1-5); the care of local prophets and teachers (13:1-7); instructions for the celebratory Sunday worship service (14:1-3); the election of congregational officials (15:3-4); and instructions for congregational discipline.[5]

A. The Wandering Charismatics, Their Examination, and Their Reception (11:1–12)

Translation

[11:1] Now, accept anyone who comes to you and teaches you everything which has already been mentioned. [2] But if the teacher himself turns away and teaches another doctrine to annul [these teachings], do not listen to him. (But if he teaches) to increase righteousness and knowledge of the Lord, receive him as the Lord.

[11:3] But as for the apostles and prophets, proceed according to the statues of the gospel: [4] receive every apostle who comes to you as you would the Lord. [5] But he may not stay longer than a day; if it is necessary, then two days; but if he stays three days, then he is a false prophet. [6] When the apostle departs, he should take nothing with him except for bread until he reaches lodging. If he asks for money, then he is a false prophet.

[11:7] Furthermore, do not test or examine every prophet who speaks in the Spirit. For "every sin will be forgiven, but this sin will not be forgiven." [8] Not everyone who speaks in the Spirit is a prophet, but only the one who behaves like the Lord. In this way will the false prophet and the prophet be recognized. [9] And every prophet who orders food at a table in the Spirit does not eat from it, but if he does, he is a false prophet. [10] Every prophet who teaches truth but does not do as he teaches, is a false prophet. [11] However, every proven, truthful prophet who acts according to the earthly mystery of the Church, but does not teach others to do what he himself does, should not be judged by you, for his judgment is with God. For this is how all prophets have

---

5. TN: This paragraph is not present within the original German text but has been added for the sake of unity and clarity in the newly formatted English edition.

behaved. [12] But if someone says in the Spirit, "Give me money" or anything of the like, do not listen to him. But if he says to give money for others who are in need, let no one judge him.

Textual Notes

11:1 and 2 give a general rule which applies to every brother who travels; but the pneumatics are certainly already in view in light of διδάσκειν, προσθεῖναι γνῶσιν, and on account of the end of v. 2; see also v. 4. For the most part, διδάσκειν has practical content; προσθεῖναι δικαιοσύνην καὶ γνῶσιν κυρίου is its purpose, where the *gnosis* is also of a predominantly practical nature (the will of God). κυρίου is a subjective genitive: *gnosis* which comes from the Lord, which he brought. On the principle δέξασθε αὐτὸν ὡς κύριον, see already 4:1. Before εἰς τὸ προσθεῖναι, supplement with ἐὰν δὲ διδάσκῃ. καταλῦσαι is absolute, though if not, supply τὴν διδαχήν. On the principle of not hearing and receiving, see 2 John 7–10.

11:3 transitions over to the particular, to the apostles and the prophets. On the very ancient trinity of apostle, prophet, and teacher (teachers are mentioned alongside the prophets in 13:2), see 1 Cor 12:28 and the explanation by Lietzmann, *Korinther*; von Harnack, *Lehre*; and von Harnack, *Mission*, 1:320ff. The Did., which is itself a sign of its antiquity, is still aware of the wandering apostle, the man called and equipped by the Spirit, who goes about proclaiming the word, houseless and homeless, without a worldly profession. But it is also aware of degeneration of the apostolate. The gullibility of the congregations, their unconditional respect for the spiritual leaders, is exploited by dubious people, wandering charlatans, who move into the congregations from the outside and exploit the communities there as Christ's apostles. The original Christian prophethood shows a corresponding degeneration; on these relationships, see Lucian, *Peregr.* 11–13, 16, for example 13: καταφρονοῦσιν (the Christians) οὖν ἁπάντων ἐξ ἴσης καὶ κοινὰ ἡγοῦνται ἄνευ τινὸς ἀκριβοῦς πίστεως τὰ τοιαῦτα παραδεξάμενοι. ἢν τοίνυν παρέλθῃ τις εἰς αὐτοὺς γόης καὶ τεχνίτης ἄνθρωπος καὶ πράγμασι χρῆσθαι δυνάμενος, αὐτίκα μάλα πλούσιος ἐν βραχεῖ ἐγένετο, ἰδιώταις ἀνθρώποις ἐγχανών. The Did. says nothing clear about the false doctrine of *gnosis* being carried into the churches by the itinerant apostles (see, however, 10:2). — κατὰ τὸ δόγμα τ. εὐ belongs with ποιήσατε, not with what comes before; the thought is similar to the instructions in Matt 10:40f as well as 10:10; 12:31; see further 1 Cor 9:14.

11:4–6 are now about the behavior toward the apostles.

11:4 is the general principle, from which immense respect for the apostle speaks; see 4:1 for the formulation.

11:5 contains the restriction which prevents the appointment of the apostle, preventing even a prolonged stay. ἐὰν ᾖ χρεία probably speaks to adverse circumstances that postpone departure, not to the congregation's needs of edification. ψευδοπροφήτης is written here instead of the less frequently attested form in ancient Christian literature ψευδαπόστολος (e.g., 2 Cor 11:13), which would have been expected here; see the broad usage of ψευδοπροφήτης in Matt 7:15.

11:6 presupposes that the Christian communities are not too thinly sown: at most a few days journey away from one another. On the prohibition of taking money, see Mark 6:8. ἄρτος probably means provisions.

11:7–12 deal with the prophet. He, too, is a bearer of the Spirit, and the word that the Spirit gives him is not to be shaken or quibbled with. But the congregation must be able to protect itself from those rare deceivers. Hermas, *Mand.* XI can be compared with what follows.

11:7 Speaking in the Spirit here and afterward is speaking in ecstasy, where the clear consciousness of the prophet is switched off, but the words are intelligible; see Hermas, *Mand.* XI 9 as well as 1 Cor 14:24f, 29f. Of course, the prophet can pray, preach, and teach even without ecstasy, but this is not discussed here (cf., however, 10:7). The prohibition of πειράζειν and διακρίνειν goes beyond Paul (1 Cor 12:10; 14:29) and 1 John 4:1. How πειράζειν and διακρίνειν differ from each other we cannot say for certain, but the former may pertain to the prophet's conduct and the latter to his speech. διακρίνειν here does not seem to be, as in Paul, a spiritual gift. On πειράζειν, see Rev 2:2.

11:8 There is also a demonic form of ecstasy (cf. Hermas, *Mand.* XI 12ff). The τρόποι κυρίου should be understood either (more narrowly) as selflessness and truthfulness in contrast to the behavior described in 11:9, 12, or else as the whole conduct of life, which should be carried out by following the Lord (cf. Hermas, *Mand.* XI 8). The idea of *imitatio* of just the poor life of Christ, so important in later church history, is echoed here.

11:9–12 now introduce rules and examples that clarify the demand in v.8b.

11:9 It is not the congregational *agape*, but a meal for the poor, which is to be provided by the congregation or by its richer members. Such meals are attested already in Acts 6:1ff; for the later time, see Hippolytus, *Canones* 32 (Achelis, *Kirchenrechtes*, 105; cf. also Riedel *Kirchenrechtsquellen*, 193ff): *Si agape fit vel coena ab aliquo pauperibus paratur* κυριακῇ *tempore accensus lucernae, praesente episcopo surgat diaconus ad accendendum. Episcopus autem oret super eos et eum, qui invitavit illos . . .* 35 (111) *Si quis*

viduis coenam parare vult, curet, ut habeant coenam et ut dimittantur, an-
tequam sol occidat. The Spirit may order such meals through the prophet;
the prophet himself returned to waking consciousness. If he is ἀληθινός, he
will not eat of them. On the merry feasting of false prophets, see Hermas,
Mand. XI 12: ἐν τρυφαῖς πολλαῖς.

11:10 On the rule, see Matt 23:3 as well as 6:15ff. The ἀλήθεια, which
the true prophet teaches, has practical content (cf. 11:2).

11:11 The prophet should do everything he teaches. There is also,
however, a case (or cases) where the prophet does not teach (i.e., does not
require the congregation to do) what he does. The prophet is a powerful person, equipped and empowered by the Spirit in a very special way. Perhaps
it would be ideal if everyone were to do what he does. But experience has
shown the congregation that human weakness, which also reigns among
Christians, too easily leads from the sublime to the ridiculous and further to
the filthy. For an explanation of the vague and much-discussed passage, see
in addition to the commentaries Taylor, *Teaching*, 82–92; Weinel, *Wirkun-*
gen, 131–38, Zahn, *Supplementum Clementinum*, 301; Zahn, "Lehre," 201–4;
the presumably correct explanation is the one found in von Harnack, Weinel,
Drews. — The vieled words within the text, which would be recognized to
those in the know, are about matters pertaining to sex, i.e., asceticism. It deals
with proven prophets, found to be genuine (δεδοκιμασμένος, ἀληθινός). The
μυστήριον ἐκκλησίας is this: the pre-existent church is the immaculate flesh
and the pure body of Christ, but also his bride, with whom he lives in pure
marriage, in heavenly syzygy, and this upper, heavenly relationship can be
reproduced on earth in meaningful, mysterious acts, comprehensible only
to the initiated. Thus heavenly things are reflected in earthly things, and the
mystery becomes earthly (κοσμικόν). On the idea of the syzygy of Christ with
the church, the one created before all eons, and on the idea of the church as
the pure body (flesh) of Christ, see Eph 5:22–32, especially 5:31f; then see
Rev 19:7, 9; 21:2, 9; 22:17; John 3:29; Ignatius, *Poly.* 5:1; Hermas, *Vis.* II 4.1;
and most of all the most noteworthy remarks in 2 Clem. 14. (Somehow the
figurative speeches of Jesus, which are connected with the messianic circle of
thoughts, also belong here: Mark 2:19; Matt 22:1–10; 25:1–13; Luke 12:36.)
In the use of the image, as it is found in Did. 11, 2 Clem. 14, as well as in
Ephesians and in Ignatius, different circles of thoughts converge: it is felt and
said that the pre-existent church is the flesh and the body of Christ, but also
that the earthly flesh of Christ is the first manifestation, the beginning of the
church, namely the earthly one, which is the image of the heavenly one and is
mysteriously connected with it. These speculations are connected with ethical and ascetic ideas: one must keep the church pure, because it is the flesh,
the bride of Christ. But one keeps the church pure by keeping one's own flesh

pure. The only true and proper way to keep oneself pure is through virginity, the ascetic life. Whoever practices it keeps his flesh pure, but also keeps the church pure; he acts according to "the earthly mystery of the church." To give our passage the proper force, however, we must not stop at the demand of simple asceticism, but must adopt the intensified form of spiritual marriage, of the cohabitation of the ascetic and the virgin; see Lietzmann, *Korinther*, at 1 Cor 7:38 and Achelis, *Virgines*, 1902. Whoever lives in this way imitates on earth the pure marriage of Christ with the church. Thus, once the thought of a replica of the heavenly syzygy comes to the fore, we can better understand μὴ διδάσκω . . . κρίσιν: for from the worldly point of view, this cohabitation of the ascetic and the virgin can be rather offensive; it also contains a great danger, since the will of the two can collapse because of their sensuality (Irenaeus, *Haer.* I 6.3 writes of the Valentian prophets and their deeds: ἄλλοι δὲ αὖ πάλιν σεμνῶς κατ᾽ ἀρχάς, ὡς μετὰ ἀδελφῶν προσποιούμενοι συνοικεῖν, προϊόντος τοῦ χρόνου ἠλέγχθησαν, ἐγκύμονος τῆς ἀδελφῆς ὑπὸ τοῦ ἀδελφοῦ γενηθείσης). This accounts for the warning that the prophet must not invite others to imitate him; with respect to criticism originating from the congregation, there is a warning that judgment is in God's hands and not in the hands of the congregation. Other interpretations of the passage are as follows: it is about outlandish, symbolic actions of the prophets like the bronze serpent of Num 21:8f, offensive marriages with whores and pagans, two wives, as reported by Moses, Jacob, and Hosea; see Justin, *Dial.* 94 and 134; Iren. *Haer.* IV 20.12 (on this cf. Harris, Taylor, Zahn). The "ancient" prophets are hardly—as in von Harnack—the prophets of the first apostolic age like Agabus, Judas, Silas, the daughters of Philip, but rather the prophets of the Old Testament. We do not know which passages of the Old Testament were interpreted as spiritual marriage; much is possible with the allegorizing method. Hosea 3:1–3 may be in view most of all.

11:12 is a close parallel to v. 9: just like for a meal, the prophet can ask for money in the Spirit, but it must be for the poor, not for himself. On the poverty and disinterestedness of the true prophet, see Herm. *Mand.* XI 8.

B. How to Treat Unostentatious, Wandering Christians (12:1–5)

Translation

12:1 Everyone who "comes in the name of the Lord" should be received. Then, when you examine him you will obtain knowledge of him; for you will have insight and be able to distinguish between right and left. ² If the one who comes is passing through, then help him as much as you can; he may stay with you only two or three days if it is necessary. ³ If he wishes to stay with you, then he should work as a craftsman and thereby be able to eat. ⁴ If he does not have a craft, then you should take care according to your understanding so that a Christian does not live idly among you. ⁵ If, however, he does not wish to comply with this, then he is playing a game with Christ. Beware of such people.

Textual Notes

The chapter is an insertion; it would perhaps be better after ch. 13, which again talks about the prophet and the teacher. The context is the reception and preservation of the traveling brothers, more simply (Did. 12), and the charismatics (Did. 13). In the Roman Empire, trade and traffic flourished within the Mediterranean community, travel was safe, and freedom of movement was great (see Stephan "Verkehrsleben," 1–136; see further Friedländer, *Sittengeschichte*, 2:1ff, as well as Zahn, *Weltverkehr*). Thus as a foundational, often-repeated admonition in the ancient Christian writings to be hospitable (cf. Rom 12:13; 1 Pet 4:9; 1 Tim 3:2; 5:10; Heb 13:2; 1 Clem. 1:2; 10:7—12:7; as well as in Justin, *1 Apol.* 67.6; etc.).

12:1 At the beginning is the exhortation to welcome any brother who is traveling. ἐν ὀνόματι κυρίου may be translated as an appeal to the fact that he is a Christian; on the whole expression, see Ps 117:26. Only after admission does the examination take place; the author does not say how it is entrusted to the congregation. δεξιὰν καὶ ἀριστεράν is connected with σύνεσιν ἕξετε adverbially (not adjectivally with σύνεσιν), which makes better sense than taking it together with γνώσεσθε (which is also possible; see γινώσκειν δεξιὰν καὶ ἀριστεράν in Jonah 4:11) and taking σύνεσιν γὰρ ἕξετε parenthetically.

12:2 If the one who has arrived and passed the examination is a transient, he may remain up to three days (cf. 11:5); the ἀνάγκη may be great fatigue or also indisposition.

12:3 This verse deals with a permanent establishment. Only the craftsman would be considered in need of assistance in this regard. The merchant in a similar situation can help himself. The traveling craftsman was probably supported in such a way that a fellow craftsman took care of him (cf. Acts 18:3); on ἐργαζέσθω καὶ φαγέτω, see 2 Thess 3:10.

12:4 The unskilled should somehow be put to work. On the σύνεσις of the congregation, see Did. 12:1. Note the name of honor used for those in the congregation: χριστιανός! No lazy person shall live in the congregation, but no one shall suffer in need. A strong force of propaganda must result from the implementation of these prescriptions, in which there is a good deal of social wisdom; see the *Clementine Homilies*; Epistles of Clement to James 8: τεχνίτῃ ἔργον, ἀδρανεῖ ἔλεος.

12:5 Not only the prophets and apostles, but also other simpler people the name Christian to go about as beggars. χριστέμπορος is a good compound word, used here for the first time. ἔμπορος already, according to its etymology, denotes the traveling merchant, the merchant (*mercator*) in contrast to the anchored grocer, the κάπηλος (*caupo*). χριστέμπορος can be traced more often in later ecclesiastical usage (the oldest passages are Hippolytus, *Ruth*, in Bonwetsch and Achelis, 120; Pseudo-Ignatius, *Trall.* 6:2; *Magn.* 9:2; Athanasius, *Ad Matth.* 7:15 in *Migne Graeca* 27, 1381), which is likely to be explained in all instances by a reliance on the Did.

C. Support of Local Prophets and Teachers (13:1–7)

Translation

¹³:¹ Every true prophet who wants to stay with you is worthy of his food. ² Similarly, a true teacher, "like the worker is worthy of his food." ³ Therefore, take every first portion of the produce of the winepress and the threshing floor, of the cattle and the sheep, and give the first portion to the prophets. For they are your high priests. ⁴ But if you have no prophet, give it to the poor. ⁵ When you bake bread, take the leaven and give it according to the commandment. ⁶ Likewise, when you have opened a jar of wine or oil, take the broken portion, and give it to the prophets. ⁷ And of your money, and of your clothing, and of all your possessions, take a portion at your pleasure and give it according to the commandment.

Textual Notes

From πᾶς ὁ ἐρχόμενος, who migrates and wishes to settle within the congregation, the focus moves on to the itinerant prophet and teacher who remain in the congregation (the apostle should not remain; 11:5).

On the teacher, see 1 Cor 12:28 (at the comments on Did. 11:3); it is the charismatically gifted preacher and catechist of the congregation whose gift is wisdom and knowledge and who edifies, admonishes, and teaches with calm, non-ecstatic speech and who interprets the Old Testament and applies it to the congregation; we can clearly see the activity of the teachers in Hebrews and 1 Peter. For the bibliographical details, see von Harnack's comments in *Lehre* on this passage.

13:1–2 As a general rule, the word of the Lord applies (cf. Matt 10:10 as well as 1 Cor 9:13f). It does not speak of a fixed salary but mainly of food and clothing (see, however, ἀργύριον in 13:7); and how these provisions are to be offered is shown in the following verses. Note the rural and country-urban conditions that are assumed: the members of the congregation have a garden, stable, vineyard, field, store-cellar, and the ability to bake and weave (?) within the house. The Did. did not originate within the city.

13:3 The commandment to give the firstfruits to the priests (= God) is a Jewish law (cf. Num 18:12ff; Deut 18:3f; 26:1ff) but is also a rather widespread, general, ancient custom (good examples come from the Syrian Bedouins, evidence of the survival of an ancient custom, in Curtis, *Ursemitische Religion*, 204–6; the firstfruits offering is based upon primitive taboo ideas). The firstfruits originally consisted of only the first yields of a newly planted field, newly planted trees, and the first births of the animals. Here, as often elsewhere, the firstfruits are taken from the harvest of each year and each field, but in the case of cattle it is also here only the true first birth (in larger herds, of course, a regular, annual ἀπαρχή is possible). Note still the high esteem in which the prophets are held: they are the high priests and precede the poor (Did. 13:4).

13:4 That the prophet should then give of his abundance to the poor is possible, but it is not mentioned: the poor could also be supported in other ways than indirectly or directly by the firstfruits.

13:5 σιτία: not the raw dough, of course, but rather the baked bread is sent to the prophet. Note here and in the following the recent expansion of the concept of ἀπαρχή: each time one bakes, puts a barrel in the cellar, puts a piece of cloth to work, collects money, and in general all property, a portion of these things are sent to the prophet. Obviously, those who have no agricultural goods of their own but buy their provisions, who live by trade and commerce are taken into account. The ἐντολή in v. 5 and v. 7 is either the Mosaic commandment or the Lord's commandment (Matt 10:10). Drews, *Untersuchungen zur Didache*, 63ff believes it to be a lost word of the Lord and for support appeals to Iren. *Haer.* IV 17.5: *sed (dominus noster) et suis discipulis dans consilium, primitias deo offerre ex suis creaturis . . . .*

13:6 This verse deals with purchased, not self-harvested (v. 3) provisions. κεράμιον, is a large earthen vessel well known to all of antiquity, the sherds of which make up, for example, the Monte Testaccio near Rome. Other types of storage can be found in Mark 2:22.

13:7 ἀργύριον is money that has been earned; ἱμάτιον is a piece of cloth that has been purchased or woven by oneself, to be cut according to size;

κτῆμα includes, as broadly as possible, any possession that might come into consideration. ὡς ἄν σοι δόξῃ, that is, according to ability and good will.

D. Celebration on Sunday (14:1–3)

Translation

14:1 Further, on the Lord's Day, come together, break bread, and give thanks, having first confessed your sins, so that your sacrifice may be pure. 2 And anyone who has a quarrel with his neighbor should not come together with you until they have reconciled, so that your sacrifice may not be profaned. 3 For this is what the Lord said, "In every place and at every time they shall offer me a pure sacrifice: For I am a great King, says the Lord, and my name is admired among the gentiles."

Textual Notes

How ch. 14 relates to what comes before it remains rather unclear. The wording of ch. 13 in no way suggests that the firstfruits are to be brought to the worship service, nor can this be inferred from Justin, *1 Apol.* 67.6. Very important pieces of the congregational worship service are missing; edification by the word is not touched upon in the slightest. It is not the author's intention to give a detailed layout of the Sunday worship service, which is determined by tradition and the congregational custom, and whose direction lies in the hands of the one called. The author only wishes to tell the congregation what they have to do to make possible a worthy celebration of the Sunday worship service. And in addition to the self-evident duty of being present, attentive, etc., belongs only one thing: the confession of sins at the Eucharist. Chapter 14 speaks of the necessity of this. The eucharistic celebration here is probably, as in Justin, *1 Apol.* 67, a celebration detached from the communal meal (*agape*), connected with the Sunday worship service accompanied by the word, in which only wine and bread are enjoyed (cf. the comments at Did. 9:1).

14:1 κυριακή κυρίου is pleonastic, see for example our "Herrensonntag,"[6] which I found in the folk song in Huggenberger, *Dorfgenossen*, 85. Or was it the case that in the Jewish circles, with which the Jewish readers of the Did. were close, the designation κυριακή "day of the Lord/God" was common terminology for the Sabbath? In this case κυρίου assures the Christian

6. TN: "The Lord's Sunday."

Lord's Day is in mind: κυριακὴ τοῦ κυρίου ἡμῶν Χριστοῦ. The oldest passages about the Sunday celebration: 1 Cor 16:2 (μία σαββάτου); Acts 20:7 (μία τῶν σαββάτων); Rev 1:10 (κυριακὴ ἡμέρα); Barn. 15:9 (ἡμέρα ὀγδόη); Ignatius, *Magn.* 9:1 (κυριακή); Pliny, *Ep.* X 96 (*status dies*); Evang. Petri 50 (κυριακή); Justin, *1 Apol.* 67.3, 7 (ἡλίου ἡμέρα); *Dial.* 24.1; 41.4; 138.1 (ἡμέρα ὀγδόη, 41.4 also μία τῶν σαββάτων). On the Hellenistic use of κυριακός and on the possibility that the celebration of the early Christian Lord's Day took place with conscious opposition to the imperial cult and the imperial day, see Deissmann, *Licht*, 268–74, as well as Deissmann, *Bibelstudien*, 44–46. This is also a possible explanation of the pleonasm κυριακὴ κυρίου. συναχθέντες, the whole congregation comes together. In the eucharistic celebration the most important element is the breaking of bread; on the ancient name, see 1 Cor 10:16; Acts 2:46; 20:7, 11, as well as κλάσμα in Did. 9:3; on εὐχαριστήσατε, see the excursus before ch. 9. προεξομολογησάμενοι (the manuscript has προσεξομολογησάμενοι "confessing thereby") probably means a brief, individual confession like in 4:14. παραπτώματα are daily transgressions; severe sins must be subject to church discipline (15:3). θυσία: the Eucharist as a sacrifice; see the excursus before ch. 9. Belonging to the purity of the sacrifice (καθαρά and κοινόν in v. 2 are technical terms) is the purity of the participants from sins, which is achieved by confession and in v. 2 freedom from hatred of the brother (ἑταῖρος).

14:2 The instruction is a narrowing of the general precept of Jesus in Matt 5:23f to inner-congregational relationships, which has become law and custom here. On the matter, see also the close connection between the allusions to the Lord's Supper with the exhortation to reconciliation in Ignatius, *Trall.* 8. τὴν before ἀμφιβολίαν is strange; von Gebhardt suggested τινά. The passage, linked with 15:3, is cited in a curiously free form in Pseudo-Cyprian, *Adv. aleat.* 4: *in doctrinis apostolorum: si quis frater delinquit in ecclesia et non paret legi, hic nec colligatur donec poenitentiam agat, et non recipiatur, ne inquinetur et impediatur oratio vestra.*

14:3 On the loose citation, especially in the first sentence, of Mal 1:11, 14, see Justin, *Dial.* (28.5); 41.2f; 117.1–4; Irenaeus, *Haer.* IV 17.5; 18.1; Tertullian, *Adv. Jud.* 5; *Adv. Marc.* III 22; Clement of Alexandria, *Strom.* 5.14.136; the true sacrifice to be offered everywhere and at all times is readily found in the Christian Eucharist.

E. Election of the Congregation's Officials (15:1–2)

Translation

¹⁵:¹ Now, choose bishops and deacons worthy of the Lord, mild men, free from greed, truthful, and tested. For they also render you the service of prophets and teachers. ² Do not, therefore, hold them in low esteem. For they are your honored ones along with the prophets and teachers.

Textual Notes

Very important, unfortunately very brief information about the church officials. See the compilation of material on early Christian congregational government in Knopf, *Nachapostolische Zeitalter*, 147ff, 152–60 for a treatment of the Did.; Leitzmann, "Verfassungsgeschichte," 97–153; very important is von Harnack's large edition of the Did. (*Lehre*) and *Entstehung*, 1 for a bibliography. — The information in the Did. shows the following:

15:1 ἐπίσκοποι καὶ διάκονοι, bishops and, closely related to them, deacons form a college, hence the plural (cf. Phil 1:1; 1 Tim 2:3–13; 1 Clem. 42:4f; Hermas, *Vis.* III 5.1; presbyters are not mentioned at all within the text, the monarchical episcopate is still remote. How many bishops and deacons there are surely depends upon local needs. χειροτονήσατε ἑαυτοῖς: the office, therefore, does not depend on *charisma* but on election, by the whole congregation; the effect of the ministers must, therefore, be confined to the individual congregation, to which the given regulations from ch. 14 onward apply. The οὖν creates a close connection between 15:1 and what precedes: ministers within the congregation must be elected so that the Sunday worship service might proceed in order and dignity. The preparation for the celebration is incumbent upon them; they will also have had, alone or together with the prophets and the teachers, the direction of the assembly. See another conjecture below on πραεῖς. On the quite general ἀξίους τοῦ κυρίου (= Christ, 11:8), see Ignatius, *Eph.* 2:1; 4:1; and *Rom.* 10:2. πραεῖς is used rather generally, but perhaps consideration is given to pastoral activity: they must be attuned to the individual confession of sin and reconciliation (14:1f) to ensure that the sacrifice is pure. Since the church officers have the administration of gifts at worship within their purview, and since they also have the administration of the church funds under their purview, as the parallels attest, they are to be ἀφιλάργυροι; see 2 Tim 3:3; Justin, *1 Apol* 67.6: οἱ εὐποροῦντες δὲ καὶ βουλόμενοι κατὰ προαίρεσιν ἕκαστος τὴν ἑαυτοῦ ὃ βούλεται δίδωσιν (namely within the Sunday worship service) καὶ τὸ συλλεγόμενον παρὰ τῷ προεστῶτι ἀποτίθεται καὶ αὐτὸς ἐπικουρεῖ ὀρφανοῖς τε καὶ χήραις, the sick, the imprisoned, generally those in need. On ἀληθεῖς and δεδοκιμασμένους, see 11:11 and 13:1f; the same demands that are made of the prophets and teachers are made of the ministers. The reasoning also corresponds to this: ὑμῖν γὰρ κτλ. The expression λειτουργία already denotes in secular Greek the service to God, the cult (then cf. Num 8:22; 16:9; Luke 1:23; Heb 8:6; 9:21; 1 Clem. 40:2; etc.). The ministers receive a share in the divine activity of those who bear the Spirit, as they pray, teach, edify, expound, and only in this do they approach the prestige of the group of prophets and teachers, who were originally far superior to them. The development toward Catholicism is clear: the office itself begins to usurp the teaching until the bishop becomes the sole bearer and guardian of the truth. The Did. writes at a time when the bearers of the Spirit have already become rarer.

15:2 For their part, the congregations are not yet readily inclined to place their ministers alongside the charismatics. τετιμημένοι, which divides the congregations into a group of leaders and a group of the broader multitude, is probably to be interpreted as those honored by God. ὑμῶν is a partitive genitive; see Clement of Alexandria, *Strom.* 6.13.107: οἱ τῇ μεγαλοπρεπεστάτῃ δόξῃ τετιμημένοι of the leaders of the congregation; the same in Clem. Alex., *Hypotyposes* in Eusebius, *Hist. eccl.* 2.1.3 (Peter, James, John): ὑπὸ τοῦ σωτῆρος προτετιμημένους.

F. Congregational Discipline (15:3–4)

Translation

3 Rebuke one another, not in anger, but in peace, as you have [learned] in the gospel. Let no one speak to anyone who transgresses against his neighbor, nor let him hear a word from you until he has repented. 4 But your prayers and alms and all you do, do these things as you have [learned] in the gospel of our Lord.

Textual Notes

The discussion clearly ties in with 14:1–3; see especially 14:2. If the case of 14:2 occurs and the parties involved cannot reconcile among themselves, then the other members of the congregation should intervene and rebuke with gentleness; on ἐλέγχετε, see 2:7; 4:3; on the entire exhortation, see (Sir 10:6); 2 Tim 4:2; Letter of Polycarp 6:1. The reference to the gospel alludes to passages such as Matt 18:15, 21f, as well as 5:22f. If the offending party

remains defiant (perhaps also: if the offended party refuses the gently re-
quested forgiveness), then the guilty party should not only stay away from
the congregational meeting, but also personal interactions with him should
be broken off until he relents. The legalism and the penitential institute of the
nascent church prepare themselves here. On ἀστοχεῖν, see 1 Tim 1:6; 6:21;
2 Tim 2:18; 2 Clem. 17:7. μηδὲ ἀκουέτω is a tautology and a difficult construction; we would expect: nor shall any among you hear from him.

15:4 These are "good works." Prayer and alms placed together; see
also Matt 6:2–6; Acts 10:4; 1 Pet 4:7f; 2 Clem. 16:4; and even previously
in Judaism in Tob 12:8. Among πάσας τὰς πράξεις then, the text may have
fasting in view (8:1), but other things pertaining to worship as well. ὡς
ἔχετε κτλ. is quite general: one is aware that he is in harmony with the
gospel. It is possible that instructions like Matt 6 are still especially in
mind (cf. already Did. 8).

IV. Conclusion (16:1–8)

At the closing of the Did., the author turns to eschatological matters, exhorting Christians to be prepared for the imminent return of Christ (16:1–2) and
warning them to be aware that as the end approaches, many false prophets
and corrupters will enter the flock, evil will increase, and one claiming to
be the Son of God will do evils that have never been seen before. Then, the
signs of the return of Christ will be seen and Christ will be seen returning
on the clouds of heaven (16:3–8).[7]

A. Be Ready at Any Hour (16:1–2)

Translation

16:1 "Watch" over your lives! "Do not let your candlesticks go out,
nor let your robes be loose," but "be ready. For you do not know
the hour when our Lord comes." [2] Come together frequently,
and search for whatever is needed for your souls. For the whole
time you remain in your faith will count for nothing if you do
not stand perfect in the last days.

---

7. TN: This paragraph is not present within the original German text but has been
added for the sake of unity and clarity in the newly formatted English edition.

Textual Notes

16:1–2 contain the exhortations. The content of these verses is: always be ready because the end will come suddenly! On 16:1, see Matt 24:42, 44; Luke 12:35. Connections with Matt 24 run throughout the entire passage. ζωή fits very well in the final exhortation because a ὁδὸς ζωῆς was mentioned at the beginning.

16:2 πυκνῶς itself can mean both "often" and "in large numbers." The meaning here is probably the latter: the individual is admonished not to stay away from the congregational worship service; see similarly at Barn. 4:10 (4:9f is parallel to Did. 16:2); Heb 10:25; Ignatius, *Eph.* 20:2; 2 Clem. 17:3. On οὐ γὰρ κτλ., see Matt 10:22; 24:13; Mark 13:13; 1 Clem. 35:4; 2 Clem. 8:2f; 19:3. Faithfulness in the last hour is so especially important because the temptations of that hour are especially severe, and ἐν οἷς ἂν ὑμᾶς καταλάβω, ἐν τούτοις καὶ κρινῶ (Justin, *Dial.* 47.5), see also the attitude of John's Revelation and of apocalypticism in general, which attempts to strengthen faithfulness especially for the end times.

B. For After a Time of Increasing Wickedness, the Lord Comes to Judge (16:3–8)

Translation

³ For in the last days false prophets and corrupters will become numerous, and "the sheep will turn into wolves, and love will turn into hatred." ⁴ For when iniquity abounds, "they will hate one another, and persecute and betray one another," and then the deceiver of the world will appear as the Son of God, and will do signs and wonders, and the earth will be delivered into his hands, and he will do iniquities which have never been done from everlasting. ⁵ Then the world of men will come into the fire of probation, and "many will fall" and perish; but those who endure in their faith will be saved by the "accursed one" himself. ⁶ And then the signs of truth will appear: first, the sign of the tearing in the heaven; then the sign of the sound of the trumpet; and third, the resurrection of the dead. ⁷ But not the resurrection of all [the dead], to be sure, as it was said, "The Lord will come, and all the saints with him." ⁸ Then the world will see "the Lord coming on the clouds of heaven."

Textual Notes

16:3–7, a small apocalypse, describes the time of increasing distress, its climax in the appearance of the Antichrist (v. 3f), the great apostasy (v. 5), and the turn to salvation (v. 6f).

16:3 See Matt 24:11, 24, as well as 7:15. The false prophets here are Satan's emissaries (different from 11:5, 8); φθορεῖς different from 5:2; on the appearance of the false teachers in recent times, see Apoc. Petri 1:1; Ascension of Isaiah 3:27ff; Sib. Or. II 165f.

16:4 See Matt 24:10, 12. The ἀνομία continues to increase (αὐξανούσης) until the climax is reached. On the Antichrist (κοσμοπλάνος only here), see Matt 24:15; 2 Thess 2:3–12; Rev 12ff; and on ancient Judaism, see Bousset, *Antichrist* and *Religion*, 291ff. On υἱὸς θεοῦ, see 2 Thess 2:4; Rev 13:11; on τέρατα and σημεῖα, see Mark 13:22; Matt 24:24; 2 Thess 2:9; Sib. Or. II 167; III 6.3ff; etc.; on world domination, see Rev 13:7 among other passages. The ἀθέμιτα are abominations, outrages, the highest among them probably the godlike worship, which the Antichrist demands for himself.

16:5 The Antichrist brings about a tremendous apostasy by cunning seduction of the whole world and by severe plagues on the faithful; almost all worship him and only a few remain faithful (cf. for instance Rev 13). Thus mankind is put to the test by a trial by fire (πύρωσις τῆς δοκιμασίας, on the image see 1 Pet 1:7). Difficult to interpret is ὑπ' αὐτοῦ τοῦ καταθέματος; the κατάθεμα (= curse) may be the ἀπώλεια, or also according to known usage (curse = object of the curse) the Antichrist. In this case, though, ὑπό would no longer fit since ἀπό would have been expected, nor would αὐτοῦ be properly understood. Or κατάθεμα (= accursed one) could refer to the *kyrios* who is blasphemed and cursed by the unbelievers. This option makes good sense of both ὑπό and αὐτοῦ, though the meaning of the expression is not entirely clear. But perhaps this was intentional; the expression was spoken in a vague manner for those who are in the know. ἐν τῇ πίστει can also be connected with σωθήσεται.

16:6 See Matt 24:30f. ἀλήθεια: the truth, the true facts will be revealed, namely that the crucified one is the heavenly Lord and not a κατάθεμα. Apocalyptic literature loves the enumeration of "signs," see already the indications in 16:3f. ἐκπέτασις dispersal = an opening; on the use of the word, see Plutarch, *Sera* 22, p. 564Bf, where ἐκπέτασις and διάχυσις are used in contrast with συστολή; on the context, see Rev 6:14. But it is quite possible that in the phrase σημεῖον ἐκπετάσεως something quite different is meant, namely a deliberately obscure reference to the fact that the Son of Man will appear hanging on the cross with outstretched hands (ἐκπέτασις) at the Second Coming. The cross went with him up to heaven; see Ev. Petri

39: . . . ὁρῶσιν ἐξελθόντας ἀπὸ τοῦ τάφου τρεῖς ἄνδρας, καὶ τοὺς δύο τὸν ἕνα ὑπορθοῦντας καὶ σταυρὸν ἀκολουθοῦντα αὐτοῖς. Sibylline Oracles VI 26f: Ὦ ζύλον ὦ μακαριστόν, ἐφ᾽ οὗ θεὸς ἐξετανύσθη, Οὐχ ἕξει σε χθών, ἀλλ᾽ οὐρανὸν οἶκον ἐσόψει. The "sign" of the outstretched hands also appears in Pss. Sol. 27: "I have stretched out my hands and sanctified the Lord, for the expansion of my hands is his sign, and my spreading out is the upright wood, Hallelujah!" Similar is Pss. Sol. 42:1–3. The idea that Jesus would return hanging from the transfigured cross was widespread in later times; see Bousset, *Der Antichrist*, 154ff and for an explanation on the whole, see Bousset, *Kyrios Christos*, 291. On φωνὴ σάλπιγγος, see 1 Thess 4:16; 1 Cor 15:52. οὐ πάντων, so perhaps a 1,000 year reign, like in Rev 20:4–6; with respect to 20:12–15 (the general judgment): the general resurrection comes later.

First Clement

Introduction

Outline

IV. The Ugly Quarrel in Corinth Should Be Settled as Soon as Possible (40:1—61:3)

    A. The Congregational Office Is Appointed by God (40:1—44:6)

    B. Noble Men Are Only Deposed by Villains (45:1—46:9)

    C. Praise of Love (47:1—50:7)

    D. Direct Admonition to the Authors of the Quarrel: They Must Repent, Submit, and Depart (51:1—58:2)

    E. Conclusion of the Letter with a Long Prayer (59:1—61:3)

V. The End of the Letter with a Concluding Admonition and Vows (62:1—65:2)

    A. Concluding Exhortations (62–63)

    B. Two Closing Vows and the Confirmation of the Emissaries (64–65)

Transmission

The letter has been preserved relatively well: in the Greek original text and in Latin, Syriac, and Coptic translations. It has been preserved in Greek within the appendix of the biblical codex Alexandrinus (A), though unfortunately with many gaps, the largest of which consists of the loss of an entire leaf containing 57:6—63:4. The complete Greek text is present within a minuscule from the eleventh century (1056), discovered by Bryennios in Constantinople and now kept in the Jerusalem Patriarchal Library. It is the same codex that contains the Did. (H). A Syriac translation (S) is written in a Cambridge manuscript (twelfth cent. CE, 1170), and a Latin translation (L) in an eleventh century codex in the Seminary at Namur. The Coptic tradition consists of two witnesses, a papyrus manuscript from the fourth century in the Staatsbibliothek of Berlin (C), and a very fragmentary papyrus manuscript from the fifth century in the Straßburg University and Landesbibliothek (C1) that contains 1 Clem. 1:1—26:2, though with many gaps. Both translations are in the Akhmimic dialect and are independent of one another. Also of significant text critical value are Clement of Alexandria's extensive quotations of 1 Clem. (see below).

Editions and Literature

O. von Gebhardt et al., *Patrum apostolicorum opera I*, 2nd ed. (Leipzig: Hinrichs, 1876). — A. Hilgenfeld, *Novum Testamentum extra canonem receptum*, 2nd ed. (Leipzig: Hinrichs, 1876). J. B. Lightfoot, *The Apostolic Fathers, Part 1: S. Clemens of Rome*, 2 vols. (London and New York: Macmillan, 1890). — F. X. Funk, *Patres Apostolici I*, 2nd ed. (Tübingen: Laupp, 1901). — In addition to these annotated editions, the well-known texts in the study editions are the following: O. von Gebhardt et al., *Patrum apostolicorum opera ed. minor*, 5th ed. (Leipzig: Hinrichs, 1906). — F. X. Funk, *Die apostolischen Väter*, 2nd ed. (Mohr Siebeck, 1907). — R. Knopf, *Der Erste Clemensbrief*, Texte und Untersuchungen 20.1 (Leipzig: Hinrichs, 1899). — The Syriac translation ed. by R. L. Bensly, *The Epistles of S. Clement to the Corinthians in Syriac* (Cambridge: Cambridge University Press, 1899); the Latin translation ed. by G. Morin, *Anecdota Maredsolana; Seu, Monumenta Ecclesiasticae Antiquitatis en Mss. Codicibus nunc Primum Edita*, vol. 2 (Maredsoli: Monasterio S. Benedicti, 1894); the Berlin Coptic ed. by C. Schmidt, *Der erste Clemensbrief in altkoptischer Übersetzung*, Texte und Untersuchungen 32.1 (Leipzig: Hinrichs, 1908); the Straßburger text by F. Rösch, *Bruchstücke des ersten Clemensbriefes: Nach dem Achmimischen Papyrus der Straßburger Universitäts- und Landesbibliothek, mit biblischen Texten derselben Handschrift* (Straßburg: Schlesier & Schweikhardt, 1910). — A German translation with a short explanation by R. Knopf, "Clemens an die Korinther," in *Neutestamentliche Apokryphen*, ed. E. Hennecke (Tübingen: Mohr, 1904), 84–112. — R. Knopf, "Clemens an die Korinther," in *Handbuch zu den neutestamentlichen Apokryphen*, ed. E. Hennecke (Tübingen: Mohr, 1904), 173–90. — W. Wrede, *Untersuchungen zum ersten Klemensbriefe* (Göttingen: Vandenhoeck and Ruprecht, 1891). — A. Stahl, *Patristische Untersuchungen: Der erste brief des romischen Clemens; Ignatius von Antiochien; der Hirt des Hermas* (Leipzig: A. Deichert, 1901). — T. M. Wehofer, "Untersuchungen zur altchristlichen Epistolographie," *Sitzungsberichte der Wiener Akademie, philosophisch-historische Klasse* 143.17 (1901) 102–37. — D. Völter, *Die apostolischen Väter neu untersucht. Vol. 1: Clemens, Hermas, Barnabas* (Leiden: Brill, 1904). — D. Völter, "Bemerkungen zum ersten Klemensbrief," *Zeitschrift für neutestamentlichen Wissenschaft* 7 (1906) 261–64. — G. Avanden Bergh van Eysinga, *Onderzoek naar de echtheid van Clemens eerste brief aan de Corinthiërs* (Leiden: Brill, 1908). — T. Schermann, *Griechische Zauberpapyri und das Gemeinde- und Dankgebet im I. Klemensbriefe*, Texte und Untersuchungen 34.2 (Leipzig: Hinrichs, 1909). — A. von Harnack, "Der erste Klemensbrief: Eine Studie zur Bestimmung des Charakters des ältesten Heidenchristentums," *Sitzungsberichte der Preußischen Akademie der Wissenschaften: Philosophisch-historische Klasse*

(1909) 38–61. — ET: A. von Harnack, "The First Letter of Clement: A Study to Determine the Character of the Oldest Form of Gentile Christianity," in *The Letter of the Roman Church to the Corinthian Church from the Era of Domitian: 1 Clement*, ed. and trans. Jacob N. Cerone, Classic Studies on the Apostolic Fathers 1 (Eugene, OR: Pickwick, 2021), 144–68. — W. Praetorius, "Die Bedeutung der beiden Klemensbriefe für die älteste Geschichte der kirchlichen Praxis (1. Hälfte)," *Zeitschrift für Kirchengeschichte* 33 (1912) 33, 347–63, 501–28. — More literature and also studies on the inidividual translations can be found in O. Bardenhewer, *Geschichte der altkirchlichen Literatur*. Vol. 1: *Vom Ausgang der apostolischen Zeitalters bis zum Ende des 2. Jahrhunderts*, 2nd ed. (Freiburg im Breisgau: Herder, 1913), §11.

Points of Contract and Attestations

There is no doubt that Polycarp of Smyrna knew 1 Clem. He uses it several times in his letter to the Philippians. Even his prescript is designed after that of 1 Clem. Explicit mention of 1 Clem. is first found in Hegesippus (Eusebius, *Hist. eccl* 4.22.1) and in Dionysius of Corinth (Eusebius, *Hist. eccl.* 4.23.11). Shortly thereafter, Irenaeus mentions him and praises him (*Haer.* III 3.3). We find extensive use of 1 Clem. in Clement of Alexandria's *Stromata*; see Eusebius, *Hist eccl.* 6.13.6, and further at Clem. Alex. *Strom.* 1.1.15; 7.38; 2.15.65; 4.6.32f; and above all 4.17–19, 105–19; 5.12.80; 6.8.64f. Also there are some echoes at other places which can be demonstrated. Origen and of course Eusebius know of the letter, which was read and used by some Greek writers until the tenth and eleventh centuries. A list of the references and quotations can be found in Gebhardt and von Harnack, *Patrum apostolicorum opera I*, xxiv–xliv; von Harnack, *Geschichte*, 1:40–47; and a very detailed and convenient treatment at Lightfoot, *Clement*, 1:148–200.

Occasion

The letter is sent from the Roman congregation to the Corinthian congregation when disputes broke out in Corinth. The majority of the congregation, led by a few leaders (1:1; 47:6), who presumably used their spiritual (pneumatic) gifts (13:1; 38:1f), stood up against the ministers, the presbyters, and dismissed some of them (47:6; 44:6). The letter from the Romans necessarily takes the side of the ousted ministers, demands their reinstatement, exhorts the congregation to repent and be converted, and instructs the leaders of the quarrel to depart from the congregation (cf. especially 51–58). But the Romans, in addition to the immediate occasion of the letter, also give a number of exhortations in an excessive number of words about the main elements of Christian conversion and life, without it being possible to see more precisely how these exhortations relate to the actual purpose of the letter; see primarily the first, more extensive main part of the letter (4–38) and the summary in 62:1f.

Provenance, Date, and Author

This document, which is very important for the history of ancient Christian piety and ancient congregational life, acquires a special value because it is not only classified according to its origin and destination, which it identifies at the outset, but also because its date of composition can be determined with a satisfying degree of certainty. The letter could not have been written too long after the deaths of Peter and Paul, at most about a human lifetime.[1] This is proven in 1 Clem. 5:1—6:2 which speaks of the two apostles and of the victims of the Neronian persecution: they all belong to the recent past, to "our generation" (1 Clem. 51). Of course, the date of the letter should not be placed too close to the actual apostolic age. This is prohibited by the already established theory of apostolic succession (1 Clem. 42), by the observation that the first ministers, appointed by the apostles, have already died (44:2f), that the church of Corinth is called ancient (47:6), that there are members of the church in Rome who from their youth until old age have walked blamelessly as Christians (63:3). These observations suggest at least the end of the second Christian generation. A more precise assessment is permitted from 1 Clem. 1:1. The dangers and hardships mentioned there should be interpreted as a persecution experienced by the Roman community. This persecution must have been a later one than the Neronian persecution, on which 5:1—6:2 reflects. According to our knowledge of early Christianity, it can be none other than the Domitian persecution. Domitian persecuted the church in Rome toward the end of his reign. The letter must have been writ-ten while there was a break in the persecution, or immediately following its conclusion, in the final phase of Domitian's reign, or even at the beginning of Nerva's reign, thus around 95 or 96 CE.

From the beginning to the end, 1 Clem. is a letter from the entire Ro-man congregation. From the first to the last sentence the 1st person plural is used. But in the tradition, the letter is transmitted under the name of a certain individual man, Clement, whose name is never mentioned within the letter: Yet Dionysius of Corinth in Eusebius, *Hist. eccl.* 4.23.11 already called 1 Clem. τὴν διὰ Κλήμεντος γραφεῖσαν (ἐπιστολὴν ὑμῶν). The tradition

---

1. TN: "Menschenalter" can mean either "generation" or "lifetime."

could very well be accurate. Even if the letter is written in the name of the Roman congregation, it is written by a singular, outstanding man, as the strictly uniform style already proves, and the author may very well have been called Clement; it was a man who belonged among the leaders of the Roman congregation in the time of the second generation and who appears in the later tradition as the second or third bishop of Rome. Unfortunately we know nothing more about him. The letter reveals a skillful homiletician with an excellent command of the LXX, but who also knows how to use forms of contemporary Greek oratory. Beyond the immediate needs of the moment, he has delivered a product of literary art that goes beyond the form of a real letter and, in broad, homiletical trains of thought and designs, portrays the ideal, proper Christian way of life.

I. Prescript (1:0)

Translation

1:0 The congregation of God which dwells in Rome as a so-journer, to the congregation of God which dwells in Corinth as a sojourner, called and sanctified according to the will of God through our Lord Jesus Christ. May grace and peace from Almighty God be given to you in fullness through Jesus Christ.

Textual Notes

The prescript is based on the prescript of 1 Corinthians, which was almost certainly intended (see 47:1–3), and on that of 1 Peter, whom the author also knows. The author of the letter does not identify himself. The whole congregation takes the floor (cf. Mart. Poly. prescript). παροικεῖν communicates the idea of temporary residence in a foreign country (see also 1 Pet 1:1, 17; 2:11; Heb 11:13; Herm. Sim. I 1). On κλητοῖς ἡγιασμένοις, see 1 Cor 1:2; both words could be equivalent to one another, but the one can also be subordinated to the other. Calling and sanctification take place according to the antecedent, salvific will of God (29:1) through the Lord Jesus. Christians are the new people, yet chosen from the very beginning, and their formation is conditioned upon the appearance of the Lord. παντοκράτωρ occurs often in the letter (cf. 2:3; 32:4; 60:4; and also 8:5), is rare in early Christian literature, with the exception of Revelation, but is used frequently in the LXX.

II. Introduction: The Occasion of the Letter, Then and Now (1:1—3:4)

In 1 Clem. 1:1—3:4, the author provides the Corinthians with the impetus for this letter (1:1) and details their former state of obedience and the great fame they had won among Christian congregations (1:2—2:8), as well as the current pitiful state of congregation (3:1–4).[2]

A. Occasion of the Letter (1:1)

Translation

1:1 Because of the dangers and hardships that suddenly and quickly occurred, one after another, we now turn our attention, a little late in our opinion, to the disputes that have arisen among you, beloved, and to the insurrection which is unfitting and is foreign for the elect of God, that ugly and godless insurrection, which has inflamed a few hasty and impudent people to such a degree of folly that your venerable and renowned name has been tremendously damaged.

Textual Notes

The apology can only refer to the persecutions that have affected the Roman congregation. The Neronian persecution is in the distant past and is referred to in 1 Clem. 5 and 6. Since the congregation still numbers itself among the Neronian martyrs (5:1), only Domitian's oppression can be meant here. On the Domitian oppression, see Lightfoot, *Clement*, 1:104–14; Knopf, *Nachapostolische Zeitalter*, 88–96, then Preuschen, *Analecta*, 1:11 and the literature mentioned there. Dio Cassius LXVII 14, along with Eusebius, *Hist. eccl.* 3.17–20, 1 Peter, and Revelation are the main sources, and Dio testifies to the Roman persecution. Added to this is the monumental tradition of the catacombs (cf. Marucchi, *Archäologie*, 36ff). The Roman persecution of Christians during Domitian's reign took place certainly toward the end of his rule. According to our passage, it took place suddenly and happened repeatedly. τὰ ἐπιζητούμενα παρ' ὑμῖν πράγματα are "the things which are in question with you" and indeed not "the things for which you have asked us." ἀλλοτρίας καὶ ξένης: 1 Clem. loves using a twofold approach to define

---

2. TN: This paragraph is not present within the original German text but has been added for the sake of unity and clarity in the newly formatted English edition.

matters more closely, and the following evidences a number of similar formations. On στάσις, the following, especially 1 Clem. 40, reveals something more detailed: It is an uprising of the congregation against its ministers, some of whom have been deposed (see introduction, pp. 61–62). That the ringleaders are few in number (ὀλίγα πρόσωπα) is more clearly articulated in 47:6. On ἀξιαγάπητος, see also 21:7. The clustered compositions with ἀξιο- are Hellenistic, starting with Xenophon. Ignatius is very fond of them. On ἀξιαγάπητος, see Ign. *Phld.* 5:2. On the rhetorically exaggerated expression πᾶσιν ἀνθρώποις, see 1 Thess 1:8; Ign. *Eph.* 8:1. — βλασφημηθῆναι in AH; (βλασφημεῖσθαι) CC[1]; but βλαφθῆναι in LS.

B. The Once-Splendid State of the Corinthian Congregation (1:2—2:8)

Translation

1:2 For who has stayed with you as a guest and did not admire your glorious and firm faith, your prudent and gentle Christian piety? And who did not praise your great hospitality and perfect and secure knowledge? [3] For you did all things without respect to the person. You walked in God's statutes, were obedient to your superiors, and showed reverence to your elders. You encouraged the younger to be humble and honorable. You commanded the women to perform all their duties with an impeccable, honorable, and pure conscience, while loving their husbands in the proper manner. You also taught them to keep themselves within the bounds of subordination, to furnish the household with honor, and to be reasonable in every respect. 2:1 You all were humble and in no way arrogant. You preferred to obey rather than command. You preferred to give more than to receive. You were content and were careful with what Christ offered you for your pilgrimage. You carefully locked up his words in your heart, and his sufferings were before your eyes.

[2] Therefore a deep and blessed peace and an unquenchable desire for good were bestowed upon all, and the Holy Spirt was poured out abundantly upon all. [3] Full of holy intent, in good confidence, with pious trust, you stretched out your hands to Almighty God, imploring him to be gracious to you if you had done wrong against your will. [4] Day and night you toiled for the entire brotherhood, so that through (your) merciful disposition and inner compassion the number of his elect might

be saved. ⁵ You were pure and without falsehood and did not hold anything against one another. ⁶ You hated all strife and division. You mourned the sins of your neighbors. You saw their mistakes as your own. ⁷ You did not repent of any good deed; you were prepared for every good work. ⁸ Adorned with a virtuous and venerable manner of life, you did everything in the fear of God. The commandments and demands of the Lord were "written on the tablets of your heart."

Textual Notes

1:2 gives the reason for σεμνὸν κτλ., especially with regard to πᾶσιν ἀνθρώποις. Note here and in what follows the practical, ethical, entirely non-mystical nature of Christianity represented by 1 Clem. παρεπιδημεῖν means to stay for a short time in a foreign place (see 1 Pet 1:1; 2:11; Heb 11:13). Many strangers came from abroad to the *bimaris Corinthus* for various reasons. The news of the dispute may have come to Rome through Roman Christians who had visited Corinth. Clement has a fondness for the rare word πάναρετος (cf. 2:8; 45:7; 57:3; 60:4), which is otherwise missing in early Christian literature as well as the LXX; see also Lucian, *Philops.* 6; Philo, *Migr.* 95 (ed. Mangey, 541); Eusebius, *Hist. eccl.* 1.2.11; 4.22.8. πίστις should be understood as broadly as possible: the Christian state of faith. εὐσέβεια, as the adjectives prove, is already put into practice. The word is foreign to the first layer of early Christian literature and is decidedly Hellenistic (cf. 1 Tim 2:2). First Clement uses it and related terms often (cf. 2:3; 11:1; 15:1; 32:4; 50:3; 61:2; 62:1). There was a special opportunity for hospitality in the oft-visited Corinth (see later at 10:7—12:8 for details). γνῶσις is also practical: it is primarily the knowledge of the divine will. First Clement shows both broadly and in detail how his will is to be determined, through *gnosis*, whose main source is the OT.

1:3 What follows in external form is a description which deals with the whole congregation, a kind of household code (*Haustafel*). On this form, which also recurs in 21:6–8 and is composed from the ethical tradition of Hellenism, see Did. 4:9–11 and also the excursus after Col 4:1 (Bisping, *Epheser, Philipper und Kolosser*). — The biblical Greek (LXX) saying πρόσωπον λαμβάνειν is also attested in the New Testament; the *adverbium* used here is also found in 1 Pet 1:17 and Barn. 4:12. Justice and fearlessness within the congregation is praised: the congregation did not allow itself to be impressed by anyone. — νομίμοις is in L and Clement of Alexandria; νόμοις in AHS. — The ἡγούμενοι of the congregation, who appear again in 21:6, are best understood to be the ministers and the leading charismatics, that is, the honored ones of Did. 15:2. Clement also recognizes them as τιμή. ἡγούμενοι occurs in Heb 13:7, 17, 24; προηγούμενοι in Herm. *Vis.* II 2.6; III 9.7. The matter is different, however, in 1 Clem. 5:7; 37:2f; 60:4, where ἡγούμενοι means the secular Roman authority. The πρεσβύτεροι spoken of here are not ministers, but the older, leading class within the congregation, some of whom had still been with Paul and Peter and had experienced the Neronian persecution. — In the ideal portrayal of women, the main features are chastity, subordination, and withdrawal from the public sphere. It is an ancient ideal for women, which is reflected here and which is also recognizable in a very similar way in the other household codes (*Haustafeln*) of early Christianity.

In 1 Clem. 2, the narration returns to general matters. Subordination, humility, love of peace are strongly emphasized anew in what follows.

2:1 On ἥδιον διδόντες, see Acts 20:35. — Since the text can be read with Χριστοῦ according to HLSCC[1] instead of θεοῦ according to A, then the ἐφόδια needs to be ascribed to Christ: It is not bodily food and physical needs that are in view, but spiritual provisions. καὶ προσέχοντες must be interpreted in connection with the previous clause not the subsequent, and the λόγοι αὐτοῦ are the words of Christ. The sense of the passage is as follows: You were humble without arrogance; you preferred to submit yourselves rather than to command others to submit; you preferred to give of your earthly goods rather than to strive for their increase. For you had no interest in external possessions: Christ gave you a different kind of allowance with which you were content and which you took care of. You took his words to heart, etc. Formulated in this manner, the passage makes a fine point: the use of τοῖς ἐφοδίοις τοῦ Χριστοῦ directs the thought away from the earthly-material to the high realm of the spiritual and religious life, and it is shown in what once consisted of the wealth which made the Corinthians happy (cf. Knopf, *Clemensbrief*, 85–93). ἐνστερνίζειν is a late word. The phrase τὰ παθήματα κτλ. is probably a remembrance of Gal 3:1.

2:2 καὶ πλήρης πνεύματος ἁγίου ἔκχυσις κτλ. within the series of the other statements seems strange. For Paul, John, and other types of piety in early Christianity, the Spirit is the first, fundamental element from which everything grows, above all moral life; for the Roman, who is still aware of the gifts of the Spirit (13:1; 38:1f; 48:5), it appears, at least at this point, as a reward for ethical action, as a kind of *conscientia bona consequens*. This corresponds fully with the rational moralism of the letter.

2:3 depicts the prayer for the forgiveness of sins. Christians only sin ἄκοντες, but of course they do sin as can be seen almost immediately hereafter in v. 6. On the form ἵλεων, which maintains its Attic declension, see Radermacher, *Gram.*, 52, Blaß-Debrunner, *Grammatik*, §44.

2:4 The toil intended here is certainly not mere prayer, but is an active help of the sort that the Roman congregation itself does. See for example the explicit testimony of Dionysius of Corinth about the Romans in Eusebius, *Hist. eccl.* 4.23.10: . . . πάντας μὲν ἀδελφοὺς ποικίλως εὐεργετεῖν ἐκκλησίαις τε πολλαῖς ταῖς κατὰ πᾶσαν πόλιν ἐφόδια πέμπειν, ὧδε μὲν τὴν τῶν δεομένων πενίαν ἀναψύχοντας, ἐν μετάλλοις δὲ ἀδελφοῖς ὑπάρχουσιν ἐπιχορηγοῦντας δι' ὧν πέμπετε ἀρχῆθεν ἐφοδίων. Here, as in 1 Pet 2:17 and 5:9 (Polycarp, *Phil.* 10:1), ἀδελφότης is the entire Christian brotherhood. The reading μετ' ἐλέους is now secure; C with its reading μετὰ δέους stands alone. συνείδησις can hardly be understood with reference to God, for example as co-knowledge, consent of God, but rather must be interpreted, as is otherwise always the case, with reference to the believer: the inner consciousness of an imposed obligation. The Corinthian community, not the ἀδελφότης, has this consciousness, and it comes down to the obligation that they must help others. Mercy should also be sought by the Corinthians. On ἀριθμὸς τῶν ἐκλεκτῶν, see 1 Clem. 58:2 and 59:2; the expression sounds like predestination, but 1 Clem. is far from this view.

2:5 There could be a Pauline allusion with εἰλικρινεῖς καὶ ἀκέραιοι (see Phil 1:10 and 2:15). ἀμνησίκακος, along with its closest relative, is a Hellenistic word as well as the forms directly connected with μνησικακεῖν, whereas the verb itself, which is the seed of the whole group, already appears in Herodotus and the Attic authors. For ἀμνησίκακος, see also (1 Clem. 62:2) Hermas, *Mand.* (XIII 10) IX 39:3; Philo, *Joseph* 246 (ed. Mangey, 75); Nicolaus of Damascus (Müller *Fragm. Hist. Graec.* III 439): ἀμνησίκακος ἦν πρὸς τοὺς κρατηθέντας.

2:6 has particular reference to the dispute within the Corinthian community.

2:7 In the active sense, ἀμεταμέλητος first appears in Aristotle. On ἕτοιμοι κτλ., see Titus 3:1. The praise in v. 7 is quite general, as befits the conclusion of the whole account. The same goes for v. 8.

2:8 With these words, the Romans describe their ideal form of Christianity. Take note again of the moralism. On the conclusion of v. 8, see Prov 7:2: ἐπίγραψον δὲ (sc. τοὺς ἐμοὺς λόγους) ἐπὶ τὸ πλάτος τῆς καρδίας σου. The combination of προστάγματα καὶ δικαιώματα appears to have originated from the liturgy, see 1 Clem. 58:2 (liturgical passage), and then Apost. Const. VIII 5.5 in the prayer for the catechumens: (ἵνα) . . . διδάξῃ αὐτοὺς τὰ προστάγματα αὐτοῦ καὶ τὰ δικαιώματα.

C. The Tragic Present State of the Congregation (3:1–4)

Translation

³:¹ Fame and abundance were given to you in full, but what has been written came about: "He ate and drank and became fat and strong—then the beloved kicked out." ² Therefore, from this came jealousy and envy, strife and discord, persecution and disorder, war and imprisonment. ³ Thus the dishonorable rose up against the honorable, the ignoble against the noble, those without understanding against those with understanding, the young against the old. ⁴ That is why justice and peace are a long way off because everyone has abandoned the fear of God and has become weak-sighted in faith, no longer walking in the ordinances of his commandments and lives a life worthy of Christ, but because everyone goes after the desires of his evil heart, filled with unjust and ungodly jealousy, through which "death came into the world."

Textual Notes

In contrast to the happy past stands the ugly present. It is described much more briefly than the former out of interest of delicacy, but also because the author wishes to come to his topic, the admonitions, and finally because in what will follow there will be plenty of opportunities to point out the damage caused to the Corinthian community in more precise terms.

3:1—within a citation of the Holy Scriptures (Deut 32:15)—indicates a reversal: when the climax was reached, the fall took place with arrogance. πλατυσμός, literally meaning "expansion, spreading out," within the LXX translates the words רְחָב (Ps 118:45) or מֶרְחָב (Ps 17:20; 117:5; etc.). The word is probably to be judged as a biblical expression by the writer since it also occurs in secular literature in a figurative sense, but as a reproach: ostentation.

3:2 Take note of the form of the clauses here and in v. 3 and in v. 4. It is not a very clear anaphora: ἐκ τούτου—οὕτως—διὰ τοῦτο, also the paired secondary or opposite order should work in these clauses; it starts with ζῆλος (2) and ends with ζῆλος (4). — Here and in the following, ζῆλος is the jealousy for reputation, position, advantages over others. In it the source of the Corinthians' quarrel is seen. In 4:7 and 5:2, as in 3:2, φθόνος appears beside ἔρις. Good parallels to the intra-community ζῆλος fought here can be found in Hermas, *Sim.* VIII 7:4: ζῆλος περὶ πρωτείων καὶ περὶ δόξης τινός or Epictetus, *Ench.* 19: . . . ἰδών τινα προτιμώμενον ἢ μέγα δυνάμενον ἢ ἄλλως εὐδοκιμοῦντα. — ζῆλος is metaplastic. First Clement uses both ὁ and τό (Radermacher, *Grammatik*, 52; Blaß-Debrunner *Gramatik*, §51) side by side, see 3:4 and 5:2 in contrast with 4:8 and 6:1, 2. διωγμός, ἀκαταστασία (= disorder, rebellion; on ἀκαταστασία as a Hellenistic word, see also 1 Clem. 14:1; 43:6), πόλεμος, and αἰχμαλωσία are, of course, to be understood in terms of the conditions within the community. αἰχμαλωσία is an exaggeration and is figurative, as is πόλεμος; the removal of officials, thus their degradation and loss of influence, may appear as αἰχμαλωσία.

3:3 Light and shadow are immediately and vigorously divided by the Roman author. He and his congregation resolutely take the side of the deposed and their followers, as they already did in 1:1. See also Isa 3:5: προσκόψει τὸ παιδίον πρὸς τὸν πρεσβύτην, ὁ ἄτιμος πρὸς τὸν ἔντιμον.

3:4 διὰ τοῦτο refers back to v. 1. Anaphora, see above at v. 2. Take note here again of the moralism. δικαιοσύνη, a word often used by Clement, refers here to the state of the congregation in which it can stand before God; εἰρήνη is the gift of God above at 2:2; on the phrase, see also Isa 59:14: καὶ ἡ δικαιοσύνη μακρὰν ἀφέστηκεν. πίστει αὐτοῦ, the genitive is an objective genitive and refers to God; what is meant is trust in God, the confidence that is placed in him, his commandments, and his promises. — νόμιμα already appears in 1:3. — πολιεύεσθαι, the expression so often attested in the Greek world, is often used in Koine in a very abbreviated way = περιπατεῖν, see also 1 Clem. 6:1; 21:1; Phil 1:27; see further Proclus, *Typi epistolares* (Hercher *Epistolographoi*, 13): οἶδα μὲν ὡς εὐσεβῶς ζῇς καὶ σεμνῶς πολιτεύῃ. ζῆλος began the series in 3:2 and ζῆλος ends it, and thus the *Stichwort* of the new section is reached. On the idea that death entered into the world through jealousy, see Wis 2:24: φθόνῳ δὲ διαβόλου θάνατος εἰσῆλθεν εἰς τὸν κόσμον and Theophilus, *Ad Autolycum* II 29: ὁ σατανᾶς . . . ἐφ᾽ ᾧ οὐκ ἴσχυσεν θανατῶσαι αὐτοὺς φθόνῳ φερόμενος, ἡνίκα ἑώρα τὸν Ἄβελ εὐαρεστοῦντα τῷ θεῷ, ἐνεργήσας εἰς τὸν ἀδελφὸν αὐτοῦ, τὸν καλούμενον Κάϊν, ἐποίησεν ἀποκτεῖναι τὸν ἀδελφὸν αὐτοῦ τὸν Ἄβελ, καὶ οὕτως ἀρχὴ θανάτου ἐγένετο εἰς τόνδε τὸν κόσμον . . . . First Clement however locates the envious jealousy with Cain, not with the devil.

III. The God-Fearing Life (4:1—39:9)

The first main half of 1 Clem. spans 4:1—39:9. This section contains a number of excessive exhortations which pertain to the Christian life. These exhortations include admonitions against jealousy (4:1—6:4); an admonition to repent (7:1—8:5); a call to live an obedient and pious life, with faith and hospitality (9:1—12:8); and to be humble before God and man (13:1—19:1). Furthermore, this section includes reflections on the benefactions of God and his order (19:2—22:9) as well as assurances of the coming parousia and future resurrection from the dead (23:1—27:7). Additional instruction includes fleeing from slander, discord, and pride (29:1—30:8) and with a sketch of the way of blessedness (31:1—36:6). In light of the breadth of instruction given and the description of the main elements of the Christian life, it is difficult if not impossible to more precisely demonstrate how the individual pieces relate to the main purpose of the letter.[3]

A. Against Jealousy (4:1—6:4)

Translation

[4:1] For thus it is written, "And it came to pass after a while that Cain offered God a sacrifice of the fruits of the earth and Abel also offered some of the first fruits of the sheep of their fat. [2] And God looked favorably on Abel and his gifts, but he paid no attention to Cain and his sacrifices. [3] And Cain was deeply distressed and his countenance grew dark. [4] And God said to Cain, "Why are you sad, and why has your countenance grown dark? Is it not true that if you sacrifice rightly but do not divide rightly you have sinned? [5] Remain clam, it will return to you and you will rule over it." [6] And Cain said to his brother Abel, "Let us go into the field." And it came about that when they were in the field, Cain rose up against his brother Abel and struck him dead. [7] See, brothers, jealousy and envy are the cause of fratricide. [8] Because of jealousy, our father Jacob fled from before his brother Esau. [9] Jealousy caused Joseph to be persecuted up to the point of death and he entered into slavery. [10] Jealousy forced Moses from the presence of Pharaoh, king of Egypt, to flee when he heard from his fellow countryman, "Who made you judge or arbitrator over us? Do you wish to kill me like you killed the Egyptian yesterday?" [11] Because of jealousy, Aaron and Miriam remained outside the camp. [12] Because of jealousy Dathan and Abiram went down to the underworld alive because they rebelled against Moses, the servant of God. [13] Because of jealousy

---

3. TN: This paragraph is not present within the original German text but has been added for the sake of unity and clarity in the newly formatted English edition. The judgments made about the relationship between this part of the letter to the main purpose of the letter have been shaped from Knopf's introduction to 1 Clem.

David not only had to endure the envy of strangers, but he was also persecuted by Saul, the king of Israel.

⁵:¹ But to stop with the examples of the past, let us move on to the fighters of the recent past. Let us take the brave role models of our generation. ² Because of jealousy and envy the greatest and most righteous pillars were persecuted and fought until death. ³ Let us place the good apostles before our eyes: ⁴ Peter, who because of unrighteous jealousy endured trials not once or twice but many times and so, after giving his testimony, departed to the place of glory due him. ⁵ Because of jealousy and strife Paul showed the (way to the) prize for patient endurance: ⁶ he was in chains seven times, was chased away, stoned, appeared as a herald in the East and in the West, and because of this he has earned glorious fame on account of his faith. ⁷ For he taught righteousness to the entire world, until he reached the furthest points of the West, and testified before the rulers: then he was taken out of the world, and he went into the holy place, the greatest example of patience.

⁶:¹ In addition to these men who have led a holy way of life, a large number of elect were gathered who, because of jealousy, endured numerous humiliations and torments, and thus became exceedingly magnificent models in our midst. ² Because of jealousy, women were persecuted who, as Danaids and Dircae, endured horrible and godless cruelty and thereby attained the secure goal in the race of faith and received glorious honors, although they were weak in body. ³ Jealousy alienated women from their husbands and changed the word of our father Adam, "Now this is bone of my bone and flesh of my flesh." ⁴ Jealousy and strife have destroyed great cities and uprooted mighty nations.

Textual Notes

The warning takes the form of a detailed series of examples, the individual members of which are intended to show how hopeless and pernicious jealousy is through which the wicked suffer severe punishment and the good suffer great harm. The series is carefully laid out. It begins with ἀρχαῖα ὑποδείγματα (5:1), the examples from the sacred books of the OT, proceeding from the primitive times, Cain, at the beginning up until David (4:1–13). Then follows by "examples of our generation": the lives of the apostles (Peter and Paul) and examples from Christian contemporary history in 5:1—6:2. Finally, examples from the gentile world, which also return later (37:2–4; 55:1), are brought forward for consideration in 6:3f, which reflects a remarkable freedom and open-mindedness in an ancient Christian writing. On the form, take note of the following: the first example, from primeval history, is given in great detail because of its fundamental importance (3:4: δι᾽ οὗ καὶ θάνατος εἰσῆλθεν εἰς τὸν κόσμον), with broad citation of the sacred text, whereas the other examples only contain a single sentence each. The long series of sentences from 3:7—6:4 is built up anaphorically: again and again the thing to be proved, ζῆλος and διὰ ζῆλος, appears at the head of the sentences. Seven examples are given from the Old Testament; the number of examples enumerated in chapters 5 and 6 are also seven (three in ch. 5 and four in ch. 6). Indeed, ζῆλος is mentioned seven times in the series of examples in 1 Clem. 4 and seven times in 1 Clem. 5f. The first series of exhortations is therefore, as might be expected, carefully constructed, and a certain rhetorical art on the part of the preacher is evident in it. On the author's great familiarity with the OT, of which we have here the first example, see especially Wrede and von Harnack (above in "Introduction," pp. 60–61).

4:1–6 On 1–6, see Gen 4:3–8. The citation is almost verbatim, with only minor deviations. The LXX deviates here strongly from the original.

4:3 τὸ πρόσωπον perhaps with C against τῷ προσώπῳ A (LXX).

4:4 The LXX understood the obviously completely distorted base text (*Grundschrift*) in such a way that Cain had offered the sacrifice in the correct outward manner, but that he did not divide it properly, that is, that he had kept the good pieces for himself and given the bad ones to God. The Fathers allegorically reinterpret the passage. They explain ὀρθῶς δὲ μὴ διέλῃς as Cain's unkindness to Abel, or as his moral and religious depravity in general, see Irenaeus, *Haer.* III 23.4; IV 18.3; Origen, *Sel. Gen.* 4:13 (Lommatzsch, *Origenis Opera*, 8:59). However, it is uncertain whether Clement was familiar with this interpretation.

4:8 See Gen 27:41ff. ὁ πατὴρ ἡμῶν, in the spiritual sense; the Patriarchs are the fathers of Christians, of spiritual Israel, see also 31:2; 60:4; then Rom 4 and Gal 3:7–18; Jas 2:21; Barn. 13:7; as well as 1 Pet 3:6.

4:9 See Gen 37.

4:10 See Exod 2:11–22, especially 2:14; the LXX has ἄρχοντα instead of κριτήν.

4:11 See Num 12; there, however, it is narrated that only Miriam remained outside of the camp (12:14f). ὁ θεράπων τοῦ θεοῦ is a frequently used title for Moses, see already Exod 4:10; 14:31; etc.; then 1 Clem. 43:1; 51:3–5; 53:5; Barn. 14:4; etc.

4:12 See Num 16. In this and the previous example, it is not the pious, who are persecuted by others, who suffer, but the wicked themselves.

4:13 See 1 Sam 19–29, especially 18:9 and 29:1–11. The ἀλλόφυλοι are the Philistines, see 1 Sam 22:10 and 29:1–4.

5:1—6:2 Contemporary examples in 1 Clem. 5:1—6:2, drawn from the history of early Christianity, join together with the previous examples from the Old Testament: the apostles, especially Peter and Paul, the martyrs as a whole, and among them especially a group of women, consist of five members. The author clearly constructed this group of five and marks it by the fivefold use of διὰ ζῆλον(ς). This is followed by the two additional examples in 1 Clem. 6:3f, which also brings the total number in the second series to seven.

5:1–7 One should not suppose based upon ἔγγιστα that the death of the great apostles and the Neronian persecution now brought as examples had just occurred, in which case 1 Clem. would possibly have had to be written before 70 CE. The author uses ἔγγιστα in contrast to the ἀρχαῖα ὑποδείγματα which were just mentioned and is immediately placed into the correct framework with τῆς γενεᾶς ὑμῶν. If the letter was written around 96 CE, then the events under Nero still belong to the experiences of the present generation. A precise parallel to 1 Clem. is the Muratorian Fragment, line 74, where the author says of Hermas that he wrote *nuperrime* (in contrast to the ancient prophets) *temporibus nostris*. In this instance, there are 40 years between the completion of Hermas and the time of the fragment. See also Irenaeus, who in *Haer.* V 30.3 said the following of Revelation: οὐδὲ γὰρ πρὸ πολλοῦ χρόνου ἑωράθη, ἀλλὰ σχεδὸν ἐπὶ τῆς ἡμετέρας γενεᾶς πρὸς τῷ τέλει τῆς Δομετιανοῦ ἀρχῆς. The persecution of Christians came about through ζῆλος and φθόνος: the hatred, envy, and jealousy of the world against the children of God! Note the echo between γενεᾶς and γεννναῖα. γεννναῖος is preferred here, see also 1 Clem. 5:6 and 6:2.

5:2 The pillars certainly come from Gal 2; it is not just the apostles, for they will come immediately after the mention of the pillars, but they along with other leaders of the earlier age: for example, Stephen, James the brother of the Lord, etc. For all the outstanding people who have been persecuted, see also Heb 13:1.

5:3 The author has the apostles in mind in a narrower sense: the Twelve and Paul. He knows about the sufferings of all the apostles, or he sees them as a matter of fact from the outset; see, for example, Acts 5:40; 12:2; 1 Cor 4:9–13 (which 1 Clem. understood of every apostle), then the possible martyrdom of John the son of Zebedee, finally the apocryphal legends of the apostles among others.

5:4, 5 Among the ranks of the thirteen apostles, the two most out-standing men are singled out: Peter and Paul. The reason for this is, on the one hand, their high reputation, but then also that they are related to the Roman community. It was well known that Paul was in Rome and that he was executed there under Nero. But also Peter's stay in Rome and his martyrdom there can hardly be doubted. On the martyrdom of Peter in general, see 1 Pet 5:1 (?); John 21:18f; 2 Pet 1:14, Dionysius of Corinth in Eusebius, *Hist. eccl.* 2.15.2; 3.39.15; Dionysius of Corinth and Gaius in Eusebius, *Hist. eccl.* 2.25.7f; Porphyrius in Macarius Magnes III 22 (cf. von Harnack, *Mission*, 1:63, 2); see also the article Sieffert, "Petrus"; Knopf, "Petrus"; Schmiedel, "Peter"). But if Peter and Paul are celebrated here as exalted examples, it is not only because of their connection with Rome, but also because of their connection with Corinth: both were active in Corinth. Peter's stay in Corinth, which is in itself very questionable, was certainly inferred very early on from passages such as 1 Cor 1:12; 3:22; 9:5; and Dionysius of Corinth in Eusebius, *Hist. eccl.* 2.25.8 is already aware of this tradition: ἄμφω (Peter and Paul) καὶ εἰς τὴν ἡμετέραν Κόρινθον φυτεύσαντες ἡμᾶς ὁμοίως ἐδίδαξαν, ὁμοίως δὲ καὶ εἰς τὴν Ἰταλίαν ὁμόσε διδάξαντες ἐμαρτύρησαν κατὰ τὸν αὐτὸν καιρόν.

5:4 Peter comes first, as usual in the compilation. Since we know so little about Peter's life, we do not know anything more detailed about his trials, see however above at v. 3. In μαρτυρήσας there is not only an indication that he faithfully endured πόνοι, but also an indication that he was martyred since his journey toward his end is immediately mentioned. On ὀφειλόμενον τόπον τῆς δόξης, see immediately afterward at 1 Clem. 5:7; Herm. *Sim.* IX 27 as well as Acts 1:25; how the view of the resting places that the blessed already have is compatible with the resurrection of the dead and a realistic es-chatology (1 Clem. 23–26) is well attested in Irenaeus, *Haer.* V 31.2: αἱ ψυχαὶ ἀπέρχονται εἰς τὸν τόπον (+ *invisibilem* Lat.) τὸν ὡρισμένον αὐταῖς ἀπὸ τοῦ θεοῦ, κἀκεῖ μέχρι τῆς ἀναστάσεως φοιτῶσι, περιμένουσαι τὴν ἀνάστασιν· ἔπειτα ἀπολαβοῦσαι τὰ σώματα, καὶ ὁλοκλήρως ἀναστᾶσαι, τουτέστι σωματικῶς, καθὼς καὶ ὁ κύριος ἀνέστη, οὕτως ἐλεύσονται εἰς τὴν ὄψιν τοῦ θεοῦ.

5:5-7 The information about Paul stands in the second place, but it is significantly longer. Paul's life was more eventful and richer in content than Peter's, and more was known about him. In addition to the reference to the abomination of ζῆλος, a second emerges from the example: the glory of ὑπομονή, which is expressly mentioned at the beginning and end of vv. 5 and 7. The example has two peaks. The commendation of ὑπομονή, which can also be heard before and afterward, is not pursued any further; but this shining virtue of the heroes of the faith should not go unmentioned.

5:5 ὑπομονῆς βραβεῖον, the pictures of the competition are popular with Paul himself and very common in the popular philosophy of the time (cf. Lietzmann, *Römer*, at Rom 9:1; Wendland, *Kultur*, 357.1). ἔδειξεν (H or ὑπέδειξεν A): he showed how to the get the prize.

5:6 We do not know how the author calculated the seven times in chains. φυγαδεύειν here means "to chase," not to exile with a judgment. On this, see 2 Cor 11:32 (Acts 9:25); Acts 9:30; 13:50; 14:6; 17:10, 14; 20:3. The entire report of Acts is evidence for φυγαδεύειν. On λιθασθείς, see 2 Cor 11:25 and Acts 14:(5), 19. In the Pastoral Epistles, Paul is described as a κῆρυξ (2 Tim 1:11). A good parallel, including content, can be found in Epictetus, *Diatr.* III 22.69, from a real Cynic: ἄγγελος καὶ κατάσκοπος καὶ κῆρυξ τῶν θεῶν. Here, the word simply means preacher, see shortly hereafter at 7:6f: κηρύσσειν.

5:7 The broad scope of the Pauline mission is sketched: ἐν τῇ ἀνατολῇ καὶ ἐν τῇ δύσει, ὅλον τὸν κόσμον, τέρμα τῆς δύσεως. The last expression can hardly be understood within a Roman letter as anything other than the fact that the author wishes to speak of Paul's activity west of Rome. It fits best with a sermon in Spain.

First Clement 5:4–7 is very important for the history of the outcome of the lives of both apostles. Along with John 21:28f, 1 Clem. 5:4 is the oldest passage from a tradition which speaks of the martyrdom of Peter (cf. see further the passages referenced above). From the end of the second century onward, the tradition is fixed and frequently attested. No place other than Rome has been identified for his martyrdom, and Peter is said to have stayed in Rome as an apostle. It is likely that 1 Clem. 5:4 already presupposes Peter's stay and martyrdom in Rome; 1 Pet 5:13 locates the apostle in Rome, as does Ign. *Rom.* 4:3; see then Dionysius in Eusebius, *Hist. eccl.* 2.25.8; Tertullian, *Praescr.* 36; Clement of Alexandria and Gaius of Rome in Eusebius, *Hist. eccl.* 2.15.2, 25.7; 6.14.6; the apocryphal Acts of Peter; and other passages. — First Clement 5:5f is also the oldest testimony to the martyrdom of Paul. This passage also represents the main piece of evidence for the hypothesis of Paul's so-called "second imprisonment" and his travel to Spain. Had Paul truly functioned as a missionary to the τέρμα τῆς δύσεως, then he must have been freed from his imprisonment mentioned in his letters and in Acts 28, and thereafter fulfilled his old plan (Rom 15:24). The Muratorian Fragment, line 38f speaks explicitly of Paul's trip to Spain (*profectione Pauli ab urbe in Spaniam proficiscentis*). Another important factor in deciding the question is how one assesses the information in the Pastoral Epistles, 2 Tim 4:16f, and then, above all, the passages from 1 Timothy and from Titus, which depict the apostle in a situation which we cannot accommodate into the life of Paul known to us (cf. especially Titus 3:12). On the much discussed question of

the end of both great apostles' lives, see Lietzmann, *Petrus und Paulus*; E.
Dubowy, *Klemens*; Bauer, "Legende," 270–307.

5:7 ἡγούμενοι, see already 1 Clem. 1:3. In 1:3, the inner congregational
rulers are in view, whereas here the secular rulers are meant, as is also the
case in 37:2f and 60:4. In both of these passages, the word seems to have
the narrower sense of the Roman emperor (cf. esp. 1 Clem. 60:4). However,
as 32:2 and 51:5 show, this ambiguous word can also be used to refer to the
nobles within the empire, the *magistratus*. In this case, the author not only
has Paul's testimony before the imperial court in Rome in mind, but also his
appearance before Sergius Paulus, Gallio, Felix, Festus, Agrippa, and other
men, including those whose names we do not know. ὑπογραμμός is a Koine
word, meaning that which is drawn in advance and to be copied, the *Vorlage* for γράφειν (= "to write, draw, paint"), then generally "model, pattern"
(cf. 2 Macc 2:21; Poly. *Phil* 8:2). On the style of 5:5–7, the long series of lau-
datory participles, see the encomia in Hellenistic decrees on honor in, for
example, Dittenberger, *Or. inscr.* II, 529: Μᾶρκον Ἀντώνιον Σεργία Ῥοῦφον
. . . διασημότατον καὶ . . . λαμπρότατον, πάσας μὲν λειτουργίας διεξελθόντα, ἐν
πάσαις δὲ φιλοτιμίαις εὐδοκιμήσαντα, ἄρξαντα καὶ θιασαρχήσαντα πολλάκις,
ἀγορανομήσαντα πλεονάκις, ποντάρχησαντα ἐν τῇ μητροπόλει Πόντου
Νεοκαισαρείᾳ, πολλὰ μὲν καὶ μεγάλα ἔργα κατασκευασάμενον δι' ἐπιμελείας,
πολὺ δὲ πλείονα ἀπὸ τῶν ἑαυτοῦ, πρῶτον μὲν ἀνοίξαντα τὸ γυμνάσιον,
ἀρχιερασάμενον . . . ; see further at 537, or 542: Τι. Κλ. Προκιλλιανὸν
γαλατάρχην Τι. Κλ. Βόκχου γαλατάρχου υἱόν, χειλιαρχήσαντος ζ′ (= ἑπτάκις)
ἀρχιερέως β′, σεβαστοφάντου, ἀγωνοθέτου, πάσας ἀρχὰς καὶ λειτουργίας καὶ
ἐπιδόσεις ἐκτελέσαντος τῇ πατρίδι . . . .

First Clement 6:1–2 The admonition proceeds from the noble leaders
of the apostles to the simpler martyrs, whom the congregation in Rome still
knew and had seen. Again, the Neronian persecution is in view here. But of
course, later blood-witnesses executed under the Flavians (Domitian) cannot be entirely excluded. Because of ἐν ἡμῖν (we = the Roman congregation)
in 6:1 and because of the clear allusion to the amphitheater in 6:2, it must be
concluded that these are Roman martyrdoms.

6:1 Commentary on the passage is mainly Tacitus, *Ann.* 44: πολὺ
πλῆθος = *multitudo ingens*; πολλαῖς αἰκίαις καὶ βασάνοις = *pereuntibus ad-
dita ludibria, ut ferarum tergis contecti laniatu canum interirent, aut crucibus
adfixi, aut flamandi atque, ubi defecisset dies, in usum nocturni luminis ure-
rentur; hortos suos ei spectaculo Nero obtulerat et circense ludicrum edebat.*
Note here again the dual example: warning of ζῆλος, but also ὑπόδειγμα
κάλλιστον! Instead of the dative πολλαῖς αἰκίαις κτλ., L and perhaps also C
and C¹ read the accusative πολλὰς κτλ., connected with παθόντες.

6:2 Contemporary rhetoric would have enjoyed the reference to the glorious deeds performed by weak women: *non tamen adeo virtutum sterile saeculum, ut non et bona exempla prodiderit; comitatae profugos liberos matres, secutae maritos in exilia coniuges* (Tacitus, *Hist.* I 3); see also the examples of the death-defying pagan women in Tertullian, *Mart.* 4; *Apol.* 50; and the examples of the *univirae* in *De exhort. castit.* 13. The clause Δαναΐδες καὶ Δίρκαι is much-discussed and difficult to interpret; the words have been transmitted unanimously in all witnesses (except for C¹, which is corrupted here). Conjectures (such as those found in Lightfoot, *Clement*, 2:32–34) are unnecessary. In the Roman amphitheater, cruel executions, severe torture, and mutilations were carried out in the guise of mythological depictions. The rich mythology, as well as the ancient legends, offered a plentitude and a variety of material to the bloodthirsty Roman population. See already the citation from Tacitus above, which at least comes into consideration as a parallel; then, see Tertullian, *Apol.* 15 (for Carthage): "You are certainly more devout in the theater, where your gods dance over human blood and the refuse of the punished and offer plots and legends for the condemned (for depiction). Often, the condemned are put behind the masks of your gods. Once, we saw (in the theater) the castration of Attis, that god from Pessinus; another man, who was burned alive, was depicted as Hercules. At the lighthearted atrocities of the midday gladiators, we laughed at Mercury, who examined the dead bodies with a red-hot iron stamp, and the brother of Jupiter who smashed the corpses of the gladiators with an iron hammer." In 80 CE, on the occasion of the inauguration of the Flavian amphitheater, Martial wrote the epigrams of his *Liber spectaculorum*: At these inaugural games, the execution of a famous robber, Laureolus, was carried out; the person in question was stuck on a cross and a Caledonian bear ate off his limbs (*epi.* 7); a Daedalus who had fallen was torn apart by a Lucanian bear (*ep.* 8); a Heracles rode a bull into heaven (*ep.* 16); an Orpheus, who had appeared with a wondrous theatrical decoration accompaniment of walking rocks and trees, tamed animals and birds, ripped up by a bear at the end (*ep.* 21). On these representations, see Friedländer, *Sittengeschichte*, 2:412f. When we speak of women who suffered as Dircae, this is easy to understand according to what has been said: Dircae, tied to the horns of the bull by the pair of brothers Amphion and Zethus and dragged to death ("Farnese bull"), could easily be depicted. Of course it still remains unclear what we are to do with Danaids. The punishment of the daughters of Danaus was to fill a barrel in the underworld, which was riddled with holes. As has been demonstrated, this would not have satisfied the cruel desires of the amphitheater. But perhaps it depicted the terrible mass murders like how Lynceus slew the Danaids. It is more probable, however, that some horrific variants of death or Tartarus like punishments of the Danaids were introduced; see above at the references to Martial who depicts the overthrown Daedalus, Heracles, and Orpheus. — βέβαιος δρόμος, the point on the racetrack where the race is decided, victory is assured, the goal.

6:3 and 6:4 include general examples from secular history. They are commonplaces that are anticlimactic in comparison to the preceding examples, but they complete the list of seven. The first sentence expresses an experience that is ordinary in everyday life. In the second sentence, the author can conjure up all kinds of political events. If he has traced the persecutions of Christians to ζῆλος, then he can also discover that ζῆλος is a motivating force behind every war and every great upheaval: it could call to mind the Babylonians, Assyrians, Lydians, Medes, Persians, Aramaeans, Egyptians, Greeks, Carthaginians, Gauls, etc.; Troy, Babylon, Sardis, Miletus, Sybaris, Carthage, Taranto, Numantia, Corinth, Artaxata, and many others; and certainly also the fall of the Jewish commonwealth and the destruction of Jerusalem under Vespasian, for the ancient Christians the most significant and relevant contemporary event.

B. Admonition to Repent (7:1—8:5)

Translation

⁷:¹ We write these things to you, beloved, not only for your exhortation but also for our own encouragement. For we are (also) in the same straights, and the same struggle is (also) before us. ² Therefore, let us leave empty and vain thoughts behind, let us live according to the magnificent and noble rule which has been handed down to us, ³ and pay attention to what is good and what is pleasing and what is pleasant before our creator.

⁷:⁴ Let us look at the blood of Christ and recognize how precious it is to his Father, for when it was shed for our salvation, it brought the grace of repentance to the whole world. ⁵ Let us walk through all generations and see that from generation to generation the Lord has given an opportunity to repent to those who would turn to him. ⁶ Noah preached repentance and those who heard him were saved. ⁷ Jonah prophesied destruction to the Ninevites, but they repented of their sins, softened God through their supplications and were spared, even though they did not belong to the people of God.

⁸:¹ The servants of divine grace preached about repentance through the Holy Spirit, ² and he himself, the Lord of all, spoke of repentance with an oath: "As surely as I live, says the Lord, I do not desire the death of the sinner,

but that he should repent." To this he added a merciful declaration, [3] "Repent, house of Israel, from your godlessness. Say to the sons of my people, 'If your sins reach from the earth up to heaven, and if they are redder than scarlet and blacker than sackcloth, and you turn to me with all your soul and say "Father," then I will hear you as a holy people.'" [4] And in another place, he also says, "Wash and clean yourselves, remove the wickedness of your souls from before my eyes. Put away your wickedness, learn to do good, seek justice, stand with the oppressed, create justice for the orphans, and help the widow's cause, and then come and let us reason with one another, says the Lord. And if your sins are like crimson, I will make them as white as snow. And if they are like scarlet, I will make them white like wool. And if you are willing and obey me, then you will eat the good of the land, but if you do not obey me, then the sword will devour you. For the mouth of the Lord has spoken." [5] Accordingly, he wants all his loved ones to partake of the repentance which he has established according to his almighty will.

Textual Notes

This section begins with a brief turn to exhortations to be delivered to the congregation itself (7:1), then the author shows again by means of historical observation (examples and quotations) that God has always been ready to accept the repentance to which his holy will has called men at all times (7:2—8:5).

   7:1 The statement shows very clearly how the author is aware of the fact that he goes beyond the present occasion for the letter and delivers a generally applicable exhortation; repentance and penance are needed everywhere, including Rome. See also the corresponding passage in 62:1f. — σκάμμα is the sand-covered practice area in the gymnasium and palaces, which got its name (verb σκάπτειν) either because it was dug deep or because it was surrounded by deep trenches. Here we have one of the many images taken from the athletic realm, which has been taken over from the diatribes into Christian paraenesis; see Rom 9:15–17; 1 Cor 9:24–27; then see Wendland, *Kultur*, 357.1; on σκάμμα, see also Epictetus, *Diatr.* IV 8.26: εἰς τοσοῦτο σκάμμα προεκαλεῖτο (Socrates) πάντα ὁντιναοῦν.

   7:2 and 7:3 describe the call to repent: (1) dismiss vain and empty thoughts; (2) live according to the noble rule that has been handed down to us; (3) do that which is pleasing to God. κεναὶ καὶ μάταιαι φροντίδες should be understood as thoughts of jealousy and strife (cf. 9:1). However, the expression should not be limited to these matters. The phrase κενὸς καὶ μάταιος occurs frequently; see Job 20:18; Hos 12:1; Plutarch, *Art.* 15: οὐ γὰρ . . . ἐκόντισα κενὸν καὶ μάταιον; Plutarch, *Adv. Col.* 17: (ἀρετάς), κενὰς καὶ ματαίας καὶ ταραχώδεις ἐχούσας τῶν καρπῶν τὰς ἐλπίδας. — The word κανών is hardly a continuation of the image of σκάμμα, such that it meant the measuring line or the measure of the athletic jump or run; it is too well-worn a word for such a technical meaning. The use of εὐκλεῆ, σεμνόν, and τῆς παραδόσεως speak more in favor for a generic usage: rule, guideline. τῆς παραδόσεως, because in the Old Testament and in Christianity, it has already been handed down from the Lord and the apostles (cf. Loofs, *Dogmengeschichte*, 78, 87).

7:3 The answer to the emphatic question (Ps 132:1: ἰδοὺ δὴ τί καλὸν ἢ τί τερπνόν, ἢ τὸ κατοικεῖν ἀδελφοὺς ἐπὶ τὸ αὐτό; cf. 1 Tim 2:3) is hardly, "repentance." Instead, the individual parts of the Christian ideal are meant, as are depicted below: repentance, faith, obedience, humility, hospitality, etc. But in all of this repentance is an important component, because it is a foundational element. Its value and necessity are presented below by pointing first to the sacrificial death of Christ that made repentance possible (7:4), then to the consistent opportunity God gave to each generation to repent (7:5—8:1), finally to God's fundamental willingness to grant forgiveness at any time upon repentance.

7:4 In order for repentance to come about, it is not only necessary that man change his will, but God must forgive his sins and thus accept his repentance. But this is the effect of the death of Jesus, which took place for the sake of general salvation; his blood enables the forgiveness of sins. On τίμιον, see 1 Pet 1:19.

7:5 But 1 Clem. goes far beyond the general Christian and speaks of constant general forgiveness of sins. The boundaries between old and new are disappearing, and it is almost impossible to say what the real meaning and virtue of Christianity has been, presumably its greater generality, certainty, and impact. — In every generation since the beginning of the world, God has granted an opportunity for repentance, which would save those βουλόμενοι ἐπιστραφῆναι ἐπ' αὐτόν. Take note of the rationalism and the moralism; there is no divine ἐκλογή here. On μετανοίας τόπον, see Heb 12:17; Wis 12:10; Tatian, *Ad Graecos* 15.3; then also 1 Clem. 63:1.

7:6 In Hellenistic Judaism, Noah has become a preacher of repentance to humanity; see Josephus, *Ant.* I 74: Νῶχος δὲ τοῖς πραττομένοις ὑπ' αὐτῶν δυσχεραίνων καὶ τοῖς βουλεύμασιν ἀηδῶς ἔχων ἔπειθεν ἐπὶ τὸ κρεῖττον τὴν διάνοιαν αὐτοὺς καὶ τὰς πράξεις μεταφέρειν, ὁρῶν δὲ οὐκ ἐνδιδόντας . . . δείσας μὴ καὶ φονεύσωσιν αὐτὸν μετὰ γυναικῶν καὶ τέκνων καὶ τῶν τούτοις συνοικουσῶν ἐξεχώρησε τῆς γῆς; Sib. Or. I 127–29. καὶ τῷ μὲν θεὸς αὐτὸς ἀπ' οὐρανόθεν φάτο τοῖα· Νῶε, δέμας θάρσυνον ἑὸν λαοῖσί τε πᾶσιν Κήρυξον μετάνοιαν, ὅπως σωθῶσιν ἅπαντες . . . ; see also Sib. Or. I 150–70 for Noah's sermon on repentance; 2 Pet 2:5; also 1 Clem. 9:4; Theophilus, *Autol.* III 19. Only Noah's own household listened to him, and eight souls were saved; 1 Pet 3:20; see also 2 Pet 2:5. σώζειν, of course, is not only used for the deliverance of life, but more generally for the salvation of the elect, for participation in the ὑπερβάλλουσαι καὶ ἔνδοξοι δωρεαί (23:2; 23–25).

7:7 An example of the salvation of pagans through repentance, the only one which Clement brings and can bring from the pre-Christian era is Jonah 3. The σωτηρία which was given to the Ninevites is of course the same which was given to the pre-Christian pious; see ἐσώθησαν of the house of Noah in v. 6. Clement has a friendly disposition toward the gentiles, and he does not connect their salvation with Christ either. On καταστροφή, see Jonah 3:4: καὶ Νινευὴ καταστραφήσεται. ἀλλότριοι τοῦ θεοῦ = pagans; the people of God is Israel; see also 1 Clem. 29:2f and Eph 2:12.

8:1 The λειτουργοὶ τῆς χάριτος τοῦ θεοῦ are the prophets. Every one of them preached repentance like Noah and Jonah. Thus 1 Clem. 7:5 is fulfilled: ἐν γενεᾷ καὶ γενεᾷ.

8:2–5 In order to demonstrate God's fundamental willingness to forgive sinners, two citations are introduced. The first has greater or lesser echoes with Ezek 33:11; 18:30f; Ps 102:11f; Jer 3:19, 22; and Isa 1:18. However, it is not a combination of these passages, but rather a citation from an unknown apocryphon that worked with Old Testament material. The main reason for this assumption is that Isa 1:18 appears immediately afterward in its correct, original context.

8:2 γνώμην ἀγαθήν: the saying is good because of the excellent promise it brings.

8:3 κόκκος is the scarlet color that antiquity obtained from the collected and dried female Kermes (*Coccus ilicis*); see Riehm, "Carmesin." The proper term κόκκινος, which occurs immediately afterward (8:4), has become the dominant word for red in modern Greek, whereas ἐρυθρός belongs only to literary Greek. This development can already be seen in Koine; see, for example, Epictetus, *Diatr.* III 22.10; IV 11.34. "Redder than scarlet" is a saying; see Dromo in Athenaeus VI 240D: τὸν Τιθύμαλλον ἐρυθρότερον κόκκου περιπατοῦντ᾽ ἐσθ᾽ ὁρᾶν.

8:4 is a citation from Isa 1:16–20, cited almost word-for-word according to our LXX text. φοινικοῦς is contracted from φοινίκεος = πορφύρεος, because the purple dye was considered to be a Phoenician invention to the ancients and was practiced to the highest level of perfection in Phoenicia (Tyre).

8:5 ἐστήριξεν etc. refers to the citations, the oath, and the promises. With πάντας τοὺς ἀγαπητούς it is once again clearly stated that Christians also need repentance, just as the Israelites and the gentiles who had been chosen in the past.

C. Obedience, Piety, Faith, Hospitality (9:1—12:8)

Translation

9:1 For this reason we should obey his majestic and glorious will and, as supplicants of his mercy and goodness, prostrate ourselves and entrust ourselves to his compassion, refraining from vain toil and strife and deadly jealousy.

9:2 Let us look to those who have served his magnificent glory perfectly. 3 Let us take Enoch, who being found righteous in obedience was transported without (a trace) of his death being found. 4 Noah, who was found to be faithful, proclaimed rebirth through his service to the world, and through him the Lord saved the living beings who had come into the ark in harmony.

10:1 Abraham, who was called "friend," was found to be faithful, because he obeyed the words of God. 2 Because of his obedience he left his land and his family and the house of his father in order to inherit the promises of God instead of a meager land and a weak family and a small house. 3 For he said to him, "Go from your land and from your family and from your father's house into the land which I will show you. And I will make you into a great people and will bless you and will make your name great and you will be blessed. I will bless those who bless you and curse those who curse you, and in you I will bless all the generations of the earth." 4 And again, when he parted from Lot, God said to him, "Lift up your eyes and look from the place where you are now, toward midnight and noon, and morning and evening. For all the land which you see I will give you and your seed forever. 5 And I will make your seed like the dust of the earth. If someone could number the sands of the earth, so also your seed will be numbered." 6 And again it says, "God led Abraham out and said to him, 'Look up at the sky and count the stars. Can you count them? So shall your seed be.' Abraham believed God and it was counted to him as righteousness." 7 Because of his faith and hospitality a son was sent to him in his old age, and in his obedience he brought him as a sacrifice to God on the mountain which he had shown him.

^{11:1} Because of his hospitality and piety Lot was saved out of Sodom when all the land around was judged with fire and brimstone. Thus the Lord made it clear that he will not abandon those who hope in him, but plunges the stubborn into punishment and torment. ² For when his wife went out with him (out of the city), who had a different disposition and was not in harmony (with him), she was established as a sign: she became a pillar of salt which remains to this day so that it would be made known to all how those who have a divided soul and who doubt the power of the Lord are condemned and made a warning sign for all generations.

^{12:1} Because of her faith and her hospitality, Rahab the whore was saved. ² For when spies were sent to Jericho by Joshua, the son of Nun, the king of the land learned that they had come in order to spy out the land, and he sent people to catch them so that they could be executed. ³ However, the hospitable Rahab took them up and hid them in the upper room under the stalks of flax. ⁴ When the messengers of the king came and said, "Those who wish to spy out the land have come to you. Give them to us, for the king has commanded it," she answered, "Indeed the men whom you seek came to me, but they immediately departed and moved along down the road." And then she pointed them in the opposite direction. ⁵ And she said to the men, "Truly I recognize that God, the Lord, is delivering this land to you, for fear and terror has fallen upon all the inhabitants because of you. When you take it, spare me and the house of my father." ⁶ And they answered her, "It will be as you have said. But as soon as you recognize that we are approaching, call all of your family under your roof and they will be spared. For whoever is found outside of your house will be destroyed." ⁷ And they gave her a sign: she should hang a red thread outside of her house. Thereby, she made it known that through the blood of the Lord there would be salvation for all who believe in God and hope in him. ⁸ You see, brothers, that there was not only faith but also prophecy in the woman.

Textual Notes

9:1 serves as the transition from the previous section and also provides a very good regulation about what belongs as a part of repentance on the part of man. βούλησις is the gracious will of God; see βουλόμενος and βούλημα in 1 Clem. 8:5. The word ματαιοπονία is, like others, composed of ματαιο-, a good Hellenistic formation; see Lucian, *Dial. mort.* 10.8: ἀμαθίαν καὶ ἔριν καὶ κενοδοξία . . . καὶ ματαιοπονίαν . . . καὶ λῆρον . . . καὶ ὕθλους καὶ μικρολογίαν . . . ; see also the compounds: ματαιοπονεῖν, ματαιοπόνος, ματαιοπόνημα, etc. ματαιοπονία is the effort which is laced on false, selfish goals, and which can thus be grouped together with ἔρις and ζῆλος. On ἔρις and ζῆλος, see chps. 3–6; there τὸ εἰς θάνατον ἄγον ζῆλος is explained. Note the rhetoric of the passage: four cola of about the same length, three of which end in αὐτοῦ. At the peak of 9:1 is the following *Leitwort*: ὑπακούσωμεν. The other *Leitwort* is λειτουργεῖν. Three examples of blameless obedient servants of God are offered: Enoch, Noah, and Abraham. On this series of examples, see Sir 44:16–23 and especially Heb 11:5–10, from which 1 Clem. seems to have drawn the examples, for he seems to betray contact with it even in the individual details; compare especially 1 Clem. 9:3 with Heb 11:5, where the similarities cannot be traced back to Gen 5:24.

9:3 δίκαιος seems to be a constant epithet for Enoch; see T. Levi 10; T. Jud. 18; T. Dan 5; T. Benj. 9; but also in 1 En. 1:2, Enoch is a ἄνθρωπος δίκαιος; in 1 En. 12:4 ὁ γραμματεὺς τῆς δικαιοσύνης; in 1 En. 14:1 his book is called a βίβλος λόγων δικαιοσύνης. On the popularity of Enoch in the Jewish and later Christian belief in miracles, see Bousset, *Antichrist*, 134ff; on Enoch in general, see the indexes of Schürer, *Geschichte*; Bousset, *Religion*; Volz, *Eschatologie*; also Gunkel, *Genesis*, at the discussion of 5:21–24. However, 1 Clem. makes as little use of the rich legend as Hebrews. He sticks to the short details from Genesis.

9:4 But in the statements about Noah, the features of Jewish legend come to light, because Gen 6 knows nothing of Noah's sermon to the world, whereas Josephus, *Ant.* I 74 (3:1) does: Νῶχος δὲ τοῖς πραττομένοις ὑπ᾽ αὐτῶν δυσχεραίνων καὶ τοῖς βουλεύμασιν ἀηδῶς ἔχων ἔπειθεν ἐπὶ τὸ κρεῖττον τὴν διάνοιαν αὐτοὺς καὶ τὰς πράξεις μεταφέρειν . . . and primarily Sib. Or. I 125–98: μοῦνος δ᾽ ἐν πάντεσσι δικαιότατος καὶ ἀληθής Ἦν Νῶε πιστότατος καλοῖς τ᾽ ἔργοισι μεμηλώς. Καὶ τῷ μὲν θεὸς αὐτὸς ἀπ᾽ οὐρανόθεν φάτο τοῖα· Νῶε δέμας θάρσυνον ἐὸν λαοῖσί τε πᾶσιν Κήρυξον μετάνοιαν, ὅπως σωθῶσιν ἅπαντες . . . ; then also see 2 Pet 2:5: Νῶε δικαιοσύνης κήρυκα. The rebirth of the world is its new creation after the flood. The expression here of course does not refer to the rebirth of the individual soul, to the ἀναγέννησις. Noah proclaimed the new aeon; see the usage of παλιγγενεσία in Matt 19:28 and then Sib. Or. I 195 (in Noah's sermon): . . . καὶ δεύτερος ἔσσεται αἰών. The word παλιγγενεσία as well as the synonymously used term ἀποκατάστασις appear in Stoic terminology, where both express the idea that in the alternating great periods of the world all things and events return back to the smallest, a view which the Stoics had again taken over from the Pythagoreans. See Marcus Aurelius XI 1: . . . ἔτι δὲ περιέρχεται (sc. the soul) τὸν ὅλον κόσμον . . .

καὶ εἰς τὴν ἀπειρίαν τοῦ αἰῶνος ἐκτείνεται καὶ τὴν περιοδικὴν παλιγγενεσίαν τῶν ὅλων ἐμπεριλαμβάνει. . . . Philo, *Aet.* 47 (ed. Mangey, 507): καὶ μὴν οἵ γε τὰς ἐκπυρώσεις καὶ τὰς παλιγγενεσίας εἰσηγούμενοι τοῦ κόσμου νομίζουσι . . . τοὺς ἀστέρας θεοὺς εἶναι and 76 (ed. Mangey, 497): Βοηθὸς γοῦν ὁ Σιδώνιος καὶ Παναίτιος, ἄνδρες ἐν τοῖς Στωϊκοῖς δόγμασιν ἰσχυκότες . . . τὰς ἐκπυρώσεις καὶ παλιγγενεσίας καταλιπόντες πρὸς ὁσιώτερον δόγμα τὸ τῆς ἀφθαρσίας τοῦ κόσμου παντὸς ηὐτομόλησαν . . . ; finally also Philo, *Vita Mosis* II 65 (ed. Mangey, 144), where the following is said of the ἀγαθοὶ ἄνδρες: παλιγγενεσίας ἐγένοντο ἡγεμόνες καὶ δευτέρας ἀρχηγέται περιόδου. In this passage, along with the Stoics and in 1 Clem. 9:4, the word has a cosmological sense; in Matt 19:28 it appears in an eschatological-messianic context; Josephus, *Ant.* XI 66 speaks of ἀνάκτησις καὶ παλιγγενεσία τῆς πατρίδος (thus political-national); and on a very important mystical-individualistic use of the word, see Titus 3:5 (and the excursus on it in Dibelius, *Briefe des Apostels Paulus*). — First Clement, like 2 Peter, presents the flood as a destruction of the old world and as a subsequent new creation. The present world will be destroyed by fire, not by water. — On πιστὸς εὑρεθείς, see 1 Clem. 10:1: faith is obedience. διὰ τῆς λειτουργίας αὐτοῦ could also be connected with πιστὸς εὑρεθείς, but then, like in 1 Clem. 10:1, ἐν τῇ λειτουργίᾳ αὐτοῦ would be more likely. In the second half of the sentence, ἐν ὁμονοίᾳ is used as a clear reference to the Corinthian discord: the animals were peaceable, the humans are not. See also 1 Clem. 20:10: τά τε ἐλάχιστα τῶν ζώων κτλ.

First Clement 10 presents Abraham as a hero of obedience.

10:1 φίλος (τοῦ θεοῦ), see also 1 Clem. 17:2, is evidently known to the author as an honorary epithet of Abraham. It seems to have already been well established in Jewish legend. It does not occur in our text of Genesis; see, however, how it is cited in Jas 2:23 from Genesis; Philo, *Sobr.* 56 (ed. Mangey, 401) cites from Gen 18:17 in the following form: μὴ ἐπικαλύψω ἐγὼ ἀπὸ Ἀβραὰμ τοῦ φίλου μου (LXX τοῦ παιδός μου); see also Isa 41:8; 2 Chrn 20:7; in the Masoretic Text; also Isa 51:2 LXX: καὶ ἠγάπησα αὐτόν; Dan 3:35 LXX; Jdt 8:22 (21) Vulgate: *dei amicus effectus est*; 4 Esd 3:14: *dilexisti eum*; Jub. 19:9: "for he was found faithful and was written on the heavenly tablets as a friend of God" (cf. also 30:20). Clement *Homil.* XVIII 13: Ἀβραὰμ ὁ φίλος . . . ; etc. In Islam, Abraham bears the honorary name *el-Khalil*.

10:3 The citation comes from Gen 12:1–3 with minor deviations from the LXX.

10:4-5 On vv. 4–5, see Gen 13:11–16.

10:6 On v. 6, see Gen 15:5f.

10:7—12:8 The citations from 10:7—12:8 must be closely grouped with the foregoing, for the series of examples runs in chronological succession from Abraham to Lot and then to Rahab. With these examples, the author discusses the topic πίστις, and the closely related idea εὐσέβεια (10:7; 11:1f; 12:1, 8). But a new theme slides itself into the examples from 10:7 onward: hospitality. It is often inculcated in the admonitions of the expanding world church; see Heb 13:2; 1 Pet 4:9; 1 Tim 3:2; Titus 1:8; Herm. *Mand.* VIII 10; Herm. *Sim.* IX 27.2; see also already 1 Clem. 1:1. It is not easy to explain why the exemplary hospitality of Abraham, Lot, and Rahab are praised here: either the author was familiar with the edifying thought that these ancient heroes of faith also showed the beautiful and popular virtue of hospitality, and he therefore does not want to miss the opportunity to mention it, or he had reason to assume that the Corinthians have recently been lacking hospitality, in which case the exhortation is probably merited.

10:7 On the hospitality of Abraham see Gen 18 (also Heb 13:2); on Isaac's birth and sacrifice see Gen 21f. πίστις and ὑπακοή are closely related alternating terms (cf. 10:1).

First Clement 11 On Lot as an example of hospitality and piety and his wife as a counter-example of doubt and discord see Gen 19. εὐσέβεια, which 1 Clem. often uses along with εὐσεβής, must exist for him in the closest relationship with πίστις. For in the following, ἐλπίζειν ἐπὶ τὸν θεόν is used to explain indirectly what πιστεύειν (and ὑπακούειν) is. On the nominative absolute which follows, see Rademacher, *Grammatik*, 17f, 178f; Blaß-Debrunner, *Grammatik*, §466.4 with the examples listed there. ἑτεροκλινεῖς means to be inclined toward the other side, deviant, stubborn. It is intended to denote the contrast to faith, obedience, and as the next sentence shows unity.

11:2 Lot's wife serves as the example for the punishment of stubbornness and doubtfulness. On the meaning of Gen 19:26, see Gunkel, *Genesis*, on this passage: she was disobedient and wished to eavesdrop on the mystery of the Godhead. Wisdom 10:7 says: ἀπιστούσης ψυχῆς μνημεῖον ἑστηκυῖα στήλη ἁλός. Here, therefore, doubtfulness is already assumed to be the woman's motive. Josephus, *Ant.* I 203 (11.4) says: ἡ δὲ Λώτου γυνὴ παρὰ τὴν ἀναχώρησιν συνεχῶς εἰς τὴν πόλιν ἀναστρεφομένη καὶ πολυπραγμονοῦσα τὰ περὶ αὐτήν, ἀπηγορευκότος τοῦ θεοῦ τοῦτο μὴ ποιεῖν, εἰς στήλην ἁλῶν μετέβαλεν· ἱστόρησα δ' αὐτήν, ἔτι γὰρ καὶ νῦν διαμένει (this last detail explains ἕως τῆς ἡμέρας ταύτης and πάσαις ταῖς γενεαῖς in our passage; a column that consisted of salt rock at the Dead Sea was interpreted to be Lot's wife; Irenaeus, *Haer.* IV 31.3: *statua salis semper manens*; see also Gunkel, *Genesis*, on this passage). Nowhere else is it said that Lot's wife was at odds with her husband; however, the connection is important to the author because he can use it against the Corinthian quarrel (cf. 1 Clem. 9:4). Easier to understand are διψυχία and διστάζειν as a contrast to πίστις (see above reference to Wis 10:7). This point of connection is also important to the author, because later he returns to speak in detail about διψυχία (see 1 Clem. 23–27 and the discussion there).

First Clement 12 See Josh 2 on the topic of Rahab the whore as an example of faith and hospitality. First Clement reproduces the Old Testament report about Rahab with only a few factual deviations that enrich the original; in form, however, he proceeds in an exceedingly free manner, rendering the account in his own words. On the whole, he shortens the narrative. Rahab is presented as a model of faith in Heb 11:31; in Jas 2:25 she is presented as an example of works righteousness; 1 Clem. unites faith and action, which is here and elsewhere (cf. 1 Clem. 31–34) the content of godly action. Since 1 Clem. has already demonstrated he has used material from Heb 11, he might have drawn his example of Rahab from there as well. Rahab also appears in Matt 15 in Christ's family tree.

12:1 First Clement, of course, finds the woman's faith in her firm confidence in the victory of God's people (12:5; further elaborated in the LXX), her hospitality in the fact that she rescued the spies despite obvious danger to her own life. On Justin's and Irenaeus' interpretations, see the comments at 1 Clem. 12:7. The reading ἡ ἐπιλεγομένη before πόρνη (HLS and both Coptic witnesses) is very old, however it is certainly not original; A and Clement of Alexandria do not have this reading; it was to exonerate Rahab of her offensive profession.

12:2 ὅπως συλλημφθέντες θανατωθῶσιν is an expansive addition by 1 Clem.

12:4 ὑποδεικνύουσα αὐτοῖς ἐναλλάξ is also an addition.

12:7 According to Josh 2:18, the matter was somewhat clearer such that the spies leave a red thread for Rahab. The thread may have been a cord amulet (cf. Gen 38:18). The color red in particular was and is very popular as a protective color; it is also possible that it is a thread on which a fixed amulet was worn. The sign, which is not conspicuous in itself, is supposed to be attached to the window by Rahab when the Israelites enter the city. On κόκκινος, see the comments at 1 Clem. 8:3. προσέθεντο αὐτῇ δοῦναι σημεῖον can also be translated: "they told her to give a sign." First Clement sees in the salvific red thread a prophecy about the blood of Christ. On the effectiveness of this blood, see 1 Clem. 7:4. On the allegorical interpretation, see also Justin, Dial. 111.4: καὶ γὰρ τὸ σύμβολον τοῦ κοκκίνου σπαρτίου, οὗ ἔδωκαν ἐν Ἰεριχῶ οἱ ἀπὸ Ἰησοῦ τοῦ Ναυῆ πεμφθέντες κατάσκοποι Ῥαὰβ τῇ πόρνῃ, εἰπόντες προσδῆσαι αὐτὸ τῇ θυρίδι δι' ἧς αὐτοὺς ἐχάλασεν ὅπως λάθωσιν τοὺς πολεμίους, ὁμοίως τὸ σύμβολον τοῦ αἵματος τοῦ Χριστοῦ ἐδήλου, δι' οὗ οἱ πάλαι πόρνοι καὶ ἄδικοι ἐκ πάντων τῶν ἐθνῶν σώζονται, ἄφεσιν ἁμαρτιῶν λαβόντες καὶ μηκέτι ἁμαρτάνοντες. Similarly, though not as clear is Irenaeus, Haer. IV 20.12: Sic autem et Raab fornicaria semetipsam quidem condemnans quoniam *esset gentilis, omnium peccatorum rea, suscepit autem tres (!) speculatores, qui speculabantur universam terram, et apud se abscondit, Patrem scilicet et Filium cum Spiritu sancto. Et cum universa civitas, in qua habitabat, concidisset in ruinam canentibus septem tubicinis, in ultimis Raab fornicaria conservata est cum universa domo sua, fide signi coccini.*

D. Humility (13:1—19:1)

Translation

¹³:¹ Let us also be humble, brothers, and let us put aside all boastfulness, arrogance, foolishness, and all anger, and let us do what has been written. For the Holy Spirit says, "Let not the one who is wise boast in his wisdom, nor the strong in his strength, nor the rich in his riches, but whoever boasts, let him boast in the Lord, that he seeks him and practices what is just and right." Let us be mindful above all of the words of the Lord Jesus, which he said when teaching about mildness and patience. ² For he said thus, "Have mercy, forgive, that you will find forgiveness. As you do, it will be done to you. As you give, it will be given to you. As you judge, so also will you be judged. As you show kindness, so also will kindness be shown to you. With whatever measure you measure, so also will you be measured." ³ With this commandment and with these precepts let us strengthen ourselves with a humble mind, so that we might walk in obedience to his holy words. ⁴ For the holy word says, "Whom will I look upon but the meek and the calm, and the one who fears my words?"

¹⁴:¹ Therefore, it is just and proper, men and brothers, that we would rather obey God than follow those who in arrogance and disorderliness have risen to become leaders of this hideous jealousy. ² For we will not bring upon ourselves little harm but rather great danger if we foolhardily entrust ourselves to the will of people who aim at quarrels and disputes in order to alienate us from what is good.

¹⁴:³ Therefore, let us be kind to one another according to the mercy and kindness of him who made us. ⁴ For it is written, "The gentle will live in the land and the innocent will remain in it. But the sinners will be exterminated from it." ⁵ And again it says, "I saw a godless person who stood up defiantly and spread out like the cedars of Lebanon. And I passed by and, behold, he was no more. And I searched for his place and did not find it. Remain

pious and hold to what is right, for there will be a progeny for the peaceful person. [15:1] Therefore, let us join together with those who piously keep peace and not those who hypocritically want peace. [2] For it says somewhere, "This people honors me with (their) lips, but their heart is far from me." [3] And again, "They blessed with their mouth, but cursed in their hearts." [4] And again it says, "They loved him with their mouths and lied to him with their tongue; but their heart was not honest with him, and they did not keep his covenant faithfully." [5] Therefore, "Let the false lips which speak lawlessness against the righteous one be silenced." [6] And again, "May the Lord exterminate all the insidious lips, the boastful tongue, the people who say, 'We will praise our tongue, our lips belong to us. Who is Lord over us?' Because of the affliction of the poor and because of the sighs of the needy, I will rise up now, says the Lord. I will bring about salvation (for him); [7] I will deal with him openly."

[16:1] For Christ belongs to the humble, not those who elevate themselves above his flock. [2] The scepter of the divine majesty, the Lord Jesus Christ, did not come with arrogant and haughty pomp, although he could have done so. Instead, he came with humility, just as the Holy Spirit announced. [3] For he said, "Lord, who believed our report? And to whom was the arm of the Lord revealed? We proclaimed before him: (He is) like a child, like a root in dry earth. He had no form or honor, and we saw him, and he had neither form nor beauty, but his form was despised, uglier than the shape of men. A man beaten and tormented and trained to endure illness: for his face was turned aside. He was despised and not respected. [4] This one bears our sins, and because of us he is tormented, and we considered him to be a tormented and beaten and tortured man. [5] But he is wounded for our sins, and broken for our iniquities. The punishment that leads to our peace rests on him; through his wound we were healed. [6] We all went astray like sheep; each one went astray in his way; [7] and the Lord gave him up for our sins. And he does not open his mouth because of misfortune. He was led to the slaughter like a sheep, and as a lamb is mute before its shearers, so also he does not open his mouth. In his humiliation justice was abolished. [8] Who will announce his generation? For his life has been torn from the earth. [9] He will die for the sins of my people. [10] And I will sacrifice the wicked for his burial and the rich for his death, for he has done nothing wrong and there is no deception found in his mouth. And the Lord wants to set him free from his torment. [11] When you offer (sacrifice) for your sin, your soul will see long-living offspring. [12] And the Lord wants to lessen the agony of his soul, show him light, and shape him with insight, to save a righteous man who has served many well. And he will bear their sins. [13] Because of this he will inherit many, and he will distribute the plunder of the strong, because his soul was given to death and he was counted among the wicked. [14] And he bore the sins of many, and because of their sins he was delivered up." [15] And again he says, "But I am a worm and not a person, a mockery and a contempt of the people. [16] All who saw me mocked me, mumbled their lips, and shook their heads: 'He had hoped in the Lord, he would help him out, let him save him, since he desired him.'" [17] You see, beloved men, the example that has been given to us. For if the Lord was so humble, what shall we do who through him have been brought under the yoke of his grace?

[17:1] Let us also become imitators of those who went about in goatskins and sheepskins and proclaimed the coming of Christ. We mean Elijah and Elisha and also Ezekiel, the prophets, in addition to those who received (from God) a (good) testimony. [2] A glorious testimony was given to Abraham; he was called the friend of God, and yet, looking at the glory of God, he said with humility, "I am but dirt and ashes." [3] And so also it is written about Job, "Job was just and without blame, sincere, God-fearing, and avoided all evil." [4] But he, too, accuses himself saying, "Nobody is clean of filth, even if his life lasts only one day." [5] Moses was called "faithful in his entire house," and through his service God punished Egypt with plagues and torments that came upon them. But even he, although greatly exalted, did not make a boastful speech, but when a divine saying was given to him from the thorn bush, he said, "Who am I that you send me?" I have a weak voice and a heavy tongue." [6] And again he says, "But I am steam (which rises) from the saucepan."

[18:1] And what should we say of David who has been given a good testimony? God said of him, "I have found a man after my heart, David, the son of Jesse; I have anointed him with everlasting mercy." [2] But he also says to God, "Have mercy on me, God, according to your great mercy, and according to the multitude of your compassion, extinguish my transgression. [3] Wash me again and again from my iniquity, and cleanse me from my sin. For I know my iniquity and my sin is always before me. [4] It is only against you that I have sinned and done evil before you, so that you may be right in your words and win when you are brought to court. [5] For behold I was begotten in iniquity and my sin is always before me. [6] For behold, you loved truth. You have made known to me the invisible and hidden secrets of wisdom. [7] You will cleanse me with hyssop and I will be pure. You will wash me and I will be whiter than snow. [8] You will let me hear joy and bliss; the broken bones will shout. [9] Hide your face from my sins and put away all my iniquities. [10] Create a pure heart in me, God, and renew in me a righteous spirit. [11] Do not cast me away from your presence or take your holy spirit from me. [12] Give me again the bliss of your salvation, and strengthen me with a royal spirit. [13] I will teach your ways to the wicked, and sinners will turn to you. [14] Deliver me from bloodshed, O God, God of my salvation. [15] My tongue will cheerfully proclaim your righteousness; Lord, you will open my mouth and my lips will proclaim your glory. [16] For had you wished for a sacrifice, I would have given it. You have no pleasure in burnt offerings. A sacrifice to God is a contrite spirit. God will not despise a contrite and broken heart.

[19:1] The humble and modest nature of such great and holy men to whom testimony was given, through obedience has improved not only us but also the generations before us, namely those who received his words in fear and truthfulness.

Textual Notes

It is a longer section, a small treatise, which bears in itself the peculiarity of the Clementine way of preaching, already clearly recognizable in the preceding: the actual paraenesis is short. In our section, it comprises 13:1, 3; 14:1–3; 15:1. It is expanded and substantiated (1) by warnings and threats from the Old Testament in 13:1, 4; 14:4, 5; 15:2–6, (2) by the words of the Lord in 13:2, (3) by a long, here particularly careful series of examples, which employs the Lord in 1 Clem. 16 and the most outstanding Old Testament saints and prophets in 1 Clem. 17 and 18. The peculiarity and dexterity of the homiletician are best seen in this passage. Also, it is particularly evident here that he lives entirely in the OT: only one citation from the words of the Lord can be found (13:2), and the example of the Lord's humility in 1 Clem. 16 is not presented with any living traits of the Gospel tradition, but with the word of the prophet.

In terms of content, it should be noted upfront that the statements flow well from the previous section, whose keyword (*Stichwort*) was obedience and faith. Obedience and humility toward God are closely related; see 13:4 and 14:1 wherein obedience is recommended in the passage's paraenesis dealing with humility. When 1 Clem. emphasizes humility so strongly in the fight against his opponents, the well-known schema of denying heresy, so often repeated later, already appears with him: the one who separates himself and causes divisions in the congregation, whether in doctrinal or constitutional matters lacks (1) humility, (2) love, (3) discernment; see, for example, 2 Tim 3:2–4 and especially Ign. *Eph.*5:3 on the matter of humility: ὁ οὖν μὴ ἐρχόμενος ἐπὶ τὸ αὐτό, οὗτος ἤδη ὑπερηφανεῖ. First Clement accuses the opponents of both a lack of insight (13:1, ἀφροσύνην; 3:3; 39:1; 51:1; etc.) as well as a lack of love (49f). First Clement is quite occupied with the demand for ταπεινοφροσύνη; the word, along with its nearest relatives ταπεινοφρονεῖν and ταπεινόφρων, occur quite frequently within the work (and within Hermas), as nowhere else in early Christian writings; see already 1 Clem. 2:1: πάντες τε ἐταπεινοφρονεῖτε κτλ. The matter itself, the demand for humility that is, naturally occurs quite frequently before 1 Clem. Jesus demands humility, and Paul is very insistent on cultivating humility in the face of all sorts of pride, boastfulness, and arrogance (e.g., 1 Cor 4:7; 13:4; Rom 12:3; Phil 2:2ff). But even before Jesus and Paul, the religious demand for humility was emphatically raised in Judaism; the pious and the wise are humble. See, for example, Ps 50:19: καρδίαν . . . τεταπεινωμένην ὁ θεὸς οὐκ ἐξουδενώσει and Sir 3:18: ὅσῳ μέγας εἶ, τοσούτῳ ταπεινοῦ σεαυτόν, καὶ ἔναντι κυρίου εὑρήσεις χάριν. It is certain that the ancient Christian demand to be humble is prepared in Jewish and generally in eastern religion, whereas it is more distant from genuine Greek religion, although it cannot, of course, be absent from any developed religion. However, . . . θεοῦ, ᾧ πᾶσα ψυχὴ ἐν τῇ σήμερον ἡμέρᾳ ταπεινοῦται μεθ᾽ ἱκετείας in the two prayers for vengeance from Rheneia (Deißmann, *Licht*, 316–18), it is impossible to conclude that it is a real Greek inscription. The piece in question is Jewish or early Christian. Also, the meaning ταπεινοφροσύνη = humility is not proper Greek. The word and its relatives are, in the Hellenistic language where they first appear in general, terms for a defect = dejection, faint-heartedness. Josephus, *J.W.* IV 494: αἰτιαθεὶς ἐπὶ ταπεινοφροσύνῃ. Epictetus, *Diatr.* III 24.56: τοῦ ἔτι κολακείας τόπος, τοῦ ταπεινοφροσύνης. Epictetus I 9.10: . . . ὅπως μὴ ταπεινοφρονήσητε μηδὲ ταπεινοὺς μηδ᾽ ἀγεννεῖς τινας διαλογισμοὺς διαλογιεῖσθε αὐτοὶ περὶ ἑαυτῶν. Plutarch, *Alex. fort.* II 4: εἴπωμεν οὖν, ὅτι μικροὺς ἡ Τύχη καὶ περιδεεῖς ποιεῖ καὶ ταπεινόφρονας. However, see also Bekker, *Anecdota Graeca*, 1:462: ἀτυφία: ταπεινοφρονσύνη (thus *sensu bono*).

13:1 The hortatory subjunctive[4] continues; see both of the preceding paraeneses (7:2f; 9:1), with which 13:1 is closely related in structure (cf.

4. TN: The German phrase "der kommunikative Plural" refers to Clement's use of the first-person plural (hortatory subjunctive), not ἀδελφοί/ἀγαπητοί as I suggested previously in von Harnack, *Letter*, 92–93n9.

further 13:3; 15:1; 19:2; etc.). The rhetoric is very simple and is pushed along with οὖν and διό. On the form, see 1 Clem. 57:2. The transition from the previous section is hard and it is not easy to understand the οὖν. However, the association πίστις = ὑπακοή is very strong, and this is easily followed by ταπεινοφρονήσωμεν. The participial clause, which unfolds the statement of the main clause, contains a small catalog of closely related vices. τῦφος is neuter, whereas otherwise it is more commonly masculine; see the similar case with ζῆλος in 4:8, 11, 13 and 5:2, 4, 5. ἀφροσύνη, insofar as it is folly for man to exalt himself, a good Jewish perspective; see Ps 13:1: εἶπεν ἄφρων ἐν καρδίᾳ αὐτοῦ· οὐκ ἔστιν θεός, among other texts. In the Old Testament, [5]נְבָלָה is more of a moral-religious deficiency than it is an intellectual one; see also אִוֶּלֶת and then its antonym חָכְמָה.

On the *citation formula*, see 1 Clem. 16:2. The quotation probably comes from Jer 9:23f and 1 Sam 2:10. With slight changes and abbreviations, the first part of the citation is in agreement with the LXX, even in the order of the three parts of the list. Difficultly however exists in the second part of the quotation. First Samuel 2:10 says: ἀλλ᾽ ἢ ἐν τούτῳ καυχάσθω ὁ καυχώμενος, συνίειν καὶ γινώσκειν τὸν κύριον καὶ ποιεῖν κρίμα καὶ δικαιοσύνην ἐν μεσῳ τῆς γῆς (Jer 9:24 deviates even more from 1 Clem.). On the other hand, Paul cites in 1 Cor 1:31: ἵνα καθὼς γέγραπται· ὁ καυχώμενος ἐν κυρίῳ καυχάσθω (cf. also 2 Cor 10:17), thus closely related to 1 Clem. Is 1 Clem. dependent upon 1 Corinthians here, and if so from where did Paul draw his citation which is not written anywhere in the OT? Did both draw from a lost source (cf. excursus on Gal 4:31)? Sirach 10:22: πλούσιος καὶ ἔνδοξος καὶ πτωχός, τὸ καύχημα αὐτῶν φόβος κυρίου however can hardly be Paul's source? On the striking construction μάλιστα μεμνημένοι κτλ., see the absolute nominative in 1 Clem. 11:1. In addition to the word of the Holy Spirit in the OT comes the second teaching and legislative entity, the Lord. The Scriptures and the Lord provide the foundational directives for the faith and life of the congregation. The words of Jesus are holy, infallible, and authoritative precisely because they are the words of the Master, but not because they are recorded in Holy Scripture, inspired by the Spirit (cf. Jülicher, *Einleitung*, §34f).

13:2 Also, our text does not introduce its citation from the "Gospel" with γέγραπται or with a similar formula, but instead with: (ὁ κύριος) εἶπεν. First Clement proceeds accordingly in another passage where he clearly and explicitly introduces a word of the Lord (1 Clem. 46:7f); see there also μνήσθητε τῶν λόγων. (He further shows an appeal to synoptic tradition

5. TN: בְּלָה appears in the German edition, which is clearly a typographical error. My thanks to Ben Horn for identifying the intended form.

only in 24:5 with ἐξῆλθεν ὁ σπείρων; 15:2, incidentally also introduced with λέγει γάρ που, is a quotation in a quotation; Isaiah in a saying of the Lord. Beyond these points of contact, there is no use of the Lord's words in the letter.) The citation in 1 Clem. 13:2 appears verbatim in Clement of Alexandria, *Strom.* 2.18.91.2, with the exception of the fact that at the end Clement of Alexandria has ἀντιμετρηθήσεται instead of ἐν αὐτῷ μετρηθήσεται: The Alexandrian Clement draws from the Roman Clement and is in no way an independent witness in the matter. The quotation in 1 Clem. at first glance looks as if it has been borrowed from Matt 7:1f and Luke 6:36–38 (cf. also Matt 5:7; 6:14; Luke 6:31); however the points of contact are not at all word-for-word, and the components ἐλεᾶτε ἵνα ἐλεηθῆτε as well as ὡς χρηστεύεσθε, οὕτως χρηστευθήσεται ὑμῖν have no parallel either in Matthew or in Luke. Polycarp, *Phil.* 2:3 says: μνημονεύοντες δὲ ὧν εἶπεν ὁ κύριος διδάσκων· μὴ κρίνετε ἵνα μὴ κριθῆτε· ἀφίετε καὶ ἀφεθήσεται ὑμῖν· ἐλεᾶτε ἵνα ἐλεηθῆτε, ᾧ μέτρῳ μετρεῖτε, ἀντιμετρηθήσεται ὑμῖν. It does not seem as if Polycarp has borrowed from 1 Clem., even though he is strongly dependent on Clement and leans on him in many instances, even in the address. If Polycarp is indeed independent of Clement in this case, then one must assume that both have cited from a third source which is neither Matthew nor Luke but is rather a lost apocryphal collection. The following sources still play a role in the matter. Didascalia II 42: ὁδὸς δὲ εἰρήνης ἐστὶν ὁ σωτὴρ ἡμῶν, Ἰησοῦς ὁ Χριστός, ὃς καὶ εἶπεν· ἄφετε καὶ ἀφεθήσεται ὑμῖν [δίδοτε καὶ δοθήσεται ὑμῖν om. Syr. Lat.]; Didascalia II 42: ὅτι λέγει ὁ κύριος· ᾧ κρίματι κρίνετε, κριθήσεσθε, καὶ ὡς καταδικάζετε, καταδικασθήσεσθε. Macarius Alexandrinus, *Hom.* 37.3: καθὼς ἐνετείλατο, ἄφετε καὶ ἀφεθήσεται ὑμῖν. On the whole matter, see Oxford, *Apostolic*, 58ff.

If one considers the content of the Lord's word, then it looks as if when Clement reproves the audience for a lack of ταπεινοφροσύνη, he thinks strongly of condemnation and uncharitable judging, which he accuses his opponents of. — On ἐλεᾶτε for ἐλεεῖτε, see Radermacher, *Grammatik*, 73, and Blaß-Debrunner, *Grammatik*, §90.

13:3 Note the richness and the rhythm of the expression at the beginning of the verse. On ὑπακοή, see the entire previous section. ἁγιοπρεπής seems to appear here for the first time in the literature; see then shortly hereafter Polycarp, *Phil.* 1:1 which is highly dependent upon 1 Clem. Meaning: befitting the sacred = holy; already ἀξιοπρεπής and μεγαλοπρεπής belong to the classical language. On the citation formula, see 1 Clem. 56:3.

13:4 The quotation is from Isa 66:2, only Isaiah has ταπεινόν instead of πραΰν. It is strange that 1 Clem. should miss this specific word, especially when he has just used ταπεινοφρονοῦντες. The three terms together illuminate what Clement means by ταπεινοφρονῶν: it is a virtue with respect to God and man.

First Clement 14 exhorts the Christian to obey God, not follow people; God loves the gentle, and he exterminates the impudent. In the next chapter, too, the admonition continues to support the peacemakers, whom God loves. The admonitions are closely related to the main content of the passage (i.e., humility) and unfold it a bit more for the present case. The opponents come into view again a bit more clearly in 14:1f and 15:1.

14:1 is linked to the end of 13:4 with an easily understandable οὖν: τρέμοντά μου τὰ λόγια. The idea that one must obey God more than people is widely used as a commonplace. For the New Testament, see Acts 4:19 and 5:29, then Socrates in Plato, *Apol.* 17 (p. 29D): ἐγὼ ὑμᾶς, ἄνδρες Ἀθηναῖοι, ἀσπάζομαι μὲν καὶ φιλῶ, πείσομαι δὲ μᾶλλον τῷ θεῷ ἢ ὑμῖν. A number of additional references from classical works and rabbinic literature can be found in Wettstein on Acts 4:19. Here it is particularly a matter of the fact that the people whom the Corinthians want to follow are morally inferior or are represented in this way (on this, cf. also 1 Clem. 47:4f). They are ἀρχηγοὶ ζήλους (3:4—6:4) and indeed ἐν ἀλαζονείᾳ (13:1; not humble and modest) and ἀκαταστασίᾳ (3:2; also 43:6). μυσερός (also in 30:1) is the Koine form for μυσαρός, prompted by the liquids (cf. see Radermacher, *Grammatik*, 33; Blaß-Debrunner, *Grammatik*, §29; Helbing, *Gramatik*, 1:5f). Its appearance comes out clearly in Koine and also in modern Greek dialects; see τέσσερα and τεσσεράκοντα, καθερίζειν, modern Greek φρένιμος: φρόνιμος (Chios), among others. H improves 14:1 and 30:1 with μυσαρός.

14:2 The warning about a not insignificant danger is alienation from the good, as the closing words of the paragraph indicate, and thus rejection by God. ριψοκίνδυνος and ριψοκινδυνεύειν belong to the language of the Hellenistic period, but the adjective already comes from Xenophon, *Mem.* I 3.9. The image seems to have been taken from a game of dice. For the transferred use of ἐξακοντίζειν, see ὅταν γλώσσῃ ματαίους ἐξακοντίζῃ λόγους in Menander, *Frag.* 87 in Meineke's ed. (in Stobaeus, *Floril.* 36.12); 1 Clem. uses the word absolutely.

14:3 A reads αὐτοῖς, H ἑαυτοῖς, and LSC also translate from ἑαυτοῖς; ἑαυτοῖς is therefore undoubtedly better attested. αὐτοῖς would have to refer to the originators of the dispute, toward whom one should be gentle. The quotation in verse 4 would fit this interpretation well along with the broader context which speaks of gentleness, meekness, and peaceableness. But the letter speaks in v. 2 and immediately again in vv. 4f and in other places before and afterward very angrily of the authors of the dispute and simply demands submission and repentance from them (57:1)—should he here, without mentioning this demand, advise the congregation to be gentle with respect to the offenders? For this reason, ἑαυτοῖς and the proposed translation is decidedly preferable. Gentleness and meekness within the congregation is recommended, and it is precisely the disputants who are guilty of violating this charge. To read αυτοις in A as αὐτοῖς does not fit since the contraction is rare in Koine (cf. Radermacher, *Grammatik*, 61).

14:4 See Prov 2:21 LXX, in which S and A offer a rather faithful reproduction of the first two parts (χρηστοὶ . . . ἄκακοι) of our text. Instead of the third part, our LXX text reads the doublet: ὁδοὶ ἀσεβῶν ἐκ γῆς ὀλοῦνται, οἱ δὲ παράνομοι ἐξωσθήσονται ἀπ᾽ αὐτῆς; see however Ps 36:38: οἱ δὲ παράνομοι ἐξολεθρευθήσονται ἐπὶ τὸ αὐτό. It seems that the memory of this last passage has influenced 1 Clem. because the citation of what is immediately in front of it is introduced in v. 5: Ps 36:35–37 verbatim, only that the LXX reads: καὶ ἐζήτησα αὐτὸν, καὶ οὐχ εὑρέθη ὁ τόπος αὐτοῦ. — ἐγκατάλειμμα does not have to be translated as descendants. It can also be interpreted as a leftover, remnant. The LXX translates here and in the next verse אַחֲרִית of the base text (*Grundtextes*), which means descendants, but can also mean fortunate outcome. In T. Sim. 6:3, ἐγκατάλειμμα can mean both descendant and remnant.

First Clement 15 urges genuine peaceableness.

15:1 Peaceableness without hypocrisy are the two keywords (*Stichworte*) of this section. The connection with the previous section is such that εἰρηνικῷ is taken up at the end of ch. 14 with εἰρηνεύειν, which at the same time forms the contrast with ἔρεις in 14:2 and ἀκαταστασία in 14:1, as it is also parallel to χρηστευσώμεθα in 14:3. κολληθῶμεν in 15:1 corresponds to ἐξακολουθεῖν in 14:1 and ἐπιδῶμεν ἑαυτούς in 14:2. The new, continuing thought is μὴ μεθ᾽ ὑποκρίσεως, which had not been introduced previously. First Clement reproaches the opponents with false, hypocritical love of peace. They talk of calm, order, and peace in the congregation, but have in truth created unrest by the partisanship they have caused and by deposing their officers. The statements which follow are carefully arranged and introduce citations in the first section (vv. 2–4) that establish a contrast between the mouth and the heart, whereas the second section from v. 5f, introduced with διὰ τοῦτο, introduces penalties for false tongues.

15:2 See Isa 29:13, where it says: ἐγγίζει μοι ὁ λαὸς οὗτος ἐν τῷ στόματι αὐτου, καὶ ἐν τοῖς χείλεσιν αὐτῶν τιμῶσίν με, ἡ δὲ καρδία αὐτῶν πόρρω ἀπέχει ἀπ᾽ ἐμοῦ. First Clement seems to have been influenced by the form of the citation in Mark 7:6 (Matt 15:8); see also 2 Clem. 3:5, where the form of the Gospel is used, but also with the citation formula: λέγει δὲ καὶ ἐν τῷ Ἡσαΐᾳ.

15:3 See Ps 61:5, with very slight change: ἔψεξαν H should probably not be read, but rather ἐψεύσαντο (LXX). εὐλογοῦσαν is 3rd person imperfect; the ending -σαν instead of -ν penetrates into Koine (cf. Radermacher, *Grammatik*,

77; Blaß-Debunner, *Grammatik*, §84). In modern Greek, the imperfect is conjugated as follows: ηὐλογοῦσα, -σες, -σε, -σαμε, -σετε, -σαν.

15:4 See Ps 77:36f.

15:5 διὰ τοῦτο does not actually belong to the citation and is a transitional formula, as well as the following καὶ πάλιν. The text should be read with S: τὰ χείλη τὰ δόλια, τὰ λαλοῦντα κατὰ τοῦ δικαίου ἀνομίαν. καὶ πάλιν· ἐξολεθρεύσαι κύριος πάντα τὰ χείλη τὰ δόλια, γλῶσσαν μεγαλορήμονα. The great homoeoteleuton τὰ χείλη τὰ δόλια has brought the text in the other witnesses into disarray, and the crippled sentence structure was then tended to by them in many ways. The basic mistake, the omission, must be very old, since AHLCC¹ and Clement of Alexandria have it. The citation in the first part up to ἀνομίαν comes from Ps 30:19. The second part in vv. 5b, 6, and 7 comes from Ps 11:4–6. Both are cited word for word. The "boasters" and the "poor" are of course interpreted by Clement as referring to the Corinthian community.

First Clement 16 After the citations and their paraenesis, the examples in 1 Clem. 16–18 follow, with Christ at the head as the most distinguished among them. He did not come with arrogance and boasting, but in humility. ταπεινοφροσύνη, the keyword (*Stichwort*) of the entire section, appears more frequently now than in 1 Clem. 14 and 15.

16:1 The γάρ is explained by the promises of salvation which immediately precede and which apply to the πτωχοί and πένητες, that is, to the humble. On ποίμνιον, see 44:3; 54:2; 57:2; 1 Pet 5:3f; Acts 20:29; Barn. 5:12; and additionally the manifold designation of Jesus as the shepherd and the arch-shepherd. Of course, this is preceded before speaking of the "flock." The root of the image is probably in the ancient designation of kings and rulers as the shepherds, which Homer already uses and which goes much further up into the east. The OT use of the image is only a branch of the generally ancient one.

16:2 The expression σκῆπτρον τῆς μεγαλωσύνης is supposed to say that God exercises his power and Lordship through Christ and exercised it even before the incarnation through the pre-existent one: he was already the σκῆπτρον τῆς μεγαλωσύνης when he came. The scepter, the long staff, has long been familiar to the eastern world and to the Greeks since ancient times as a symbol of the sovereign power, and they have depicted their gods and kings with the ruler's staff countless times; see the example of the famous scepter of Zeus in the house of Atreus in *Iliad* II 101–9, the image in Greßmann et al., *Altorientalische Texte und Bilder*, #106ff (the Egyptian gods), the שֵׁבֶט in the OT (e.g., Amos 1:5; Ps 44:7; etc.). Our passage can be explained on the basis of this widespread idea, but there is hardly any reference to Heb 1:8 and the quotation given there, especially because Heb 1:8

speaks of ῥάβδος and σκῆπτρον. First Clement, like Hebrews, is supported by the views of the Christology of the Logos, to the extent he shows his Christology at all (cf. also at 1 Clem. 36). Christ is pre-existent, the reflection of divine glory, the mediator through whom God exercises his power, created and rules the world. The expressions are deliberately chosen to be strong and full-sounding σκῆπτρον . . . κύριος Ἰησοῦς Χριστός in order to make the humility of the great stand out all the more by contrast. Perhaps the expressions are taken from the liturgy. A mystery weaves around the divine Lord of the congregation: he suffered for his own people and died for them, an uncommon paradox. On this, see the Pauline Christology, especially 2 Cor 8:9 and Phil 2:6ff; these two passages also explain well καίπερ δυνάμενος. It is very important to note that the picture of the humble Lord is not drawn with any features from the life of Jesus or with words that were handed down from him, but according to the OT, that is, from the "prophets."

16:3–14 Two citations are used in this passage. The first appears in 1 Clem. 16:3–14 and is taken from Isa 53:1–12. No other text from the OT is used in early Christian literature as frequently, either in part or in whole, than Isa 53. The chapter has a great, foundational significance for ancient Christian piety and for the emerging messianic doctrines; see Mark 15:28; Matt 8:17; Luke 22:37; Rom 10:16; John 1:29; 12:38; Acts 8:22f; 1 Pet 2:22ff; Barn. 5:2; Justin, *1 Apol.* 50.2–11; 51.1–5; very frequently in Justin *Dial.*, especially *Dial.* 13, as well as in 14.8; 32.2; 89.3; 97.2; etc.; Melito, fragment in von Otto, *Corpus Apologetarum* IX, 416–18; in Goodspeed, *Apologeten*, Fragm. IX, 312. The original text, which is at times difficult to understand, has not become clearer in the LXX translation. The speakers, 1st person plural, are to be thought of as the prophets; see 1 Clem. 16:15 where the Lord is introduced as the speaker with αὐτός. In the vision the prophets foresaw the Lord who appeared on earth in his humility and humiliation, and Isaiah describes him. The long citation is of course not given from memory but has been looked up and written out and thus it corresponds very precisely to our LXX manuscripts.

16:3 The LXX with its text ἀνηγγείλαμεν ὡς παιδίον ἐναντίον αὐτοῦ does not make sense. The adjustment, which appears in other places as well (cf. Justin, *Dial.* 13.3), is supposed to mean that "he" is weak and inconspicuous like a little child, a root in dry land, and that the prophets declare this of him. The entire passage has a different form in the Masoretic Text. — Instead of παρὰ τὸ εἶδος τῶν ἀνθρώπων, the LXX has παρὰ [πάντας] τοὺς ἀνθρώπους; in the next section, it lacks ἐν πόνῳ. His face was turned away: he hides and veils it because he is ashamed and because he is despised.

16:7 Instead of ὑπὲρ τῶν ἁμαρτιῶν ἡμῶν, the LXX has ταῖς ἁμαρτίαις ἡμῶν. ἐν τῇ ταπεινώσει κτλ. . . . these and the followings words have the following messianic interpretation: since he humbled himself to the point of agony and death, he was removed from the judgment of death (cf. also Phil 2:8f).

16:8 Nobody can describe his generation, for it is innumerable; all believers who join him belong to it. This great effect of his comes from the fact that his life is taken up from earth to heaven.

16:10 The wicked and the rich will die as punishment for his death.

16:11 In the 2nd person plural, the believers are addressed; the long-living seed was of course also understood as spiritual descendants.

16:15 In this verse the Lord himself speaks: αὐτός. The pre-existent Messiah speaks the words of the Psalm and prophecies about his humiliation. The citation comes from Ps 21:7–9 (reproduced verbatim). Psalm 21 is, like Isa 53, already of great significance for the piety and theology of the most ancient form of Christianity. It also serves as a messianic proof and, as is well known, plays a role in the synoptic narrative of suffering (cf. Matt 27:43; then also Heb 2:12; Barn. 6:6).

16:16 On shaking the head as a sign of mockery, see also Matt 27:39 and then Ps 43:15; 108:25; *Threnoi* 2.15. Instead of ἐλάλησαν ἐν χείλεσιν, the original text (*Urtext*) has: "they open their lips," which probably means that they open their mouths mockingly (cf. *Thren* 2.16).

16:17 On ὑπογραμμός, see 1 Clem. 5:7. εἰ γὰρ κτλ., conclusion *a maiore ad minus*, in contrast with ὁ κύριος and ἡμεῖς. On the yoke of grace, see Matt 11:29f. δι᾿ αὐτοῦ, namely through his kindness and humility just mentioned.

First Clement 17 and the following chapter contain two more groups of examples, which follow the example of the Lord's humbleness: very briefly the prophets in v. 1.

17:1 We are to become imitators of them, of course with the humility that no longer needs to be expressly repeated in this context. The prophets are described according to their role, which is foretelling the coming of Christ. This is of course a very important assignment, and those chosen for it are chosen and imparted with grace by God in a special way. Nevertheless, they were full of humility, which itself can be seen in their poor dress. On this, see especially Heb 11:37, which is the source of the wording; then on the sheepskins, see 1 Kgs 19:13 (Elijah when God appeared to him at Horeb): ἐπεκάλυψεν τὸ πρόσωπον αὐτοῦ ἐν τῇ μηλωτῇ ἑαυτοῦ and 1 Kgs 19:19 (Elijah takes Elisha as a companion): καὶ ἐπέρριψε τὴν μηλωτὴν αὐτοῦ ἐπ᾿ αὐτόν; see additionally 2 Kgs 2:8, 13, 14 (Elijah's ascension, his μηλωτή, with which he parted the Jorden, remains behind with Elisha). On the prophetic garb, see Zech 13:4: . . . οἱ προφῆται . . . ἐνδύσονται δέρριν τριχίνην ἀνθ᾿ ὧν ἐψεύσαντο, where the original text (*Urtext*) identifies the prophetic garb even more clearly than the LXX through the negation. What is translated as μηλωτή in the LXX is אַדֶּרֶת and signifies only the wide, enveloping cloak. Zechariah 13:4 says: אַדֶּרֶת שֵׂעָר, the hairy cloak. Sheepskin skirt or cloak occasionally occurs outside of the LXX. The goat skins are not mentioned anywhere in the OT as the garb of the prophets, but see Heb 11:37. They are an even rougher form of dress than those of sheepskins. Ἐλισαιέ or Ἐλισσαιέ (better perhaps *properispomenon*) is the form of the name in LXX; Josephus has Ἐλισσαῖος. That Ezekiel dressed himself in sheepskin is reported nowhere in the OT, but the austerity of the man, his zeal against idolatry, has probably prompted him to be removed from the ranks of the great prophets and be placed next to Elijah and Elisha.

17:2 The μεμαρτυρημένοι follow (up to 1 Clem. 18:17). These are people about whom God has given an explicit testimony in the Holy Book, which ensures their piety and the divine satisfaction in them. On the use of μαρτυρεῖν here and in the following, including (30:7); 38:2; 44:3; 47:4, see also Acts 6:3; 10:22; 13:22; 16:2; 22:12; Heb 11:2, 4, 5, 39; 3 John 12; Ign., *Phld.* 11:1; etc., as well as Dittenberger, *Sylloge*, #197.37f: . . . πολλάκις μεμαρτύρηκεν αὐτῶι ὁ βασιλεὺς (it is Lysimachus) πρὸς τοὺς πρεσβεύοντας Ἀθηναίων πρὸς ἑαυτόν . . . ; Orient. Inscr. 504.10f (Asia, Hadrian's time): . . . εὔλογον ἡγησάμεθα μαρτυρῆσαι αὐτῶι παρ᾽ ὑμεῖν . . . . Very similar in Orient. Inscr. 505.13f and 507.8. See also μαρτυρία in the inscriptions 504.18 and 507.5; further in 646.7 (263–67 CE, Palmyra): . . . μαρτυρηθέντα ὑπὸ τῶν ἀρχεμπόρων . . . and above all in 640.15 (242/3 CE, Palmyra): . . . ὡς διὰ ταῦτα μαρτυρηθῆναι ὑπὸ θεοῦ Ἰαριβώλου . . . . This testimony of God must have been determined by an oracle, thus, like 1 Clem., it must have been an explicit testimony. Even the OT words are often referred to by Christians as χρησμοί, thus likewise in v. 5 as χρηματισμός. The section on the μεμαρτυρημένοι is carefully constructed. Three prophets were named in v. 1, four μεμαρτυρημένοι are listed below: Abraham, Job, Moses, David, all four especially holy and famous men. The additional examples are presented in such a way that immediately after the testimony of praise by God follows an utterance of the greatest modesty and deepest humility of the one praised. Also, note the chronological order of the series (Job is considered a man of the distant past; according to Jewish tradition he lived beyond Moses; he was a son of Esau according to Aristeas in Eusebius, *Praep. ev.* IX 25). Finally, note the law of increase followed here: the examples increase in scope, one after the other. — Abraham, the patriarch, is the first example. On φίλος, see 1 Clem. 10:1. The brief citation ἐγὼ κτλ. is taken verbatim from Gen 18:27 LXX. In Gen 18, Abraham negotiates with God face to face about the possible deliverance of Sodom. The refined consciousness of God of a later era can no longer admit this, and the old theophany must be reinterpreted: Abraham only saw the δόξα, the radiance, the light of God; on this notion, see already Exod 33:18–23 and Deut 5:22ff. The implemented Logos theology would require that man does not see anything of God, but only that the splendor of the Logos appears to him (cf. John 12:41).

17:3–4 See Job 1:1 and 14:4f; both citations in 1 Clem. have not been cited verbatim but flowed from the author's memory.

17:5 On the praise of Moses, see Num 12:7 (also Heb 3:2, 5 is cited); in Hebrew and in the LXX, the οἶκος is the house, the family of God, which is probably also what is meant here. On the punishment of Egypt, see Exod 8–12. Moses' words are a composite from Exod 3:11 (τίς εἰμι ἐγὼ ὅτι πορεύσομαι πρὸς Φαραὼ βασιλέα Αἰγύπου . . .) and 4:10 (ἰσχνόφωνος καὶ βραδύγλωσσος ἐγώ εἰμι).

17:6 The source of the citation is unknown; it must come from a lost Apocryphon, probably a book of Moses (Assumption of Moses?); see also J. R. Harris, "Obscure," 190–95. On the image, see Jas 4:14; Hos 13:3 (ἀπὸ δακρύων, LXX is obviously corrupt). The idea of the frailty of all human beings, which was also very old and often emphasized in classical antiquity, is often illustrated by the Stoics with the image of smoke: Marcus Aurelius, Εἰς ἑαυτόν X 31.3: οὕτως γὰρ συνεχῶς θεάσῃ τὰ ἀνθρώπινα καπνὸν καὶ τὸ μηδέν, XII 33: πῶς ἑαυτῷ χρῆται τὸ ἡγεμονικόν; ἐν γὰρ τούτῳ τὸ πᾶν ἐστι. τὰ δὲ λοιπὰ ἢ προαιρετικά ἐστιν ἢ ἀπροαίρετα, νεκρὰ καὶ καπνός, Seneca, Tro. 392ff: Ut calidis fumus ab ignibus Vanescit . . . Sic hic quo regimur spiritus effluent, already in Empedocles, Περὶ φύσεως Frag. 2 (Diels, Fragmente der Vorsokratiker, 1:223) ὠκύμοροι καπνοῖο δίκην ἀρθέντες ἀπέπταν, see also Schiller, Siegesfest: "Every earthly creature is smoke: as the column of steam ripples, all earthly greetings vanish, only the gods remain." — κύθρα = χύτρα with shifting aspiration; see κιθών = χιτών, πάθνη = φάτνη.

18:1 See Ps 88:21: εὗρον Δαυεὶδ τὸν δοῦλόν μου, ἐν ἐλέει ἁγίῳ ἔχρισα αὐτὸν and 1 Sam 13:14: ζητήσει κύριος ἑαυτῷ ἄνθρωπον κατὰ τὴν καρδίαν αὐτοῦ (said of David); on the amalgamation of the two quotations, see also Acts 13:22; the son of Jesse in 2 Sam 23:1: πιστὸς Δαυεὶδ υἱὸς Ἰεσσαί, see also Ps 71:20. AHL attest to ἐλέει, Clement of Alexandria SC have ἐλαίῳ. The LXX manuscripts are also split on this reading.

18:2–17 See Ps 50:3–19, also verbatim agreement with our LXX, as is to be expected with a lengthy citation. The penitential psalm not only speaks of contrition and humility, but also expresses the humble person's good confidence and plea for salvation (7ff) and therefore fits well with the end of the whole series of examples. The conclusion in v. 17 is also very effective and cleverly closes the entire series of warnings from 16:1 on the topic of humility!

18:5 A few more details: in v. 5 κισσάω (τινός) is used of the pregnant woman's desire. Epictetus, Diatr. IV 8.35: ἰδοῦ σου τὴν ὁρμήν, μὴ κακοστομάχου ἢ κισσώσης γυναικός ἐστιν. The LXX uses the word only here in translation of the *piel* יָחַם and clearly understands by this, as the original text (*Urtext*) and parallelism show, the pleasure of procreation; hence the connection with the accusative.

18:7 ὕσσωπος, Hebrew אֵזוֹב, like many plant names from the east that have come into Greek, is *hyssopus officinalis*, a half-shrub up to 50 cm high, with dense aromatic leaves. The branches are used for sprinkling in purification rites, but also for the preparation of the purifying water itself; see Exod 12:22; Lev 14:4, 6, 49; Num 19:6, 18.

18:8 ἀκουτίζειν, a Hellenistic word, often in the LXX and used by the other Bible translators.

18:12 ΠΝΕΥΜΑ ΗΓΕΜΟΝΙΚΟΝ, the LXX translates here רוּחַ נְדִיבָה of the original text (*Urtext*), as parallels to this usage, see also Symmachus Ps 110:3 and Prov 8:6 and Theodotion Prov 8:6 (in Origen's Hexapla, ed. by Field). נָדִיב means willing, generous, then noble and noble minded; the substantive נְדִיבָה, which is present in Ps 50:14, means willingness, then majesty, nobility. It is this second meaning which the LXX grasped. Objectively, for the Christian and before that in the LXX, the πνεῦμα ἡγεμονικόν is the same as the just-mentioned πνεῦμα ἅγιον: the Holy Spirit is the leading and royal Spirit. By choosing this expression, the LXX followed a philosophical, Stoic manner of expression, in which τὸ ἡγεμονικόν is a very common term. There, it designates reason as the basic force of the soul; all other forces of the soul are only the lower forces and subordinate parts of this foundational force. ἡγεμονικόν has its seat in the chest (or in the head), and the I, the personality, is posited in it; see Zeller, *Philosophie*, 3.1:197ff. See then the texts in von Arnim, *Stoicorum veterum fragmenta*, 2:217–63, above all Aetius, *De placitis philosophorum* IV 21 (Diels, *Doxographi*, 410): οἱ Στωϊκοί φασιν εἶναι τῆς ψυχῆς ἀνώτατον μέρος τὸ ἡγεμονικόν, τὸ ποιοῦν τὰς φαντασίας καὶ συγκαταθέσεις καὶ αἰσθήσεις καὶ ὁρμάς, καὶ τοῦτο λογισμὸν καλοῦσιν. ἀπὸ δὲ τοῦ ἡγεμονικοῦ ἑπτὰ μέρη ἐστι τῆς ψυχῆς ἐκπεφυκότα καὶ ἐκτεινόμενα εἰς τὸ σῶμα καθάπερ αἱ ἀπὸ τοῦ πολύποδος πλεκτάναι· τῶν δὲ ἑπτὰ μερῶν τῆς ψυχῆς πέντε μέν εἰσιν τὰ αἰσθητήρια, ὅρασις ὄσφρησις ἀκοὴ γεῦσις καὶ ἁφή . . . τῶν δὲ λοιπῶν τὸ μὲν λέγεται σπέρμα . . . τὸ δὲ "φωνᾶεν" ὑπὸ τοῦ Ζήνωνος εἰρημένον, ὃ καὶ φωνὴν καλοῦσιν . . . αὐτὸ δὲ τὸ ἡγεμονικὸν ὥσπερ ἐν κόσμῳ <ἥλιος> κατοικεῖ ἐν τῇ ἡμετέρᾳ σφαιροειδεῖ κεφαλῇ. On the later Stoa, see ἡγεμονικόν in the indexes on Epictetus and Marcus Antoninus in Schenkl; for example, Εἰς ἑαυτόν II 2.1: ὅ τί ποτε τοῦτό εἰμι, σαρκία ἐστὶ καὶ πνευμάτιον καὶ τὸ ἡγεμονικόν. See further Tertullian, *De anima* 15: *summus in anima gradus vitalis . . . quod* ἡγεμονικὸν *appellant, id est principale.* The Stoic expression πνεῦμα ἡγεμονικόν, which is already present in the LXX and refers to the Holy Spirit, was then adopted by Christians and also used to designate the Holy Spirit; for the earliest reference, see Muratorian Fragment, line 19f: *cum uno ac principali spiritu declarata sint in omnibus* [scil. evangeliis] *omnia* . . . . αἷμα, especially in the plural = bloodshed, murder; see already *Iliad* 11.164; 19.214; then Plato, *Leg.* IX 12 (p. 872E): ἡ τῶν ξυγγενῶν αἱμάτων τιμωρὸς δίκη.

19:1 concludes the section: The great ones have shown humility and in it they have been obedient. In doing so, they make us better, we who read of them in the Scriptures; in doing so, they have already made the past generations better, who were their contemporaries and who were able to stand up by their example and therefore accepted God's word in fear and truthfulness. Regarding the generations of the past and their conversion, see already 1 Clem. 7:5. — On the form of the clause τοσούτων καὶ τοιούτων, as in 1 Clem. 63:1, see also Heb 12:1. ὑποδεής, which is almost always used in the comparative, means inadequate, but it is used here in a positive sense: modest. For a good parallel, see the closely related ἐνδεής in Herm. *Mand.* VIII 10: μηδενὶ ἀντιτάσσεσθαι, ἡσύχιον εἶναι, ἐνδεέστερον γίνεσθαι πάντων ἀνθρώπων. The other option of ὑποδεές as a reference to voluntary poverty, the lack of physical goods of those who are praised should probably be rejected. The unique τε simply reinforces and explains.

E. God's Benefactions and His Order (19:2—22:9)

Translation

² Since we have been a part of so many great and glorious deeds (of the blessing), let us run toward the goal of peace that has been set out for us from the beginning, to look to the Father and founder of the whole world and to adhere to his glorious and abundant gifts of peace and benefactions. ³ Let us look at him in spirit and contemplate his long-suffering will with the eyes of our soul; let us pay attention to how kind he is toward all his creation. 20:1 The heavens circle at his command, and they obey him in peace. ² Day and night complete the course that he has prescribed for them without hindering one another. ³ Sun and moon and the choir of stars roll along according to his command in harmony and steadfastly follow the paths prescribed for them. ⁴ According to his will, the earth bears fruit at the appropriate time and allows sufficient nourishment for people and animals and everything that lives on it to grow without hesitation and without changing anything in his statutes. ⁵ The mysterious courts of the abyss and the unspeakable courts of the dead are maintained by the same commands. ⁶ The depth of

the infinite sea remains as he created it, in the place where it is collected, and it does not break through the bars placed around it, but does as he commanded. ⁷ For he said, "You shall come as far as here, and your waves shall crush in on you." ⁸ The *oceanos*, which has no end for the people, and the worlds beyond are ruled by the same commands of the Lord. ⁹ Spring and summer and autumn and winter peacefully follow one another. ¹⁰ The established orders of the winds carry out their service in their time, without disturbance. Never ending springs, created for enjoyment and health, offer life-giving breasts to people, without running out. Yes, even the smallest animals hold their meetings in peace and harmony. ¹¹ The great creator and Lord of the universe appointed all this to be in peace and harmony, showering everything with benefits, but especially we who have taken refuge in his mercy through Jesus Christ, our Lord, ¹² to whom be honor and glory forever and ever. Amen.

²¹:¹ Brothers, see that his many benefits do not bring us to damnation if we do not walk worthy of him and do that which is good and pleasing to him in unity. ² For it says somewhere, "The Spirit of the Lord is a light that shines through the chambers of the body." ³ Let us see how close he is and that not a single one of our thoughts and our intentions which we have had remain hidden from him. ⁴ It is proper, therefore, that we do not deviate from his will. ⁵ We would rather give offense to foolish and unintelligent people who puff themselves up and exalt themselves in their boastful speech than offend God.

²¹:⁶ Let us dread the Lord Jesus Christ, whose blood was given for us. Let us show respect to our leaders, honor our elders, educate our young in the fear of the Lord, encourage our wives to do good. ⁷ Let them display a kind, chaste manner, show an unadulterated, gentle disposition, make known the moderation of their tongues through silence. They should not exercise their loving activity arbitrarily, but apply it with a pure mind in the same way to all who fear God. ⁸ Let our children participate in the education in Christ, let them learn what God can do with humility, what God can do with holy love, how the fear of him is good and glorious and saves all who walk holy in him with a pure conscience. ⁹ For he is an investigator of thoughts and attitudes. His breath is in us, and when he wishes, he will take it back.

²²:¹ Faith in Christ ensures all of this. For he himself calls us through the Holy Spirit: "Come here, children, listen to me, I will teach you the fear of the Lord. ² Who is the person who

desires life, who wishes to see good days? [3] Protect your tongue from evil and your lips from speaking falsehood. [4] Forsake evil and do what is good; [5] seek peace and chase after it. [6] The eyes of the Lord (are directed) at the righteous, and his ears at their entreaties. But the face of the Lord is (situated) upon the wrong-doers, that he may cut off their memory from the earth. [7] The righteous one cried out, and the Lord heard him, and he delivered him from all his tribulations. [[8] Many are the afflictions of the righteous, and the Lord will save him from all of them." Then,] [9] "The plagues of the sinner are numerous, but mercy will surround those who hope in the Lord."

Textual Notes

The section quickly begins to describe the benefactions of God, which this time are not sought in history and the offering of salvation, but in creation. Peace and order reign in the cosmos (19:3—20:12). Mankind must also emulate this goal of peace, fear of God, obedience, and order; peace must reign in the congregation (21:1—22:8; 21:6–9, the congregational rules [*Gemeindetafel*]).

19:2 The transition is abrupt; from God's benefactions in history, which are based on the examples of humility, there is a transition to his benefactions in creation. But the liturgy already tied both together, the God of nature and the God of sacred history, and in this passage 1 Clem. leans most strongly on the congregational liturgy (cf. below). The God of creation is a God of peace and benefactions.

19:2 The πράξεις are the deeds and examples of the holy men of the primordial age and also of the Lord Christ, of whom we spoke previously. On the other hand, εἰρήνης σκοπόν already looks forward to the following: a goal of peace to strive after is established in creation from the beginning. God is called πατὴρ καὶ κτίστης τοῦ σύμπαντος κόσμου: the genitive also belongs with πατήρ. The double epithet here is one of the numerous expressions and phrases that 1 Clem. uses to praise God the creator. On πατὴρ τοῦ κόσμου, see Philo, *Leg.* I 18 (p. 47): πατὴρ . . . τῶν γιγνομένων and *Her.* 205 (p. 501): ὁ τὰ ὅλα γεννήσας πατήρ. On κτίστης, see also 1 Clem. 59:3; 62:2 (cf. also 60:1); 1 Pet 4:19 (the only passage in the NT); 2 Sam 22:32; Jdt 9:12; Sir 24:8; 2 Macc 1:24; 7:23; 13:14 (B); 4 Macc 5:25; 11:5 (thus seven times in the apocrypha, once in the older books); frequently in Philo; Let. Aris. 16 (Josephus does not use the expression); Table of Hadrumet (*Antike Fluchtafeln*, ed. Wünsch, #5.10): ὁρκίζω σε τὸν κτίσαντα τὸν οὐρανὸν καὶ τὴν θάλασσαν. Leiden Magical papyrus (Dieterich, *Abraxas*, 176.2f): τὸν τὰ πάντα κτίσαντα, etc. The benefactions of God are strongly emphasized here and in what follows (cf. 1 Clem. 20:11; 21:1). The idea of God as the great benefactor is not foreign to the OT; see Ps 12:6; 56:3; 114:7 (here, however, applied personally); Wis 16:2 (εὐεργετήσας τὸν λαόν σου). See also Ps 103:27f: πάντα πρὸς σὲ προσδοκῶσιν, δοῦναι τὴν τροφὴν αὐτοῖς εὔκαιρον. δόντος σου αὐτοῖς συλλέξουσιν, ἀνοίξαντος δε σου τὴν χεῖρα τὰ σύμπαντα ἐμπλησθήσεται χρηστότητος. See the entire psalm in general as well as Ps 102, among others. But the thought in form, application, as well as the connection (the order of the cosmos) in which 1 Clem. sets it is a layer of a widespread Hellenistic thought which is often attested in religion and philosophy. εὐεργέτης, next to σωτήρ, is one of the most beloved epithets for God: because of the benefactions of the course of nature, of agriculture and viticulture, of manifold inventions, the gods are praised as εὐεργέται and also the earthly rulers, the visible gods, are affectionately called εὐεργέται; in the enlightened absolutism of the Hellenistic kingship εὐεργεσία and φιλανθρωπία are the main virtues of the ruler (also otherwise deserving people, officials and citizens, are gladly praised by the grateful fellow citizens as εὐεργέται or because of their εὐεργεσία, as the inscriptions prove a hundred times over); besides Luke 22:25, see the indexes by Dittenberger under εὐεργέτης, εὐεργετεῖν, and εὐεργεσία, then see Wendland, *Kultur*, 448 under εὐεργέτης, εὐεργεσίαι .... Possibly even more clearly in the religion of philosophy, especially in the Stoa, the all-pervading, foreseeing deity is described and venerated as the all-benevolent being, and it is in the spiritual sphere of this religion that we stand in 1 Clem. 20 (see below): Arius Didymus (written around the time of the birth of Christ) in Eusebius, *Praep. ev.* XV 15.5: ... νομιστέον, προνοεῖν τῶν ἀνθρώπων τὸν τὰ ὅλα διοικοῦντα θεόν, εὐεργετικὸν ὄντα καὶ χρηστὸν καὶ φιλάνθρωπον, δίκαιόν τε καὶ πάσας ἔχοντα τὰς ἀρετάς. Musonius in Stobaeus, *Flor.* 117.8 (Hense, *Musonii*, 90.11). God is κρείττων ... φθόνου καὶ ζηλοτυπίας, μεγαλόφρων δὲ καὶ εὐεργετικὸς καὶ φιλάνθρωπος. Plutarch, *Stoic. rep.* 38 (p. 1051 F): Ἀντίπατρος ὁ Ταρσεὺς (written around 150 BCE) ἐν τῷ περὶ θεῶν γράφει ταῦτα κατὰ λέξιν· ... θεὸν ... νοοῦμεν ζῷον μακάριον καὶ ἄφθαρτον καὶ εὐποιητικὸν ἀνθρώπων. Frequently in Philo; see, for example, *Spec.* I 209 (p. 242): ὁ γὰρ θεὸς ἀγαθός τέ ἐστι καὶ ποιητὴς καὶ γεννητὴς τῶν ὅλων καὶ προνοητικὸς ὢν ἐγέννησε, σωτήρ τε καὶ εὐεργέτης, μακαριότητος καὶ πάσης εὐδαιμονίας ἀνάπλεως. Seneca, *Ep.* 95.49: *quae causa est dis benefaciendi? natura. errat, si quis illos putat nocere nolle: non possunt.* Seneca, *Ben.* II 29.3: *quanto satius est ad contemplationem tot tantorumque beneficiorum reverti et agere gratias ...* [6] *carissimos nos habuerunt di immortales habentque et, qui maximus tribui honos potuit, ab ipsis proximos conlocaverunt.* Seneca, *Ben.* IV 3–9 is about divine benefactions; see there 9.1: *plurima beneficia ac maxima in nos deus defert sine spe recipiendi.*

19:3 ἀόργητος sounds truly philosophical (Stoic); see Ignatius, *Phld.*
1:2 and Polycarp, *Phil.* 12:2 (*sine iracundia*); Justin, *1 Apol.* 16.1; then
further Marcus Aurelius, *In semet ipsum* 1.1; Epictetus, *Diatr.* III 20.9.
Conquering anger is part of the Stoic ideal of *ataraxia* and apathy, and
freedom from anger is also a characteristic of the immortal gods: *natura
enim illis mitis et placida est, tam longe remota ab aliena iniuria quam a
sua* (Seneca, *Ira* II 27.1).

First Clement 20: The benefactions of God and his goodness toward
everything that lives are shown in the order and peace that rule all creation.

LITURGY

Drews brought the correct approach to the whole section in his very important study (*Liturgie*, esp. 12ff). According to Drews' investigation of
1 Clem. 20, we have undoubtedly received a piece of the ancient Roman
liturgy, albeit of course used freely. Liturgy is further evident in the related sections of 1 Clem. 33:2–6 and in 34:5f. In the continuation of the
last piece in 1 Clem. 34:7, we clearly recognize the congregation united in
worship. The question about the peculiarity of 1 Clem. 20, as well as the
other two pieces, demands, however, an answer to the origin of the material. The influence of the LXX is self-evident; Psalms and Job contribute
descriptions of nature and praise the all-powerful creator God. Genesis
1 reports on the creation of the universe; the Trisagion in 1 Clem. 34:6
comes from Isa 6. First Clement 20, 33, and 34 also expressly refer to the
OT in several places. But the passages can by no means be sufficiently explained with reference to the Holy Books. Already the great, foundational
idea of 1 Clem. 20 is as follows: the regularity and order of the cosmos.
This regularity and order of the cosmos is the perfect expression of the
divine creative activity, and is entirely non-Jewish and generally not an
eastern idea. The spirit of Greek philosophical piety makes itself known
here most clearly. Additionally, there is a strong Greek influence in the
presentation of the material, as well as in the substantial material parallels
which can be proven: from the fragments of the Stoics, from Cicero, *Nat.
de.* II, from passages out of Seneca, such as *Marc.* 18; *Helv.* 8.6; *Nat.* V 13ff;
Ben. IV 25; from Pseudo-Aristotle, *De mundo* (mainly printed in the Greek
reader by von Wilamowitz-Moellendorff, *Griechisches Lesebuch*: contains
the thoughts of Posidonius and the later Stoa with Aristotelian material),
from the prayers in Firmicus Maternus, *Mathesis* V, *Praefatio* 3–5 and VII
Praefatio 2, from the magical papyri, which contain a significant amount
of Stoic material, and from other sources of Hellenistic theology. See also

Skutsch, "Liturgie," 291–305 (deals with the prayers of Firmicus) and also Wendland, "Politik," 330–34; see further Schermann, *Griechische Zauber-papyri*. — The whole passage in 1 Clem. 20 has two peaks. One consideration is that the glorious well-ordered creation is a blessing from God; see the framing of the passage in 19:2f and then in 20:11 (εὐεργετῶν), 21:1 (εὐεργεσίαι). The paraenesis then is that we must show ourselves worthy of the great benefactions. The second peak is that obedience and peace are shown in creation. This is carried out in detail and logically in every single clause from 20:1–11; other than the recurring repetition of εἰρήνη and ὁμόνοια, see also δίχα παρεκβάσεως, δίχα ἐλλείψεως, and others, as well as the constant use of derivatives of the root ταγ. The paraenesis is then: let us also submit and maintain peace and harmony (21:1). Incidentally, the author himself couples the two approaches very closely together by speaking of δωρεαὶ τῆς εἰρήνης in 19:2.

20:1 The use of διοίκησις, a frequently used word among the Stoics, with which they denoted the world-ordering and world-administering activity of the god of the Logos, is quite noteworthy; a parallel expression is διακόσμησις (cf. the comments at 1 Clem. 33:3). On διοίκησις, see already Zeno according to Aristocles in Eusebius, *Praep. ev.* XV 14.2 p. 817a (von Arnim, *Stoicorum veterum fragmenta*, 1:#98): . . . ταύτῃ δὲ πάντα διοικεῖσθαι τὰ κατὰ τὸν κόσμον ὑπέρευ, καθάπερ ἐν εὐνομωτάτῃ τινὶ πολιτείᾳ. Also Stobaeus, *Eclogae* I 17.3 (von Arnim, *Stoicorum veterum fragmenta*, 1:#102): . . . τοιαύτην δὲ δεήσει εἶναι ἐν περιόδῳ τὴν τοῦ ὅλου διακόσμησιν ἐκ τῆς οὐσίας . . . . See also numbers 103 and 107 . . . ; see further at Chrysippus in Eusebius, *Praep. ev.* XV 15.5 (von Arnim, *Stoicorum veterum fragmenta*, 2:#528): οἷς ἀκολούθως νομιστέον προνοεῖν τῶν ἀνθρώπων τὸν τὰ ὅλα διοικοῦντα θεόν . . . . Cleanthes, *Praep. ev.* 15.7 (*Stoicorum veterum fragmenta*, 1:#499): ἡγεμονικὸν δὲ τοῦ κόσμου Κλεάνθει μὲν ἤρεσε τὸν ἥλιον εἶναι διὰ τὸ μέγιστον τῶν ἄστρων ὑπάρχειν καὶ πλεῖστα συμβάλλεσθαι πρὸς τὴν τῶν ὅλων διοίκησιν . . . . Epictetus, Cornutus, Marcus Aurelius, and others like to use διοικεῖν and διοίκησις frequently, speaking of the διοίκησις τοῦ θεοῦ, of the διοίκησις τοῦ κόσμου, τῶν ὅλων, etc.; see the indexes of Schenkl on Epictetus and Marcus Aurelius and of Lang on Cornutus. The use of σαλεύεσθαι to denote the regular, God-ordered revolutions of the heavens is noteworthy. σαλεύεσθαι, otherwise *sensu malo*, means "to waver, be shaken, be thrown into confusion"; see the abundantly attested usage of the LXX, for example, Ps 17:7: ἐσαλεύθη . . . ἡ γῆ καὶ τὰ θεμέλια τῶν ὀρέων . . . ἐσαλεύθησαν, as well as Ps 45:6; 76:19; 81:5; 96:4; 97:7; 98:1; Sir 16:18: ἄβυσσος καὶ γῆ σαλευθήσονται ἐν τῇ ἐπισκοπῇ αὐτοῦ . . . and Mic 1:4; Hab 3:6; etc., then Mark 13:25 (Matt 24:29; Luke 21:26); Matt 11:7; Heb 12:26f; see further Asclepius, *Prom.* 1081: χθὼν σεσάλευται. Improvements have therefore been proposed: μὴ σαλευόμενοι (thus already in Young, the first editor). The conjecture is impossible, however, because the whole chapter elaborates the idea of change and movement with constant order and because here we do not have the solid vault of other worldviews, but the revolving spheres of the Greeks. σαλεύεσθαι must therefore mean here: "to turn."

20:2 It is strange that day and night are mentioned here, detached from the sun. But see also the independence of day and night at 24:3. Genesis 1:1–13 is known for the repetitive mention of day and night before the creation of the heavenly lights is reported in 1:14ff. But Cicero, *Nat. d.* II 98–104 also describes the order and beauty of the world and says of the air in 101: *exin mari finitumus aër die et nocte distinguitur* . . . and mentions the sun first in 102: *isque oriens et occidens diem noctemque conficit* . . . ; see also the liturgy in Apost. Const. VIII 12.9 (Lietzmann, *Klementinische Liturgie*): ὁ πήξας στερέωμα καὶ νύκτα καὶ ἡμέραν κατασκευάσας ὁ ἐξαγαγὼν φῶς ἐκ θησαυρῶν καὶ τῇ τούτου συστολῇ ἐπαγαγὼν τὸ σκότος εἰς ἀνάπαυλαν τῶν ἐν τῷ κόσμῳ κινουμένων ζῴων, ὁ τὸν ἥλιον τάξας εἰς ἀρχὰς τῆς ἡμέρας ἐν οὐρανῷ καὶ τὴν σελήνην εἰς ἀρχὰς τῆς νυκτός . . . . Here we have, admittedly in a strongly Old Testament mythologizing form of expression, an explanation of 1 Clem. 20:2: Day and night depend not only on the sun, but also on "light" in general, which has other sources than the sun. The position of v. 2 between vv. 1 and 3 proves that in 1 Clem. day and night are viewed as cosmic, not just as earthly phenomena.

20:3 The heavenly bodies follow in the self-evident, often documented order: sun, moon, stars. The choirs = the rounds of the stars are a very old image, and popular among the Stoics. The author uses the plural because he has the numerous constellations in mind. In the Christian liturgy, see Apost. Const. VIII 12.9: . . . ὁ τὸν ἥλιον τάξας εἰς ἀρχὰς τῆς ἡμέρας ἐν οὐρανῷ καὶ τὴν σελήνην εἰς ἀρχὰς τῆς νυκτὸς καὶ τὸν χορὸν τῶν ἀστέρων ἐν οὐρανῷ καταγράψας εἰς εἶνον τῆς σῆς μεγαλοπρεπείας . . . . Pseudo-Cyprian (Novatian) *De spectaculis* 9: . . . *astrorum micantes choros* . . . *Martyrdom of the Three Cappadocians*: . . . ἀστέρων χοροὺς ἐν οὐρανῷ φαιδρύνας (text in Weyman, "Analecta," 577). See also Theophilus, *Autol.* I 6: ἄστρων χορείαν. Philo, *De victimis* 207 (ed. Mangey, 242): . . . συγχορεύειν ἡλίῳ καὶ σελήνῃ καὶ τῇ τῶν ἄλλων ἀστέρων . . . στρατιᾷ. Then Euripides, *El.* 467: ἄστρων τ' αἰθέριοι χοροί etc. παρεκβάσεως ALK; H has παραβάσεως, which is highly unlikely to be the original reading because of its scant testimony. The verb παρεκβαίνειν, shortly hereafter in v. 6 means "to cross over to the side." ἐξελίσσουσιν: the image of the rounds made by the heavenly bodies is retained; on the word, see Plutarch, *Is. Os.* 42 p. 368A: . . . τοσαύταις ἡμέραις τὸν αὐτῆς κύκλον ἐξελίσσει (sc. ἡ σελήνη). The ὁρισμοί are the circles in which, as it appears to the eye, the heavenly bodies move across the sky;

they are firmly outlined and delimited, hence ὁρισμοί. The paths are different for the individual heavenly bodies; different for the sun and the moon, for Orion and for the Big Dipper (Ursa Major). On the whole reference to the beautiful, well-ordered heavenly world, see also Cicero, *Nat. d.* II 101: *restat ultimus et a domiciliis nostris altissimus omnia cingens et coërcens caeli complexus, qui idem aether vocatur, extrema ora et determinatio mundi, in quo cum admirabilitate maxima igneae formae cursus ordinatos* (= τοὺς ἐπιτεταγμένους αὐτοῖς ὁρισμούς) *definiunt* (then *sol* follows in 102, *luna* and *stellae, quas vagas dicimus* in 103, *stellarum inerrantium maxima multitudo* in 104); see also the remarks about the heavenly bodies in *Nat. d.* II 47–57, then Cicero, *Somnium Scipionis* 15; (Aristotle) *De mundo* 6.

20:4–5 From here on, the contemplation descends from the heavenly regions to the sublunar regions. Earth and the abyss in their fixed order are presented in vv. 4–8. Although the cosmos of the Greeks confronts us here in decisive ways, and the religious mood of the joyful trust in the all-regulating and determining effectiveness of God continues to resonate, mythology and the relation to the OT now occupy a broader space (cf. 20:5, 6).

20:4 The earth is the mainland, and as v. 8 demonstrates, the well-known οἰκουμένη determines the borders of the ocean. For the joyful contemplation of the colorful earth that nourishes men and animals, see the Stoic theodicy in Cicero, *Nat. d.* II 98: *Ac principio terra universa cernatur . . . vestita floribus, herbis, arboribus, frugibus, quorum omnium incredibilis multitudo insatiabili varietate distinguitur*; see further in 120f and *De mundo* 3 and 5. The form θήρ used here is noteworthy since already in Attic prose as well as further into Hellenism θηρίον is the dominant form. The θῆρες are the quadrupeds, especially the larger wild ones, whereas the "other animals" of the earth are the crawling and flying creatures. μὴ διχοστατοῦσα: without hesitation, which fits well with the remarks in 1 Clem. 20; within the broader context of the whole letter, however, the actual meaning of the word also fits well: διχοστατεῖν means "to fight."

20:5 The contemplation moves from the fruit bearing surface of the earth, lying in the light of the sun, to the spaces below the earth. There, in the underworld, is the place of the dead and in particular the place of punishment for the great sinners. Here we are no longer in the Stoic cosmology but in the popular Hades mythology, in which eastern ideas of Sheol merge together with Greek images of Tartarus. The fact that we are dealing especially with a Jewish-Christian tradition is already seen by the use of the word ἄβυσσος, which when used as the substantive ἡ ἄβυσσος for the abyss of the world (Gen 1:1) or the depths of Hades occurs first in the LXX and almost always as a translation of תְּהוֹם. The plural form of the word occurs frequently in the LXX. See for example Deut 8:7; Ps 32:7; 76:17; Prov 3:20;

Dan 3:55 (LXX and Theodotion); the corresponding Greek mythological and cosmological expression is βυθός. The reading κρίματα which is unanimously attested by tradition should be maintained; κλίματα is a very nice but unnecessary improvement. κρίματα can mean "regulations, statues," and that would fit the context here quite nicely: already at the end of the Epic of Gilgamesh, Tablet XII, the hero asks his dead friend about the "statutes of the earth" (i.e., the laws of the underworld) and receives information about the various lots of the dead and what causes the differences (Greßmann et al., *Altorientalische Texte*, 61). The otherwise documented meaning of κρίματα, however, corresponds better to the translation "courts, judgments." Already after the death of everyone a preliminary judgment is made over his soul; see also in 1 Clem. 5:4, 7; further at 1 Clem. 50:3, and then in detail in 1 En. 22; 4 Esd 7:75–99. Serious punishments are imposed on particular evildoers immediately after death or after their fall into hell: Clement must have known the old stories of Ixion, Sisyphus, and Tantalus; the Jewish apocalyptic tradition reported the bondage and torment of Satan and his helper angels, who had been pushed in the underworld (1 En. 10f; 14; 21); and it is also possible that the Orphic-Pythagorean conceptions of hell were known to Clement, as the author of the Apocalypse of Peter also adopted them. — If we wish to divide the expressions in our passage, then the mysterious courts of the abyss would mean the condemnation of Satan and his helpers, while the unspeakable judgments of the world of the dead must have in mind the verdicts for the various custodies of the souls in the places of the deceased.

20:6–8 The structure of the earth element, the solid land, in 20:4–5[6] is followed by the water element, the sea and the *oceanos*. The Old Testament influence can be seen in the explicit citation from Job 38:11. It can be seen further in the phrase συσταθὲν εἰς τὰς συναγωγάς; see Gen 1:9: συναθήτω τὸ ὕδωρ τὸ ὑποκάτω τοῦ οὐρανοῦ εἰς συναγωγὴν μίαν . . . καὶ συνήχθη τὸ ὕδωρ τὸ ὑποκάτω τοῦ οὐρανοῦ εἰς τὰς συναγωγὰς αὐτῶν. Job 38:10 also mentions the bars laid before the sea: ἐθέμην δὲ αὐτῇ ὅρια, περιθεὶς κλεῖθρα καὶ πύλας. Note the echo of the Old Testament myth that runs through the passage: In primeval times, God tamed and enclosed the sea; see the passages in Gunkel, *Schöpfung*, 91ff.

20:8 Here, the Greek view, and indeed that of science, comes to the fore again and pushes back that of the OT view. ἀπέραντος should be read according to AHLC Clem. Al., Dion. Al., and Didymus against the reading ἀπέρατος according to S Origen. ἀπέραντος means "unending." ἀπέρατος means "impenetrable, not to be overstepped." ἀπέρατος of course also fits

6. TN: Knopf's text originally read in 4:4, 5, which cannot be correct because 1 Clem. 4:4, 5 speaks of Cain and Abel.

quite well in the context. Both words are very closely related in derivation and in meaning. For ἀπέραντος ἀνθρώποις does not in itself mean "unending" but only "for the people without end," and comes very close to the sense of ἀπέρατος. The ring of the *oceanos* lies around the οἰκουμένη. Even in the Roman Empire it was firmly believed that the Western Sea as well as the North Sea would become impenetrable at a certain distance from the coast; see Friedländer, *Sittengeschichte*, 2:100f; Ukert, *Geographie*, 3.1:85; Peschel, *Erdkunde*, 22. In contrast, Greek science says soberly and calmly, based on experience that the Atlantic Sea is navigable and those who tried it are only turned around ὑπὸ ἀπορίας καὶ ἐρημίας (Strabo, *Geogr.* I 1.8 [p. 5 Cas.]), and that if the size of the Atlantic Sea did not prevent it (εἰ μὴ τὸ μέγεθος τοῦ Ἀτλαντικοῦ πελάγους ἐκώλθε, cf. our ἀνθρώποις ἀπέραντος!), we could sail from Spain on the same parallel circle to India (Eratosthenes in Strabo, *Geogr.* I 4.6 [p. 64 Cas.)]; from the west of the οἰκουμένη, one would have to sail with the east wind, reach India after a distance of 70,000 stadia (Posidonius in Strabo, *Geogr.* II 3.6 [p. 102 Cas.]). — If one goes beyond the *oceanos*, they arrive at new worlds (continents) according to some ancient traditions. Clement unhesitatingly joins these traditions, which were very much alive in the Hellenistic period and which mostly presuppose the spherical shape of the earth. Plato already tells of the island of Atlantis in an old myth traced back to Solon (*Timaeus* p. 21A–25D; *Cratylus* p. 108E–121C). Later authors speak much more clearly and purely scientifically; compare not as much Aristotle, *De caelo* II 14 [p. 298] and *Mete.* II 5 [p. 362] on the western route to India as primarily Cicero, *Rep.* VI; *Somn. Scip.* 20 (21): *cernis autem eandem terram quasi quibusdam redimitam et circumdatam cingulis* (the five zones are meant) *e quibus duos maxime inter se diversos et caeli verticibus ipsis ex utraque parte subnixos obriguisse pruina vides, medium autem illum et maximum solis ardore torrere. Duo sunt habitabiles, quorum australis ille, in quo qui insistunt, adversa vobis urgent vestigia, nihil ad vestrum genus; hic autem alter subiectus aquiloni, quem incolitis, cerne quam tenui vos parte contingat. omnis enim terra, quae colitur a vobis . . . parva quaedam insula est circumfusa illo mari, quod Atlanticum, quod magnum, quem Oceanum appellatis in terris, qui tamen tanto nomine quam sit parvus, vides.* Aristotle, *De mundo* 3: τὴν μὲν οὖν οἰκουμένην ὁ πολὺς λόγος εἴς τε νήσους καὶ ἠπείρους διεῖλεν, ἀγνοῶν ὅτι καὶ ἡ σύμπασα μία νῆσός ἐστιν, ὑπὸ τῆς Ἀτλαντικῆς καλουμένης θαλάσσης περιρρεομένην. πολλὰς δὲ καὶ ἄλλας εἰκὸς τῆσδε ἀντιπόρθμους (= located opposite the sea) ἄπωθεν κεῖσθαι, τὰς μὲν μείζους αὐτῆς τὰς τὲ ἐλάττους, ἡμῖν δὲ πάσας πλὴν τῆσδε ἀοράτους. Eratosthenes in Strabo, *Geogr.* I 4.6 [p. 65]): ἐνδέχεται δὲ ἐν τῇ αὐτῇ εὐκράτῳ ζώνῃ καὶ δύο οἰκουμένας εἶναι ἢ καὶ πλείους, καὶ μάλιστα ἐγγὺς τοῦ δι᾽ Ἀθηνῶν κύκλου (latitudinal circle) τοῦ διὰ τοῦ Ἀτλαντικοῦ πελάγους γραφομένου. On the testimonies of the ancients, see von Humboldt, *Untersuchungen*, 119–87. Here, too, Clement is dependent upon ancient traditions. Later Church Fathers (Tertullian, *Pall.* 2; *Herm.* 25 is the first for us) reject the acceptance of worlds beyond the *oceanos*, and in this passage L reads simply *et omnis orbis terrarum* instead of οἱ μετ᾽ αὐτὸν κόσμοι. Photius (*Lex.* 126) expressly rebukes Clement for accepting the notion of worlds beyond the *oceanos*.

20:9–10 This is followed by the last section in vv. 9–10, which, with the exception of the last part of v. 10 (τά τε ἐλάχιστα κτλ.), is essentially about the order of the element of the air. Although this element, the ἀήρ, is not itself named, the seasons of the year, the wind, and the fountains belong in its domain. A very close parallel to vv. 9f can be found in Cicero, *Nat. d.* II 101: *exin mari finitumus aër die et nocte distinguitur, isque tum fusus et extenuatus sublime fertur, tum autem concretus in nubes cogitur umoremque colligens terram auget imbribus, tum effluens huc et illuc ventos efficit; idem annuas frigorum et calorum facit varietates* (the springs and rivers that are fed by the rain are of course already listed within the realm of the *terra* in II 98); see further in Firmicus Maternus Mathesis V, *Praef.* 3: *qui omnem operis tui substantiam salutaribus ventorum flatibus vegetas, qui fontium ac fluviorum undas . . . profundis, qui varietatem temporum certis dierum cursibus reddis . . . .* See also VII 1.2: *qui terram . . . rigat fontibus, qui ventorum flatus . . . facit . . . variari*, whereby clearly, as the progress shows, the element of the air and its effect is considered. Rain and the winds together with other phenomena of the air belong to the realm of the ἀήρ (cf. also *De mundo* 2). — Thus, even according to its arrangement, 1 Clem. 20 betrays a Stoic cosmology perfectly clearly: heaven and stars, that is, fire (or aether, the heavenly fire) precedes. The three spheres of the earthly world follow: the solid earth, the innermost and deepest element, is mentioned first; next the water that covers the earth is mentioned; finally, the third element is mentioned, the kingdom of the air. To mention only two relevant passages, see Cicero, *Nat. d.* II 98–104 which describes in turn *terra, mare, aer, caelum* (= *aether*) or *De mundo* 2f (where admittedly the five, not the older four, elements are distinguished): οὐρανός + ἄστρα (= αἰθήρ); the earthly fire, the φλογώδης οὐσία of lightning, meteors, etc.; air; earth; sea. On the cosmology and the four or five elements of the Stoics, see also Zeller, *Philosophie*, 3rd ed., 179ff; 4th ed., 182ff.

20:9 On the seldom used μεταπαραδιδόναι, here intransitive, see Adamantius, *Dialog* 26: μεταπαραδιδοὺς τῷ δεσπότῃ τοὺς μαθητάς and μεταπαραδοθῆναι.

20:10 On ἀνέμων σταθμοί, see Job 28:25: ἐποίησεν ἀνέμων σταθμόν ὕδατος μέτρα, where σταθμός means the weight and the heaviness of the wind; see for example 4 Esd 4:5: "Now, weigh for me the weight of the fire or measure the weight of the wind." However, this meaning cannot be applied here. The ambiguous σταθμός must mean the established order, perhaps the fixed quarters, the stations. ἀέναοι πηγαί: In the Mediterranean countries, springs, especially those that do not fail even in hot weather, are valued above all and can be seen as forceful proof of the divine πρόνοια; see the nice, literal parallels in Cicero, *Nat. d.* II 98 in the description of the *terra*: *adde huc fontium gelidas perennitates* and Firmicus Maternus Mathesis VII 1.2: *qui terram perennibus rigat fontibus*; also *De mundo* 3 highlights the springs. The use of ὑγείαν seems to have the effect of healing springs in mind. On the phrase πρὸς ζωῆς, see Acts 27:34; πρός with the genitive (= on the side of, in the interest of) is literary Greek. Blaß-Debruner, *Grammatik*, §240 refers to Thucydides III 59.1: οὐ πρὸς τῆς ὑμετέρας δόξης τάδε. The image of the breasts is pleasant and straightforward and has certainly not been prompted by Jer 18:14 (LXX): μὴ ἐκλείψουσιν ἀπὸ πέτρας μαστοί. The final clause is an addendum. The animals have nothing to do with the kingdom of the air, unless only flying creatures are in view; see Cicero, *Nat. d.* II 101, speaking of the air: *idemque et volatus alitum sustinet.* The fact that order in the animal world is referred to at all is certainly not so much an imitation of the Old Testament model (e.g., Jer 8:7 or Job 38:39—39:30) as it is a borrowing from Stoic theodicy; see the order in the animal kingdom in Cicero, *Nat. d.* 120–27. The συνελεύσεις refer perhaps to the orderly, unanimous gathering of small animals such as ants and bees, to the dances of mosquitoes. If so, the letter indirectly holds up these little creatures to the Corinthians as models of peace and unity, as Walther does to the Germans in a similar way: "So woe unto thee, German tongue, how stand thy orders! That now the mosquito has its king and that your honor thus perishes."[7] But perhaps συνέλευσις should be understood as copulation, which the word can denote quite well.

20:11 concludes the preceding (εἰρήνη καὶ ὁμόνοια, προσέταξεν) and at the same time (εὐεργετῶν) ties in with 19:2f and prepares for 21:1 (εὐεργεσίαι); on the dual outlook, see above in the excursus. The use of δημιουργός as an epithet for God occurs also in 26:1; 33:2; 35:3; 59:2. In the New Testament, it only occurs in Heb 11:10. In the LXX, it does not appear at all. In the second century, the apologists use the epithet and the related verb more frequently (Goodspeed, *Index apologeticus*, s.v.; cf. also Diogn. 8:7). Philo and Josephus use the term frequently. The epithet δημιουργός is genuinely Greek, especially

---

7. TN: The original medieval German reads: "sô wê dir, tiuschiu zunge, wie stêt dîn ordenunge! daz nû diu mugge ir kunec hât, und daz dîn êre alsô zergât." My thanks to Friederike Kunath for providing the following contemporary German rendering: "So weh dir, deutsche Zunge, wie stehen deine Ordnungen! Dass nun die Mücke ihren König hat und dass deine Ehre so vergeht."

Platonic: in Timaeus, God, the world builder, is often called δημιουργός (cf. Plato, *Timaeus* p. 28A, 29A, 31A, etc.; *Republic* VII p. 530A; cf. also Xenophon, *Mem.* I 4.7, 9. In the history of Greek religion, including philosophy, word and concept have great significance. On δεσπότης τῶν ἁπάντων, see 1 Clem. 8:2. What God's benefits are to believers in particular are enumerated in 1 Clem. 35:2f, but 1 Clem. 23–27 also discusses in detail one of his greatest gifts, the resurrection.

20:12 The doxology is to Christ (L reads *per quem deo et patri sit honor* etc. is alone in its reading); see 1 Clem. 50:7. The end of the liturgically based construction has prompted the doxology. A deeper break does not exist. On doxologies, which in no way denote the ends of sections in the letter, see 1 Clem. 32:4; 38:4; 43:6; 45:7f; 50:7; 58:2; 61:3; 64; 65:2.

First Clement 21 mainly features paraenesis and shows what peace, unity, and subordination in the church must look like.

21:1 On εὐεργεσίαι, see 20:11 and 19:2. ἀξίως πολιτεύεσθαι in Phil 1:27; on πολιτεύεσθαι, see 1 Clem. 3:4. — τὰ καλὰ καὶ εὐάρεστα ἐνώπιον αὐτοῦ is according to LXX usage (cf. Deut 12:25, 28; 13:18; 21:9; cf. also Ps 114:9 as well as Heb 13:21).

21:2 See 21:9. The citation is loosely cited from Prov 20:21: φῶς κυρίου πνοὴ ἀνθρώπων, ὃς ἐρευνᾷ ταμεῖα κοιλίας.

21:3 ἐγγύς does not depend on the timeliness of the *parousia*, like (23:5) and Phil 4:5, but like 1 Clem. 27:3; Ign. *Eph.* 15:3; Ps 33:19; et al.

21:4 λειποτακτεῖν is a military image, like 28:2 and especially 37:2f (cf. the discussion there); an exact parallel is in Ign. *Pol.* 6:2: μή τις ὑμῶν δεσέρτωρ εὑρεθῇ, only that Ignatius uses the Latin loan word. On warriordom in the church, see von Harnack, *Militia*, ch. 1.

21:5 is a clear reference to the leaders of the controversy: They are accused of folly and arrogance, as are the schismatics and heretics of all times; the third usual major accusation, lack of love, is missing here, but comes later in 49–51. On folly and arrogance, see also 1 Clem. 39:1.

21:6 In vv. 4 and 5, the beginning to the household code (*Haustafel*) is already given, which is clearly shown in vv. 6–8, and is also delimited in external form: (God), the Lord Jesus, the church officials, the old and the young, the women and children are listed. Regarding the household codes (*Haustafeln*), see the excursus at Col 4:1 in Bisping, *Epheser, Philipper und Kolosser* and at Did. 4:9–11; see also above at 1 Clem. 1:3. — Clement of Alexandria, *Strom.* 4.107.8f (p. 611f) introduces the household code (*Haustafel*) in a slightly different way: τὸν κύριον Ἰησοῦν λέγω . . . οὗ τὸ αἷμα ὑπὲρ ἡμῶν ἡγιάσθη. ἐντραπῶμεν οὖν τοὺς προηγουμένους ἡμῶν καὶ αἰδεσθῶμεν, τοὺς πρεσβυτέρους τιμήσωμεν, τοὺς νέος παιδεύσωμεν κτλ. — On the blood of Jesus and its significance for salvation, see 7:4; 12:7. The προηγούμενοι are the ἡγούμενοι of 1:3; see the discussion there. The πρεσβύτεροι and the νέοι are to be understood as in 1:3; see also 3:3. On the exhortation for the νέοι, see Prov 15:33: φόβος θεοῦ παιδεία and Sir 1:27: παιδεία φόβος κυρίου.

21:7 The generally broad ἀγαθόν of v. 6 is unfolded in four parts. What is described here is not how the women should behave in the house, but how they should behave in the community. In the schism within the community, women could do considerable harm by passionate partisanship, gossiping, and scheming. This should be resisted. On ἀξιαγάπητος, see 1:1. ἁγνεία is, of course, not merely physical chastity, but the respectable, demure disposition in general, relatable to σωφροσύνη (1 Clem. 64). On the silence of women, see 1 Cor 14:34f and 1 Tim 2:11. The acts of love carried out by the women in the church are manifold; see for example 1 Tim 5:10 and in later times Tertullian, *Ux.* II 4, which lists: she visits the brethren from alley to alley, even in strange, poor huts, sneaks into the prison to kiss the chains of the martyrs, kisses the brethren, washes the feet of the saints, gives food and drink, hospitably receives foreign brethren, gives generously from storehouse and cellar.

21:8 On παιδεία ἐν Χριστῷ (ἐν Χριστῷ abraded = Christian), see above παιδεία τοῦ φόβου τοῦ θεοῦ; also φόβος τοῦ θεοῦ will be mentioned shortly afterward. In τοὺς ἐν αὐτῷ ἀναστρεφομένους the phrase ἐν αὐτῷ probably means ἐν θεῷ and not ἐν τῷ φόβῳ τοῦ θεοῦ, for shortly thereafter in v. 9, God is the subject.

21:9 See above at v. 2. On the expression, see Heb 4:12: κριτκὸς ἐνθυμήσεων καὶ ἐννοιῶν καρδίας. On πνοή, see Prov 20:21 (mentioned above at v. 2) and on the statement, see Gen 2:7: ἐνεφύσησεν εἰς τὸ πρόσωπον αὐτοῦ πνοὴν ζωῆς, Prov 24:12: ὁ πλάσας πνοὴν πᾶσιν αὐτὸς οἶδεν πάντα, Ps 103:29: ἀντανελεῖς τὸ πνεῦμα αὐτῶν καὶ ἐκλείψουσιν, among others (on the divine spirit of life in man, according to the Old Testament conception, see also Volz, *Der Geist Gottes*, 49–51). But as certainly as the formulation of thought is conditioned upon the Old Testament, so also must the Stoic parallel be pointed out: God is *pneuma*, the rational breath which pervades everything; the soul of man relates to the divine world-soul as the part to the whole. The soul of man stands, by its reasonableness, in a special and close relationship to God, and it returns to the primordial breath and the primordial fire of the Godhead. Athenagoras, *Leg.* 6.4: οἱ . . . ἀπὸ τῆς Στοᾶς . . . ἕνα νομίζουσι τὸν θεόν . . . τὸ δὲ πνεῦμα αὐτοῦ διήκει δι' ὅλου τοῦ κόσμου . . . Ζεὺς μὲν κατὰ τὸ ζέον τῆς ὕλης ὀνομαζόμενος (cf. Zeller, *Philosophie*, 3rd ed., 3:138ff, 194ff; 4th ed., 141ff; 197ff). On the future ἀνελεῖ, see Radermacher, *Grammatik*, 77; Blaß-Debrunner, *Grammatik*, §74.3.

First Clement 22 contains a lengthy quotation from the OT, which confirms the paraenesis of what preceded, but also hints at the thoughts of the whole section. The quotation comes from Ps 33:12–18 and Ps 31:10, and is reproduced almost verbatim. The two quotations are separated from each other in HS since v. 8 is introduced with εἶτα. After ἐρύσατο αὐτόν in v. 7, S also reads πολλαὶ αἱ θλίψεις τοῦ δικαίου καὶ ἐκ πασῶν αὐτῶν ῥύσεται αὐτὸν ὁ κύριος, which comes from Ps 33:20 (Lightfoot and Funk follow S, though hardly correctly against AHLCC[1]).

22:1–8 On the pre-existent Christ, see also 16:2. The quote fits so well here because it contains demands and promises: but the preceding has pointed to the benefactions and commands of God; see the relationships between the following: φόβος κυρίου in v. 1 with 21:6, 8; spiritualized and eschatologically conceived in v. 2 with 20:11; sins of the tongue and cunning in v. 3 with 21:7; v. 4 with 21:6, at the end; εἰρήνη in v. 5 with 19:2; 20; 21:4–8; v. 6 with 21:2, 9; ἔλεος in v. 8 with the strong emphasis on the benefactions of God in the preceding.

F. Parousia and Resurrection (23:1—27:7)

Translation

23:1 The all-merciful and benevolent Father has compassion on those who fear him, and he bestows his grace gently and kindly on those who draw near to him with a simple heart. ² Let us have no doubts about it, and may our souls not waver about his exuberant and glorious gifts. ³ Let the Scripture be far from us that says, "Unhappy are those who doubt, those who are ambivalent in their souls and say, 'We have already heard this in the days of our fathers, and behold, we have grown old and none of this has happened to us.' ⁴ You fools, compare yourselves to a tree. Look at the vine. First, it drops its leaves, then a sapling emerges, then a leaf, then a flower, and then an unripe grape, and finally the ripe grape appears." You see, the fruit of the tree becomes ripe in such a short period of time. ⁵ Truly, swiftly, and suddenly his plan will be accomplished since the Scriptures testify, "He will come quickly and not hesitate, and suddenly the Lord will come to his temple and the Holy One whom you await."

24:1 Let us consider, beloved, how the Lord continually shows us the future resurrection, the firstfruits of which he made the Lord Jesus Christ by raising him from the dead. ² Let us look at the resurrection that happens regularly. ³ Day and night show us the resurrection: night goes to rest, and day breaks in, day disappears, and night arrives.

⁴ Let us consider the fruits: how and in what way does the sowing take place? ⁵ "The sower went out" and threw each of the seeds on the earth. They fall on the field, dry and naked, rotten; and then, after rotting, the Lord resurrects them, and then one becomes many and they bring forth fruit.

²⁵:¹ Let us consider the miraculous sign that happens in the east, in the regions of Arabia. ² There is a bird (there) called the phoenix. It is the only one of its kind and lives five hundred years. But when the end of its life draws near, and it has to die, it makes a coffin out of incense and myrrh and other spices, and when the time of its life is up it sits down and dies. ³ While its flesh decays, a worm emerges which feeds on the putrefactive sap of the deceased animal and it grows wings. Then, when it is stronger, it takes the coffin in which the bones of the earlier bird are contained and flies with it from Arabia to Egypt, to the city called Heliopolis. ⁴ And in the light of day, in front of everyone, it flies to the altar of Helios and lays down its burden upon it, and then flies back again. ⁵ Then the priests look at the chronological tables and find that five-hundred years had passed.

²⁶:¹ Should we then think it is a great and marvelous matter that the creator of the universe will raise those who have served him in a holy manner and with the confidence of good faith, when he makes clear to us his magnificent promise even in the form of a bird? ² For it says somewhere, "You will raise me up, and I will praise you" and, "I lay down and slept, I woke up because you are with me." ³ And again Job says, "And you will raise up this flesh of mine, which endured all this."

²⁷:¹ In this hope, then, may our souls cling to him who is reliable in his promises and righteous in his judgments. ² He who has forbidden lying will all the less lie himself. Because with God nothing is impossible except for lying. ³ So may belief in him be kindled in us, and let us consider that all things are near to him. ⁴ By one word from his majesty he founded the universe and with one word he can destroy it again. ⁵ "Who will say to him, 'What have you done?' or who will withstand his mighty strength. For when he wishes and how he wishes, he will do all things, and nothing of what he has established will pass away." ⁶ All things are before his face, and nothing is hidden from his counsel, ⁷ since "the heavens declare the glory of God and the firmament proclaims the work of his hands. One day speaks to the other and one night proclaims knowledge to the other. And there is no speech or words whose voices cannot be heard."

Textual Notes

The resurrection occupies a special place among the blessings of God toward believers (1 Clem. 23:1—27:7). It is important to hold on to it and not doubt it. It is secured by a series of evidences.

It is not easy to determine why the resurrection is treated so broadly in this context. There is no suggestion that the opponents in Corinth objected to the traditional eschatology. But if the author, as the letter also says elsewhere, feels obligated to explain the faith and life of the true Christian (62:2), he can of course deal with this important part of the faith, the Christian hope, in detail. In addition, there are two factors: (1) in the post-apostolic period, we see in many passages the traditional early Christian eschatology exposed to doubts, which arose against it within the congregations, because the *parousia* had not yet taken place, because the resurrection of the dead and the kingdom of God contradicted Greek sensibilities, and because the *gnosis* made an impression with its criticism; (2) in 1 Corinthians Paul already had to correct the doubts of the same church about πῶς ἐγείρονται οἱ νεκροί; however 1 Corinthians is used extensively in 1 Clem. and there are similarities between 1 Cor 15 and our section here. How the church leaders of the second and third generation repeatedly inculcate the early Christian hope, the nearness of the end, can be seen well in passages like Rev 1:1; 22:10, 12, 20; 1 Pet 4:7; 1 John 2:18; Ign. *Eph.* 11:1; Barn. 4; Hermas, *Vis.* III 8.9; *Sim.* X 4.4.

23:1 The transition ties in well with the preceding; see οἰκτίρμων and σπλάγχνα with ἔλεος in 22:8 and οἰκτιρμοί in 20:11; εὐεργετικός with 21:1; 20:11; 19:2f; the thought of special graces for the believers with 20:11; προσέρχεσθαι with προσφεύγειν in 20:11; and with the invitation in 22:1f.

23:2 only suggests the topic of the section, which then comes into view more clearly in v. 3, even if the word ἀνάστασις is not mentioned until 24:1. Verse 2 and then 27:1 are the only paraenetic statements in the whole section, everything else is evidence and citation. — ἰνδάλλεσθαι "appear to oneself, become visible, show oneself," must have a strongly modified meaning here. L translates with *diffidat*, and this meaning, which Bryennios had assumed in his explanation, fits best here. This meaning is perhaps conveyed by ἰνδάλλεσθαι = "imagine, mistakenly so," and this meaning is actually proven in Dio Chrysostom, *Orat.* XII 53 (p. 209M): πρότερον μὲν γὰρ ἅτε οὐδὲν σαφὲς εἰδότες ἄλλην ἄλλος ἀνεπλάττομεν ἰδέαν, πᾶν τὸ θνητὸν κατὰ τὴν ἑαυτοῦ δύναμιν καὶ φύσιν ἰνδαλλόμενοι καὶ ὀνειρώττοντες, Sextus, *Math.* XI 122: ὁ τὸν πλοῦτον μέγιστον ἀγαθὸν ἰνδαλλόμενος, Clement of Alexandria, *Protr.* X 103.2 (p. 81): μηδὲ χρυσὸν ἢ λίθον ἢ δένδρον ἢ πρᾶξιν ἢ πάθος ἢ νόσον ἢ φόβον ἰνδάλλεσθαι ὡς θεόν (as well as other passages found in Lightfoot).

23:3f The origin of the citation cannot be determined. It appears again with a few deviations and with the expansion of a clause (i.e., independent of 1 Clem) in 2 Clem. 11:2–4 and is introduced there as follows: λέγει γὰρ καὶ ὁ προφητικὸς λόγος. It is an apocryphal book that went under the flag of the Old Testament and was probably of Jewish origin. Related to the subject matter of the image, though different in its application, is Epictetus, *Diatr.* I 14.3: πόθεν γὰρ οὕτως τεταγμένως καθάπερ ἐκ προστάγματος τοῦ θεοῦ, ὅταν ἐκεῖνος εἴπῃ τοῖς φυτοῖς ἀνθεῖν, ἀνθεῖ, ὅταν εἴπῃ βλαστάνειν, βλαστάνει, ὅταν ἐκφέρειν τὸν καρπόν, ἐκφέρει, ὅταν πεπαίνειν, πεπαίνει, ὅταν πάλιν ἀποβάλλειν, ἀποβάλλει, καὶ φυλλορροεῖν, φυλλοροεῖ, καὶ αὐτὰ εἰς αὑτὰ συνειλούμενα ἐφ᾽ ἡσυχίας μένειν καὶ ἀναπαύεσθαι μένει καὶ ἀναπαύεται; and I 15.7f: οὐδὲν ... τῶν μεγάλων ἄφνω γίνεται, ὅπου γε οὐδ᾽ ὁ βότρυς οὐδὲ σῦκον. ἄν μοι νῦν λέγῃς ὅτι θέλω σῦκον, ἀποκρινοῦμαί σοι ὅτι χρόνου δεῖ. ἄφες ἀνθήσῃ πρῶτον, εἶτα προβάλῃ τὸν καρπόν, εἶτα πεπανθῇ· εἶτα συκῆς μὲν καρπὸς ἄφνω καὶ μιᾷ ὥρᾳ οὐ τελειοῦται, γνώμης δ᾽ ἀνθρώπου καρπὸν θέλεις οὕτω δι᾽ ὀλίγου καὶ εὐκόλως κτήσασθαι; μηδ᾽ οὖν, ἐγώ σοι λέγω, προσδόκα. — πατέρων = at the time of our fathers, when our fathers were still alive. — On ἐν καιρῷ ὀλίγῳ, see ταχύ, ἐξαίφνης in v. 5. — οὐ χρονιεῖ: here it is strongly emphasized that the parousia will come soon; from 1 Clem. 24 on, it is about the resurrection, something related and yet different.

23:5 The citation is composed of Isa 13:22: ταχὺ ἔρχεται καὶ οὐ χρονιεῖ and Mal 3:1: καὶ ἐξαίφνης ἥξει εἰς τὸν ναὸν αὐτοῦ κύριος ὃν ὑμεῖς ζητεῖτε καὶ ὁ ἄγγελος τῆς διαθήκης, ὃν ὑμεῖς θέλετε. The "Lord" and the "Holy One" is, of course, Christ.

First Clement 24 deals with the resurrection of the body in more detail than the imminence and certainty of the second coming. First Clement is the first author since Paul to attempt to provide a rational justification of this belief. The apologists follow thereafter: Justin (?), *De resurrectione*; Athenagoras, *De resurrectione*; Tertullian, *De resurrectione carnis* (1 Clem. 24f is used in chs. 12f); also, occasional remarks are made by apologists such as Theophilus, *Autol.* I 13 (where 1 Clement seems to have been used), Tertullian, *Apol.* 48; Minucius Felix, *Oct.* 34. First Clement brings two proofs of the resurrection from the natural order.

24:1 On ἀπαρχή, see 1 Cor 15:20, 23; here, 1 Clem. shows evidence of contact with 1 Corinthians for the first time. Other points of contact will follow. On the thought, see also the πρωτότοκος (ἐν νεκρῶν) in Rom 8:29; Col 1:18; Rev 1:5.

24:2 κατὰ καιρόν: at the right time, in its time.

24:3 A very good, detailed paraphrase of thought can be found in Tertullian, *Res.* 12: *Dies moritur in noctem et tenebris usquequaque sepelitur. funestatur mundi honor, omnis substantia denigratur. sordent, silent, stupent cuncta, ubique iustitium est, quies rerum. ita lux amissa lugetur. et tamen rursus cum suo cultu, cum dote, cum sole, eadem et integra et tota universo orbi revivescit, interficiens mortem suam, noctem, recindens sepulturam suam, tenebras, heres sibimet existens, donec et nox reviviscat cum suo et illa suggestu. reaccenduntur et stellarum radii, quos matutina succensio extinxerat, reducuntur et siderum absentiae, quas temporalis distinctio exemerat; reornantur et specula lunae, quae menstruus numerus adtriverat.* Very briefly in Theophilus, *Autol.* I 13: κατανόησον τὴν τῶν καιρῶν καὶ ἡμερῶν καὶ νυκτῶν τελευτήν, πῶς καὶ αὐτὰ τελευτᾷ καὶ ἀνίσταται.

24:4f The second image is based on 1 Cor 15:35–38, but in the version in 1 Clem., there are also echoes of the parable of the sower; see especially Mark 4:3, 8. On the entire image, see also John 12:24, as well as Theophilus, *Autol.* I 13: τί δὲ καὶ οὐχὶ ἡ τῶν σπερμάτων καὶ καρπῶν γινομένη ἐξανάστασις καὶ τοῦτο εἰς τὴν χρῆσιν τῶν ἀνθρώπων; εἰ γὰρ τύχοι εἰπεῖν, κόκκος σίτου ἢ τῶν λοιπῶν σπερμάτων ἐπὰν βληθῇ εἰς τὴν γῆν, πρῶτον ἀποθνήσκει καὶ λύεται, εἶτα ἐγείρεται καὶ γίνεται στάχυς, 3 Cor 28 (von Harnack, *Apokrypha*): *neque enim, viri Corinthii, sciunt trilici semina sicut aliorum seminum quoniam nuda mittuntur in terra et simul corrupta deorsum surgunt in voluntate dei corporata et vestita*, and on the Jewish origin of the image, see the rabbinic parallels on this passage in Hennecke, *Handbuch*, 393).

24:4 On λάβωμεν, see 1 Clem. 37:5, also 5:1; 9:3. σπόρος = sowing, which is the meaning the word has in the first place. On γυμνά, see 1 Cor 15:37.

First Clement 25 contains the third evidence of the resurrection: the example of the phoenix.

The myth of the phoenix, originating from Egypt, was known early on in antiquity. Hesiod already mentions the long lifespan of the miraculous bird, but otherwise mentions nothing else within the story: the crow lives nine human generations, the deer lives four times as long as the crow, the raven three times as long as the deer, the phoenix nine times as long as the raven (Rzach, *Carmina*, frag. 171; the fragment obtained from Plutarch, *Def. orac.* 11, p. 415c.). But Herodotus already completes the narrative in a few main respects in *Hist.* II 73: ἔστι δὲ καὶ ἄλλος ὄρνις ἱρός, τῷ οὔνομα φοῖνιξ. ἐγὼ μέν μιν οὐκ εἶδον εἰ μὴ ὅσον γραφῇ (in pictures). καὶ γὰρ δὴ καὶ σπάνιος ἐπιφοιτᾷ σφι δι᾽ ἐτέων, ὡς Ἡλιοπολῖται λέγουσι, πεντακοσίων. φοιτᾶν δὲ τότε φασὶ ἐπεάν οἱ ἀποθάνῃ ὁ πατήρ. ἔστι δε, εἰ τῇ γραφῇ παρόμοιος, τοσόσδε καὶ τοιόσδε· τὰ μὲν αὐτοῦ χρυσιόκομα τῶν πτερῶν τὰ δὲ ἐρυθρά. ἐς τὰ μάλιστα αἰετῷ περιήγησιν ὁμοιότατος καὶ τὸ μέγαθος. τοῦτον δὲ λέγουσι μηχανᾶσθαι τάδε, ἐμοὶ μὲν οὐ πιστὰ λέγοντες, ἐξ Ἀραβίης ὁρμώμενον ἐς τὸ ἱρὸν τοῦ Ἡλίου κομίζειν τὸν πατέρα ἐν σμύρνῃ ἐμπλάσσοντα καὶ θάπτειν ἐν τοῦ Ἡλίου τῷ ἱρῷ. κομίζειν δὲ οὕτω· πρῶτον τῆς σμύρνης ᾠὸν πλάσσειν ὅσον τε δυνατός

ἐστι φέρειν, μετὰ δὲ πειρᾶσθαι αὐτὸ φορέοντα, ἐπεὰν δὲ ἀποπειρηθῇ, οὕτω δὴ
κοιλήναντα τὸ ᾠὸν τὸν πατέρα ἐς αὐτὸ ἐντιθέναι, σμύρνῃ δὲ ἄλλῃ ἐμπλάσσειν
τοῦτο κατ' ὅ τι τοῦ ᾠοῦ ἐκκοιλήνας ἐνέθηκε τὸν πατέρα, ἐσκειμένου δὲ τοῦ
πατρὸς γίνεσθαι τὠυτὸ βάρος, ἐμπλάσαντα δὲ κομίζειν μιν ἐπ' Αἰγύπτου ἐς
τοῦ Ἡλίου τὸ ἱρόν. ταῦτα μὲν τοῦτον ὄρνιν λέγουσι ποιέειν. From Herodotus to Roman times, for example, there is hardly a fleeting mention of the
phoenix in the literature that has survived, although the story was clearly
known. In the imperial era, the evidence increased, the miraculous birth of
the young bird is mentioned and the story shows features of the character
that 1 Clem. has. Ovid, *Metam.* XV 392–407: *Una est, quae reparet seque
ipsa reseminet, ales: Assyrii phoenica vocant, non fruge neque herbis, sed turis
lacrimis et suco vivit amomi. Haec ubi quinque suae complevit saecula vitae,
Ilicet in ramis tremulaeque cacumine palmae Unguibus et puro nidum sibi
construit ore. Quo simul ac casias et nardi lenis aristas Quassaque cum fulva
substravit cinnama murra Se super imponit finitque in odoribus aevum. Inde
ferunt, totidem qui vivere debeat annos, Corpore de patrio parvum phoenica
renasci. Cum dedit huic aetas vires, onerique ferendo est Ponderibus nidi
ramos levat arboris altae Fertque pius cunasque suas patriumque sepulcrum,
Perque leves auras Hyperionis urbe potitus Ante fores sacras Hyperionis aede
reponit.* The younger contemporary of Ovid, Pomponius Mela, mentions
the phoenix in his geography when describing the borderlands of the Red
Sea and says of it that it will not be conceived and born, *putrescentium
membrorum tabe . . . rursus renascitur* (Pomponius Mela, *De situ orbis* III
8.10). Pliny the Elder in *Nat.* X 2 tells of the phoenix with reference to a
previous author, Manilius, who wrote toward the end of the first cent. BCE:
*neminem exstitisse, qui viderit vescentem: sacrum in Arabia Soli esse, vivere
annis quingentis quadraginta. senescentem casiae turisque surculis constru-
ere nidum, replere odoribus et supermori. ex ossibus deinde et medullis eius
nasci primo seu vermiculum, inde fieri pullum, principioque iusta funera
priori reddere et totum deferre nidum prope Panchaiam in Solis urbem et in
ara ibi deponere.* Pliny also describes the bird: *aquilae narratur magnitu-
dine, auri fulgore circa colla, ceterum purpureus, caeruleam roseis caudam
pennis distinguentibus, cristis fauces captuque plumeo apice honestante.* How
fixed and widespread the story was, especially among the Romans at the
time of 1 Clem., may ultimately be found in Tacitus, *Ann.* VI 34 (28): *Paulo
Fabio L. Vitellio consulibus* (= 34 CE) *post longum saeculorum ambitum
avis phoenix in Aegyptum venit praebuitque materiem doctissimis indigena-
rum et Graecorum multa super eo miraculo disserendi: de quibus congruunt
et plura ambigua sed congnitu non absurda promere libet. sacrum Soli id
animal et ore ac distinctu pinnarum a ceteris avibus diversum consentiunt,
qui forman eius effinxere; de numero annorum varia traduntur: maxime*

volgatum quingentorum spatium; sunt qui adseverent mille quadringentos sexaginta unum interici, prioresque alites Sesoside primum, post Amaside dominantibus, dein Ptolemaeo qui ex Macedonibus tertius regnavit, in civitatem, cui Heliopolis nomen, advolavisse multo ceterarum volucrum comitatu novam faciem mirantium. sed antiquitas quidem obscura: inter Ptolemaeum ac Tiberium minus ducenti quinquaginta anni fuere; unde nonnulli falsum hunc phoenicem neque Arabum e terris credidere nihilque usurpavisse ex his quae vetus memoria firmavit: confecto quippe annorum numero, ubi mors propinquet, suis in terris struere nidum eique vim genitalem adfundere, ex qua fetum oriri; et primam adulto curam sepeliendi patris, neque id temere sed sublato murrae pondere temptatoque per longum iter, ubi par oneri, par meatui sit, subire patrium corpus inque Solis aram perferre atque adolere. haec incerta et fabulosis aucta: ceterum aspici aliquando in Aegypto eam volucrem non ambigitur. The phoenix appeared on Roman imperial coins since Antoninus Pius as a symbol of the *aeternitas*.

A larger number of later Roman and Greek writers mentioned the bird in the second, third, and fourth centuries in shorter or longer descriptions; Martial, *Epigr.* V 7; Artemidor, *Oneirocritica* IV 47; and Philostratus, *Apollon. Tyan.* III 49 are the first to tell of the self-immolation of the old bird. The fable of the phoenix came from the Greeks to the Jews already in the earlier Hellenistic era. Ezekiel the Tragedian, an Alexandrian Jew who probably lived in the second century BCE (on him, see Schürer, *Geschcihte*, 3:373–76) has the following in his drama: the exodus from Egypt gives the description of a miraculous bird that appears at Elim, the glorious camp, and that is clearly described in the manner of the phoenix, without, of course, mentioning its name (Fragment in Eusebius, *Praep. ev.* IX 29.16). — In Job 29:18, the phoenix is found in the word חול according to rabbinic tradition; see Henrichsen, *Phoenicis*, 2:15ff. See also the LXX version of Job 29:18: εἶπα δε· ἡ ἡλικία μου γηράσει ὥσπερ στέλεχος φοίνικος, πολὺν χρόνον βιώσω. In Ps 91:31, the LXX reads: δίκαιος ὡς φοῖνιξ ἀνθήσει, which Tertullian, who to our knowledge is the first, interprets as the phoenix (*Res.* 13). — Of the Christian authors, after 1 Clem., the next to use the story is Tertullian (see above), and thereafter many have followed them. See Origen, *Cels.* IV 98; Apost. Const. V 7; Cyril, *Hieros. Catech.* XVIII 8; Rufin, *Symbol. Apost.* 11 p. 73; Epiph. *Ancor.* 84; among others. There is a poem about the phoenix under the name of Lactantius. Photius (*Lex.* 126) of course rebukes Clement for the example of the phoenix: αἰτιάσαιτο δ᾽ ἄν τις αὐτὸν ἐν ταύταις (namely the letters) ... ὅτι ὡς παναληθεστάτῳ τῷ κατὰ τὸν Φοίνικα τὸ ὄρνεον ὑποδείγματι κέχρηται. For literature about the phoenix, see Henrichsen, *Phoenicis*; Wiedemann, *Herodots*, 312–16; Roscher, "Phönix," 3450–72, where even more literature and a series of pictorial representations can be found; Erman, *Die ägyptische*

Religion, there, on p. 30, there is also a picture from a grave in Hau, which clearly shows the phoenix as a heron, reprinted in Greßmann et al., *Altorientalische Texte*, fig. 111, whereas other images depict it as an eagle, as Herodotus described it; Zimmermann, "Phönixsage," 202–23.

First Clement uses the story in a broad form and the components of his report can be substantiated without exception from the cited passages.

25:2[8] τοῦ ἀποθανεῖν αὐτό: genitive with the infinitive functioning as a purpose clause; see Luke 2:21: ἐπλήσθησαν ἡμέραι ὀκτὼ τοῦ περιτεμεῖν αὐτόν, 1 Cor 10:13: τὴν ἔκβασιν τοῦ δύνασθαι ὑπενεγκεῖν. LS have τοῦ χρόνου + τοῦ βίου, however this may be a gloss of the translator.

25:3 γενναῖος here simply means "strong, powerful," which the word often means. Heliopolis is the ancient, famous city that is called Onu in Egyptian (On in the Old Testament) and is located on the southern tip of the delta. It had a temple of the sun god, "the house of Rê," which was founded in the 12th dynasty around 2,000 BCE, and in the new kingdom it was the largest and richest temple after the temple of Amon in Thebes. It held the Mnevis. The priests of Heliopolis were considered particularly wise; Plato is said to have stayed with them for 13 years (Strabo, *Geogr.* XVII 29, p. 806). At the time of 1 Clem., the city was already empty; the temples, which still stood in their grand splendor, had become lonely (cf. Strabo, *Geogr.* XVII 27–29, p. 805f).

25:5 The ἀναγραφαὶ τῶν χρόνων are the public records. They were particularly old in Egypt and were also considered especially reliable by the Greeks; see Tatian, *Or. Graec.* 38: Αἰγυπτίων δέ εἰσιν ἀκριβεῖς χρόνων ἀναγραφαί, Josephus, *C. Ap.* I 6 (28): ὅτι μὲν οὖν παρ' Αἰγυπτίοις . . . ἐκ μακροτάτων ἄνωθεν χρόνων τὴν περὶ τὰς ἀναγραφὰς ἐπιμέλειαν . . . οἱ ἱερεῖς ἦσαν ἐγκεχειρισμένοι . . . ἐπειδὴ συγχωροῦσιν ἅπαντες, ἐάσειν μοι δοκῶ.

26:1 concludes the previous proof. On δημιουργός, see 1 Clem. 20:11; on the conclusion *a minore ad maius*, see Tertullian, *Res.* 13: *multis passeribus antestare nos dominus pronuntiavit; si non et phoenicibus, nihil magnum. sed homines semel interibunt, avibus Arabiae de resurrectione securis?*

26:2 adds the scriptural evidence as the last link in the chain of evidence: each member in the series ἐξαναστήσεις, ἐξηγέρθην, ἀναστήσεις carries the heavy tone. The origin of the first citation cannot be determined, though it sounds like Ps 27:7: . . . καὶ ἀνέθαλεν ἡ σάρξ μου· καὶ ἐκ θελήματός μου ἐξομολογήσομαι αὐτῷ, see also Ps 87:11: ἢ ἰατροὶ ἀναστήσουσιν καὶ ἐξομολογήσονταί σοι. The second citation seems to be a composite of Ps 3:6

---

8. TN: Knopf's German text has 25:1 here, but the phrase under discussion and those that follow come from 25:2, not v. 1.

and 22:4: ἐγὼ ἐκοιμήθην καὶ ὕπνωσα, ἐξηγέρθην ὅτι κύριος ἀντιλήψεταί μου and οὐ φοβηθήσομαι κακά, ὅτι σὺ μετ’ ἐμοῦ εἶ.

26:3 See Job 19:26, where the manuscripts strongly diverge from one another. First Clement is closest to A: ἀναστήσει δε μου τὸ σῶμα, τὸ ἀναντλοῦν ταῦτα. Because they are short, all three citations have been reproduced in the text from memory and are therefore very free.

First Clement 27 brings the final warning to believe in the true, reliable, and at the same time omnipotent God.

27:1 On τῷ πιστῷ ἐν ταῖς ἐπαγγελίαις, see Heb 10:23 and 11:11, but also Ps 145:14: πιστὸς κύριος ἐν τοῖς λόγοις αὐτοῦ, Deut 7:9; 32:4; 3 Macc 2:11. God the righteous judge is one of the most common concepts in the OT and in Christianity. This justice is highlighted here because it deals with eschatology.

27:2 In the OT, God forbade lies and threatened the liar; see already the Decalogue: οὐ ψευδομαρτυρήσεις. On the truthfulness of God, see Titus 1:2; John 3:33; among others. On the version of the sentence, see also Heb 6:18: (ἐν οἷς) ἀδύνατον ψεύσασθαι θεόν and Mark 10:27: πάντα γὰρ δυνατὰ παρὰ τῷ θεῷ along with other OT parallels. See also the many passages in the OT where the truthfulness and reliability of God are mentioned and finally Plato, *Rep.* II p. 382 E: πάντη ἄρα ἀψευδὲς τὸ δαιμόνιόν τε καὶ τὸ θεῖον.

27:3 ἀναζωπυρεῖν here is intransitive as also in Ignatius, *Eph.* 1:1: ἀναζωπυρήσαντες ἐν αἵματι θεοῦ. The words πίστις αὐτοῦ can also mean: his loyalty (cf. Rom 3:3). On πάντα ἐγγύς, see 21:2f, 9.

27:4 See Wis 9:1: θεὲ πατέρων καὶ κύριε τοῦ ἐλέους σου, ὁ ποιήσας τὰ πάντα ἐν λόγῳ σου, see also Heb 1:3 φέρων τὰ πάντα τῷ ῥήματι τῆς δυνάμεως αὐτοῦ. Clement uses the well-known, old, widespread *theologumenon* of the word of God, which has creative power (cf. Gunkel, *Genesis*, at Gen 1:3): he speaks, so it happens; he commands, and so it is (Ps 32:9). However, a reference to the doctrine of the Logos should not be assumed here, which 1 Clem. does not use in other passages of his writing, although he does represent the idea of the preexistence of Christ along with Paul and other early Christian theologians (cf. σκῆπτρον μεγαλωσύνης in 1 Clem. 16:2).

27:5 See Wis 12:12: τίς γὰρ ἐρεῖ· τί ἐποίησας; ἢ τίς ἀντιστήσεται τῷ κρίματί σου; and 11:21: καὶ κράτει βραχίονός σου τίς ἀντιστήσεται; the quotations have been mixed up in memory. L (*quia cum*) seems to have read ὅτε as ὅτι. The strong emphatic negation οὐδὲν μή fits well here, but the construction is shortened. It should read οὐδὲν οὐ μή; see Herm. *Mand.* IX 5: οὐδὲν οὐ μὴ λήψῃ.

27:7 εἰ introduces the citation and does not belong to the citation itself. The citation from Ps 18:2–4 is reproduced almost verbatim, only the LXX has λαλιαὶ οὐδὲ λόγοι. The meaning of the citation arises from its connection with vv. 5b and 6; see also v. 3b: the almighty God, who sees and hears everything, will also be able to raise dead bodies.

G. Transition (28:1–4)

Translation

28:1 Since everything is seen and heard, we should fear him and let go of ugly desires for evil deeds, so that we are protected by his mercy from the approaching judgment. 2 For where could any of us flee from his strong hand? What world would accept one who has fled his service? 3 For the Scriptures say somewhere, "Where should I go and where can I hide from your face? If I ascend to heaven, you are there; if I go to the ends of the earth, your right hand is there; if I make my bed in the underworld, your spirit is there." 4 Where then can anyone go, and where can they flee from the one who embraces everything?

Textual Notes

First Clement 28 is a transitional section that ties in closely with what came before and clearly leads over to the paraenesis of the subsequent chapters. Since God sees and hears everything, we must abandon the desire for evil works.

28:1 The thought that everything is seen and heard by God ties in with the quotation from which 1 Clem. found not only the omnipotence but also the omniscience of God (cf. further 1 Clem. 27:3 and 21:2f, 9). On the paraenesis, see 30:1. On μέλλοντα κρίματα, see 27:1 and the eschatology in general previously.

28:2 ποῖος κόσμος, on the idea of other worlds, see 1 Clem. 20:8. αὐτομολούντων is a military image, as in 21:4 and 37:1–4. γραφεῖον is actually the instrument with which one paints or writes, the pen or brush; then its meaning is transferred and used for that which is written. In the church, probably previously also in Jewish-Hellenistic language, γραφεῖα is used occasionally as a name for the third part of the Hebrew canon, the Ketubim, which is also called the ἁγιόγραφα. The oldest witness to this designation is found here; see also Epiphanius, Pan. 29 7.2 (of the Nazarenes): οὐ γὰρ ἀπηγόρευται παρ' αὐτοῖς νομοθεσία καὶ προφῆται καὶ γραφεῖα τὰ καλούμενα παρὰ Ἰουδαίοις βιβλία and 7.4: παρ'αὐτοῖς γὰρ πᾶς ὁ νόμος καὶ οἱ προφῆται καὶ τὰ γραφεῖα λεγόμενα ... Ἑβραϊκῶς ἀναγινώσκεται; see further De mensuris et ponderibus

4: . . . τὰ καλούμενα γραφεῖα, παρά τισι δὲ ἁγιόγραφα λεγόμενα [following him very similarly is John Damascus, *De fid. orthod.* IV 17].

28:3 The citation comes from Ps 138:7–10, but it is quite different in the LXX: ποῦ πορευθῶ ἀπὸ τοῦ πνεύματος σου, καὶ ἀπὸ τοῦ προσώπου σου ποῦ φύγω; ἐὰν ἀναβῶ εἰς τὸν οὐρανόν, σὺ εἶ ἐκεῖ· ἐὰν καταβῶ εἰς τὸν ᾅδην, πάρει· ἐὰν ἀναλάβω τὰς πτέρυγάς μου κατ' ὀρθὸν καὶ κατασκηνώσω εἰς τὰ ἔσχατα τῆς θαλάσσης, καὶ γὰρ ἐκεῖ ἡ χείρ σου ὁδηγήσει με, καὶ καθέξει με ἡ δεξιά σου. It's very difficult to say how Clement came by the form of the text he uses. Influence from Amos 9:2f is hardly likely. In καταστρώσω, the Hebrew text seems to be taken into account, which otherwise corresponds to the LXX.

28:4 τοῦ τὰ πάντα ἐμπεριέχοντος does not depict the God of the OT, whose throne is heaven and whose footstool is the earth, nor the god of the academy and the Peripatos on the other hand, but the god of the Stoa, who pervades and holds everything in the world "in whom we live, weave, and are" (cf. Norden, *Agnostos Theos*, 19ff); the characteristic word ἐμπεριέχειν seems to be taken directly from the Stoic doctrine of god. On the Stoic god, see the fragment that has been handed down numerous times: οἱ Στωϊκοὶ νοερὸν θεὸν ἀποφαίνονται, πῦρ τεχνικὸν ὁδῷ βαδίζον ἐπὶ γενέσει κόσμου (= *ignem artificiosum ad gignendum progredientem viâ*; Cicero, *Nat. d.* II 22.57), ἐμπεριειληφὸς πάντας τοὺς σπερματικοὺς λόγους, καθ' οὓς ἕκαστα καθ' εἱμαρμένην γίνεται· καὶ πνεῦμα μὲν διῆκον δι' ὅλου τοῦ κόσμου, τὰς δὲ προσηγορίας μεταλαμβάνον διὰ τὰς τῆς ὕλης, δι' ἧς κεχώρηκε, παραλλάξεις (Diels, *Doxographi*, 305f); see further at Origen, *Cels.* VI 71: τῶν Στωϊκῶν φασκόντων ὅτι ὁ θεὸς πνεῦμά ἐστι διὰ πάντων διεληλυθὸς καὶ πάντ' ἐν ἑαυτῷ περιέχον. Marcus Aurelius, *In semet ipsum* VIII 54.1: μηκέτι μόνον συμπνεῖν τῷ περιέχοντι ἀέρι, ἀλλὰ ἤδη καὶ συμφρονεῖν τῷ περιέχοντι πάντα νοερῷ, X 1.3: . . . τοῦ τελείου ζῴου, τοῦ ἀγαθοῦ καὶ δικαίου καὶ καλοῦ καὶ γεννῶντος πάντα καὶ συνέχοντος καὶ περιέχοντος . . . . What is very noteworthy at our point is the direct combination of OT and Greek conceptions, which have entered into the sacred text.

H. The Holy and Chosen Ones Must Flee from Slander, Discord, and Pride (29:1 — 30:8)

Translation

29:1 Let us draw near to him with a holy soul, to lift up pure and immaculate hands to him and to love our kind and merciful Father, who has made us his chosen portion. 2 For thus it is written, "When the Most High divided the nations by scattering the sons of Adam, he set the boundaries of the nations according to the number of the angels of God. (However) his nation, Jacob, became the portion of the Lord, Israel the cord of his inheritance." [3] And in another place it says, "Behold, the Lord takes a nation from among the nations as a man takes the first fruits of his threshing floor. And the most holy of holies will emerge from this people.

[30:1] So since we are a holy portion, we should do everything that belongs to holiness and flee slander, hideous and unclean embraces, drunkenness and novelties, and ugly passions, detestable adultery, ugly pride. [2] "For God," it says, "opposes the proud, but gives grace to the humble." [3] So let us attach ourselves to those who have been given grace by God. Let us put on concord, be humble and abstinent, and keep away from all blasphemy and slander, becoming righteous by works, not by words. [4] For it says, "The one who speaks much must also listen in return. Or does the one who talks believe he is righteous? [5] Blessed is the one born of a woman who lives only a short period of time. Do not be a chatterbox." [6] Let our praise be in God and not from ourselves. For God hates those who praise themselves. [7] Let the testimony of our good works be given by others, as it was given to our righteous fathers. [8] Insolence and arrogance and presumptuousness is characteristic of those who are condemned by God! Mildness and humility and meekness is characteristic of those blessed by God!

Textual Notes

First Clement 29 describes the election of the blessed people of God.

29:1 On the paraenesis, see 28:1 and 30:1. The posture of prayer alluded to here is the well-known, ancient posture of prayer: hands raised to heaven and of course with the head looking up. See already Homer, *Il.* III 318: λαοὶ δ᾽ ἠρήσαντο θεοῖς ἰδὲ χεῖρας ἀνέσχον or Homer, *Od.* XIII 355: αὐτίκα δὲ νύμφης ἠρήσατο χεῖρας ἀνασχών. As a visual representation, see the well-known "Adoranten" and for the Christian posture of prayer, see the numerous orans figures on the catacombs and sarcophagi (cf. von Sybel, *Christliche Antike*, 1:255ff). That hands raised in prayer are holy and undefiled is an ancient, widespread cultic demand, which here is naturally transferred from the cultic to the moral realm. — ἐκλογῆς μέρος: the Christians are the true people of God, they are the elect people of God, the Ἰσραὴλ τοῦ θεοῦ. That is the view of all early Christian writings. That is why the holy books, inspired by God, are believed by Christians to be their property without further ado, and all the high, honorific names in them are claimed by them. This view appears very clearly in 1 Clem. 29; see for example 1 Pet 2:9f; Justin, *Dial.* 11.5: Ἰσραηλιτικὸν γὰρ τὸ ἀληθινόν, πνευματικόν, καὶ Ἰούδα γένος καὶ Ἰακὼβ καὶ Ἰσαὰκ καὶ Ἀβραάμ . . . ἡμεῖς ἐσμεν. Christians also feel themselves to be a new people, the τρίτον γένος after the gentiles and Jews. The old nationalistic associations from which they emerged have lost their meaning to them, and they have acquired a whole new consciousness of belonging together, and also of belonging together politically, so to speak: φανερὸν γάρ ἐστιν ἡμῖν, ὦ βασιλεῦ, ὅτι τρία γένη εἰσιν ἀνθρώπων ἐν τῷδε τῷ κόσμῳ· ὧν εἰσιν οἱ τῶν παρ' ὑμῖν λεγομένων θεῶν προσκυνηταὶ καὶ Ἰουδαῖοι καὶ Χριστιανοί (Aristid., *Apol.* 2.1; on the notion of the third generation, cf. von Harnack, *Mission*, 1:238 [Book II 7] 260 [excursus]). The expressions λαός (v. 2) and ἔθνος (v. 3) should be understood in light of the consciousness of the new people.

29:2 See Deut 32:8f, which is reproduced here verbatim. The original text (*Urtext*), which instead of the angels of God has the sons of Israel, is to be improved according to the LXX: read בְּנֵי אֵל instead of בְּנֵי יִשְׂרָאֵל. Every nation received a guardian angel, a patron, when Yahweh divided the earth. But he has reserved his people for himself. According to another tradition, of course, he handed it over to the most eminent of the archangels, Michael. On the angels of the nations, see Deut 4:19; 17:3, as well as very clearly in Sir 17:17: ἑκάστῳ ἔθνει κατέστησεν ἡγούμενον καὶ μερὶς κυρίου Ἰσραήλ ἐστιν and Jub. 15:31f: "the nations are many and the people are numerous, and they all belong to him; and he gave the spirits power over all, that they might make them stray from him. But he has not given any angel or spirit power over Israel; he alone is their ruler." λαός of the people of God; the Jews do not like to refer to themselves as ἔθνος. λαός = עַם is Israel; ἔθνη = גּוֹיִם are the gentiles; see the concordance of the NT and a passage like Deut 32:43 (= Rom 15:10). σχοίνισμα, from σχοῖνος, is the land delimited and assigned by the measuring line.

29:3 is a strangely thrown together and imprecise quotation; if Clement read it in a certain place (ἐν ἑτέρῳ τόπῳ), it must have been in a lost apocryphon. But, of course, this assumption is not necessary; Clement could have reproduced the text from memory. See also the following passages. Deuteronomy 4:34: εἰ ἐπείρασεν ὁ θεὸς εἰσελθὼν λαβεῖν ἑαυτῷ ἔθνος ἐκ μέσου ἔθνους, Deut 14:2: καὶ σὲ ἐξελέξατο κύριος ὁ θεός σου γενέσθαι σε αὐτῷ λαὸν περιούσιον ἀπὸ πάντων τῶν ἐθνῶν τῶν ἐπὶ προσώπου τῆς γῆς, see further Num 18:27: λογισθήσεται ὑμῖν τὰ ἀφαιρέματα ὑμῶν ὡς σῖτος ἀπὸ ἅλω καὶ ἀφαίρεμα ἀπὸ ληνοῦ, 2 Chrn 31:14: δοῦναι τὰς ἀπαρχὰς κυρίου καὶ τὰ ἅγια τῶν ἁγίων, and finally Ezek 48:12: ἔσται αὐτοῖς ἡ ἀπαρχὴ δεδομένη ἐκ τῶν ἀπαρχῶν τῆς γῆς, ἅγιον ἁγίων ἀπὸ τῶν ὁρίων τῶν Λευιτῶν. The genitive ἅλω belongs to ἡ ἅλως; the LXX often uses this Attic form of the word next to ἡ ἅλων, ἅλωνος, which predominates in the NT as is generally the case in the Hellenistic language.

First Clement 30 contains some of the admonitions that are quite general, but their primary meaning is clearly a warning against arrogance, quarreling, and gossip, which the author believed had been evident in Corinth.

30:1 The connection with the end of 29:3 is obvious. Read ἁγία οὖν μερίς with LS; A has ἁγίου οὖν μερίς, H has ἅγια οὖν μέρη, C has ἁγίων οὖν μερίς. On the thought, see 1 Pet 1:15. The seven-part catalog of vices (*Lasterkatalog*) is general and also disordered; take note however the following καταλαλιάς, νεωτερισμούς, ὑπερηφανίαν, and furthermore the form of the same sounds (rhymes) in the 1st to the 3rd, and then again in the 6th and the 7th parts (pronounced *mychían*!).

30:2 The quotation that follows the last section comes from Prov 3:34 and is reproduced verbatim. The LXX differs in that it has κύριος instead of θεὸς γάρ; see, however, 1 Pet 5:5 and Jas 4:6, which also have ὁ θεός.

30:3 follows on from v. 2 and then demonstrates the behavior through which the grace of God is obtained. On ψιθυρισμοῦ καὶ καταλαλιᾶς, see 1 Clem. 35:5 as well as 2 Cor 12:20 and Rom 1:30. The conclusion ἔργοις καὶ μὴ λόγοις already indicates the subject that will be treated in the following, from 1 Clem. 31 onward.

30:4f See Job 11:2f, verbatim. Even the senseless error in the original text (*Urtext*) εὐλογημένος γεννητὸς γυναικὸς ὀλιγόβιος in the LXX has been reproduced. In context, it can only be interpreted as follows: whoever lives briefly will also speak little, and thus be saved from sin.

30:6 On the thought, see Rom 2:29. The word αὐτεπαίνετος so far only found here, but other corresponding compositions with αὐτο- are not uncommon.

30:7 On μαρτυρία and μαρτυρεῖν, see the comments at 1 Clem. 17:2. The fathers are not the living descendants, and also not the Christians of the previous generations, but the spiritual fathers, the holy men of the OT (cf. below at 1 Clem. 31:2). How the "testimony" was given to them was demonstrated in 1 Clem. 17f; the letter refers back to the explanations there. ὑπ᾽ ἄλλων, however, cannot be a reference to God here; on the idea, see Prov 27:2: ἐγκωμιαζέτω σε ὁ πέλας καὶ μὴ τὸ σὸν στόμα, ἀλλότριος καὶ μὴ τὰ σὰ χείλη and our text which says that self-praise stinks but foreign praises sound good, etc.

30:8 Note the exact parallelism and the same conclusion of the two links.

I. The Way of Blessedness (31:1 — 36:6)

Translation

31:1 Therefore, let us hold fast to his blessings and pay attention to the paths of blessing. Let us go over the old story in our minds. 2 Why was our father Abraham blessed? Was it not because he did righteousness and what is true in faith?

31:3 Isaac gladly allowed himself to be led there as a sacrifice with good confidence, since he knew the future beforehand.

31:4 Jacob humbly fled his country for his brother's sake, went to Laban and served him, and the twelve tribes of Israel were given to him.

32:1 If one looks closely at these individual matters, he will realize the greatness of the gifts bestowed by him [God]. 2 For from him came all the priests and the Levites who serve at God's altar. From him comes the Lord Jesus according to the flesh. From him come the kings and the rulers, and the princes through Judah. And the rest of his tribes have no small honor, since God promised, "Your seed will be as the stars of heaven." 3 All now were honored and glorified not by themselves or their works or by the good deeds they performed, but by his will. 4 And now we also, who are called by his will in Jesus Christ, are not justified by ourselves, not by our wisdom, understanding, piety, or by the works we do in purity of heart, but by faith, through which almighty God has justified all from the beginning. To him be the glory forever and ever. Amen.

33:1 What then should we do, brothers? Should we stop doing good and should we put love aside? May the Lord never let this happen to us, but let us hasten with perseverance and willingness to complete every good work. 2 For the creator and Lord of all things himself rejoices over his works. 3 With his power which surpasses everything he established the heavens, and with his incomprehensible wisdom he arranged them. He separated the earth from the water that encompasses it all around and established it on the secure foundation of his will. He called into being the animals that walk on it according to his command, the sea and the animals that are in it he created beforehand, and with his power he established boundaries for them. 4 On top of that, with his holy and blameless hands he created the most excellent and greatest of his creations, man, an imprint of his image. 5 For

thus says God, "Let us make man in our image and in our like-
ness. And God created man, male and female he created them."
⁶ When he had finished all these things, he praised it and blessed
it and said, "Be fruitful and multiply." ⁷ Let us (therefore) note
that all the righteous ones have been adorned with good works
and that the Lord himself adorned himself with good works and
rejoiced in them. ⁸ Since we have such an example, let us submit
to his will without hesitation and perform works of righteousness with all our might.

³⁴:¹ The good worker accepts the wages for his work; the lazy and
nonchalant worker does not dare look his employer in the face.
² We must therefore be willing to do good works, since everything comes from him. ³ He also warns us in advance: "Behold,
the Lord, and his reward is before him, to reward everyone according to his work." ⁴ Therefore he urges us to believe in him
wholeheartedly and not be lazy and casual about any good work.
⁵ Our boast and our joy should be in him. We should submit to
his will. Let us see how all the multitude of his angels stand with
him and serve him. ⁶ For the Scriptures say, "Ten thousand times
ten thousand stood with him, and a thousand times a thousand
served him, and they shouted, 'Holy, holy, holy is the Lord of
hosts, all creation is full of his glory." ⁷ And we too, gathered in
one accord, reverently, should call out to him emphatically, as
with one mouth, that we may be partakers of his great and glorious promises. ⁸ For it says, "No eye has seen, nor ear heard, nor
has it entered into the heart of man, the things which the Lord
has prepared for those that await him."

³⁵:¹ How blessed and admirable are the gifts of God, beloved. Life
in immortality, happiness in righteousness, truth in joyfulness,
faith in confidence, abstinence in sanctification. We know these
things already. ³ But what are the gifts that will be prepared for
those who persevere? The creator and Father of the eons, the
All-Holy One, alone knows their number and gloriousness. ⁴ Let
us therefore strive to be found among the number of those who
persevere so that we may share in the promised gifts. ⁵ But how
can this be, beloved? When our minds are faithful and steadfast
in God, when we strive for what is pleasing and agreeable to
him, when we carry out what corresponds to his irreproachable
will and follow the path of truth, and in doing so cast off from
us all injustice and wickedness, covetousness, contentiousness,
malice and deceit, gossip and slander, hatred of God, pride and
arrogance, empty boasting and inhospitality. ⁶ For those who do

these things are hated by God, not only those who do them, but also those who are pleased with them. ⁷ For the Scripture says, "But God says to the sinner, 'Why do you count my commandments and put my covenant in your mouth? ⁸ For you hated my discipline and cast my words behind you. If you saw a thief, you ran with him and you had fellowship with adulterers. Your mouth overflowed with malice and your tongue wove falsehood. You sat and spoke against your brother, and you insulted your mother's son. ⁹ You did this, and I was silent. You thought, O wicked one, I was like you. ¹⁰ I will convict you and place you before yourself. ¹¹ Take note, you who forget God, so that he does not carry you away like a lion, and there be no savior. ¹² A sacrifice of thanksgiving will praise me, and that is the way I will show him the salvation of God.'"

³⁶:¹ This is the way, beloved, in which we found our salvation, Jesus Christ, the high priest of our sacrifices, the protector and helper of our weaknesses. ² Through him we look into the heights of the heavens. Through him we behold God's unadulterated and exalted face, as if in a mirror. Through him the eyes of our hearts were opened. Through him our (once) incomprehensible and darkened mind grows up into the light. Through him the Lord made us taste immortal knowledge: he, as the reflection of his glory, is so much greater than the angels, for the name he has inherited surpasses them. ³ For thus it is written, "He makes his angels winds, and his servants a flame of fire." ⁴ But of his Son the Lord said, "You are my Son, today I have begotten you. Ask of me, and I will give you (the) gentiles for your inheritance, and the ends of the earth for your possession." ⁵ And again he says to him, "Sit at my right hand until I make your enemies as a footstool for your feet." ⁶ Who then are these enemies? The wicked and those who oppose his will.

Textual Notes

First Clement 31–36 form a larger, reasonably coherent unit: The Way of Blessing; see the theme which is raised in 31:1 and which is echoed again in 35:11 and 36:1. One must have faith, but not omit works. This is the main conclusion the author reaches. The Pauline formula is connected with Jewish-Hellenistic moralism, as can be seen in numerous examples in the post-apostolic age.

31:1 The theme of εὐλογία and ὁδοὶ τῆς εὐλογίας ties in directly with the closing verse of 30:8. Clement loves this type of transition. ἀνατυλίσσειν:

"rewind, unwind again," transferred "to consider, reconsider," *revolvere*; a
rare, selected word. See Lucian, *Nigrinus* 7: τοὺς λόγους, οὓς τότε ἤκουσα,
συναγείρων καὶ πρὸς ἐμαυτὸν ἀνατυλίττων.

31:2 The first solution to the question raised is given in the manner
we have become accustomed to, by means of examples, and is presented in
1 Clem. 31f. Referring to the example of the three patriarchs, it is shown that
"to do righteousness and truth by faith" (31:2) is the way to obtain a glorious
reward. This very general formula, however, is then turned around in 32:4f to
the effect that no merit of one's own, but rather faith brings about justification
before God, which Clement seeks to prove using the same examples.

31:2 The examples begin, and this time they are the three patriarchs.
On πατὴρ ἡμῶν, see 4:8. The blessings of Abraham are the glorious promises
mentioned to him numerous times in Genesis; see Gal 3:14 and Gen 12:2f:
καὶ ποιήσω σε εἰς ἔθνος μέγα καὶ εὐλογήσω σε καὶ μεγαλυνῶ τὸ ὄνομά σου καὶ
ἔσῃ εὐλογητός καὶ εὐλογήσω τοὺς εὐλογοῦντάς σε, καὶ τοὺς καταρωμένους σε
καταράσομαι καὶ εὐλογηθήσονται ἐν σοὶ πᾶσαι αἱ φυλαὶ τῆς γῆς, Gen 18:18:
Ἀβραὰμ δὲ γινόμενος ἔσται εἰς ἔθνος μέγα καὶ πολύ, καὶ ἐνευλογηθήσονται ἐν
αὐτῷ πάντα τὰ ἔθνη τῆς γῆς. — The characteristic feature of the formula is
the combination of πίστις and ποιεῖν. διά here, as is often the case, denotes
not so much the means as the accompanying circumstance "with"; see Rom
2:27: σὲ τὸν διὰ γράμματος καὶ περιτομῆς παραβάτην νόμου. See also Rom
14:20 and 2 Cor 2:4. Thus, the meaning *in faith, by which he trusts God*.
πίστις is of course not the Pauline faith, but rather trust in God, building
on him and on the truth of his promise; see both of the following examples,
especially μετὰ πεποιθήσεως in v. 3. — The formula ποιεῖν δικαιοσύνην is very
common in the LXX, and it is applied both to God and to man; on the
second usage, see for example 1 Sam 2:10; 2 Sam 8:15; Ps 105:3; Isa 56:1;
58:2; Tob 4:5; 13:6; among others. The meaning is this: doing what is right,
godly. In the NT, see in addition to Rev 22:11 also 1 John 2:29; 3:7, 10: ὁ
ποιῶν (or μὴ ποιῶν) τὴν δικαιοσύνην. Another construction that is not rare in
the LXX is ποιεῖν ἀλήθειαν, and again this construction is used for both God
and people; on the second usage, see Josh 2:14; Tob 13:6; 4:6 (here alongside
ποιεῖν δικαιοσύνην: ποιοῦντες σου τὴν ἀλήθειαν εὐοδίαι ἔσονται ἐν τοῖς ἔργοις
σου καὶ πᾶσι τοῖς ποιοῦσι τὴν δικαιοσύνην). In the NT, see again John's well-
known usage of the phrase: John 3:21; 1 John 1:6; see also 1 John 3:18 and
2 John 4. But the Johannine view has a different, deeper content than that of
1 Clem. or Tob, in which ἀλήθεια is simply the true will of God.

31:3 See Gen 22:7f. Nowhere in the OT does it say that Isaac know-
ingly and willingly allowed himself to be offered as a sacrifice, but this detail
is a part of Jewish tradition; see Josephus, *Ant.* I 13.4 (232): Ἴσακος δὲ . . .
δέχεται πρὸς ἡδονὴν τοὺς λόγους καὶ φήσας, ὡς οὐδὲ γεγονέναι τὴν ἀρχὴν ἦν

δίκαιος, εἰ θεοῦ καὶ πατρὸς μέλλει κρίσιν ἀπωθεῖσθαι καὶ μὴ παρέχειν αὐτὸν τοῖς ἀμφοτέρων βουλήμασιν ἑτοίμως . . . ὥρμησεν ἐπὶ τὸν βωμὸν καὶ τὴν σφαγήν; see then the rabbinic parallels in Beer, *Leben*, 65-67. μετὰ πεποιθήσεως picks up διὰ πίστεως which comes immediately beforehand. In γινώσκων τὸ μέλλον there could perhaps still be allegorism: he knew in advance of the sacrifice of Christ. In four preserved fragments (Goodspeed, *Apologeten*, 312f; von Otto, *Corpus Apologetarum* IX, 416-18), Melito interprets the story of Isaac's offering allegorically to Christ; see what he says in fr. 9: ὡς γὰρ κριὸς ἐδέθη, φησὶ περὶ τοῦ κυρίου ἡμῶν Ἰησοῦ Χριστοῦ, καὶ ὡς ἀμνὸς ἐκάρη καὶ ὡς πρόβατον εἰς σφαγὴν ἤχθη καὶ ὡς ἀμνὸς ἐσταυρώθη, καὶ ἐβάστασε τὸ ξύλον ἐπὶ τοῖς ὤμοις αὐτοῦ, ἀναγόμενος σφαγῆναι ὡς Ἰσαὰκ ὑπὸ τοῦ πατρὸς αὐτοῦ, and in another place in fr. 10: ὑπὲρ Ἰσαὰκ τοῦ δικαίου ἐφάνη κριὸς εἰς σφαγήν, ἵνα δεσμῶν Ἰσαὰκ λυθῇ. ἐκεῖνος σφαγεὶς ἐλυτρώσατο τὸν Ἰσαάκ· οὕτως καὶ ὁ κύριος σφαγεὶς ἔσωσεν ἡμᾶς καὶ δεθεὶς ἔλυσε καὶ τυθεὶς ἐλυτρώσατο.

31:4 The same spirit of mourning and abandonment is indicated by μετὰ ταπεινοφροσύνης in v. 4. The place which this virtue occupies in the piety and paraenesis of the letter is already familiar to us (cf. primarily 1 Clem. 16-19). On the allusion, see Gen 28f. δωδεκάσκηπτρον seems to be a *hapaxlegomenon*, but similar compositions with δώδεκα are common; see the lexicons and especially δωδεκάφυλον in 55:6 and Acts 26:7. σκῆπτρον is metaphorical for φυλή, so also in 32:2 and already in the OT (LXX and MT שֵׁבֶט); see for example 1 Sam 2:28; 9:21; 10:20; 1 Kgs 8:16; 11:35f; 12:20f. The image is not conveyed by "twig" or "rod," but by the ruler's staff of the tribal prince (Num 17:6).

First Clement 32 at first ties in closely with the end of 31:4 (δωρεῶν: ἐδόθη) but then more broadly elaborates on the thought of δωρεά: God's will grants and bestows his grace, such that faith and not works is the watchword.

32:1f enumerates the gifts to Jacob. On μεγαλεῖα see Acts 2:11; the expression is biblical Greek. In the LXX, the substantivized (τὸ) μεγαλεῖον or (τὰ) μεγαλεῖα is not rare; as a parallel to our passage, see Sir 17:9: ἵνα διηγῶνται τὰ μεγαλεῖα τῶν ἔργων αὐτοῦ.

32:2 ἐξ αὐτοῦ here is a reference to Jacob. The style is loose. ὑπ᾽ αὐτοῦ also lacks a grammatical subject. Note the anaphora, the threefold use of ἐξ αὐτοῦ. Romans 9:4f certainly has had an influence; see especially λειτουργία and τὸ κατὰ σάρκα both here and there. The tribe of priests and kings are listed, with the Lord Jesus in between, who belongs to both. Christ is known as a high priest from Hebrews and other ancient Christian writings (cf. 1 Clem. 36:1; 61:3). For an assessment of the priestly tribe, see also 1 Clem. 40-43, especially 43. On κατὰ τὸν Ἰούδαν (in accordance with, according to modality), see Gen 49:10, where also, as here, ἄρχων and ἡγούμενος are used beside one another: οὐκ ἐκλείψει ἄρχων ἐξ Ἰούδα καὶ ἡγούμενος ἐκ τῶν μηρῶν αὐτοῦ. The promise is not taken from Genesis verbatim (cf. Gen 15:5; 22:17; 26:4). It is also not given to Jacob, but to Abraham in 15:5 and 22:17 (it is the εὐλογία of 1 Clem. 31:2), and to Isaac 26:4. First Clement does not have spiritual Israel in mind here but physical Israel, which he sees as very large in number and to which he does not deny a certain honor from God (see also Rom 9:4f).

32:3 πάντες is again loose. With the expression Clement means not only the previously mentioned Jewish tribes, but above all the patriarchs, Levites, priests, the tribe of Judah, and the kings. αὐτοῦ at the end of v. 3 is also loose. δικαιοπραγία and δικαιοπραγεῖν, δικαιοπραγής are common words from the time of Aristotle onward. On the idea of the sentence, see Titus 3:5 as well as Rom 9:16, among other passages.

32:4 πίστις corresponds to the gracious will of God on the part of man, by which the pre-Christian righteous ones were saved. σοφία and σύνεσις appear near each other also in 1 Cor 1:19 (Isa 29:14) and Col 1:9 (see also Matt 11:25 and Luke 10:21). πάντας is imprecise. Of course not all people are meant, but all saved people (cf. 7:5). Here too the doxology does not demarcate a larger division within the text, but rather only a sub-section. As in 20:11, it is prompted by the mention of the great blessing of God. ἀπ' αἰῶνος and παντοκράτωρ also have a liturgical sound. On παντοκράτωρ, see the prescript.

First Clement 33 In addition to the formula of sola fide-ism[9] adopted by Paul a synergism immediately appears, as was to be expected from 31:2 as well as from 10:7 and 12:1. On this, see from the post-Pauline period Jas 2:22, but also Eph 2:10 and then the frequently repeated formula of the ἀγαθὰ (or καλὰ) ἔργα in the Pastoral Epistles: 1 Tim 2:10; 5:10; 5:25; 6:18; 2 Tim 2:21; 3:17; Titus 1:16; 2:7, 14; 3:1, 8, 14 (as well as Titus 3:5 and 2 Tim 1:9). Faith (grace) and good works, this new formula that characterizes the early church and with which it starts on the path of development toward the ancient Catholic Church. The pre-Christian sins are erased by baptism; for what follows, man must take comfort in faith in divine grace and must have his own good deeds to show, without which he cannot be saved. Judaism—or perhaps better articulated—an easily comprehensible, general form of human moralism pushes itself to the light in the post-Pauline communities.

33:1 Well-known formulas of the Pauline dialectic, more precisely from Romans (τί οὖν ἐροῦμεν seven times in Romans; four times with subsequent question and negation: 3:5; 6:1; 7:7; 9:14), are imitated here, probably consciously. Romans 6:1 in particular may be on the author's mind. ἀγάπη was already mentioned above in 21:7f as an outstanding

9. TN: The German term used here is "Solafidismus."

Christian virtue. The full praise of ἀγάπη is articulated later in 1 Clem. 49f. In the present passage, its mention shows that it appears to Clement to be the most outstanding of good works, as their summary. On this, see 1 Pet 4:8: ἀγάπη καλύπτει πλῆθος ἁμαρτιῶν. Giving alms, showing hospitality, caring for the sick and prisoners, serving the congregation, and other such works fall under the umbrella of love. δεσπότης appears here as it has frequently beforehand (cf. 7:5; 8:2; 9:4; 11:1; etc.) and immediately afterward (cf. 33:2; 36:2; etc.). The form μηθαμῶς, which also occurs in 45:7 (53:4), is not common (cf. Blaß-Debrunner, *Grammatik*, §33 and Radermacher, *Grammatik*, 40). It is parallel to μηθείς, οὐθείς. ἔργον ἀγαθόν is a keyword (*Stichwort*) in the chapter (cf. also 34:1–4).

33:2–6 proves the need for good works by pointing to God who did so many good works in creation. The view is closely related to that of 1 Clem. 20, and here too the connection between Judeo-Christian ideas and Stoic and generally Greek ideas returns: the primary stream is clearly visible; secondary streams originated on Greek soil. The ecclesiastical liturgy should be regarded as a direct source for Clement: vv. 2–6 have their parallels in the "*praefationen*" of the eastern liturgies. For example Apost. Const. VIII 12.6ff; see Leitzmann, *Klementinische Liturgie*, 12ff and Drews, *Clementinische*, 14ff; Skutsch, "Liturgie," 291ff.

33:2 On δημιουργὸς καὶ δεσπότης τῶν ἁπάντων, see the comments at 1 Clem. 20:11.

33:3 On παμμεγεθεστάτῳ, see παμμέγεθες in 33:4. The word is not attested in the LXX or the NT, but otherwise is not entirely uncommon. The choice of the word ἐστήρισεν is probably influenced by the similar sounding στερέωμα, which Gen 1 repeatedly uses for the heavens (cf. also Ps 18:1; Sir 43:8; et al.). Nowhere does the LXX say στηρίζειν τὸν οὐρανόν (or τοὺς οὐρανούς). The designation στηρίζειν is familiar to Greek cosmology: κόσμον . . . στηρίξατο (Abel, *Orphica*, frag. 170.3); αὐτὸς γὰρ τά γε σήματ᾽ ἐν οὐρανῷ ἐστήριξεν (Arat Phänom. 10). The heavens are fixed because they are tied up around the polar axis, but they rotate (see 1 Clem. 20:1). — The expression διεκόσμησεν is genuinely Greek, and in Stoic cosmology, it is used abundantly (similar to διοικεῖν in 20:1); see Zeno in Aristocles (Eusebius, *Praep. ev.* XV 14.2 p. 817 A; von Arnim, *Stoicorum veterum fragmenta*, 1:#98): ἔπειτα δὲ καὶ κατά τινας εἱμαρμένους χρόνους ἐκπυροῦσθαι τὸν σύμπαντα κόσμον, εἶτ᾽ αὖθις πάλιν διακοσμεῖσθαι, see further at Stob. *Ecl.* I 17.3 in Wachsmuth, *Anthologium*, 152, 19 (von Arnim, *Stoicorum veterum fragmenta*, 1:#102): τοιαύτην δὲ δεήσει εἶναι ἐν περιόδῳ τὴν τοῦ ὅλου διακόσμησιν ἐκ τῆς οὐσίας, the Stoics in Arius (Eusebius, *Praep. ev.* XV 18.3, p. 820): πάλιν ἐκ τούτου (i.e., the fire) αὐτὴν ἀποτελεῖσθαι τὴν διακόσμησιν, οἵα τὸ πρότερον ἦν (with reference to Zeno,

Cleanthes, Chrysippus). See also Eusebius, *Praep. ev.* XV 19.2, p. 821, et al. The Stoics took over the word and view from the Ionian natural philosophers; see Anaxagoras in Diog. Laert. *Lives* II 3: πάντα χρήματα ἦν ὁμοῦ· εἶτα νοῦς ἐλθὼν αὐτὰ διεκόσμησεν (for additional references, see Diels, *Doxographi*, index, s.v.), but also see the old Heraclitus in Hippolytus, *Haer.* IX 10 (Diels, *Vorsokratiker I*, fragm. 65): καλεῖ δὲ (Heraclitus) αὐτὸ (the primordial fire) "χρησμοσύνην καὶ κόρον"· χρησμοσύνη δε ἐστιν ἡ διακόσμησις κατ᾽ αὐτόν, ἡ δὲ ἐκπύρωσις κόρος, and additionally Parmenides in his *Lehrgedichte* (Diels, *Fragmente der Vorsokratiker I*, fragm. 8, 60): τόν σοι ἐγὼ διάκοσμον ἐοικότα πάντα φατίζω. — The respective formation of the new world after the old one is destroyed by fire or water is called διακόσμησις by the Stoics, the διοίκησις is the preservation of the world and of government. The expression is entirely lacking in the LXX. Only διακοσμεῖν and διακόσμησις come over into 2 Macc 2:29; 3:25; 4:5. — On γῆν κτλ., see Gen 1:9f. διαχωρίζειν is frequently used in Gen 1, though admittedly not for the division between water and land. In περιέχοντος αὐτήν, the idea of the *oceanos* returns (cf. 20:8). ἑδράζειν describes the mountains in Ps 89:2 and Prov 8:25; also the LXX has θεμέλια as a reference to the earth in Ps 17:16; 81:5; Sir 10:16; 16:19; Isa 13:13, et al. The idea of the foundations of the earth, on which it stands without wavering, is authentic and in general an eastern-mythological idea. — τὰ ἐν αὐτῇ ζῶα describes the creation of the land animals (Gen 1:24f). θάλασσαν is a reference to the creation of the sea (Gen 1:9f), and the creation of the animals in the sea (Gen 1:20ff). Since the aquatic animals were created before the already mentioned land animals, the expression προετοιμάσας is used (thus H and LSC, προδημιουργήσας A). In ἐνέκλεισεν the ancient mythological view of the taming of the sea and the hostile monsters in it, often attested in the OT, is softly echoed (cf. 1 Clem. 20:6f).

33:4 The construction of the sentence is not clear, nor is the reading fixed. τὸ ἐξοχώτατον καὶ παμμέγεθες can either be the object of ἔπλασεν, whereby ἄνθρωπον is in apposition to this accusative, as it has been translated above. Or τὸ ἐξοχώτατον κτλ. is an absolute nominative: "and on top of all that, the most excellent and greatest: he created man." In this reading, κατὰ διάνοιαν is not certain: it is included in AH, but is omitted in LSC. Presumably it will have to be deleted as a gloss which, however, does not help make a decision about the ambiguity just mentioned. Nothing can be inferred from the lack of the article before ἄνθρωπον since οὐρανούς, γῆν, θάλασσαν were also introduced without articles in the preceding clauses. If διάνοιαν is kept, then in the first interpretive option, followed in the translation above, it is the διάνοια of man, whereas in the second interpretive option, it is the διάνοια of God. — On v. 4, see Gen 1:27: καὶ ἐποίησεν ὁ θεὸς τὸν ἄνθρωπον, κατ᾽ εἰκόνα θεοῦ ἐποίησεν αὐτόν (1:26: ποιήσωμεν ἄνθρωπον κατ᾽ εἰκόνα ἡμετέραν καὶ καθ᾽ ὁμοίωσιν) and Gen 2:7: ἔπλασεν ὁ θεὸς τὸν ἄνθρωπον χοῦν ἀπὸ τῆς γῆς. The fact that God created man with his hands is not explicitly stated in Genesis, but is certainly presupposed in Gen 2:7. In any case, the OT speaks often enough of the hand and hands of God; see especially Ps 18:1: ποίησιν . . . χειρῶν αὐτοῦ, Ps 101:26: ἔργα τῶν χειρῶν σου. The whole manner of thinking is non-Greek; the addition of ταῖς ἱεραῖς καὶ ἀμώμοις gives the impression of a softening of the anthropomorphism. χαρακτήρ, in Heb 1:3 Christ is the χαρακτὴρ τῆς ὑποστάσεως.

33:5 is composed from pieces of Gen 1:26f. The reference to the creation of man in vv. 4 and 5 is essentially based on Genesis, and at most a parallel to the sense of the passage can be recalled from the Stoic view of man as the crown of creation, created both for his own sake and for God and for the sake of the rest of the world; see Cicero, *Nat. d.* II 62.154: *principio ipse mundus deorum hominumque causa factus est, quaeque in eo sunt, ea parata ad fructum hominum et inventa sunt. Est enim mundus quasi communis deorum atque hominum domus aut urbs utrorumque. Soli enim ratione utentes iure ac lege vivunt,* or Chrysippus (von Arnim, *Stoicorum veterum fragmenta.* 2:#527, and similarly in Cicero, *Fin.* III 20.67): κόσμον δὲ εἶναί φησιν ὁ Χρύσιππος . . . τὸ ἐκ θεῶν καὶ ἀνθρώπων σύστημα καὶ ἐκ τῶν ἕνεκα τούτων γεγονότων.

33:6 As a neuter ταῦτα . . . αὐτά cannot only apply to human beings, but must apply to all of the aforementioned creatures. The quotation is not only from Gen 1:28, but probably also takes 1:22 into account (cf. also 8:17; 9:1, 7); ηὐλόγησεν is in both passages. — Finally, note the contact 1 Clem. 33:2–5 has with the liturgy; Apost. Const. VIII 12.9 (Lietzmann, *Klementinische Liturgie*): σὺ γὰρ εἶ ὁ τὸν οὐρανὸν ὡς καμάραν στήσας καὶ ὡς δέρριν ἐκτείνας καὶ τὴν γῆν ἐπ᾽ οὐδενὸς ἱδρύσας γνώμῃ μόνῃ, ὁ πήξας στερέωμα . . . . VIII 12.12: ὁ τὴν μεγάλην θάλασσαν χωρίσας τῆς γῆς . . . καὶ τὴν μὲν ζώοις μικροῖς καὶ μεγάλοις πληθύνας, τὴν δὲ ἡμέροις καὶ ἀτιθάσοις πληρώσας . . . . VIII 12.15: ἐπλήρωσας γάρ σου τὸν κόσμον καὶ διεκόσμησας αὐτὸν . . . . VII 12.16: καὶ οὐ μόνον τὸν κόσμον ἐδημιούργησας ἀλλὰ καὶ τὸν κοσμοπολίτην (notice the expression, which is of Cynic-Stoic origin) ἄνθρωπον ἐν αὐτῷ ἐποίησας, κόμου κόσμον αὐτὸν ἀναδείξας· εἶπας γὰρ τῇ σῇ σοφίᾳ Ποιήσωμεν ἄνθρωπον κατ᾽ εἰκόνα ἡμετέραν κτλ. See further Apost. Const. VII 34.1: ὁ διαχωρίσας ὕδατα ὑδάτων στερεώματι καὶ πνεῦμα ζωτικὸν τούτοις ἐμβαλών, ὁ γῆν ἑδράσας καὶ οὐρανὸν ἐκτείνας καὶ τὴν ἑκάστου τῶν κτισμάτων ἀκριβῆ διάταξιν κοσμήσας . . . . VII 34.3: αὐτὴν δὲ τὴν θάλασσαν πῶς ἄν τις ἐκφράσειεν; ἥτις ἔρχεται μὲν ἀπὸ πελάγους μαινομένη παλινδρομεῖ δὲ ἀπὸ ψάμμου τῇ σῇ προσταγῇ κωλυομένη· εἶπας γὰρ ἐν αὐτῇ συντριβήσεσθαι αὐτῆς τὰ κύματα, ζῴοις δὲ μικροῖς καὶ μεγάλοις καὶ πλοίοις πορευτὴν αὐτὴν ἐποίησας . . . . VII.34.5: ἔπειτα

διαφόρων ζῴων κατεσκευάζετο γένη . . . . VII.34.6: καὶ τέλος τῆς δημιουργίας τὸ
λογικὸν ζῷον, τὸν κοσμοπολίτην, τῇ σοφίᾳ διαταξάμενος κατεσκεύασας εἰπών·
ποιήσωμεν ἄνθρωπον κατ᾽ εἰκόνα καὶ καθ᾽ ὁμοίωσιν ἡμετέραν.

33:7 Paraenesis follows the example. The manuscript evidence unanimously attests to the reading ἴδωμεν and not εἴδομεν, as in von Gebhardt,
von Harnack and Lightfoot. εἴδομεν would in itself be a very good reading.
Clement would thus point to the many examples of good works that he has
already shown among the pious of all previous generations (see especially
5f and 9–18). Even with the reading ἴδωμεν, he asks the listener to think
about the previous statements. According to the context, κύριος refers to
God and not Christ.

33:8 ὑπογραμμός as in 5:7 and 16:17.

First Clement 34 leads to a second thought that prevails in this and in
the next chapter: the reward that is in view for the one who does good works
is glorious. This, in turn, supports the paraenesis: do good!

34:1 presents an example from daily life. παρρησία has nothing to do
with πίστις, which appears again in v. 5, but is simply the consciousness of
a job well done, the sure confidence that the reward cannot be missed. See
the parallels in terms of vocabulary and sense in Epictetus, *Diatr.* III 26.27:
καὶ στρατιώτῃ μὲν ἀγαθῷ οὐ λείπει ὁ μισθοδοτῶν οὐδ᾽ ἐργάτῃ οὐδὲ σκυτεῖ. On
νωθρὸς καὶ παρειμένος, see Sir 4:29: μὴ γίνου τραχὺς ἐν γλώσσῃ σου καὶ νωθρὸς
καὶ παρειμένος ἐν τοῖς ἔργοις σου. The word ἐργοπαρέκτης has not yet been
found. The customary word is ἐργοδότης.

34:2 interweaves a piece of paraenesis and follows it immediately with
justification. ἐξ αὐτοῦ = from God; τὰ πάντα, everything, both reward and
punishment, comes from him.

34:3 And this is proved by the citation, which is strangely patched together if it is not from an apocryphon; see Isa 40:10: ἰδοὺ κύριος κύριος μετὰ
ἰσχύος ἔρχεται . . . ἰδοὺ ὁ μισθὸς αὐτοῦ μετ᾽ αὐτοῦ καὶ τὸ ἔργον ἐναντίον αὐτοῦ,
Isa 62:11: ἰδοὺ ὁ σωτήρ σοι παραγέγονεν ἔχων τὸν ἑαυτοῦ μισθόν, καὶ τὸ ἔργον
αὐτοῦ πρὸ προσώπου αὐτοῦ, Prov 24:12: ὃς ἀποδίδωσιν ἑκάστῳ κατὰ τὰ ἔργα
αὐτοῦ, Ps 61:13: ὅτι σὺ ἀποδώσεις ἑκάστῳ κατὰ τὰ ἔργα αὐτοῦ. Then, see also
Rev 22:12; Rom 2:6; Job 34:11; among others.

34:4 Note again the connection between faith and works. ἐπ᾽ αὐτῷ of
course must be a reference to God; see 34:2, 5 where αὐτός is always God
and not μισθός. On the second part of the sentence, see 2 Tim 2:21: εἰς πᾶν
ἔργον ἀγαθὸν ἡτοιμασμένον.

34:5 παρρησία is used as it is in 34:1; on καύχημα ἐν θεῷ, see Rom 2:17;
4:2; 5:11; and then the price of ταπεινοφροσύνη and the divine μαρτυρία
in 1 Clem. 16–19. On ὑποτασσώμεθα, see 1 Clem. 19–21. — The hosts of
the divine angels, who are much more majestic than humans, are brought

forward as an example of subordination. λειτουργεῖν = to minister, and likely in the cult (cf. Acts 13:2; Heb 10:11; and very frequently in the LXX; see also 1 Clem. 34:7).

34:6 The first part of the citation comes from Dan 7:10 (Theodotion): χίλιαι χιλιάδες ἐλειτούργουν αὐτῷ (the LXX has ἐθεράπευον αὐτόν) καὶ μύριαι μυριάδες παριστήκεισαν αὐτῷ. The change attested to in Clement also occurs in Iren. Haer. II 7.4; Eusebius, Praep. VII 15 (p. 326); and in other church fathers. The second part of the citation comes from Isa 6:3: καὶ ἐκέκραγον (B -εν) ἕτερος πρὸς τὸν ἕτερον καὶ ἔλεγον· ἅγιος ἅγιος ἅγιος κύριος σαβαώθ, πλήρης πᾶσα ἡ γῆ τῆς δόξης αὐτοῦ. First Clement deviates from the source text in a not insignificant manner (see below).

34:7 We are led here in one fell swoop into the congregation gathered together for worship. Clement speaks here in such a manner as if he stood before the gathered congregation and he presupposes that the letter would be read at Corinth when the congregation gathered together for worship. ἐπὶ τὸ αὐτό and συνάγεσθαι (or συνέρχεσθαι) are technical expressions (cf. 1 Cor 5:4; 11:20; Acts 1:15; 2:1, 44; Ign. Eph. 13:1; Did. 14; etc.). σύναξις becomes the term for liturgical worship in later ecclesiastical language. συνείδησις here does not mean a good conscience, but inner sympathy; see the translation above for the use of the word in 2:4; see further at Eccl 10:20: καὶ γε ἐν συνειδήσει σου βασιλέα μὴ καταράσῃ ("even in your mind do not curse the king").

But in our passage there are also other aspects that come from the liturgical context; see Probst, Liturgie, 41–46: ἐκτενῶς is a technical expression for the liturgy, which is used over and over again in the early church liturgies of the fervent devotional prayer; see the oft-repeated use of ἐκτενής ἐκτένεια in the Clementine liturgy, the oldest we have, in Apost. Const. VIII 5ff (Lietzmann, Klementinische Liturgie). See Apost. Const. VIII 6.5: ἐκτενῶς τὸν θεὸν παρακαλέσωμεν. VIII 7.1: ἐκτενῶς πάντες . . . δεηθῶμεν. VIII 8.1: ἐκτενῶς, οἱ πιστοί, πάντες ὑπὲρ αὐτῶν παρακαλέσωμεν. VIII 9.1: ἐκτενῶς πάντες . . . παρακαλέσωμεν. VIII 10.22: δεηθέντες ἐκτενῶς. In the Greek liturgy, a passage is called εὐχὴ τῆς ἐκτενῆς; see for example the Constantinopolitan Liturgy, ed. by Baumstark (Messliturgie), 12: εὐχὴ τῆς ἐκτενῆς· κύριε ὁ θεὸς ἡμῶν, τὴν ἐκτενὴν ταύτην ἱκεσίαν πρόσδεξαι. Furthermore, as far as we can see, the Trisagion is always an integral part of the liturgy; Clement has just brought it over. Also, its connection with Dan 7:10 belongs to the ancient liturgical tradition; see the beautiful intertwining of the heavenly angelic service with the cult of the faithful in the liturgy of the Apostolic Constitutions, which is still very characteristic of Greek worship today. Apost. Const. VIII 12.27: σὲ (God) προσκυνοῦσιν ἀνάριθμοι στρατιαὶ ἀγγέλων, ἀρχαγγέλων, θρόνων, κυριοτήτων, ἀρχῶν, ἐξουσιῶν,

δυνάμεων, στρατιῶν αἰωνίων· τὰ Χερουβὶμ καὶ τὰ ἑξαπτέρυγα Ζεραφὶμ . . .
λέγοντα ἅμα χιλίαις χιλιάσιν ἀρχαγγέλων καὶ μυρίαις μυριάσιν ἀγγέλων
ἀκαταπαύστως καὶ ἀσιγήτως βοώσαις (as far as the priest) καὶ πᾶς ὁ λαὸς
εἰπάτω· ἅγιος, ἅγιος, ἅγιος κύριος Σαβαώθ, πλήρης ὁ οὐρανὸς καὶ ἡ γῆ τῆς
δόξης αὐτοῦ· εὐλογητὸς εἰς τοὺς αἰῶνας· ἀμήν. The same connection of the
prophetic passages can also be found in other Greek liturgies, for example
in the Chrysostom liturgy (Baumstark, *Messliturgie*, 8), in the Anaphora of
Serapion (Lietzmann, *Klementinische Liturgie*, 31), in the Markan liturgy
(Swainson, Greek Liturgies, 48; Brightman, *Liturgies*, 131f). As is assumed
in 1 Clem. (ὡς ἐξ ἑνὸς στόματος βοήσωμεν), in these liturgies the Trisagion
is spoken, or at least repeated, by the community. The ἐπινίκιος ᾠδή, as
the Trisagion is often called in the liturgies of the east, is one of the oldest
and most secure components of the liturgy. Incidentally, the saying from
34:8 also recurs in the prayers of various early Christian liturgies. See also
Drews, *Clementinische Liturgie*, 21f.

34:8 See 1 Cor 2:9, only 1 Clem. turns the relative clause into a main
clause and instead of ἀγαπῶσιν he has ὑπομένουσιν, which is an effect of
LXX Isa 64:4: ἀπὸ τοῦ αἰῶνος οὐκ ἠκούσαμεν οὐδὲ οἱ ὀφθαλμοὶ ἡμῶν εἶδον
θεὸν πλὴν σοῦ καὶ τὰ ἔργα σου ἃ ποιήσεις τοῖς ὑπομένουσιν ἔλεον. According to Origen's absolutely credible statement (in Matt 27:9, Lommatzsch,
Origenis Opera, vol. 29), the quote from Paul comes from the lost Apocalypse of Elijah (and is therefore not a combination of Isa 64:4 with 65:16f).
First Clement, however, takes it from Paul or from the church liturgy (see
above), which in turn took it from Paul. Evidence of passages where the
word still occurs in Resch, *Agrapha*, 111.

First Clement 35 speaks in a little more detail about the gifts of God
and the behavior of man through which he participates in these gifts.

35:1–3 The reward, the promise, already mentioned in 1 Clem. 34, is
of two types: gifts that the believers already have and gifts that are to be
bestowed upon them in the future.

35:2 lists the present gifts. It is strongly spiritualized, mystically determined piety that speaks here. The Hellenistic element is also clear, which is
already evident in the first part of the verse: ζωὴ ἐν ἀθανασίᾳ tangibly emerges
(cf. also Did. 9:3). The nominative of the five-part series always indicates
a piece of inner possession, the more detailed determinations with ἐν then
indicate the sphere, the means, the accompanying circumstance in which
the good is grasped and enjoyed. The two concepts, the nominative and the
ἐν determination, are closely related to each other; one could usually reverse
them. For example, παρρησία ἐν ἀληθείᾳ, πεποίθησις ἐν πίστει, etc. Life here
is the personal, inner good of salvation, which is already presently grasped
and experienced in the community in the immortality that is already granted

to the individual; this ἀθανασία for Clement probably also depends on the gnosis; see 36:2: τῆς ἀθανάτου γνώσεως, and then in our series ἀλήθεια. We are reminded of Johannine literature (cf. John 5:24); but the relationship of course is not conveyed in literary terms, and Paul already knows how to speak of the present life. ζωὴ ἐν ἀθανασίᾳ, however, is a surprising sound in 1 Clem. I wonder if the liturgy still echoes here in Clement's comments about the gifts of salvation? λαμπρότης, considered within the whole series, must also mean an internal present good, not future glory: λαπρός also means brave and happy, cheerful; see Soph. *Oed. Tyr.* 80f: ὦναξ Ἄπολλον, εἰ γὰρ ἐν τύχῃ γέ τῳ Σωτῆρι βαίη, λαμπρὸς (= cheerful) ὥσπερ ὄμματι, Xenophon, *Hell.* IV 5.10: οὗτοι δ' ὥσπερ νικηφόροι λαμπροὶ καὶ ἀγαλλόμενοι τῷ οἰκείῳ πάθει περιῄεσαν, Plutarch, *Cimon* 17: ἐλθόντων δὲ τὴν τόλμαν καὶ τὴν λαμπρότητα (happy, brave confidence) δείσαντες ἀπεπέμψαντο. Diodorus IV 40: ῥώμη σώματος καὶ ψυχῆς λαμπρότητι . . . τι πρᾶξαι. Put this way, λαμπρότης has contact here with παρρησία and πεποίθησις. ἀλήθεια must be the truth possessed by Christians and revealed to them. According to this sense, it has strong contact with the sense of γνῶσις. Thus, ἀλήθεια makes good sense in a series with ζωή and πίστις. And also the precise definition of ἐν παρρησίᾳ probably fits with it. ἐγκράτεια primarily has to do with sexual purity (cf. 38:2); also ἁγιασμός points in this direction (cf. 30:1). However, the words also have another, not so precise sense. — On the whole series, see also Did. 10:2 (γνῶσις, πίστις, ἀθανασία); 2 Pet 1:5f; then the Acts of John 109 (Bonnet, *Acta*, 2.1:208): τὸν χαρισάμενον ἡμῖν τὴν ἀλήθειαν, τὴν ἀνάπαυσιν, τὴν γνῶσιν, τὴν δύναμιν, τὴν ἐντολήν, τὴν παρρησίαν, τὴν ἐλπίδα, τὴν ἀγάπην, τὴν ἐλευθερίαν, τὴν εἰς σὲ καταφυγήν. σὺ γὰρ εἶ μόνος κύριε ἡ ῥίζα τῆς ἀθανασίας καὶ ἡ πηγὴ τῆς ἀφθαρσίας καὶ ἡ ἕδρα τῶν αἰώνων, and Poimandres XII (XIV) 18 (Reitzenstein, *Poimandres*, 346): αἱ δυνάμεις αἱ ἐν ἐμοὶ ὑμνεῖτε τὸ ἓν καὶ τὸ πᾶν . . . γνῶσις ἁγία, φωτισθεὶς ἀπὸ σου διὰ σοῦ τὸ νοητὸν φῶς . . . καὶ σύ μοι ἐγκράτεια . . . ὕμνει, δικαιοσύνη μου τὸ δίκαιον ὕμνει δι᾿ ἐμοῦ, κοινωνία ἡ ἐμὴ τὸ πᾶν ὕμνει δι᾿ ἐμοῦ, ὕμνει ἀλήθεια τὴν ἀλήθειαν, τὸ ἀγαθὸν, ἀγαθὸν ὕμνει· ζωὴ καὶ φῶς, ἀφ᾿ ὑμῶν εἰς ὑμᾶς χωρεῖ ἡ εὐλογία. See also Schermann, *Griechische Zauberpapyri*, 43–45. — ὑποπίπτοντα should be read in agreement with LS, against ὑπέπιπτεν πάντα in A and ὑποπίπτει πάντα in H. [C has a gap due to the loss of five pages, spanning 1 Clem. 34:5 to 42:2.]

35:3 What are meant here are the unspeakable good things and glories of the future eon (cf. 34:8 and earlier in 23:2). ὑπομένειν, as in 34:8; δημιουργός, as in 20:11; 26:1; 33:2; also in 59:2 (cf. discussion at 20:11). As in 20:11 and 33:2, there is also a second designation in addition to δημιουργός, the πατὴρ τῶν αἰώνων, which only occurs here in 1 Clem.; see θεὸν τῶν αἰώνων in 55:6 and βασιλεῦ τῶν αἰώνων in 61:2, as well as πατὴρ . . . τοῦ σύμπαντος κόσμου in 19:2. Here, as often elsewhere, in the church and

with the Gnostics, the eons are great angelic beings. πανάγιος is also used in
3 Maccabees, which was written about the same time as 1 Clem. (see 4 Macc
7:4; 14:7). These are the three oldest passages where the word occurs. But
it then found a very rich use in Christianity and is now one of the most
common words in the Greek cultic language: the *pánaja* is the Virgin Mary,
Panajótis is a very common modern Greek proper name.

35:4 Paraenesis sets in. τῶν ὑπομενόντων should be read in agreement
with HL and αὐτόν, which is present in AS, should be deleted; ὑπομενόντων
picks up ὑπομένουσιν again from v. 3.

35:5 In the first part, the paraenesis says: believe. In the second and
third parts, it says: do. Finally, the paraenesis adds a catalog of vices. Also
note the rhetoric of the passage: question and answer, three parallel terms,
εὐάρεστα and εὐπρόσδεκτα, and the structure of the vice catalog (*Lasterkata-
loges*). In ἐκζητῶμεν: ἐπιτελέσωμεν, there is also a deliberate intensification.
— ὁδὸς τῆς ἀληθείας repeats the keyword of the section. The catalog of vices
(*Lasterkatalog*) relies most clearly on Rom 1:29–31. After ἀδικίαν is the reading πονηρίαν in HLS against ἀνομίαν in A, although πονηρίαν is suspected to
be a harmonization with Rom 1:29. In addition, the whole series of vices has
been taken over from Rom 1:29f with the exception of the two elements in the
last position: κενοδοξίαν and ἀφιλοξενίαν. A certain order in 1 Clem. is easy
to recognize. The author builds five pairings that place alongside each other
what belongs together. The final term ἀφιλοξενίαν should be read in agreement with HS; A has *inhumilitatem*, which perhaps presupposes φιλοδοξίαν.
The meaning of hospitality within the moral teachings of 1 Clem. has already
been encountered in 1:2; 10:7; 11:1; 12:1. Since the catalog of vices is quite
general and taken from Rom 1, one must refrain from seeing in it any allusion
to the conditions of the church in Corinth.

35:6 Compare Rom 1:32 with στυγητοὶ τῷ θεῷ and θεοστυγεῖς in Rom
1:30 with θεοστυγία in 1 Clem. 35:5; however in both passages, the constructions are active not passive like here.

35:7–12 See Ps 49:16–23. The citation is almost verbatim, though
1 Clem. deviates only in some places from the text of B and follows the
form of the text in S. The only deviation that comes into consideration is ὡς
λέων in v. 11: these words are missing in the LXX and MT. They come from
Ps 7:3: μή ποτε ἁρπάσῃ ὡς λέων τὴν ψυχήν μου. In terms of content, the
citation contains a woe for the sinner, which is why Clement has adopted it.
It follows well after v. 5f: κακία, δολιότης, καταλαλιά are also threatened in
the citation, and at the beginning of v. 8 one can recognize θεοστυγία. But
the citation also fits well because of its ending, which mentions the path of
salvation: Clement wishes to talk about the path of blessing in this section
(cf. at 31:1), and 36:1 looks back to and takes up ὁδός and σωτήριον.

35:8 σκάνδαλον, this is how the LXX translates the word דְּפִי, which means "insult, ridicule." For this reason σκάνδαλον should be translated with this word, which also fits the context better than "pitfall."

First Clement 36 brings the treatise on the way of blessing to a conclusion. On the way of blessing, one finds Christ and this glorious goal is praised by Clement, though not with his own words, but with the sentences and thoughts of Hebrews and the statements of the OT, which Hebrews had already used in his Christology. This is characteristic for Clement. He lives strongly within tradition, and especially within the area of theology he is the heir of the past. Also, the remarks in 1 Clem. 36, which cannot be accounted for on the basis of Hebrews, give the impression that they have been taken over: before Hebrews and 1 Clem., as Drews has demonstrated (*Liturgie*, 23ff), was the liturgy. As in other places (1 Clem. 20; 33), Clement is also dependent on the liturgy here. As a whole, 36:1 with its parallel clauses and the fivefold anaphora gives the impression of a liturgical character, and some of it can be shown to have come from the liturgy.

36:1 The connection with 35:12 is very close. The salvation of God referred to there is Jesus Christ, and the way by which one comes to him is already described in 35:5. On the description of Christ as the high priest, see Heb 2:17; 3:1; 4:14; 5:10; 6:20; 7:26; 8:1; 9:11; see further Ign. *Phld.* 9:1; Pol. *Phil.* 12:2; Mart. Pol. 14:3; Justin, *Dial.* 33.2; 42.1; 116.1; also T. Reu. 6; T. Sim. 7. First Clement was not just moved to use the title because of Hebrews but also found it in the liturgy (cf. 1 Clem. 61:3 and 64). For him, Christ is the ἀρχιερεὺς τῶν προσφορῶν ἡμῶν. He brings the prayers of the Christians before God, in particular the congregational prayers. On the church service and its importance for Clement, see later at chapters 40–44. First Clement does not testify to the notion that Christ also performed the high priestly work through his death (Hebrews), but may very well have shared that idea. The terms προστάτης and βοηθός also belong to the liturgy (cf. 1 Clem. 61:3; 64; and 59:3f). On ἀσθένεια, see Heb 4:15. Jesus Christ is now up in heaven, and there he graciously cares for his own before God.

36:2 The fact that 1 Clem. stands on the ground of pneumatic Christology is already seen in 16:1, and it is also the assumption of the constructions here. Christ is of divine nature and carries the fullness of divine being in him. He communicates it to believers and reveals God to them, giving them life and light. The Christ-mysticism of the churches comes across clearly in these statements, Pauline and Johannine thoughts are echoed, other features can be found in the communion prayers of the Did., and a very noticeable breath of Hellenistic piety permeates the whole, of a very different kind than the moralism that the letter otherwise represents. ἀτενίζομεν: Christ, coming from heaven, revealed heavenly mysteries; these mysteries are continually made known to believers who are in communion with him. ἐνοπτριζόμεθα: Christ is the mirror in which the image of the Most High appears. Reitzenstein, *Historia*, 242–55 dealt with the view of the mirror in its various gradations in connection with 2 Cor 3:18. In Christ, says 1 Clem., God's highest visage is reflected (cf. a little later ἀπαύγασμα), and so the highest God is recognized through the Son of God in the mystical θέα of Christ (cf. also John 1:8; 6:40 [1 John 3:2]). αὐτοῦ after ὄψις must refer to God, not to Christ. On the self-evident fact that αὐτός refers to God here, see 1 Clem. 32:1. — In the case of the following passages, note that here the consciousness of converts speaks particularly clearly, more precisely of converted gentiles (cf. a parallel in 2 Clem. 1:4–8). On ἀσύνετος καὶ ἐσκοτωμένη διάνοια, see Rom 1:21 and Eph 4:18. εἰς τὸ φῶς should be read in agreement with LS and Clem. Alex.; the reading εἰς τὸ θαυμαστὸν αὐτοῦ φῶς in A and εἰς τὸ θαυμαστὸν φῶς in H have been influenced by 1 Pet 2:9. On φῶς, see the frequent use of the word in the religious sense in Job, then in 1 Pet 2:9, and in Wetter, *Phōs*). The word has a long history, beginning with the natural religions and leading up to the highest religions. On ἀθάνατος γνῶσις, see earlier at 1 Clem. 35:2. When paired together γνῶσις and ζωή seem to be very closely connected with one another. Of course, whoever has received ἀθάνατος γνῶσις also receives ζωή itself. Is there an allusion to the Eucharist in τῆς ἀθανάτου γνώσεως γεύσασθαι? Didache 9:1 (10:2) gives thanks at the Eucharist for γνῶσις and ζωή, and 1 Clem. 36:1f, as has been demonstrated, gives the impression that it has been taken from the liturgy in other respects as well. On ὃς ὢν ἀπαύγασμα κτλ., see Heb 1:3f, which is reproduced in a very abbreviated form by 1 Clem. On ἀπαύγασμα τῆς μεγαλωσύνης, see 1 Clem. 16:2: τὸ σκῆπτρον τῆς μεγαλωσύνης.

36:3 See Heb 1:7 and Ps 103:4. First Clement follows Hebrews, which differs from the LXX.

36:4 See Ps 2:7f and Heb 1:5, but where only the first part of the quotation appears.

36:5 See Heb 1:13 and Ps 109:1.

36:6 closes with a not indistinct glimpse at the "disobedient" in Corinth; obedience was already a major theme of the discussion above (cf. esp. chs. 19–20).

J. Conclusion (37:1—39:9)

Translation

37:1 Let us then, men and brothers, do battle with all our might under his blameless commands. 2 Let us look at those who serve as soldiers under our own rulers, how precisely, how willingly, how obediently they carry out orders. ³ By no means are all prefects and tribunes and centurions and leaders of fifty and so on, but each one does in his own place what he is ordered to do by the king and the leaders. ⁴ The great cannot exist without the small, nor can the small exist without the great. There is a certain mixture in everything and therein lies the benefit.

37:5 Let us take our own body as an example: the head is nothing without the feet, and in the same way the feet are nothing without the head. Even the smallest members of our body are necessary and useful for the whole body. But all members are of one accord and give themselves over to one harmonious obedience so that the whole body may be preserved.

38:1 In the same way, let our whole body be preserved in Christ Jesus, and let everyone submit to his neighbor, on the basis of his own gift. ² The strong should take care of the weak, and the weak should respect the strong; the rich should offer help to the poor, and the poor should give thanks to God that he has given him one through whom his needs can be relieved; the wise should show his wisdom not only through words but also through good works; the humble should not praise himself, but should allow himself to be praised by another; he who is pure in this flesh should not boast but should recognize that it is someone else who gives him (the power for) abstinence. ³ Let us consider, brothers, the material from which we were made and the sort of nature we had when we entered the world, from what kind of grave and darkness our creator and former introduced us into his world (in which) he had prepared his benefactions (for us) before we were born. ⁴ Now since we have all of this from him, let us thank him everywhere. To him be the glory forever and ever, amen!

39:1 Unintelligent, unreasonable, foolish, and uneducated people (are those who) mock and ridicule us, because they puff themselves up in their imagination. ² For what power does the mortal have? Or what power does the earth-born have? ³ For it is written, "There was no form before my eyes, I heard only a breath and a voice. ⁴ What then? Should a mortal be pure in the sight of the Lord, or a man blameless because of his works? For he does not trust his own servants and perceives folly in his own angels. ⁵ Heaven is not pure before him. How much more then those who inhabit houses of clay, to which we, (who are) formed of the same clay, also belong. He struck them like a worm, and from

morning until evening they are no more. Because they could not
help themselves they perished. ⁶ He breathed on them and they
perished because they had no wisdom. ⁷ Call, then, see if anyone
hears you, or if you see one of the holy angels. For indeed, anger
kills a fool, and zeal kills an unwise man. ⁸ I have seen fools take
root, but in a moment their dwelling place was destroyed. ⁹ May
their sons be far away from salvation, may they be mocked at
the doors of the lowly, and may there be none to save them. For
what is prepared for them, the righteous will consume. But they
themselves will not come out from wickedness.

Textual Notes

First Clement 37–39 concludes the first main part of the letter. Obedience
to God and mutual submission must reign in the church. Only fools exalt
themselves.

37:1 ties in closely with the final thought of 36:6 and already prepares
the image that fills out the following sentences.

37:2–3 The Roman army is an example of perfect obedience. The images of the army and soldiers have been an integral part of the early Christian language of edification since Paul. Here, too, Christianity takes over the
legacy of previous Hellenistic tradition: in the diatribe and popular philosophy in general, and then in the language and custom of the mysteries, we
find plenty of images and expressions taken from the life of the soldiers; see
Epictetus, *Diatr.* III 26.29f: τί γὰρ ἄλλο ἢ ὡς ἀγαθὸς στρατηγὸς τὸ ἀνακλητικόν
μοι σεσήμαγκεν; πείθομαι, ἀκολουθῶ, ἐπευφημῶν τὸν ἡγεμόνα, ὑμῶν αὐτοῦ
τὰ ἔργα. καὶ γὰρ ἦλθον, ὅτ' ἐκείνῳ ἔδοξεν, καὶ ἄπειμι πάλιν ἐκείνῳ δοκοῦν καὶ
ζῶντος μου τοῦτο τὸ ἔργον ἦν ὑμνεῖν τὸν θεόν. Seneca, *Ep.* 107.9: *optimum est
pati, quod emendare non possis, et deum, quo auctore cuncta proveniunt, sine
murmuratione comitari: malus miles est, qui imperatorem gemens sequitur.*
(Pseudo-Aristotle) *De mundo* 6 describes the order of the cosmos: ἔοικε
δὲ κομιδῇ τὸ δρώμενον τοῖς ἐν πολέμου καιροῖς μάλιστα γινομένοις, ἐπειδὴ ἡ
σάλπιγξ σημήνη τῷ στρατοπέδῳ. τότε γὰρ τῆς φωνῆς ἕκαστος ἀκούσας ὁ μὲν
ἀσπίδα ἀναιρεῖται, ὁ δὲ θώρακα ἐνδύεται, ὁ δὲ κνημῖδας ἢ κράνος ἢ ζωστῆρα
περιτίθεται, καὶ ὁ μὲν ἵππον χαλινοῖ, ὁ δὲ συνωρίδα ἀναβαίνει, ὁ δὲ σύνθημα
παρεγγυᾷ· καθίσταται δὲ εὐθέως ὁ λοχαγὸς εἰς λόχον, ὁ δὲ ταξίαρχος εἰς τάξιν,
ὁ δὲ ἱππεὺς ἐπὶ κέρας, ὁ δὲ ψιλὸς εἰς τὴν ἰδίαν ἐκτρέχει χώραν· πάντα δὲ ὑφ'
ἕνα σημάντορα κινεῖται κατὰ πρόσταξιν τοῦ τὸ κράτος ἔχοντος ἡγεμόνος. In
the Mithras cult, which had developed strongly the idea of the *militia dei*,
the third degree of the mystic was that of the *miles*, and Tertullian preserved features of the military ritual of the Mithras cult in two well-known

passages: *De corona* 15 and *De praescript. haeret.* 40. In Apuleius, *Metam.*
XI 14, *e cohorte religionis* occurs as a designation of the Isis mysteries. On
the whole question, see the excursus by Dibelius, *Briefe des Apostels Paulus*,
at Eph 6:10–17, then von Harnack, *Militia*; Cumont, *Religion*, xi n1; von
Harnack, *Monuments*, 1:317n1; Reitzenstein, *Mysterienreligionen*, 66ff; von
Soden, "Μυστήριον," 206ff; Eidem, *Athletae*, 187ff. — First Clement refers
to the authorities with the broad title οἱ ἡγούμενοι; the fact that he adds
ἡμῶν is a notable feature of friendliness toward the order of this world; the
Roman is proud of "our army" (cf. also 60:4).

37:3 ἔπαρχος is a very flexible term. It is the highest official of the
province (i.e., the legate or the proconsul). In Egypt it is the prefect of the
rank of knight, who was also called ἡγεμών. The *praefectus praetorio* is also
referred to as ἔπαρχος. χιλίαρχος and ἑκατόνταρχος are the Greek terms for
the Roman titles given in translation. πεντηκόνταρχος probably denotes
the *optio*, the lieutenant of the Roman army. βασιλεύς is the popular title
for the Roman emperor throughout the entirety of the east. Our passage
shows that it was also familiar to the Greek-speaking circles in the capital.
The official Greek titles are Αὐτοκράτωρ = *imperator*, Καῖσαρ = *Caesar*,
Σεβαστός = *Augustus*. The combination of βασιλεύς and ἡγούμενοι also
appear in 1 Pet 2:14; the secular ἡγούμενοι also appear in 1 Clem. 5:7; 60:4
(ἄρχοντες καὶ ἡγούμενοι).

37:4 is not intended to be a new example; the new beginning is λάβωμεν
in v. 5, which corresponds to κατανοήσωμεν in v. 2. Rather, the image of the
army is painted a little further, with generally valid words, perhaps with
memories of the words of the poet (οἱ μεγάλοι δίχα τῶν μικρῶν and οὔτ'
οἱ μικροὶ δίχα τῶν μεγάλων clearly have rhythm). See now Sophocles, *Ajax*
158–61: καίτοι σμικροὶ μεγάλων χωρὶς Σφαλερὸν πύργου ῥῦμα πέλονται·
Μετὰ γὰρ μεγάλων βαιὸς ἄριστ' ἂν Καὶ μέγας ὀρθοῖθ' ὑπὸ μικροτέρων. Plato,
Leges X p. 902 DE: οὐ μὴν οὐδὲ κυβερνήταις οὐδὲ στρατηγοῖς οὐδ' οἰκονόμοις
οὐδ' αὖ τισὶ πολιτικοῖς οὐδ' ἄλλῳ τῶν τοιούτων οὐδενὶ χωρὶς τῶν ὀλίγων καὶ
σμικρῶν πολλὰ ἢ μεγάλα· οὐδὲ γὰρ ἄνευ σμικρῶν τοὺς μεγάλους σαφὶν οἱ
λιθολόγοι λίθους εὖ κεῖσθαι. Euripides, *Fragm.* 21 in Nauck, *Tragoediae* (from
the *Aeolus*): δοκεῖτ' ἂν οἰκεῖν γαῖαν, εἰ πένης ἅπας Λαὸς πολιτεύοιτο πλουσίων
ἄτερ; Οὐκ ἂν γένοιτο χωρὶς ἐσθλὰ καὶ κακά, Ἀλλ' ἔστι τις σύγκρασις, ὥστ'
ἔχειν καλῶς. Ἃ μὴ γὰρ ἔστι τῷ πένητι πλούσιος Δίδωσ'· ἃ δ' οἱ πλουτοῦντες
οὐ κεκτήμεθα, Τοῖσιν πένησι χρώμενοι θηρώμεθα. On the rich and poor that
immediately follow, see 1 Clem. 38:2.

37:5 The image of the body and the limbs is also one of the most common images in ancient literature, especially Hellenism; see the collection
of passages in Lietzmann, *Korinther*, at 1 Cor 12:12; see also Weiß, *Korintherbrief*, on this passage. Clement, however, is not directly dependent

on ancient proverbs and instructional wisdom, as in the previous example, but instead his model is Paul in 1 Cor 12:12–26. This conclusion follows from the specific individual features; for example, the κεφαλή and πόδες in 1 Cor 12:21, the ἀσθενέστερα μέλη, which are nevertheless ἀναγκαῖα in v. 22, the χρεία in v. 21 (εὔχρηστα in 1 Clem. 37:5; χρῆσις in 1 Clem. 37:4), ὅλον τὸ σῶμα in v. 17, συνπάσχει, συνχαίρει in v. 26 (συνπνεῖ in 1 Clem.). The application of the image in 38:1f is thus also determined in Pauline terms: the various χαρίσματα (cf. 1 Cor 12 and also Rom 12:4ff). Only the mystical truth, which resides in the Pauline image (i.e., the ἐν σῶμα ἐν Χριστῷ) is missing in Clement.

First Clement 38: The two illustrations are followed by the application, paraenesis, which then again (v. 3) points to a motive for moral action.

38:1 χάρισμα must be interpreted very broadly here; as the following shows, it is by no means merely understood to mean spiritual gifts, but also see the broad version of the *charismen* in Rom 12:6–8. ἐτέθη can also be understood personally: just as he, the neighbor, was established in his gift.

38:2 Two double examples and then three individual examples indicate a range of gifts. On ἰσχυρός . . . ἀσθενής, see Rom 15:1. However, 1 Clem. does not think of the spiritually strong and weak like Paul, but, as the following πλούσιος shows, of the strong in general (cf. ἰσχυρός and πλούσιος, also 1 Clem. 13:1). On πλούσιος . . . πτωχός, see the Euripides fragment just quoted at 37:4, and then Hermas, *Sim.* II, especially *Sim.* II 5f: ἐπιχορηγεῖ οὖν ὁ πλούσιος τῷ πένητι πάντα ἀδιστάκτως· ὁ πένης δὲ ἐπιχορηγούμενος ὑπὸ τοῦ πλουσίου ἐντυγχάνει αὐτῷ, τῷ θεῷ εὐχαριστῶν περὶ τοῦ διδόντος αὐτῷ. But the judgment concerning the rich and poor is completely different in Hermas than in Clement. After λόγοις, the reading μόνον should probably be read in agreement with L and Clem. Alex. For the wise must also contribute to the edification of the church in words. That is part of the *charismas*. Except this should not be exhausted in words. For a reminder, see 1 Clem. 30:3 and then Jas 3:13. The ταπεινόφρων must be one who somehow stands out from the congregation, probably with respect to spiritual gifts, but yet feels himself to be and designates himself as a servant of others, subordinate to them. On this gift, which was later especially highly valued in monasticism at all times, see the catalog of virtues (*Tugendkatalog*) in Herm. *Mand.* VIII 10: μηδενὶ ἀντιτάσσεσθαι, ἡσύχιον εἶναι, ἐνδεέστερον γίνεσθαι πάντων ἀνθρώπων. See further Herm. *Mand.* XI 8 speaking of the true prophet: πραῢς ἐστι καὶ ἡσύχιος καὶ ταπεινόφρων καὶ ἀπεχόμενος ἀπὸ πάσης πονηρίας καὶ ἐπιθυμίας ματαίας τοῦ αἰῶνος τούτου, καὶ ἑαυτὸν ἐνδεέστερον ποιεῖ πάντων τῶν ἀνθρώπων. On ταπεινοφρονεῖν see 1 Clem. 16–18, and on μαρτυρεῖν see 1 Clem. 17:1f. ὁ ἁγνὸς ἐν τῇ σαρκί is the ascetic in the community who lives as a virgin; he should especially be aware that he has the *donum continentiae* from God. On the warning that recurs frequently in early Christians texts, see Ign. *Pol.* 5:2: εἴ τις δύναται ἐν ἁγνείᾳ μένειν, εἰς τιμὴν τῆς σαρκὸς τοῦ κυρίου ἐν ἀκαυχησίᾳ μενέτω. ἐὰν καυχήσηται, ἀπώλετο. Tertullian, *Virg.* 13: *Et si a deo confertur continentiae virtus, quid gloriaris, quasi non acceperis.* The question in v. 2 is: to what extent does Clement have the opponents in Corinth in mind with this characteristic?

38:3 One cannot help but think of the liturgy or of some liturgical tradition, such as prayer or hymn. The idea is as follows: from v. 2, where God was already very clearly referred to at the end, attention is diverted to the general benefactions God bestows on all of us, that is upon mankind as a whole. We have all received great things from him when we entered the world and received a share in its beauty and its benefits. ἐκ ποίας ὕλης, what must be meant is: from contemptible, perishable material (ὕλη = matter, which only occurs seldomly like this in the LXX, and at that only in the Apocrypha). ποῖοι καὶ τίνες: weak and incomprehensible; see, for example, Justin, *1 Apol.* 61.10: ἐπειδὴ τὴν πρώτην γένεστιν ἡμῶν ἀγνοοῦντες κατ᾽ ἀνάγκην γεγεννήμεθα ἐξ ὑγρᾶς σπορᾶς . . . . The κόσμος, on the other hand, is the beautiful, well-ordered world as it was already praised in 1 Clem. 20 and 33. There, also the εὐεργεσίαι of God in the world were already enumerated. ἐκ ποίου τάφου καὶ σκότους should be compared with Ps 138:15: οὐκ ἐκρύβη τὸ ὀστοῦν μου ἀπὸ σοῦ, ὃ ἐποίησας ἐν κρυφῇ, καὶ ἡ ὑπόστασίς μου ἐν τοῖς κατωτάτω τῆς γῆς. It is an echo of ancient belief in "mother earth," which can be heard in the psalm and which is perceptible in 1 Clem.; for Clement cannot understand τάφος as the mother's womb if already σκότος could potentially be construed with it. τάφος and σκότος are the great kingdom under the earth, out of which the souls of the unborn come. Note also here the clash of diverse views and the joyful optimism of the worldview.

38:4 Note the liturgical conclusion: εὐχαριστεῖν and the doxology. εὐχαριστεῖν does not fit at all within the context. ὑποτάσσεθαι would have been expected.

First Clement 39: The strength of the earthborn which exalts itself is nothing before God; only fools puff themselves up in the feeling of their own strength.

39:1 The accumulated expressions ἄφρονες κτλ. are meant to paint a picture of the utter folly of the pompous. Clement thinks here strongly of the opponents in Corinth and wants to strike them.

39:2 γηγενεῖς here are simply people, and the word denotes the nothingness of their origin; the giants (γηγενεῖς) and their defiance are not in mind in any way.

39:3–9 The quotation comes from Job 4:16—5:5, the first speech of Eliphaz, and reflects rather precisely our LXX text. The sentence οὐρανὸς δὲ οὐ καθαρὸς ἐνώπιον αὐτοῦ in v. 5 comes from Job 15:15, the second speech of Eliphaz: [εἰ κατὰ ἁγίων οὐ πιστεύει] οὐρανὸς δὲ οὐ καθαρὸς ἐναντίον αὐτοῦ. The same setting here and there facilitated bringing the text over, for Job 15:14–16 repeats the material of Job 4:17–19 heavily. Clement uses the quotation because it (1) paints the nothingness of man, and (2) contains the heavy threat against the fools who exalt themselves.

39:3 The speaker in Job 4 is Eliphaz, and the opening words depict his dream vision.

39:4 In v. 4 the words of the night revelation begin. The παῖδες of God are the angels.

39:7 ὀργή and ζῆλος are probably the fool's own wrath and zeal that ruin him. The rare κολαβρίζειν, according to Suidas, who uses a false etymology, means "to mock, mockery." The word also appears in Hesychius and Athenaeus VIII p. 364A in the form καλαβρίζειν.

IV. The Ugly Quarrel in Corinth Should Be Settled as Soon as Possible (40:1—61:3)

The second main section is 1 Clem. 40–61. The quarrel in Corinth is extremely ugly and should be dismissed as soon as possible. Chapters 40–50 apply mainly to the congregation as a whole; 51–58 address the originators of the dispute directly; 59–61 conclude the admonitions in a solemn manner with prayer.

A. The Congregational Office Is Appointed by God (40:1—44:6)

Translation

40:1 Since (all) this is clear to us, and since we have peered into the depths of divine knowledge, we must do everything the Lord has asked us to do in an orderly way, at the appointed times: 2 He did not order the sacrifices and cultic rites to be carried out at random and in disarray, but at the fixed times and hours. 3 According to his most supreme council he arranged where and by whom he wants them to be performed, so that everything might be done with pious timidity according to his pleasure and thus be agreeable to his will. 4 Those, therefore, who offer their sacrifices at the appointed times are well pleasing and blessed. For since they follow the statutes of the

Lord, they do not go astray. [5] For special worship services have been prescribed for the high priest, and the priests are assigned their own place, and the Levites have their own ordinances. The layman is assigned to the regulations that apply to the laity. [41:1] Let each of us, brothers, please God in his own place, keeping a good conscience and not exceeding the appointed measure of his service, in reverent timidity. [2] Burnt offerings and vow offerings and sin offerings and trespass offerings are not offered everywhere, brothers, but only in Jerusalem. And even there, sacrifices are not offered in every place, but (only) before the sanctuary on the altar, by the high priest and his aforementioned ministers after the offering has been carefully examined. [3] Now, those who do something contrary to the order of his will receive death as their due fate. Behold, brothers, the greater the knowledge of which we have been made worthy, the greater the danger to which we are exposed.

[42:1] The gospel was proclaimed to the apostles for us by the Lord, and Jesus was sent out by God. [2] Christ, therefore, came from God, and the apostles from Christ: both of these things happened in an orderly manner according to the will of God. [3] Now when they had received their commissions, had been filled with certainty by the resurrection of the Lord Jesus Christ, and had been strengthened in the word of God, they went out in the joyfulness of the Holy Spirit to proclaim the good news of the nearness of the kingdom of God. [4] They preached in village and town and, after being tested by the Spirit, appointed their firstfruits as bishops and deacons of the future believers.

[42:5] And this was nothing surprisingly new, for this was written about bishops and deacons a long time ago. For the Scripture says thus in one place: "I will establish their bishops in righteousness, and their deacons in faith."

[43:1] And what is surprising about the fact that those entrusted by God in Christ with such a great work appointed the aforementioned, when the blessed servant Moses, faithful in his house, recorded in the Holy Books everything that was assigned to him? The rest of the prophets follow him, bearing witness to what he had decreed in the law. [2] When jealousy had broken out over the priesthood, and the tribes quarreled with each other over which of them should be adorned with the glorious name, he ordered the twelve tribal chiefs to bring him twelve rods, each with the name of their tribe upon it. He took them, bound them together, sealed them with the rings of the tribal chiefs, and placed them in the tabernacle on the table of God. ³ Then he closed the tent, sealed the keys in a similar way as he did the rods, ⁴ and he said to them, "Men and brothers, the tribe whose rod breaks forth is the one God has chosen to be his priests and to serve him." ⁵ On the next day, he called together all of Israel, 600,000 men, and showed them the seals of the chiefs of the tribes, and he opened the tabernacle, and took out the rods. And it came to pass that the rod of Aaron had not only broken forth, but had also borne fruit. ⁶ What do you think, beloved? Did not Moses know that this was going to happen? Of course he knew. But so that there might be no disorder in Israel, he did this so that the name of the one who is true and unique might be glorified. To him be the glory forever and ever! Amen.

⁴⁴:¹ And our apostles also knew (in advance) through our Lord Jesus Christ that there would be a dispute over the name of the bishop. ² For this reason, knowing this in advance, they appointed those already mentioned and then gave orders that when they fell asleep, other proven men would take over their office. ³ Therefore, we consider it wrong to dismiss such men from the office of bishop, men who were appointed by them or later by other proven men, with the consent of the whole congregation, and who served the flock of Christ in an unimpeachable, humble, peaceful, and modest manner, to whom everyone gave a good testimony for a long time. ⁴ For we consider it no slight sin if we remove from the office of the bishop those who have brought the offerings blamelessly and in a holy manner. ⁵ Blessed are the earlier presbyters who came to a fruitful and perfect end. For no longer do they need to fear that someone will expel them from the place assigned to them. ⁶ For we see that you have removed some of them from their office which they administered with honor, even though they were walking well.

Textual Notes

The order of the office arose from the will of God, who is a God of order (1 Clem. 40–44). The connection to the foregoing is good, since order and mutual submission and subordination to the will of God were already mentioned there (see 1 Clem. 37–39). First Clement 40:1 also refers back to the content of these last remarks: τούτων.

40:1 On ἐγκύπτειν, see 1 Clem. 45:2; 53:1; 62:3. In these three passages, the word is about the study of the Holy Scriptures being full of love and full of understanding: ἐγκύπτειν εἰς τὰ βάθη τῆς θείας γνώσεως. For 1 Clem., gnosis above all is the correct understanding of the Sacred Writings and the will of God set forth in them. He himself lives in the OT, has just quoted from it, and will immediately refer to it again (1 Clem. 40f), concluding with a reference to the γνῶσις (41:4). On βάθη τῆς γνώσεως, which means "the last, hidden knowledge," see 1 Cor 2:10; Rev 2:24. In Dan 2:22 LXX it is said of God: ἀνακαλύπτων τὰ βαθέα καὶ σκοτεινὰ καὶ γινώσκων τὰ ἐν τῷ σκότει καὶ τὰ ἐν τῷ φωτί (Theodotion: αὐτὸς ἀποκαλύπτει βαθέα καὶ ἀπόκρυφα, γινώσκων τὰ ἐν τῷ σκότει καὶ τὸ φῶς μετ' αὐτοῦ ἐστιν). In Plato, *Theaet.* p. 183 E, it is said of Parmenides: καί μοι ἐφάνη βάθος τι ἔχειν παντάπασιν γεναῖον. See also Irenaeus, *Haer.* II 22.3: *profunda dei adinvenire*; II 28.9: *altitudines dei exquirere.* The term βάθη τῆς θείας γνώσεως sounds strongly mystic, gnostic, but by no means does Clement understand it in this way. κατὰ καιροὺς τεταγμένους: here is already implied what then becomes quite clear in the following from the choice of the example and the expressions used, namely, that the cultus is the field on which the church officials find their activity, that they are entrusted with the order of the worship service and that their position in the cultus has been attacked by the opponents. τάξις must be in the worship service, and it has been disturbed in Corinth.

40:2–5 offers the evidence for the existence and the necessity of order from the OT. But the individual expressions and the whole manner of expression are chosen in such a way that the direct application to the church conditions is easy and clear for everyone involved: if v. 5 were missing, we would not be able to say with certainty whether Christian or Jewish issues were in mind. The statement in v. 4 is even in the present tense.

A peculiarly high *estimation of the cultic institutions of Judaism* is present in 1 Clem. 40–41. Already, in 32:2 Clement lists among the great gifts of God to Jacob: priests and Levites who serve at the altar of God, then the Lord Jesus, the kings and princes from the tribe of Judah, and the honor of the other tribes. In 1 Clem. 40–41, the priesthood and sacrificial order are derived from God's holy will. God is a God of order; whoever violates his revealed will certainly will die. The precepts of worship also belong to the holy, revealed order, which is laid down in the scrolls of the Scriptures, and they naturally had to be observed carefully and literally by Israel. But the law of worship was not only a norm of the past for Israel, it is also now a type of the constitutional and religious relationships that exist in the congregation. Just as God gave a fixed order then in the old covenant about how, where, when, by whom the sacrifices were made, so also in the new covenant there must be order within the congregation. One cannot simply say here that the Old Testament is evaluated as a prophetic document or moral law, as so often in the epistles, but the use of the Holy Scriptures passes over here into that of permanently valid constitutional documents, and the cultic commandments begin to move to the moral legislation. But of course the author does not even remotely think of transferring the Old Testament ceremonial law in the literal sense to Christian congregational relations. Correspondence takes place here and there, and it is the will of God that has an effect on both orders. See also Wrede, *Untersuchungen*, 38–50, 91–93.

40:2 After λειτουργίας, AH read ἐπιτελεῖσθαι καί, LS omit the words. They probably are found there due to the influence from ἐπιτελεῖν in v. 1 or ἐπιτελεῖσθαι in v. 3.

40:3 ὑπερτάτῳ, the superlative is only used here with two endings, as it is occasionally elsewhere (cf. Kühner-Blaß, *Grammatik*, 1:§152).

40:4 Here and also in what follows, Clement speaks of temple service in the present tense, from which, of course, it cannot be concluded that the temple was still standing when he wrote. For him, the cultic system is fixed in the Holy Books of the OT, and this order of God remains, even if the temple is destroyed; on this whole way of looking at things, see Hebrews, which continually speaks of sacrifice and the cult of the Jews without saying that the temple no longer stands, and which speaks generally much more of the tabernacle than of the temple. See then further at Barn. 7f; Diogn. 3; and Josephus, *Ant.* III 9f, which explains to the Greeks at length certain pieces of the Jewish cult in the present tense. Finally, see the Talmud, which speaks frequently of the conditions of the Jewish community as of present conditions.

40:5 The three types of priestly individuals probably have been wrongly judged as types of Christ: (1) presbyters and deacons or (2) bishops, presbyters, and deacons. Clement wishes to speak only of the order of the old covenant. Also, the types of sacrifices in 1 Clem. 41:2 do not need to be interpreted in view of Christian cultic practices. λαϊκός is used in contrast to the priests and Levites. It is missing in the LXX, which instead often speaks of the λαός in this sense. In later Greek translations, so far as they have been preserved, λαϊκός occurs sparingly: Aquila, Symmachus, and Theodotion have it in 1 Sam 21:4 and Symmachus has it in 1 Sam 22:26. Our passage seems to be the oldest in which the word is found; see the ancient Christian writings of Clem. *Ep. ad Jacob.* 5 (de Lagarde, *Clementina*, 7.38); Clem. Alex. *Strom.* 3.90.1 (p. 552); 5.33.3 (p. 665); Tert. *De bapt.* 17; *De fuga* 11; *De praescr.* 41; Euseb. *Hist. eccl.* 5.28.12; Apostolic Constitutions frequently; etc. It should be noted that 1 Clem., this letter from the Roman congregation, uses the expression λαϊκός in contrast to priest: though speaking of Jewish matters, the application of 1 Clem. 41:1 is very closely connected, and in the whole part the ministers are spoken of in contrast to the congregation. The Christian *ordo* appears in its nascent form. Instead of δέδοται (HSL), read δέδεται as attested to in A.

41:1 introduces a short paraenesis, then immediately turns back to the examples from the OT. On ἐν τῷ ἰδίῳ τάγματι, see 37:3. εὐαρεστείτω should be read with HLS against εὐχαριστείτω in A; thus the inferences which have occasionally been attached to this second reading collapse. First Clement unfortunately does not say what the λειτουργία of the layman is, but there is probably little more for him to do than to listen and enjoy the Eucharist. κανών also appears in 1:3 and 7:2.

41:2 presupposes this beyond the general idea of the order of worship: the members of the congregation are not to worship without the ministers. The program found in Ign. *Smyr.* 8:1f is found here: μηδεὶς χωρὶς τοῦ ἐπισκόπου τι πρασσέτω τῶν ἀνηκόντων εἰς τὴν ἐκκλησίαν. . . . — The types of sacrifices are taken from the LXX. Clement lists the main types known from the OT. The first offering listed is the burnt offering, תָּמִיד, which is constant and offered daily, thus θυσία ἐνδελεχισμοῦ = the offering of uninterrupted continuation. (The translation: burnt offering is not entirely fitting. Better would be: constant burnt offering of the congregation.) The *tamid* offering consists of a year old lamb in the morning and in the evening, which are brought together with food and drink offerings. The regulations are found in Exod 29:38–42 and Num 28:3–8. Furthermore, Clement counts the free-will offerings and the special offerings. There are three types: (a) the vow offering נֶדֶר (Num 6:13f et al.); (b) the sin offering חַטָּאת (Lev 4:3ff; 9:2ff et al.); finally (c) the guilt offering אָשָׁם (Lev 14:13–17, 24–28), which is closely related to the sin offering (thus καί, not ἤ). The determination of the place ἔμπροσθεν τοῦ ναοῦ denotes the place in front of the actual temple building (ναός; the temple complex as a whole with all its buildings, courtyards, walls, and gates is called ἱερόν). In front of the temple building, in the forecourt of the priests, there is a great altar for burnt offerings, the "altar" *par excellence*, on which all sacrifices were offered except the incense offering, which is offered on the golden altar of incense in the sanctuary of the temple building. On the whole sacrificial system and the temple with its topography, see Schürer, *Geschichte*, 2:279–305 (§24 IV: "Der tägliche Cultus" ["The daily cult"]). — μωμοσκοπηθέν τὸ προσφερόμενον is a nominative absolute. μῶμος is the LXX translation of מוּם, the technical- cultic term for the defect of a sacrificial animal. The Greek word has been chosen because of its consonance with the Hebrew term. μωμοσκοπεῖν and μωμοσκόπος seem to be Jewish-Hellenistic terms, which have so far only been attested in Jewish and Christian writers; see Philo, *Agr.* 29.130 (p. 320) (where the explanation of μωμοσκόπος is given): πρόνοιαν ἔχειν . . . τῶν . . . καταθυομένων ζῴων ὡς οὐδὲν οὐδεμιᾷ τὸ παράπαν ἀλλ᾽ οὐδὲ τῇ βραχυτάτῃ χρήσεται λώβῃ, καί τινας δεῖ ὅσους ἐπ᾽ αὐτὸ τοῦτο χειροτονεῖν τὸ ἔργον, οὓς ἔνιοι μωμοσκόπους ὀνομάζουσιν, ἵνα ἄμωμα καὶ ἀσινῆ προσάγηται τῷ βωμῷ ἱερεῖα. Clement of

Alexandria, *Strom.* 4.117.4 (ed. Mangey, 617): ἦσαν δὲ κἂν ταῖς τῶν θυσιῶν προσαγωγαῖς παρὰ τῷ νόμῳ οἱ τῶν ἱερείων μωμοσκόποι: from both passages it can be seen that the term was unfamiliar to Greek readers. — According to the word order, διὰ τοῦ ἀρχιερέως κτλ. can also be connected with προσφερόμενον, but Clement probably wants to emphasize the offering of the sacrifice itself by the high priest and his assistants.

41:3 παρὰ τὸ καθῆκον is a Stoic *terminus technicus*; see Lietzmann, *Römer*, at Rom 1:28. Violation of the cultic order is punishable by death, which is a fact that is attested several times in the OT; see, for example, Lev 17 and Deut 12f. πρόστιμον is a good, Hellenistic word (Attic ἐπιτίμιον).

41:4 On gnosis, see 1 Clem. 40:1.

First Clement 42 proceeds to describe the NT order. Note the stark, determined theory of succession, which is presented within the chapter: God, Christ, the apostles, the bishops, and the deacons.

42:1 ἡμῖν should be read with AHS against the reading in L, which is the easier reading and perhaps intended to align better with 44:1.

42:2 On the thought, see John 17:18, which is however inwardly filled with a completely different spirit than the statements in 1 Clem.; see further Tertullian, *Praescr.* 37: *in ea regula incedimus, quam ecclesia ab apostolis, apostoli a Christo, Christus a deo tradidit.*

42:3 Note the compounded expressions that highlight the special outfitting and commissioning of the apostles: παραγγελίας, πληροφορηθέντες, πιστωθέντες, μετὰ πληροφορίας. On the proposition of the sentence, see Iren. *Haer.* III 1.1: *Non enim per alios dispositionem salutis nostrae cognovimus, quam per eos, per quos evangelium pervenit ad nos; quod quidem tunc praeconaverunt, postea vero per dei voluntatem in scripturis nobis tradiderunt* ... *Postea enim quam surrexit dominus noster a mortuis, et induti sunt supervenientis spiritus sancti virtutem ex alto, de omnibus adimpleti sunt et habuerunt perfectam agnitionem: exierunt in fines terrae, ea quae a deo nobis bona sunt evangelizantes, et caelestem pacem hominibus annuntiantes.* On ἐξῆλθον, see also the fragment of the kerygma of Peter in Clem. Alex. *Strom.* 6.48.1 p. 765 (Hennecke, *Apokryphen*, 170, frg. 1); Aristides, *Apol.* 2; Justin, *1 Apol.* 39.3; 45.5; 49.5; et. al. Everywhere here, the program of the Twelve is reported after the resurrection.

42:4 The proclamation of the apostles thus happened everywhere: κατὰ χώρας καὶ πόλεις. On καθίστανον, see Titus 1:5: ἵνα ... καταστήσῃς κατὰ πόλιν πρεσβυτέρους. Before καθίστανον, L reads: *eos qui obaudiebant voluntati dei baptizantes*, an addition which fits the context quite well and receives a firm connection through αὐτῶν after ἀπαρχάς, but which cannot be maintained against the reading in AHSC. — αὐτῶν can refer to either the ἀπόστολοι or the χῶραι καὶ πόλεις. On ἀπαρχαί, see Rom 16:5 and 1 Cor 16:15, two passages on which 1 Clem. is certainly dependent. On τῷ πνεύματι, see πνεύματος ἁγίου in v. 3. The ministers are not only the firstfruits, but also those chosen by the Holy Spirit. ἐπισκόπους καὶ διακόνους, see Phil 1:1; 1 Tim 3:1–13; Did. 15; Herm. Vis. III 5.1 (and Ignatius frequently, who however already knows of the monarchical episcopate and the threefold hierarchical office). On the municipal constitution in 1 Clem., see Knopf, *Nachapostolischen Zeitalter*, 160; Lietzmann, "Verfassungsgeschichte," 134ff.

42:5 After the historical proof, Clement provides still the scriptural proof, Isa 60:17 LXX, but with a strangely strong deviation: καὶ δώσω τοὺς ἄρχοντάς σου ἐν εἰρήνῃ καὶ τοὺς ἐπισκόπους σου ἐν δικαιοσύνῃ.

First Clement 43 continues the scriptural proof with an example from narrative. On the use of the OT here, see 1 Clem. 12 where, as here, the OT report is reproduced by the author in his own words in quite some detail. The OT narrative is very important for 1 Clem. because it deals with the divine institution of the priesthood. The meaning of the chapter in context is as follows: It is not at all surprising that Christ's apostles instituted the *episkopen* and *diakonen*. Only Levi's tribe was clothed with the priesthood, and by a miracle, when the twelve tribes disputed among themselves which of them should become the priestly tribe, the tribe of Levi's dignity was conferred upon it. Similarly, the apostles, knowing beforehand that there would be a dispute about the office, gave a firm order concerning it.

43:1 On the personal construction πιστεύομαι τι, see Rom 3:2; 1 Cor 9:17 et al.; it is quite familiar in the Hellenistic language of Xenophon. On πιστὸς θεράπων ἐν ὅλῳ τῷ οἴκῳ, see Num 12:7: οὐχ οὕτως ὁ θεράπων μου Μωϋσῆς ἐν ὅλῳ τῷ οἴκῳ μου πιστός ἐστιν and then see Heb 3:5. On θεράπων, see 1 Clem. 4:12, then 51:3, 5; 53:5. On μακάριος, see Justin, *Dial.* 56.1: Μωϋσῆς οὖν, ὁ μακάριος καὶ πιστὸς θεράπων θεοῦ. The epithet μακάριος (μακαρίτης) is very common in the classical era in Greek and, like our "blessed," simply denotes the dead; see Rohde, *Pysche*, 1:308.1 (otherwise, however, it is used in the sense of congratulation, which is how it is used in 1 Clem. 40:4; 44:5; 50:5; see the Beatitudes of the Sermon on the Mount). ἐσημειώσατο, the sense is: Moses already reported the divine institution of the priesthood, which is an example and a type for the present. οἱ λοιποὶ προφῆται, for Moses is also a prophet in Deut 18:15; see Acts 3:21f; 7:37; and more: the historical books are also written by prophets, David prophesies in the Psalter, and so the whole OT can be called a work of the prophets, as it seems to be the case here.

43:2 The narrative comes from Num 17. This narrative is also used by Philo, *Vita Mosis* II [III] 21, 175–80 (ed. Mangey, 161f) and by Josephus, *Ant.* IV 4.2. On the haggadic embellishment of the Old Testament account, the individual features of which are listed in the explanation, see what has already been said on 1 Clem. 31:3. — τῷ ἐνδόξῳ ὀνόματι, see 1 Clem. 44:1: τοῦ ὀνόματος τῆς ἐπισκοπῆς. — ἑκάστης φύλης can either be connected with κατ᾽ ὄνομα or else the construction is ἐπιγράφω τί τινος, passive ἐπιγράφομαί τινος, which in addition to the more common ἐπιγράφομαί τι also occurs; see Plutarch, *Pyth. orac.* 13 p. 400 E: ἐβούλοντο Κορίνθιοι καὶ τὸν ἐν Πίσῃ χρυσοῦν ἀνδριάντα καὶ τὸν ἐνταῦθα τουτονὶ θησαυρὸν ἐπιγράψαι τῆς πόλεως; on the other construction, see Dionysius of Halicarnassus, *Ant. rom.* IV 58: ἀσπὶς ἐπιγεγραμμένη τὰς ὁμολογίας. On λαβὼν ἔδησεν and in general what follows, note that in 1 Clem., it is Moses who acts throughout the narrative, whereas the narration in Numbers is much more focused on God's activity. First Clement, however, can much more easily bring Moses into parallel with the apostles, as he clearly does in 44:1. Philo and Josephus modernize, as does Clement. ἔδησεν καὶ ἐσφράγισεν τοῖς δακτυλίοις τῶν φυλάρχων and shortly thereafter in v. 3 κλείσας τὴν σκηνὴν ἐσφράγισεν τὰς κλεῖδας ὡσαύτως ὡς καὶ τὰς ῥάβδους and in v. 5 ἐπεδείξατο τοῖς φυλάρχοις τὰς σφραγίδας are connections that 1 Clem. makes beyond Num 17. Their sense is easily recognizable: Moses is presented in such a manner that he eliminates all human intervention, excluding every possibility of a scam.

43:5 Also πρωΐας δὲ γενομένης συνεκάλεσεν πάντα τὸν Ἰσραήλ reflects the same intention. In Numbers, Moses and Aaron go to the tent and then show the rods to the people who are depicted as waiting outside. On 1 Clem., however, see Philo: τῇ δὲ ὑστεραίᾳ λογίῳ πληχθείς, ἅπαντος τοῦ ἔθνους παρεστῶτος εἰσέρχεται, and also, in Josephus, Aaron is not mentioned. The 600,000 men is the number known from Numbers (cf. Num 1:46; 2:32; 11:21; 26:51; 31:32. καρπόν: almonds (שְׁקֵדִים) according to Num 17:23 MT and Josephus (ἀμύγδαλα); κάρυα according to the LXX and Philo, but κάρυον is an ambiguous term and can refer to the seed of the stone fruit in general.

43:6 τοῦ ἀληθινοῦ καὶ μόνου is quite strikingly reminiscent of John 17:3: σὲ τὸν μόνον ἀληθινὸν θεόν. What is meant is: The only one who really deserves the name God; see the parallel with Demochares (ca. 300 BCE) in Athenaeus VI 62, p. 253 C: τὸν Δημήτριον (Poliorcetes is meant) οἱ Ἀθηναῖοι ἐδέχοντο . . . ἐπάδοντες ὡς εἴη μόνος θεὸς ἀληθινός, οἱ δ᾽ ἄλλοι καθεύδουσιν ἢ ἀποδημοῦσιν ἢ οὐκ εἰσίν. The epithets μόνος and ἀληθινός for God are separated quite frequently in the ancient Christian literature. The precise reading in any case is not entirely certain: A omits it; H has τοῦ ἀληθινοῦ καὶ μόνου κυρίου; SC have τοῦ ἀληθινοῦ καὶ μόνου θεοῦ (John 17:3); L simply has τοῦ ἀληθινοῦ καὶ μόνου. One must choose between L and H.

44:1 links up with προήδει in 43:6 and 43:2 and the dispute over the name of the priesthood. διὰ τοῦ κυρίου does not mean: by the heavenly Christ, but instead Clement has in mind the instruction given by the earthly Christ to his own. Afterward, in 1 Clem. 46:8, he cites a word of the Lord, which he has in mind here and in which he finds the dispute about the office prophesied. But other words about strife and conflict are also found in a word of the Lord and may have been in the author's mind. ἐπισκοπή is the office of bishop (cf. 1 Tim 3:1). The later church also experienced the great disputes due to ambition to obtain the bishop's chair; see already Hermas, *Sim.* VIII 7.4, 6; then the anti-montanists in Eusebius, *Hist. eccl.* 5.16.7: Μοντανὸν . . . ἐν ἐπιθυμίᾳ ψυχῆς ἀμέντρῳ φιλοπρωτείας, the anti-modalists in Eusebius, *Hist. eccl.* 5.28.8–12 on Natalius: δελεαζόμενος τῇ . . . πρωτοκαθεδρίᾳ, Cornelius on Novatus: προπάλαι ὀρεγόμενος τῆς ἐπισκοπῆς . . . καὶ κρύπτων ἐν αὐτῷ τὴν προπετῆ ταύτην αὐτοῦ ἐπιθυμίαν (Euseb., *Hist. eccl.* 6.43.5), Tertullian, *Bapt.* 7: *episcopatus aemulatio schismatum mater est* . . . .

44:2 τοὺς προειρημένους points back to 42:4f. ἐπινομήν should be read with A and L (*legem*); ἐπιδομήν H; ἐπὶ δοκιμήν S; C apparently did not understand the expression; ἐπινομή has to be brought together with ἐπινέμω "to assign, allocate," but remains a curious word in the non-attested sense of "arrangement." ἔδωκαν, namely the apostles; κοιμηθῶσιν, namely the *episkopen* and *diakonen*, to which αὐτῶν also refers. μεταξύ = afterward (cf. Acts 13:42; Barn. 13:5).

44:3 ὑπ᾽ ἐκείνων sc. the apostles. The style in the entire sentence is strongly reminiscent of Hellenistic official style, as it appears in the documents (*Urkunden*) about official installation and official honors; on κατασταθέντας ὑπ᾽ ἐκείνων κτλ., see for example Dittenberger, *Sylloge*, 1:297.2f: Ἱκέσιος Μητροδώρου Ἐφέσιος ὁ κατασταθεὶς ἐπ᾽ Αἰγίνας ὑπὸ τοῦ βασιλέως Εὐμένεος. Dittenberger, *Sylloge*, 737.136f in the well-known, much-treated inscription that contains the statutes of the Iobacchae association: εὔκοσμος δὲ κληρούσθω ἢ καθιστάσθω ὑπὸ ἱερέως (the chairman of the meeting should be drawn by lot or appointed by the priest). 2:451.16–18: καὶ λόγον ἐνεγκόντω περὶ τᾶς γεγενημένας δαπάνας τοὺς ἐπὶ ταῦτα κατασταθέντας. 2:554.9: καταστήσει δὲ καὶ νεωκόρον, among other texts. On the phrase συνευδοκησάσης τῆς ἐκκλησίας πάσης, see 2:514.52f: ἔδοξε Λατίοις καὶ Ὀλοντίοις κοινᾶι βουλευσαμένοις, συνευδοκησάντων καὶ Κνωσίων . . . . 2:514.44–48: ὁ παραγενόμενος πρεσβευτὰς παρὰ τᾶς πόλεος τᾶς Κνωσίων Ἀγησίπολις Ἀγαθάνδρω ποτανέγραψε τὸ ὑποτεταγμένον ψάφισμα, συνευδοκιόντων καὶ τῶν παραγενομένων πρεσβευτᾶν. 2:854.1–4: ἀπέδοτο Ἀλέξων Χαριξένου συνευδοκεόντων καὶ τῶν υἱῶν αὐτοῦ Δίωνος, Χαριξένου τῶι Ἀπόλλωνι τῶι Πυθίωι σῶμα ἀνδρεῖον ὧι ὄνομα θραικίδας. And quite appropriate 2:855.6–10: ἀνέθηκε Ἀγησιβούλα Φυσκίς, συνευδοκεόντων τοῦ τε πατρὸς αὐτᾶς Λύκωνος καὶ τᾶς ματρὸς Ἁρμοξένας, τῶι Ἀπόλλωνι τῶι Πυθίωι σῶμα γυναικεῖον, αἴ ὄνομα Μνασώ. On the honorable description of the administration in the following, see Pap. Amherst 139 (Wilcken, *Papyruskunde I.2*, num. 406): οὖσπερ ἐγγυώμεθα καὶ παραστησόμεθα ἐξ ἀλληλεγγύης ἀμέμπτως <ἀποπληροῦντας> τὴν ἐνχιριστῖσαν (= ἐγχειρισθεῖσαν) αὐτοῖς λιτουργίαν ἐν μηδενὶ μεμφθῆναι. Dittenberger, *Or. inscr.* 1:339.49–53: ἔν τε ταῖς ἄλλαις ἀρχαῖς καὶ λειτουργίαις, εἰς ἃς ὁ δῆμος αὐτὸν προκεχείρισται, ἴσον ἑαυτὸν καὶ δίκαιον παρείσχηται βουλόμενος . . . κατὰ μηθὲν ἐνλείπειν τῆι πρὸς τὸ πλῆθος εὐνοίαι. 2:566.6–11: Μάρκον Αὐρήλιον Ἀρτέμωνα . . . ἄρξαντα πᾶσαν ἀρχὴν καὶ λειτοργίαν ἐπιφανῶς καὶ μεγαλοφρόνως. On μεμαρτυρημένους, see at 1 Clem. 17:1. On the overall style, the honorific participles, see after 1 Clem. 5:7. On ἀμέμπτως καὶ ὁσίως, see 1 Thess 2:10: ὡς ὁσίως καὶ δικαίως καὶ ἀμέμπτως. The phrase προσφέρειν τὰ δῶρα consists in the offering of the congregational prayers, especially those that accompany the Eucharist, and in the offering of the Eucharist itself, see Knopf, *Nachapostolischen Zeitalter.*

44:5 On ἔγκαρπον καὶ τελείαν, see 1 Clem. 56:1. The fixed place now assigned to the deceased presbyters is the heavenly place of honor (cf. 5:4, 7).

44:6 makes a statement that is very important for the occasion of the letter: some presbyters have been deposed by the Corinthian majority. Unfortunately, we do not learn why. ἀμέμπτως as in vv. 3 and 4. τετιμημένης is a difficult reading, but it is present in AHS and, it seems, in C; L has *facto*, but this does not decide the matter as to whether it reflects the reading πεποιημένης. Hilgenfeld suggests τετηρημένης. On πολιτεύεσθαι, see at 1 Clem. 3:4.

B. Noble Men Are Only Deposed by Villains (45:1—46:9)

Translation

45:1 Be contentious and zealous, brothers, for what belongs to salvation! 2 You have searched the Holy Scriptures, the true writings which have been given by the Holy Spirit. 3 You know that there is nothing written in them that is false and forged. You will not find (in them) that the righteous men were driven out by holy men. 4 Righteous men were persecuted but by wicked men; they were thrown into prison, but by wicked men; they were stoned by transgressors of the law; they were killed by those who had given place to detestable and unjust jealousy. 5 When they suffered this, they endured bravely. 6 What then should we say (about this), brothers? Was Daniel thrown into the lion's den by those who feared God? 7 Or were Ananias and Azarias, and Misael put into the furnace of fire by the servants of the magnificent and glorious worship of the Most High? This could never be! Who then are the ones who have done these things? The hateful ones and those who are full of wickedness stirred up their anger to such an extent that they plunged into the torment of those who served God with a holy, blameless spirit, without considering that the Most High is the protector and shield of those who serve his holy name with a clear conscience. To him be the glory for all eternity! Amen. ⁸ But those who endured with confidence inherited glory and honor, were exalted and inscribed by God in his memory for all eternity. Amen.

⁴⁶:¹ We must hold fast to such examples, brothers. ² For it is written, "Hold fast to those who are holy, for those who hold on to them will be made holy." ³ And again, in another place, it says, "With an innocent man you will be innocent, and with a chosen man you will be chosen, and with a wicked man you will be corrupted." ⁴ Let us hold fast to the innocent and righteous; these are God's chosen ones. ⁵ Why is there strife, anger, dissension, division, and war among you? ⁶ Do we not have one God and one Christ and one Spirit of grace poured out upon us? And (is there not) one calling in Christ! ⁷ Why do we tear apart and rend the members of Christ and separate ourselves from our own bodies, and push folly so far as to forget that we are members of one another? Remember the words of the Lord Jesus. He said, "Woe to that man. It would be better for him not to have been born than to have offended one of my elect. It would be better for him if a millstone were put upon him and he were cast into the sea than to offend one of my elect." ⁸ Your division has brought many to confusion, many to discouragement, (prompted) many to doubt, and (plunged) all into sorrow. And your quarrel persists even now.

Textual Notes

First Clement 45–46 describes how noble men are only supplanted by evil men. We should, however, not adhere to them, but should adhere to the good men. The evidence for this is supplied by examples and citations.

45:1 Since the praise of the Corinthians, when φιλόνεικοί ἐστε is read, is unqualified, it is advisable to write the imperative φιλόνεικοι ἔστε, which HL read. There is also a particular subtlety: you should argue and fight, but only for what is necessary for salvation. The only difficulty is that ἔστε as an imperative is extremely rare. γίνεσθε and ἔσεσθε are used for the command; in the NT, however, see the variant in Eph 5:5. On ἀνήκοντα εἰς σωτηρίαν, see Barn. 17:1.

45:2 On ἐνκεκύφατε κτλ., see 1 Clem. 40:1 and then 53:1 and 62:3; the author loves this expression.

45:3b The topic of the entire construction from 45f is found in 45:3b.

45:4 In v. 4, take note of the clear, deliberate rhetoric with short, parallel links and consonance and intensification of sense. On ζῆλος, see 1 Clem. 4–6; here as there we also find the exhortation and the examples directed at both sides: the persecutors are unjust, those persecuted because of ζῆλος are noble.

45:6 See Dan 6, especially 6:16f.

45:7 On θρησκεία τοῦ ὑψίστου, see ὁ ὕψιστος, then 59:3 and in the citations at 29:2 and 52:3; in the NT and in the LXX it occurs frequently; see then Pariser Zauberpapyrus 1068 (Wessely, "Griechische Zauberpapyrus"): ἱερὸν φῶς τοῦ ὑψίστου θεοῦ, both Jewish prayers for vengeance from Rheneia (Deißmann, Licht, 315ff), which begin with the words: ἐπικαλοῦμαι καὶ ἀξιῶ τὸν θεὸν τὸν ὕψιστον. On the syncretic communities of the σεβόμενοι θεὸν ὕψιστον, see Schürer, "Juden," 200–225 and also Schürer, Geschichte, 3:124. The entirely general name, grown on polytheistic ground, has had a significant place (see Wendland, Kultur, 193f). ἐξήρισαν, ἐξερίζω means to persist with the dispute; Plutarch, Pompej. 56: οὐκ ἐξερίσας ἀλλ' οἷον ἡττηθείς. Appian, Bell. civ. II 151: φιλονεικότατοι δὲ τοῖς ἐξερίζουσιν ὄντες. On the construction εἰς τοσοῦτο θυμοῦ, see 1 Clem. 1:1: εἰς τοσοῦτον ἀπονοίας ἐξέκαυσαν. In ὕψιστος ὑπέρμαχος καὶ ὑπερασπιστής, note the consonance. ὑπερασπίζω together with ὑπερασπιστής and ὑπερασπισμός (45:7) are Koine Greek, which are often used in the LXX.

45:8 Praise of those who suffer, as in v. 5f. — δόξαν καὶ τιμὴν ἐκληρονόμησαν is probably not meant eschatologically, but is said of the glory they received from people and from the testimony about them in the Scriptures; see 1 Clem. 5:6: τὸ γενναῖον τῆς πίστεως αὐτοῦ κλέος ἔλαβεν. On the other hand, ἐπήρθησαν is probably to be understood as the exaltation in the ὀφειλόμενον τόπον τῆς δόξης (5:4; cf. 5:7), for ἔγγραφοι ἐγένοντο is also about the otherworldly reward for the faithful. τὸ μνημόσυνον is a very common expression in the LXX and usually means, as in other Greek texts, the memory of someone (A therefore also reads αὐτῶν for αὐτοῦ; cf. also 22:6); thus, it means μνημοσύνη.

46:1 The innocent who are persecuted are presented as ὑποδείγματα (cf. 1 Clem. 5f, especially 5:1 and 6:1).

46:2 is an apocryphal citation. On the expression κολλᾶσθαι τοῖς ἁγίοις, see however Herm. Vis. III 6.2; Sim. VIII 8.1; also Did. 5:2; et al.

46:3 See Ps 17:26f, which is reproduced here verbatim.

46:5 Note the rhetoric here and in the following (up to v. 7), the questions, the same beginnings, the synonyms in v. 5, arranged in ascending order, the clustering of εἷς in v. 6, and the image in v. 7.

46:6 A Trinitarian formula like the present one recurs in 58:2; see also the well-known passages at Matt 28:19; 2 Cor 13:13; 1 Pet 1:2; et al. Additionally, Eph 4:4f evidences close contact with our passage; then compare with 1 Cor 8:6; 12:12f; and also Ign. *Mag.* 7:1. κλῆσις here is, as with Paul, the *vocatio efficax*.

46:7 On the image of the body and its members, see comments at 1 Clem. 37:5. μνήσθητε τῶν λόγων Ἰησου κτλ. εἶπεν γάρ, on this introductory formula see 1 Clem. 13:1f. Both passages are the only explicit citations of a word of the Lord in the entire letter. The reading Ἰησοῦ τοῦ κυρίου ἡμῶν in A is probably correct, against τοῦ κυρίου ἡμῶν Ἰησοῦ Χριστοῦ in HSC and *domini Jesu* in L.

46:8 On the citation, see Mark 14:21 (Matt 26:24), the word about the traitor: οὐαὶ δὲ τῷ ἀνθρώπῳ ἐκείνῳ, δι᾽ οὗ ὁ υἱὸς τοῦ ἀνθρώπου παραδίδοται· καλὸν (+ ἦν Matt 26:24) αὐτῷ εἰ οὐκ ἐγεννήθη ὁ ἄνθρωπος ἐκεῖνος, and then Mark 9:42 (Matt 18:6f; Luke 17:1f); the word about the vexation of the little ones and the millstone: καὶ ὃς ἂν σκανδαλίσῃ ἕνα τῶν μικρῶν τούτων τῶν πιστευόντων, καλόν ἐστιν αὐτῷ μᾶλλον εἰ περίκειται μύλος ὀνικὸς περὶ τὸν τράχηλον αὐτοῦ καὶ βέβληται εἰς τὴν θάλασσαν, where Matthew reads καταποντισθῇ ἐν τῷ πελάγει τῆς θαλάσσης and Matthew and Luke, the one after, the other before, also have a woe. It is in itself possible that Clement freely joins the words of the Lord from the synoptic tradition, just as freely as he uses the OT writings, following Jewish and early Christian scriptural usage. But it is more likely that he uses extra-canonical tradition; see at 1 Clem. 13:2 and then Oxford, *Apostolic*, 61f. The reading ἕνα τῶν ἐκλεκτῶν μου διαστρέψαι should be accepted in agreement with LSC and Clem. Alex. against AH, which provide a harmonization: ἕνα τῶν μικρῶν μου σκανδαλίσαι.

46:9 Take note of the anaphora and the climax. On the rarely used δισταγμός, see Herm., *Sim.* IX 28.4: ὅσοι δὲ δειλοὶ καὶ ἐν δισταγμῷ ἐγένοντο and Plutarch, *Laconica* 77 p. 214 F: ὑπέφαινε δισταγμὸν καὶ προσποίησιν ἔχειν ἀποροῦντος.

C. Praise of Love (47:1 — 50:7)

Translation

⁴⁷:¹ Take the letter of the blessed apostle Paul in your hands.
² Above all, what did he write you at the beginning of his

preaching? ³ Truly, full of the Holy Spirit, he gave orders concerning himself and Cephas and Apollos, because you had divisions at that time too. But that division brought a lesser sin upon you. ⁴ For you were partisans of apostles, to whom a testimony had been given (from God), and of a man who was approved by them. ⁵ But behold who has now brought you into discord and diminished the glory of your widely known brotherly love! ⁶ It is ugly, beloved, very ugly, and unworthy of the walk in Christ, to hear that the eminently reliable and ancient church of the Corinthians has risen up against the presbyters because of one or two persons. ⁷ And this report has not only reached us, but also those of a different mind, so that by your folly you even bring blasphemy on the name of the Lord and danger upon yourselves.

⁴⁸:¹ Let us therefore quickly put this to rest and let us fall down before the Lord and pray to him with tears that he might reconcile with us again in grace and lead us back to our honorable and holy walk (filled) with brotherly love. ² For this is a gate of righteousness, opened up unto life, as it is written, "Open up to me the gates of righteousness, and I will go in and glorify the Lord. ³ This is the gate of the Lord, and the righteous will enter in." ⁴ Although many gates have been opened, the gate of righteousness is the one which (is opened) in Christ. Blessed are all who have gone in, walking their way in holiness and righteousness, accomplishing all things without swerving. ⁵ Let a person be faithful, let him be able to utter (deep) knowledge, let him be wise in discernment of speeches, let him be holy in his works: ⁶ the greater he seems to be, the humbler he must be and must strive for that which benefits all and not him alone.

⁴⁹:¹ Whoever has love in Christ, let him keep Christ's commandments. ² Who can describe the bond of divine love? ³ Who is able to exhaust the sublime nature of its beauty? ⁴ The height to which love leads is inexpressible. ⁵ Love connects us to God, "love covers a number of sins," love endures all things, love bears all things. There is nothing mean in love, nothing arrogant. Love knows no division, love causes no strife, love does all things in harmony. In love, all of God's elect were brought to perfection. Without love, nothing is pleasing in the sight of God. ⁶ In love, the Lord has accepted us. Because of the love he had for us, our Lord Jesus Christ, according to the will of God, gave his blood for us, and his flesh for our flesh, and his soul for our souls. ⁵⁰:¹ You see, beloved, how great and marvelous a thing

love is, and its perfection cannot be exhausted. ² Who is able
to be found in it except those whom God deems worthy. Let
us therefore implore his mercy and ask that we may be found
blameless in love without partiality. ³ All generations from
Adam to this day have passed away, but those who have been
perfected in love by divine grace have a place among the pious,
and will be seen in the day of the appearance of the kingdom of
Christ. ⁴ For it is written, "Enter into the chambers a little while,
until my wrath and anger pass away. And I will remember a
good day, and will raise you up out of your graves." ⁵ Blessed are
we, beloved, if we carried out the commandments of God in the
harmony of love, so that sins might be forgiven us because of
love. ⁶ For it is written, "Blessed are those whose transgressions
have been forgiven and whose sins have been covered. Blessed
is the man to whom the Lord does not attribute sin and in
whose mouth there is no falsehood." ⁷ This blessing came upon
all who were chosen by God through our Lord Jesus Christ. To
him be the glory forever and ever! Amen.

Textual Notes

First Clement 47–50: Paul already had to admonish the Corinthians toward
unity. It is ugly to hear about division in the church. Let us dismiss it. Unanimous humble love helps us obtain God's forgiveness.

47:1 τὴν ἐπιστολήν: from this type of reference, it is not necessary
to conclude that 1 Clem. knows, for example, only 1 Corinthians and not
2 Corinthians; see how later church writers cite from 1 Corinthians or 2 Corinthians, Thessalonians or Timothy. For example, see Iren. *Haer.* I 8.2: τὸν
Παῦλον λέγουσιν εἰρηκέναι ἐν τῇ πρὸς Κορινθίους (*in prima ad Corinthios*, the
Latin improves the text); *Haer.* IV 27.3: *et hoc autem apostolum in epistola,
quae est ad Corinthios, manifestissime ostendisse dicentem*; *Haer.* IV 27.4: *et
apostolo in ea, quae est ad Thessalonicenses, epistola ita praedicante*; Origin,
Cels. I 63: ἀλλὰ καὶ ὁ Παῦλος ἐν τῇ πρὸς Τιμόθεον φησι, III 20: φέρ' εἰπεῖν τῇ
πρὸς Ἐφεσίους καὶ πρὸς Κολοσαεῖς καὶ τῇ πρὸς Θεσσαλονικεῖς καὶ Φιλιππησίους
καὶ πρὸς Ῥωμαίους, et al. The authors here and elsewhere can assert that the
readers know which of the two letters is meant. Something else is also possible, namely that for 1 Clem., Paul's entire collection of letters has the title:
ἐπιστολὴ Παύλου τοῦ ἀποστόλου. This view is put forward with good reasons
by Hartke, *Paulusbriefe*. He supports the view with Irenaeus, *Haer.* III 16.5ff,
where the Johannine letters are referred to as the *epistola Johannis* and where
he wishes to deduce *epistola* = "written instruction" from the legal language.

Incidentally, 1 Clem. uses 1 Corinthians explicitly and precisely, whereas 2 Corinthians is not taken into account by him at all, unless there is a slight echo in 1 Clem. 36:2 (2 Cor 3:18; however, cf. the comments at 1 Clem. 36:2). On μακάριος, see the comments at 1 Clem. 43:1 and take note of Polycarp, *Phil.* 3:2: τοῦ μακαρίου καὶ ἐνδόξου Παύλου.

47:2 τί πρῶτον is read in all the witnesses against L: *quemadmodum* (τίνα τρόπον). πρῶτον can refer to the position of the exhortation in question at the entrance of 1 Corinthians, or it can underline the importance of the content to follow; a much more satisfactory interpretation, following Zahn, has been pointed out by W. Hartke, *Paulusbriefe*: in the collection of Paul's letters used by 1 Clem., the Corinthian letters stood at the front. This is, among witnesses, the order presupposed by the Muratorian Fragment line 42: *primum omnium Corintheis*; line 50f: *ordine tali: ad Corinthios prima* etc. Our canonical 1 Corinthians still clearly bears the trace of this position of 1 Corinthians at the beginning of the Pauline collection, though they could not have originated from Paul: σὺν πᾶσιν τοῖς ἐπικαλουμένοις τὸ ὄνομα τοῦ κυρίου ἡμῶν Ἰησοῦ Χριστοῦ ἐν παντὶ τόπῳ αὐτῶν καὶ ἡμῶν, see Weiß, *Korintherbrief*; and on this oldest order of Paul's letters, see also Zahn, *Theophilus*, 344ff and on 1 Clem. 47:2, see Zahn, *Tatians Diatessaron*, 811ff and 835ff. Then εὐαγγέλιον could refer to the preaching of the apostle as it is currently available in writing in the collection of his letters. This is a usage of language that is explained by Paul's well-known expressions that designate his sermon as the gospel of God or Christ, or as my gospel. This interpretation of ἐν ἀρχῇ τοῦ εὐαγγελίου is not absolutely necessary. The expression that alludes to Phil 4:15 can simply mean: Paul wrote to you at the beginning of his great mission to the gentiles. That 1 Corinthians was the oldest of the Pauline letters was claimed by its position at the beginning of the collection, and so it was written ἐν ἀρχῇ τοῦ εὐαγγελίου τοῦ Παύλου.

47:3 πνευματικῶς, in 1 Corinthians Paul speaks frequently of the Spirit, and especially in the opening chapters (1–4), which deal with the parties in Corinth, he appeals to the Spirit (cf. 2:4). Note that 1 Clem. only lists three, not four parties in his rendering of 1 Cor 1:12. The Christ party was either as mysterious to him as it is to more recent interpretation, or else he had not yet read ἐγὼ δὲ Χριστοῦ in his text of 1 Corinthians (cf. Weiß, *Korintherbrief*, xxxvi–xxxix and 15–18). First Corinthians 3:22 lists only the three. Note also that in 1 Corinthians, in both places, the order Paul, Apollos, Cephas appears. First Clement, however, places the apostles first.

47:4 Corresponding to this is also the fact that Apollos is expressly distinguished from the apostles in v. 4. On μεμαρτυρημένοις, see at 1 Clem. 17:1; on δεδοκιμασμένῳ, see 1 Clem. 44:2, as well as 42:4; Did. 11:11; 15:1.

On τὸ σεμνὸν τῆς περιβοήτου φιλαδελφίας, see 1:1: τὸ σεμνὸν καὶ περιβόητον
. . . ὄνομα ὑμῶν, see also 48:1.

47:6 αἰσχρὰ . . . καὶ ἀνάξια . . . ἀκούεσθαι = αἰσχρὸν . . . καὶ ἀνάξιόν
(ἐστιν) . . . ἀκούεσθαι; for examples of this plural instead of the singular,
see Kühner, *Grammatik II*, §366. See also Thucydides I 125: ἀδύνατα ἦν
ἐπιχειρεῖν ἀπαρασκεύοις οὖσιν. Herodotus, *Hist.* I 91: τὴν πεπρωμένην
μοῖραν ἀδύνατά ἐστιν ἀποφυγέειν καὶ θεῷ. Herodotus, *Hist.* IX 2: χαλεπὰ
εἶναι περιγίνεσθαι καὶ ἅπασιν ἀνθρώποισιν. Euripides, *Hec.* 1240: ἀχθεινὰ μέν
μοι τἀλλότρια κρίνειν κακά. The Corinthian congregation as a congregation
founded by Paul is already an ancient congregation; see, for example, the
assessment of the apostolic founding in Polycarp, *Phil.* 1:2 and 11:3. On ἐν
ᾗ δύο πρόσωπα see 1 Clem. 1:1: ὀλίγα πρόσωπα προπετῆ καὶ αὐθάδη, and on
πρεσβύτεροι see Knopf, *Nachapostoliche Zeitalter*, 161–67.

47:7 The ἑτεροκλινεῖς are the gentiles and Jews. The outward honor of
the congregation already appears in the Synoptics and in Paul as a driving
motive for moral action; see Matt 5:14 and then 1 Cor 10:32: ἀπρόσκοποι
καὶ Ἰουδαίοις γίνεσθε καὶ Ἕλλησιν. First Thessalonians 4:12: ἵνα περιπατῆτε
εὐσχημόνως πρὸς τοὺς ἔξω. Then, see further 1 Tim 6:1; 1 Pet 2:15; Ign.
Trall. 8:2; and very detailed in 2 Clem. 13. There, βλασφημία of the "name"
is explained very well. κίνδυνος is the danger of divine damnation, not an
earthly danger (cf. 14:2; 41:4; 59:1).

First Clement 48 mainly contains paraenesis with a citation in v. 2.

48:1 On repentance, see 2:3. ἐπικαταλλάσσεσθαι has not yet been prov-
en elsewhere, but see τοῦ χαλκοῦ τὴν ἐπικαταλλαγήν = "the premium of cop-
per coins" in Theophrastus, *Characteres* 30.15. On σεμνὴν τῆς φιλαδελφίας
κτλ., see 1 Clem. 47:5. καί is read before ἀγνήν in LS and Clem. Alex.

48:2f HLS read εἰς ζωὴν ἀνεῳγυῖα. The quotation comes from Ps
117:19f verbatim.

48:4 πολλῶν οὖν πυλῶν could be an allusion to the word of the Lord in
Matt 7:13f if necessary; however this is not very probable. The πύλαι were
mentioned in the citation; the image of the various gates or paths is widespread (cf. at Did. 1:1).

48:5 Spiritual gifts are enumerated (cf. comments at 1 Clem. 38:1 and
13:1). πίστις, γνῶσις, σοφία, ἀγνεία appear here, and the series is not far off
from that of 38:1f. It must be assumed that the opponents of the ministers in
Corinth boasted that they possessed these gifts. πίστις also appears in 1 Cor
12:9 and 13:2 among the spiritual gifts and in Paul it is the miracle-working
faith. What is meant here is only a particularly large measure of the general
Christian faith, which Clement has already frequently praised in what has
come before. On γνῶσις, see already 1 Clem. 1:2, then 40:1, 41:4, and also
36:2. σοφός is further defined by the addition; it is not a matter of the person

himself speaking wisely, but of his being able to examine and rightly judge a matter put forward by others. The gift is of course not the same as the Pauline διάκρισις πνευμάτων. ἁγνεία is chastity as in 38:2. Note the rhetoric throughout the series: short parallel constituents, same beginnings, rhyme.

48:6 On ταπεινοφρονεῖν, see 2:1; 13; 16–19; 21:8; 30:8; 31:4. μᾶλλον μείζων, double comparative as in Phil 1:23: πολλῷ γὰρ μᾶλλον κρεῖσσον (cf. Blaß-Debrunner, *Grammatik*, §246). In Modern Greek, one also encounters πλιὸ καλίτερος (= πλέον καλλίων). κοινωφελές is an intentionally chosen word, but is only attested from Philo onward; see Philo, *Joseph* 7.34 (ed. Mangey, 47): διὰ τὸ κοινωφελὲς φθάνοντα τοὺς ἄλλους αὐτουργίᾳ, Epictetus IV 10.12: ἀνθρωπικόν, εὐεργετικόν, κοινωφελές, γενναῖον, Marcus Aurelius, *In semet.* I 16.4: καὶ τὸ ἀκουστικὸν τῶν ἐχόντων τι κοινωφελὲς εἰσφέρειν, III 4.1: ὁπόταν μὴ τὴν ἀναφορὰν ἐπί τι κοινωφελὲς ποιῇ, IV 12.2: ὡς δικαίου καὶ κοινωφελοῦς, et al. πᾶσιν is pleonastic amplification.

First Clement 49–50 offers a praise of love; the word ἀγάπη occurs fourteen times in 1 Clem. 49 and five times in 1 Clem. 50. Even this constant repetition has a rhetorical effect, especially in 1 Clem. 49. The different cases in which ἀγάπη occurs act as a *polyptoton*. Note further the *anaphora* (e.g., 49:5), the intensifications, the rhetorical questions, parallelism, and antithesis. The author is certainly aware that he is giving a masterpiece of edifying rhetoric. And when he admonishes the Corinthians in 47:1 to take Paul's letter in hand, the great example from 1 Cor 13 is surely before his eyes. There are also some literal echoes.

49:1 On the idea here, see John 14:15: ἐὰν ἀγαπᾶτέ με, τὰς ἐντολὰς τὰς ἐμὰς τηρήσετε, as well as 1 John 5:3: αὕτη γάρ ἐστιν ἡ ἀγάπη τοῦ θεοῦ, ἵνα τὰς ἐντολὰς αὐτοῦ τηρῶμεν. On the construction ἐν Χριστῷ, see 2 Tim 1:13. δεσμὸς τῆς ἀγάπης, see Col 3:14: ἐπὶ πᾶσιν δὲ τούτοις τὴν ἀγάπην, ὅ ἐστιν σύνδεσμος τῆς τελειότητος. The genitive τοῦ θεοῦ is a subjective genitive (ownership or authorship); see the love of God and of Christ in v. 6. Besides, the love which the chapter speaks of is the love that fills the pious human heart.

49:3 However, v. 3, which closely follows v. 2, still continues to praise divine love. Note also the close parallelism in which v. 3 stands in relation to v. 2. αὐτοῦ of course is connected with δεσμός. In καλλονή, a Greek sound seems to resound; see already Eros in Agathon's speech in Plato, *Symposium* 19, p. 197 C: Ἔρως πρῶτος αὐτὸς ὢν κάλλιστος καὶ ἄριστος and p. 197E: ξυμπάντων τε θεῶν καὶ ἀνθρώπων κόσμος, ἡγεμὼν κάλλιστος καὶ ἄριστος.

49:4 A parallel can be found in Ign. *Eph.* 9:1: ἀναφερόμενοι εἰς τὰ ὕψη διὰ τῆς μηχανῆς Ἰησοῦ Χριστοῦ.

49:5 The saying ἀγάπη καλύπτει πλῆθος ἁμαρτιῶν also occurs in 1 Pet 4:8 (Jas 5:20). It seems very doubtful that this is a loose citation from Prov 10:12. Instead, it may come from a lost apocryphon, and its original meaning was to recommend almsgiving (cf. Oxford, *Apostolic*, 56f). Clement, however, understands ἀγάπη in a much broader sense (see below at 1 Clem. 50:5). On πάντα ἀνέχεται, see 1 Cor 13:7: πάντα στέγει . . . πάντα ὑπομένει. On πάντα μακροθυμεῖ, see 1 Cor 3:4: ἡ ἀγάπη μακροθυμεῖ. On οὐδὲν ὑπερήφανον, see 1 Cor 3:4: οὐ φυσιοῦται. Note also the antithesis of βάναυσον and ὑπερήφανον. In the following σχίσμα . . . στασιάζει . . . πάντα ἐν ὁμονοίᾳ, there is an intensification, from the broadest to the finest. On πάντες οἱ ἐκλεκτοὶ τοῦ θεοῦ, see the explanation below at 1 Clem. 50:3.

49:6 God's and Christ's love is emphasized at the end. δεσπότης here, as in the preceding, is a reference to God. The threefold use of αἷμα, σάρξ, ψυχή seems to be determined by the choice and pre-position of αἷμα by the idea of sacrifice, perhaps also by the sacrament (αἷμα and σάρξ). ψυχή is not simply the breath of life in the human being, but bears more the Greek sense of the rational soul that dwells in the body. As the higher force in man, ψυχή also appears in other parts of the letter (cf. 19:3; 23:2; 29:1; 55:6; 64). On the thought that Jesus gave up his life because of love, see John 13:1; 15:13; Gal 2:20; Eph 5:2, and on the whole construction, see Irenaeus, *Haer.* V 1.1, which probably has our passage in mind: τῷ ἰδίῳ οὖν αἷματι λυτρωσαμένου ἡμᾶς τοῦ κυρίου καὶ δόντος τὴν ψυχὴν ὑπὲρ τῶν ἡμετέρων ψυχῶν καὶ τὴν σάρκα τὴν ἑαυτοῦ ἀντὶ τῶν ἡμετέρων σαρκῶν.

First Clement 50: The main point of the discussion is the application of the praise of love to the behavior of the Corinthian church: we obtain forgiveness of sin in true genuine love.

50:1 On the τελειότης of ἀγάπη, see ἐτελειώθησαν in 49:5 and τελειωθέντες in 50:3. See also 1 Clem. 53:5 and then 1 John 2:5: ἐν τούτῳ ἡ ἀγάπη τοῦ θεοῦ τετελείωται (cf. also 1 John 4:12, 18).

50:2 On καταξιώσῃ, note the predestination of God, which does not fit in all places with the moralism of the letter, and see on this κατὰ τὴν τοῦ θεοῦ χάριν in v. 3 and ἐκλελεγμένους in v. 7. πρόσκλισις is clearly a reference to the Corinthian dispute (cf. 47:3f).

50:3f refer to the deceased generations. All went to death, not in the torments of hell, not even into dissolution, but certainly in the unconsciousness of a shadowy existence. But the great pious ones of the OT, including those who have died among the first Christian generation, have been given a wonderful, chosen resting place; see the τόπος τῆς δόξης, the ἅγιος τόπος in 1 Clem. 5:4, 7. κατὰ τὴν τοῦ θεοῦ χάριν is connected with τελειωθέντες. χῶρος εὐσεβῶν is a firmly established expression of Greek mythology; as a counterpart, see χῶρος ἀσεβῶν in Lucian, *Vera hist.* II 17, 23, 26. But 1 Clem. does not need to have thought of the place of the pious directly in accordance with the Greek model; see 1 En. 22 and above all 4 Esdr 7:78–80, 88–99. Here it is said that after a person dies, his soul goes to the chambers of the

dead and there, guarded by angels, enters into rest with a sevenfold joy,
whereas the souls of the wicked have to wander around constantly sighing
and mourning with a sevenfold torment. On the last day, the final judgment
will take place: then the righteous will receive the glory prepared for them
and shine like the sun, whereas the wicked will wander and go into eternal
torment. — This idea of the chambers of Hades is also present in 1 Clem.,
which is seen especially in the following citation in 50:4, where chambers
are spoken of and at the same time the resurrection from the graves is mentioned. Thus the author has the view that the souls of the pious who have
died from the beginning are kept in a place assigned to them. When the
kingdom of Christ becomes visible, they too will be brought out of their
hidden place to enjoy the glory prepared for them.

50:4 On ἐπισκοπή, see Luke 19:44 and 1 Pet 2:12, then Wis 3:7: ἐν
καιρῷ ἐπισκοπῆς αὐτῶν ἀναλάμψουσιν and furthermore the letter of
Polycrates of Ephesus in Eusebius, *Hist. eccl.* 5.24.5: [Melito] ὃς κεῖται
ἐν Σάρδεσιν περιμένων τὴν ἀπὸ τῶν οὐρανῶν ἐπισκοπὴν ἐν ᾗ ἐκ νεκρῶν
ἀναστήσεται. The reading Χριστοῦ is to be preferred in agreement with LC
Clem. Alex. against θεοῦ in HS; A is uncertain.

50:4 The origin of the citation cannot be determined exactly. The beginning seems to be a free reproduction of Isa 26:20: εἴσελθε εἰς τὰ ταμεῖά
σου, ἀπόκλεισον τὴν θύραν σου, ἀποκρύβηθι μικρὸν ὅσον ὅσον, ἕως ἂν παρέλθῃ
ἡ ὀργὴ κυρίου. The following words καὶ μνησθήσομαι ἡμέρας ἀγαθῆς are nowhere to be found, and at the end ἀνάξω ὑμᾶς ἐκ τῶν μνημάτων ὑμῶν in
Ezek 37:12 is only an imprecise parallel. Five Esdras 2:16 is more closely
related to our passage: *et resuscitabo mortuos de locis suis et de monumentis
educam illos,* but 5 Esdras is later than 1 Clem.; on the dating of 5 Esdras,
see Hennecke, *Apokryphen,* 307. ὅσον ὅσον = a small matter; see Heb 10:37;
Luke 5:3 D (BS etc. have ὀλίγον). Then see Aristophenes, *Wespen* 213: τί
οὐκ ἀπεκοιμήθημεν ὅσον ὅσον στίλην; see Blaß-Debrunner, *Grammatik,* §304
footnote and Radermacher, *Grammatik,* 57n2.

50:5 The construction of the conditional clause is strange. If it is a
realis construction (i.e., corresponds to reality), then ἐποιοῦμεν is not easy
to explain. It would have to be assumed that the writer, putting himself
into the time of the parousia, says ἐποιοῦμεν retrospectively, which would
then make the present tense ἐσμέν incorrect. But an *irrealis* clause (i.e.,
contrary to fact) would require ἦμεν, which is a reading attested to in HSC;
but then the statement would mean: we do not do the commandments
of God in truth, which is a statement the author would not so carelessly
make. Thus, one must assume a mixed construction: the sentence begins
as a *realis* clause in order to then more carefully consider an occurrence of
irrealis; see the readings of SA in John 19:11: οὐκ ἔχεις ἐξουσίαν κατ’ ἐμοῦ

οὐδεμία, εἰ μὴ ἦν δεδομένον σοι ἄνωθεν. Koine often left out the particle ἄν in the subordinate clause of an *irrealis* conditional construction (cf. Radermacher, *Grammatik*, 127; Blaß-Debrunner, *Grammatik*, §360). On εἰς τὸ ἀφεθῆναι κτλ., see 1 Clem. 49:5.

50:6 contains a citation from Ps 31:1f and is reproduced verbatim; but there is no mention of love, which is so urgently demanded in v. 5.

50:7 Psalm 31:1f is also used by Paul in Rom 4:7f, which continues in Rom 4:9: ὁ μακαρισμὸς οὖν οὗτος ἐγένετο ἐπὶ τὴν περιτομὴν κτλ.; this is imitated by 1 Clem.

D. Direct Admonition to the Authors of the Quarrel: They Must Repent, Submit, and Depart (51:1—58:2)

Translation

51:1 For what we are lacking and for what we have done because of some deceitful plots of the adversary, let us implore (God) for forgiveness. Furthermore, those who were the leaders of the dispute and division must look to the common ground of our hope. 2 For those who walk in fear and love would rather suffer pain themselves than see their neighbor suffer. They would rather bring judgment upon themselves than the harmony gloriously and justly delivered to us.

51:3 It is better for a man to confess his sins than to harden his heart, as the heart of those who rose up against Moses, the servant of God, was hardened, whose condemnation also became evident, 4 for they went down into the underworld alive and "death will shepherd them." 5 Pharoah and his army and all the princes of Egypt, the chariots and those who ride upon them, were thrown into the Red Sea and perished for no other reason than because their foolish hearts were hardened after the miracles and signs were performed in Egypt by Moses, the servant of God.

52:1 Brothers, the Lord is not in need of anything at all and he requires nothing at all, except that one confesses his sins. 2 For the chosen one, David, says, "I will confess my sins to the Lord, and he will be more pleased in that than a young calf, growing horns and hooves. Let those who are miserable see it and rejoice." 3 And elsewhere he says, "Offer to God a sacrifice of thanksgiving, and pay your vows to the Most High, and call upon me in the day of your distress, and I will deliver you, and you will praise me. 4 For a sacrifice to God is a bruised spirit."

⁵³:¹ You know the Holy Scriptures quite well, beloved, and you have searched the words of God. So we write this just to remind you. ² When Moses had gone up the mountain and had spent forty days and forty nights in fasting and in humility, God said to him, "Go down from here in haste, for your people have fallen away, whom you brought out of the land of Egypt. Quickly they have left the way which you commanded them. They have made for themselves graven images." ³ And the Lord said to him (further), "I have already said this to you once and then a second time, 'I have seen this people, and behold, they are stiff-necked.' Let me cut them off, and I will destroy their name from under heaven, and I will make a great and marvelous nation from you, far greater than this one." ⁴ And Moses answered, "By no means, Lord. Forgive this people its sin, or blot me also out of the book of the living." ⁵ O great love, O unsurpassable perfection! The servant speaks boldly to the Lord. He asks for forgiveness for the crowd or wishes to be destroyed together with it.

⁵⁴:¹ Who is brave among you, who is compassionate, who is filled with love? ² Let him say, "If there is discord or strife or schism because of me, then I will depart and I will go wherever you desire and do what is required by the majority; only let the flock of Christ live in peace along with it's appointed presbyters." ³ The one who does this will obtain great fame in Christ and will be received everywhere. For "the earth is the Lord's and everything that is in it." ⁴ Those who have lived as citizens of the divine kingdom have acted in this manner, without regretting it, and so they will continue to act.

⁵⁵:¹ But to bring in examples from the gentiles: many kings and princes have surrendered to death in times of plague after having received oracles, in order to save their citizens by their blood. Many departed from their hometowns so that they no longer suffered from unrest.

⁵⁵:² We know that many among us have volunteered to go into captivity in order to buy others. Many sold themselves into slavery and fed others with the prices they received.

⁵⁵:³ Many women, strengthened by divine grace, have performed many brave deeds. ⁴ The blessed Judith, when her homeland was besieged, asked the elders for permission to go into the foreigner's camp. ⁵ She voluntarily put herself in danger, went out, (driven) by love of her homeland and her people, who were besieged, and the Lord delivered Holofernes into the hand of a woman. ⁶ No

less did Esther, who was perfect in faith, put herself in danger in order to save the twelve tribes of Israel, who were in peril. For through her fasting and her humility she moved the all-seeing Lord, the God of the eons. He saw the humility of her soul and saved the people for whom she put herself in danger.

⁵⁶:¹ Therefore, let us also pray for those who are guilty of any offense, that meekness and humility might be given to them, so that they might yield, not to us but to the will of God. In this way, it will be fruitful and perfect for them when we mention (them) before God and the saints. ² Let us accept discipline which should not discourage us, beloved. The admonition we give one another is good and very useful. For it unites us with the will of God. ³ For thus says the Holy Word, "The Lord disciplined me well, but he did not hand me over to death. ⁴ For the one whom the Lord loves, he disciplines. He punishes every child in whom he is pleased." ⁵ "The righteous one will discipline me in mercy," it says, "and will convict me, but do not let the oil of sinners anoint my head." ⁶ And again it says, "Blessed is the man whom the Lord punishes; do not push away the chastening of the Almighty. For he causes pain and then restores. ⁷ He hits and his hands heal. ⁸ Six times he will deliver you from tribulation, and the seventh time no evil will disturb you. ⁹ During famine he will save you from death; in wartime he will deliver you from the hand of the sword. ¹⁰ He will hide you from the scourge of the tongue, and you will not be afraid when evil ones come. ¹¹ You will mock the wicked and the sinner, and you will not be afraid of the wild beasts, ¹² for the wild beasts will keep peace with you. ¹³ Then you will know that your house will have peace, and that your tent will not be lacking. ¹⁴ And you will know that your seed will be many, and your children will be like the plants of the field. ¹⁵ And you will come into the grave like ripe grain cut in its season, or like a heap in the threshing floor brought in at the right hour." ¹⁶ You see, beloved, how great a protection there is for those who are disciplined by the Lord. Like a good Father, he disciplines so that we might find mercy through his discipline.

⁵⁷:¹ Therefore, you who have started the quarrel, submit to the presbyters, accept discipline for repentance, and bow the knees of your heart. ² Learn to submit, put away the boastful and proud insolence of your tongue. For it is better for you to be found lowly but chosen in Christ's flock than to be excluded from the hope he gives by excessive gloating. ³ For thus says the

all-glorious Wisdom, "Behold, I will speak to you a word of my breath, I will teach you my word. [4] Because I called and you did not listen, and offered words and you did not pay attention, but rather did not heed my advice and did not obey my admonitions, therefore I will also laugh at your downfall, rejoice when destruction comes upon you, and when confusion suddenly breaks over you, and your downfall is like a thunderstorm, or when distress and besiegement come upon you. [5] Then you will call upon me, and I will not hear you. For they hated wisdom and have not accepted the fear of the Lord; neither would they listen to my counsel and mocked my reproof. [6] Therefore they will eat the fruit of their deeds, and they will be filled with their iniquity. [7] For because they violated minors, they will be slain, and judgment will strangle the wicked. But the one who listens to me will live in hope with good courage and will have rest from all evil without fear."

[58:1] Let us, therefore, be obedient to his holy and glorious name, and be wary of the threats which Wisdom pronounced against the disobedient, so that we might live full of good confidence in his holy and glorious name. [2] Take our counsel, and you will not regret it. For as God lives, and the Lord Jesus Christ, and the Holy Spirit, and the faith and hope of the elect, whosoever faithfully, humbly, and with persevering gentleness performs the requirements and commandments given by God, the same will be numbered and reckoned among those who are saved by Jesus Christ, through whom be glory forever and ever. Amen.

Textual Notes

In 1 Clem. 51–58, the originators of the dispute are addressed directly (on the division, see above before 1 Clem. 40), and with various explanations they are instructed what they must do to settle the dispute.

First Clement 51–52 exhorts the leaders of the opposing party to repent and admit their sin. The connection ἀφεθῆναι in 51:1 goes back to 50:5f, and then goes back to the related keyword ἐξομολογεῖσθαι (cf. 51:3; 52:1, 2) as well as σκληρυνθῆναι τὰς καρδίας in 51:5 and πνεῦμα συντετριμμένον in 52:4. The paraenesis, which is in 51:1–3a, is supported in the manner that is so exceedingly familiar to the author with examples (51:3–5) and citation (1 Clem. 52).

51:1 The reading from AH is διά τινος τῶν τοῦ ἀντικειμένου, which should be translated "by any of the plots (or servants) of the adversary."

However, perhaps the reading from Clem. Al. (who paraphrases our passage in *Strom.* 4.113.1, p. 614) and LC should be accepted: διά τινας παρεμπτώσεις τοῦ ἀντικειμένου. The ἀντικείμενος is Satan: 1 Tim 5:14; Mart. Pol. 17:1 (the antichrist in 2 Thess 2:4); Justin, *Dial.* 116.1, 3; Clem. Al., *Strom.* 4.113.1, p. 614; Lugdunum martyrs in Eusebius, *Hist. eccl.* 5.1.5, 23, 42, et al.; see also 1 Pet 5:8 and Barn. 2:1. — ἀρχηγοί as in 1 Clem. 14:1 — τὸ κοινὸν τῆς ἐλπίδος: substantive neuter of the adjective instead of the abstract, so = τὴν κοινωνίαν τῆς ἐλπίδος ἡμῶν; see 19:1 and 47:5. On the use in general, see Blaß-Debrunner, *Grammatik*, §263.2.

51:2 πολιτεύεσθαι is one of the author's favorite words (cf. 3:4; 6:1; et al.). Peace is "condemned" by sin against it.

51:3 On καλὸν . . . ἤ, see Matt 18:8; Mark 9:43, 45; and Blaß-Debrunner, *Grammatik*, §245.

51:3b–4 The first example appears in 51:3b–4 and is taken from Num 16: The mob of Korah and of Dathan and Abiram. On their punishment, see especially Num 16:31–33 and see earlier at 1 Clem. 4:12. There, the title θεράπων τοῦ θεοῦ is used of Moses. θάνατος ποιμανεῖ αὐτούς is a citation from Ps 48:15. On ὧν τὸ κρίμα κτλ., see also Rom 3:8: ὧν τὸ κρίμα ἔνδικόν ἐστι.

51:5 The second example comes from Exod 14 (cf. especially 14:23–28). On τά τε ἄρματα καὶ οἱ ἀναβάται αὐτῶν, see further at Exod 14:23, 26, 28 as well as Exod 15:19; Jer 28:21 (= MT 51); Hag 2:22.

First Clement 52: The epithet of God as ἀπροσδεής has grown on Greek soil. Passages like Ps 49:10–14; Isa 1:10–20; Micah 6:6–8 and related ones in the OT are not to be recalled here. The choice of the word ἀπροσδεής leads over into Hellenism, where the thought is commonplace: In the *Timaeus*, Plato refers to the world, the god who has become, the εἰκὼν τοῦ νοητοῦ θεὸς αἰσθητός (p. 92 B) as αὔταρκες and not προσδεὲς ἄλλων (p. 33 D), as οὐδενὸς ἑτέρου προσδεόμενον; see further at Euripides, *Heracl.* 1345f: δεῖται γὰρ ὁ θεός, εἴπερ ἔστ᾽ ὀρθῶς θεός, Οὐδενός, the Sophist Antiphon, *fragm.* 10 (Diels, *Vorsokratiker II.1*, 293): διὰ τοῦτο οὐδενὸς δεῖται οὐδὲ προσδέχεται οὐδενός τι, ἀλλ᾽ ἄπειρος καὶ ἀδέητος. The Stoics often spoke of their god-world, thus Chrysippus in Plutarch, *Stoic rep.* 39, p. 1052d: αὐτάρκης δ᾽ εἶναι λέγεται μόνος ὁ κόσμος, similarly in their opponent Plutarch himself in *Comp. Arist. et Caton.* 4: ἀπροσδεὴς ἁπλῶς ὁ θεός, see further the Epicurean Lucret., *De rerum nat.* II 646–50: *omnis enim per se divom natura necessest Immortali aevo summa cum pace fruatur . . . Ipsa suis pollens opibus nil indiga nostri*, finally the New Platonists, for example Plotinus, *Enneads* V 4.1, p. 516: δεῖ μὲν γάρ τι πρὸ πάντων εἶναι ἁπλοῦν τοῦτο καὶ πάντων ἕτερον τῶν μετ᾽ αὐτό, . . . αὐταρκέστατόν τε τῷ ἁπλοῦν εἶναι καὶ πρῶτον ἁπάντων. From Hellenism, the idea penetrated into Hellenistic Judaism. Philo emphasizes the self-sufficiency of God more often; see *Leg.* II 1.2, p. 66: χρήζει γὰρ οὐδενὸς τὸ

8888888888888

παράπαν, and entirely similarly in *Mut.* 4.28 p. 582: χρῇζον ἑτέρου τὸ παράπαν οὐδενός, *De fortit.* 2.9 p. 377: ἔστι γὰρ ὁ μὲν θεὸς ἀνεπιδεής, οὐδενὸς χρεῖος, ὤν, ἀλλ' αὐτὸς αὐταρκέστατος ἑαυτῷ etc., Josephus, *Ant.* VIII 4.111: ἀπροσδεὲς γὰρ τὸ θεῖον ἁπάντων, 2 Macc 14:35: σύ, κύριε, τῶν ὅλων ἀπροσδεὴς ὑπάρχων, 3 Macc 2:9: σοὶ τῷ τῶν ἁπάντων ἀπροσδεεῖ. In the Christian tradition, see primarily Acts 17:25, then Acts of Paul and Thecla 17 (θεὸς ἀπροσδεής), Clem. *Hom.* XI 9 (θεὸς . . . ἀνενδεής . . .), and then the Apologists: Justin, *1 Apol.* 13.1; *Dial.* 23.2; Athenagoras, *Suppl.* 13.1 and 29.2; *Res.* 12; Tatian, *Apol.* 4.2; Theophilus, *Autol.* II 10; *Ep. ad Diogn.* 3.3f. — The words τῶν ἁπάντων can of course also be connected with δεσπότης (cf. 1 Clem. 20:11; 33:2).

52:2 On ἐξομολογήσομαι τῷ κυρίῳ, see Ps 7:18; 117:19; and in general the numerous corresponding demands in the Psalter. On καὶ ἀρέσει αὐτῷ κτλ., see Ps 68:32f (almost verbatim).

52:3 On v. 3, see Ps 49:14 (verbatim).

52:4 On v. 4, see Ps 50:19.

First Clement 53–55 contends that the leaders of the strife should volunteer to depart from Corinth. The short forms of this council are found in 54:1f. Everything else is justification for this council, mostly in the form of example (1 Clem. 53 and 55).

In 1 Clem. 53 Moses, the man of God, wished to suffer death along with his sinful people.

53:1 On the form of the introduction, the repetition, see 47:6: αἰσχρά, ἀγαπητοί, καὶ λίαν αἰσχρά. As ἀγαπητοί demonstrates, the whole congregation is being addressed; this can also be found in the use of ὑμεῖς in 54:1. The immediate address to the author of the dispute comes only in 57:1. On the praise of the congregation as a correspondent and on ἐγκύπτειν, see 45:1f; 40:1; as well as Polycarp, *Phil.* 12:1: *confido enim vos bene exercitatos esse in sacris literis et nihil vos latet.* Also take note of ἱεραὶ γραφαί here, in 45:2, and in the passage in Polycarp; ἱεραὶ βίβλοι in 43:1 and ἱερὰ γράμματα in 2 Tim 3:15. — The following narrative of the magnanimity of Moses stems from the parallel accounts in Exod 32 and Deut 9.

53:2 On forty days and forty nights, see Deut 9:9; Exod 34:28. On God's speech in vv. 2 and 3, see Deut 9:12–14; Exod 32:7f.

53:4 See Exod 32:32. First Clement takes over what he uses from the LXX pretty much verbatim, but he abbreviates the text heavily. As a parallel, see Barn. 4:7f and 14:2f.

53:5 Take note of the rhetoric. On Moses as θεράπων, see earlier at 51:3. The useful application that the leaders of the dispute should take from the example is clear; the groundwork for the counsel in 54:1f has been prepared.

54:1f Note again the form. The council given here to the opponents is that they should voluntarily emigrate for peace, and the congregation should decide where they should go. The matter is such for 1 Clem.: The Romans hope that their admonitions in Corinth make the intended impression, that the congregation will return to its former order, and that the discernment and magnanimity among the few leaders of the opponents might ripen such that they make the decision to leave Corinth voluntarily and let the congregation, which has returned to its former state, decide where they should go, whether somewhere close by or far away. Certainly, the congregation should also give recommendations to the emigrants to their new place of residence, because they will probably emigrate to other congregations. The strange advice is a bit easier to understand if the opponents in Corinth were itinerant charismatics of the sort found in Did. 11 and 13. But this assumption is not necessary. Didache 12 bears witness to the great permissiveness that prevailed in the empire at that time; see the explanation of the passage in the commentary on the Did. On Stoic-Hellenistic parallels to 1 Clem. 54, see below. On πληροφορεῖν, see at 1 Clem. 42:3. προστάσσειν and πλῆθος are technical terms of public life, as is attested in several places in the inscriptions of the Hellenistic and classical eras, where they speak of decisions and gatherings and the municipality; see Dittenberger, *Sylloge I*, 8.21f: βουλεύσο ός (= βουλεύσω ὡς) ἂν δύνομαι ἄριστα καὶ δικαιότατα Ἐρυθραίον τῶι πλέθει καὶ Ἀθεναίον καὶ τὸν χσυνμάχον, 84.21, 32: καθ᾽ ὅτι ἂν τῶι πλήθει τῶν συμμάχων δοκῆι, 552.12ff: θείας ἐπινοίας καὶ παραστάσεως γενομένης τῶι σύμπαντι πλήθει τοῦ πολιτεύματος, 928.14f: καὶ τὸ πλῆθος εὐχάριστον φαίνεσθαι πρὸς τοὺς καλοὺς καὶ ἀγαθοὺς ἄνδρας, 519.38: ὧν αὐτοῖς ἡ βουλὴ καὶ ὁ δῆμος προστάττει, 187.40f: ὅσα πώποτε αὐτοῖς ὑπὸ τοῦ δήμου προσετάχθη, etc. On καθεσταμένοι πρεσβύτεροι, see Knopf, *Nachapostolische Zeitalter*, 161ff.

54:3 μέγα κλέος ἐν Χριστῷ; the sense of this phrase is "within the Christian congregation." πᾶς τόπος δέξεται αὐτόν: the place he visits probably has a Christian congregation, which then gladly receives him (see above). κύριος in the citation (Ps 23:1) can be either Christ or God. — To properly assess the advice, which is strange to our sensibilities, the following must be taken into consideration: in the whole of antiquity, it is considered a sign of great patriotism to go into exile voluntarily so that the state is not torn apart by parties, just as voluntary death for the fatherland is praised to the highest degree. The text immediately speaks of the illustrious examples of this sort in 1 Clem. 55:1. Here, we are dealing with a commonplace of rhetoric, also of historiography (cf. below). Furthermore, the voluntary emigration from a city in the time of the Roman Empire and its cosmopolitanism, its freedom of movement, was no longer considered to be such a grim sacrifice as it was in the era of the old city-state. Ancient Christianity also knew of the itinerate charismatic. Finally, see also the stoic cosmopolitan with his indifference to banishment, a punishment which can never lead him out of the world and communion with god; Epictetus, *Diatr.* III 22.22: φυγή; καὶ ποῦ δύναταί τις ἐκβαλεῖν ἔξω τοῦ κόσμου; οὐ δύναται. ὅπου δ᾽ ἂν ἀπέλθω, ἐκεῖ ἥλιος, ἐκεῖ σελήνη, ἐκεῖ ἄστρα, ἐνύπνια, οἰωνοί, ἡ πρὸς θεοὺς ὁμιλία (cf. 1 Clem. 54:3).

54:4 Here begin the examples that fill the following chapter. Clement thinks of Christians and of men from the sacred stories narrated in the OT. But what examples he has in mind we cannot say precisely. He also suggests that such heroic acts occurred in congregations during his time (cf. 55:2).

First Clement 55: Note the strong secular element, and see also 1 Clem. 20; 25; 33; 37:2 and the comments supplied there. Among the kings and leaders who sacrificed themselves in times of misfortune, the author thinks of Codros, Sperthias, and Bulis (Herodotus. *Hist.* VII 14ff), of Menoikeus, son of Creon, of Leonidas and other men from Greek history; furthermore, he thinks of P. Decius Mus, father and son, M. Curius, who jumped into the crevice, and of similar examples from Roman history. How common the reference to the sacrificial death of famous men is can be seen in Cicero, *Tusc.* I 116: *Clarae vero mortes pro patria oppetitae non solum gloriosae rhetoribus sed etiam beatae videri solent. Repetunt ab Erechtheo, cuius etiam filiae cupide mortem expetiverunt pro vita civium; Codrum commemorant . . . Menoeceus non praetermittitur . . . Iphigenia Aulide duci se immolandam iubet, "ut hostium eliciatur suo." Veniunt inde ad propiora. Harmodius in ore est et Aristogiton, Lacedaemonius Leonidas, Thebanus Epaminondas viget. Nostros non norunt, quos enumerare magnum est; ita sunt multi, quibus videmus optabiles mortes fuisse cum gloria.* The *nostri* are mentioned as a selection in *Tusc.* I 89: *quotiens non modo ductores nostri, sed universi etiam exercitus ad non dubiam mortem concurrerunt,* after which are enumerated L. Brutus, the Decians, the Scipions Paulus and Geminus, Marcellus, Albinus, Gracchus. — On ἐξεχώρησαν, see ἐκχωρῶ in 1 Clem. 54:2. Among those who voluntarily leave the fatherland, Solon, Lycurg, and Scipio Africanus Maior are the most famous.

55:2 The ἡμεῖς in focus here are certainly not the Romans as a people, but either the Romans as a congregation or Christians in general. The latter seems more probable with reference to 6:1. On the special love of the Roman congregation, see Ign. *Rom.* 0.1; Herm. *Mand.* VIII.10, Dionysius of Corinth in Eusebius, *Hist. eccl.* 4.23.10: ἐξ ἀρχῆς γὰρ ὑμῖν ἔθος ἐστὶν τοῦτο, πάντας μὲν ἀδελφοὺς ποικίλως εὐεργετεῖν ἐκκλησίαις τε πολλαῖς ταῖς κατὰ πᾶσαν πόλιν ἐφόδια πέμπειν, ὧδε μὲν τὴν τῶν δεομένων πενίαν ἀναψύχοντας, ἐν μετάλλοις δὲ ἀδελφοῖς ὑπάρχουσιν ἐπιχορηγοῦντας δι᾽ ὧν πέμπετε ἀρχῆθεν ἐφοδίων πατροπαράδοτον ἔθος Ῥωμαίων Ῥωμαῖοι φυλάττοντες. Certain examples of the self-sacrifice praised here are not known to us from the ancient Roman community or from early Christianity in general, for even

Const. Apost. V 1.3 does not go that far: εἰ δὲ καὶ οἷός τέ ἐστιν ἅπαντα τὸν βίον αὐτοῦ ἀποδόμενος ῥύσασθαι αὐτοὺς (sc. τοὺς ἁγίους) ἐκ τοῦ δεσμωτηρίου, μακάριος ἔσται καὶ φίλος τοῦ Χριστοῦ.

55:3 Even the weak women; see 1 Clem. 6:2 and what is noted there. Take note also of the rhetoric: γυναῖκες . . . ἀνδρεῖα.

55:4f See Jdt 8–13. Our passage is the oldest reference to this book, which was probably written during the Maccabean era (cf. Schürer, *Geschichte*, 3:171). The city is Bethulia. ἐν χειρὶ θηλείας is a literal allusion; see Jdt 13:15: ἐπάταξεν αὐτὸν ὁ κύριος ἐν χειρὶ θηλείας. See also Jdt 16:5: ἠθέτησεν αὐτοὺς ἐν χειρὶ θηλείας.

55:6 ἧττον, attested in all the witnesses except A, should be read instead of ἥττονι. On content, see Esth 7–9; on fasting, see Esth 4:16. On δωδεκάφυλον, see Acts 26:7; Prot. Jas. 1; see also δωδεκάσκηπτρον in 1 Clem. 31:4. παντεπόπτης is connected with 1 Clem. 64:1; see also 1 Clem. 59:3. This word does not appear in the LXX or the NT. See, however, Polycarp, *Phil.* 7:2; *Clementine Homilies* IV 14, 23; V 27; VIII 19; parallels in sense are not rare in the OT; see also Luke 1:48. The word is, however, attested several times in the Magical Papyri; see Schermann, *Griechische Zauberpapyri*, 28f and parallels in sense are otherwise numerous within Hellenism. On θεὸς τῶν αἰώνων, see 1 Clem. 35:3. ὧν χάριν, plural according to sense, as is also the case of οὕς in 1 Clem. 53:2.

First Clement 56 contends that accepting discipline is beneficial to everyone. Let us plead that sinners might submit to God's will.

56:1 As τινι proves, the promise of intercession does not refer to the Corinthian sinners in particular, but to all transgressors in general. μνεία πρὸς τὸν θεὸν καὶ τοὺς ἁγίους (i.e., the Christians; cf. the excursus on Rom 15:25 in Lietzmann, *Römer*) takes place in the worship service before the gathered congregation and is done during the congregation's liturgy. There, one prays for the repentance of sinners and for God's grace; how this is done, the letter demonstrates immediately afterward (cf. 1 Clem. 59:2, 4). In this prayer, the opponents in Corinth are of course included. But the wording does not seem to mean the kind of intercession that is granted to the repentant sinner after the *exhomologesis* (cf. Tert., *Paen.* 9 and anonymously in Eusebius, *Hist. eccl.* 5.28.12), because the opponents have not yet repented. The fact that the words of the letter proclaim the divine and not the human will is also said in 1 Clem. 59:1. On ἔγκαρπος καὶ τελεία, see also 1 Clem. 44:5. Also take note of the rhetoric: ἐπιείκεια . . . εἶξαι.

56:2 παιδεία is the keyword (*Stichwort*), which is found throughout, up to 57:1; see 56:2, 3, 4, 5, (6), 16; 57:1. It is the divine discipline (παιδεία) to which the admonition of mankind should lead. The goal of discipline is bending to the will of God.

56:3–15 The necessity and glory of the divine discipline is proved with three constructions, which are separated from each other by the citation formulas in vv. 3, 5, 6.

56:3–4 The first construction is a composite; on v. 3 see Ps 117:18, and on v. 4 see Prov 3:12. Both citations are cited verbatim. On the citation formula, see 1 Clem. 13:3.

56:5 See Ps 140:5, which is cited verbatim.

56:6–15 See Job 5:17–26, which is also almost in verbatim agreement with our text of the LXX. The construction praises the gloriousness and the benefits of divine discipline. The word παιδεία does not occur in this text, but rather the related terms ἐλέγχειν and νουθετεῖν.

56:14 παμβότανον appears to be a *hapaxlegomenon*.

56:16 ὑπερασπισμός occurs frequently in the LXX; see ὑπερασπιστής at 1 Clem. 45:7.

First Clement 57f exhorts the leaders of the dispute to repent and submit themselves to God. Woe to the one who disobeys God, and blessed is the one who submits himself to him. Finally, the author addresses the opponents directly, the connection to what comes before is tight and good, and the letter reaches its objective conclusion here.

57:1 ὑποτάγητε τοῖς πρεσβυτέροις, see 1 Pet 5:5 ὑποτάγητε πρεσβυτέροις. The author links what precedes with παιδεύθητε. This type of bracketing can be seen often in the letter. κάμψαντες τὰ γόνατα τῆς καρδίας, the bold image recurs in the Prayer of Manasseh 11: καὶ νῦν κλίνω γόνου καρδίας. First Clement could very well be dependent upon the apocryphon, which is admittedly only attested in Const. Apost. II 22. The prayer of Manasseh perhaps already emerged in the Maccabean era, and according to its content it is a prayer of repentance, so that its use here recommended itself. Compare, however, similar images also present in 1 Clem. such as 1 Clem. 2:8: τὰ πλάτη τῆς καρδίας, 19:3: τὰ ὄμματα τῆς ψυχῆς, and both 36:2 and 59:3: οἱ ὀφθαλμοὶ τῆς καρδίας.

57:2 The opponents are therefore eloquent and were apparently superior to the presbyters in their eloquence. God hates the bragging tongue, says the OT frequently; however, see also Soph., *Ant.* 127f: Ζεὺς γὰρ μεγάλης γλώσσης κόμπους Ὑπερχθαίρει. On ποίμνιον τοῦ Χριστοῦ, see 1 Clem. 16:1, 44:3, 54:2; on δοκοῦντες, see Gal 2:2, 6, 9.

57:3–7 This is a severe threat against the impenitent; the citation from Prov 1:23–33 agrees almost verbatim with our version of the LXX.

57:3 Proverbs is readily called ἡ πανάρετος σοφία by early Christian writers; see the explicit testimony of Eusebius, *Hist. eccl.* 4.22.9: οὐ μόνος δὲ οὗτος (namely Hegessipus) καὶ Εἰρηναῖος δὲ καὶ ὁ πᾶς τῶν ἀρχαίων χορὸς πανάρετον Σοφίαν τὰς Σολομῶνος Παροιμίας ἐκάλουν. The term probably comes from Judaism, where חָכְמָה is attested as the title of the book among the rabbis, and it is explained by the leading position that the hypostasized wisdom occupies right at the beginning of the book and then again at 8:22f; see immediately before our citation Prov 1:20, the "I" in 1:23–33 is wisdom. The epithet *ornans* πανάρετος is first attested in our passage. At the end of v. 6, a larger gap begins in codex A due to the loss of a leaf, which extends to the end of 1 Clem. 63; see above on page 59.

57:7 πεποιθώς following ἐλπίδι is attested in LCS against H, which omits it along with the LXX; that it belongs in the text is also proved by 58:1: κατασκηνώσωμεν πεποιθότες.

58:1 The reading ἁγίῳ which is in agreement with LS should be preferred against H παναγίῳ; C is uncertain; the same grouping also speaks afterward for ὅσιον instead of ὁσιώτατον. On the entrance of ὑπακούσωμεν κτλ. see 9:1; on φυγόντες κτλ. see 30:1. The Book of Proverbs is often called σοφία without πανάρετος; see Justin, *Dial.* 129.3; Melito in Eusebius, *Hist. eccl.* 4.26.14; and frequently in Clem. Alex. κατασκηνώσωμεν πεποιθότες is picked back up in 57:7.

58:2 ἀμεταμέλητα: on the word, see ἀμεταμελήτως which appears shortly afterward as well in 2:7; 54:4; on the plural, see 47:6. The second ζῇ should be erased in agreement with L, Basil (who cites the passage in *De spiritu sancto* 29), and apparently C, against the reading in HS. The words ἥ τε πίστις καὶ ἡ ἐλπὶς τῶν ἐκλεκτῶν are probably in apposition with the preceding. On the Trinitarian formula, see the comments at 46:6. — ταπεινοφροσύνη and ἐπιείκεια are placed next to each other in 30:8 and 56:1; on ἐκτενοῦς ἐπιεικείας, see 62:2; on δικαιώματα καὶ προστάγματα, see 2:8; on ἐλλόγιμος, see 44:3; 57:2; 62:3; on ἀριθμὸς τῶν σωζομένων, see 2:4; 35:4; 59:2. On ἐλλόγιμος εἰς τὸν ἀριθμόν, Plato, *Phileb.* 17E is a parallel: οὐκ ἐλλόγιμον οὐδ᾽ ἐνάριθμον.

E. Conclusion of the Letter with a Long Prayer (59:1—61:3)

Translation

⁵⁹:¹ But if some disobey the (admonitions) spoken by him through us, let them realize that they will be plunged into transgression and no small danger. ² But we will be innocent of this sin and will pray with persistent supplication and entreaty that the creator of all might preserve unharmed the numbered multitude of his elect throughout the world through his beloved servant, Jesus Christ, through whom he called us from darkness to light, from ignorance to the knowledge of the glory of his name,

³ that we might hope in your name which gave life to all created things, who opened the eyes of our heart, that we might know you, the only Highest among the Highest, the Holy One resting among the saints, the one who humbles the pride of those who boast, who puts to shame the pretentions of the pagans, who exalts the humble and humbles the exalted, who makes rich and makes poor, who kills and makes alive, the only benefactor of the spirits and the God of all flesh. He is the one who looks into the underworld, who investigates the works of men, the helper of those endangered, the savior of those who despair, the creator and overseer of every spirit, who multiplies the nations of the earth, and who has chosen from among all of them those who love you, through Jesus Christ your beloved servant, through whom you have raised us up, sanctified us, honored us.

⁵⁹:⁴ We pray, Lord, be our helper and take care of us. Save those who are in distress among us, have mercy on the oppressed, raise up the fallen, show yourself to those who pray, heal the sick, guide the erring among your people back to the right path. Feed the hungry, release our prisoners, heal the sick, comfort the fainthearted. Let all the nations know that you are the only God and Jesus Christ is your servant, and we are your people and the sheep of your pasture.

⁶⁰:¹ You have revealed the eternal nature of the world through the working of the powers. You, Lord, have founded the earth, you who are faithful in all generations, just in (your) judgments, marvelous in power and glory, wise in creating and understanding to uphold that which has been created, good in that which is seen, and mild toward those who trust in you.

Merciful and gracious one, forgive us our sins and trespasses and transgressions.

² Do not impute sin to your servants and handmaids, but purify us with the cleansing of your truth, and make our steps straight, that we might walk in purity of heart and do what is good and pleasing in your sight and in the sight of our princes. ³ Yes Lord, let your face shine upon us in peace for salvation, that we might be protected by your strong hand and kept from every sin by your exalted arm, and save us from those who hate us unjustly.

⁴ Grant unity and peace to us and to all who dwell on earth, as you gave these things to our fathers when they called on you in a holy manner in faith and truth.

Let us be obedient to your almighty and glorious name and to our rulers and princes on earth. [61:1] You, Lord, by virtue of your exalted and ineffable power, have given them kingship, that we may be mindful of the glory and honor you have bestowed upon them and submit to them in nothing that is contrary to your will. Lord, give them health, peace, concord, stability, that they may conduct without fault the dominion which you have bestowed upon them. [2] For you, heavenly Lord, King of the eons, give glory and honor to the sons of men and power over what is on earth. Guide their minds, O Lord, according to what is good and pleasing in your sight, so that in peace and meekness they may piously conduct the dominion you have given them and be partakers of your grace.

[61:3] You alone are able to do this and many more good things for us. We praise you through the high priest and protector of our souls, Jesus Christ, through whom be glory and majesty to you now and from generation to generation and from eternity to eternity. Amen!

Textual Notes

First Clement 59:1f forms the transition into the prayer.

59:1 Note again the strong self-consciousness of the church sending the letter (cf. above at 56:1, and then 1 Clem. 62 and 63:2). ὑπ' αὐτοῦ = from God. παράπτωσις is a Hellenistic word, attested several times in Polybius XV 23.5; XVI 20.5; among other places; in the LXX only Jer 22:21; in the early Christian literature, only here and in Justin, *Dial.* 141.3f. ἐνδήσουσιν should be read in agreement with HSC against L ἐνδώσουσιν (*se tradent*).

59:2 On ἐκτενῆ, see 58:2 and at 34:8. The transition to the prayer is done well. The common hope of Christians as well as the great danger of disobedience were just mentioned. Now the author uses the 1st person plural (which includes the author and the sending church) to pray that this danger which arises from disobedience may not become reality and that none of the elect—neither in Rome nor in Corinth nor in the whole world—may fall out of the number of the elect. But even though the transition fits in so well here, it was not freely composed by Clement but was taken over by him: at the beginning of the Roman congregational prayer there was a request for a heartfelt plea to almighty God through Jesus Christ; the plea was made for the congregation and for all of Christendom, and its content was that God may save and preserve his own. In the great liturgy of the Apost, Const. VIII, it says in 10.19–22: ὑπὲρ ἀλλήλων δεηθῶμεν, ὅπως ὁ κύριος διατηρήσῃ ἡμᾶς καὶ φυλάξῃ τῇ αὐτοῦ χάριτι εἰς τέλος καὶ ῥύσηται ἡμᾶς τοῦ πονηροῦ . . . καὶ σώσῃ εἰς τὴν βασιλείαν αὐτοῦ τὴν ἐπουράνιον. ὑπὲρ πάσης ψυχῆς Χριστιανῆς δεηθῶμεν. . . . δεηθέντες ἐκτενῶς ἑαυτοὺς καὶ ἀλλήλους τῷ ζῶντι θεῷ διὰ τοῦ Χριστοῦ αὐτοῦ παραθώμεθα, and this is followed by a portion of a prayer (11.1ff) which shows close contact with 1 Clem. 59:3; see then also VIII 22.3 (consecration prayer for the readers): ὁ θεὸς ὁ αἰώνιος ὁ . . . τὸν ἀριθμὸν τῶν ἐκλεκτῶν σου διαφυλάττων. Therefore, we must recognize a tradition of the congregational liturgy, which is present here as well as there. — Also, the archaic designation of Jesus as the παῖς θεοῦ clearly shows that the liturgy begins here; see the repeated use of the title below in vv. 3 and 4; see further Did. 9:2f; 10:2f in the prayers over the communion; see also Acts 4:27, 30, among other places (even more material in Bousset, *Kyrios Christos*, 68). Light and knowledge are the two most closely related goods, which Jesus Christ bestowed according to the will of the Father. ζωή, the other great good of salvation, which is often connected with *gnosis*, is not mentioned here; however, see 35:2 and φῶς in 36:2. The spiritual worth of light and knowledge can be illustrated well by 2 Clem. 1; the use of light (knowledge) and life in John's Gospel is also well known (cf. also Wetter, *Phōs*). The object of the blessed knowledge is the glory of the name of God revealed through Christ, the unique one, as will be shown in the comments on v. 3.

The prayer, which is offered in 59:3—61:3 and already begins in 59:2, is one of the most valuable parts of the whole letter, in general a particularly precious piece of the whole of early Christian literature. It is generally admitted that it is taken from the Roman congregational liturgy. This can be inferred from the content as well as from the style of its designs. However, it is not as if Clement has added to his letter an exact prayer of the Roman congregation as it was prayed on Sundays during the worship service. We do not even know to what extent this text was already fixed at that time, at the end of the first century. Even 60 years later, the words of Justin, *1 Apol.* 67.5 show that not even the liturgy of the eucharistic celebration was fixed verbatim: ὁ προεστὼς εὐχὰς ὁμοίως καὶ εὐχαριστίας, ὅση δύναμις αὐτῷ (cf. Did. 10:6!) ἀναπέμπει. But it is certain that the nature and the style of the present piece was part of the liturgy of prayer, which in Rome had its fixed place in the Sunday worship service, and that, as Justin again proves, it took place after the sermon: ἔπειτα (namely, according to the νουθέσια of the superintendent) ἀνιστάμεθα κοινῇ πάντες καὶ εὐχὰς πέμπομεν (*1 Apol.* 67.5). Just as Clement was accustomed to pray in the service before the assembled congregation, now the words come into his mouth when he writes to the Corinthian congregation without following a literal model. The reason he concludes with the prayer in such a broad way is not that he wanted to give the Corinthians an example of correct prayer pleasing to God after all the good admonitions of the preceding. For it is impossible to assume that the Corinthians did not also have their own liturgical tradition, and that there were not also men among them to offer this prayer correctly. There is no question that Clement regarded the prayer as a fixed holy formula that was to be recited verbatim. Moreover, if the Romans communicated their congregational prayer to the Corinthians as a model, this would somehow have to be expressed in the letter itself, in the context of 59–61. Thus, the reason for the letter has come to its conclusion, and the liturgical prayer sits like a crown upon its head. The lengthy designs of the letter have come to an end, and the author himself is clearly aware of this (1 Clem. 62). He has sketched a model for genuine Christian change. Now the whole thing must receive a sounding, rich, heartfelt conclusion. Clement, who is accustomed from the Sunday celebrations of his congregation to conclude the address, the sermon, with a prayer, and who is already in the spirit of the intercessory prayer for the congregation in 56:1 and 59:2, is reminded of the sentences of the liturgy, its praise of God, and its supplication, and he lets the stream of his speech flow out in its broad, familiar course. After all, he has preached in the letter, and he wants and knows that the letter should be read out loud in the church service before the assembled congregation. From the words of Dionysius of Corinth in Eusebius (*Eccl. hist.* 4.23.11), we also learn that the Corinthians accepted the Roman letter into the cycle of ecclesiastical readings, and that they continued to enjoy its reading in the church service for decades. — The content and structure of the prayer is as follows: after the transition (59:2) comes an elaboration containing the praise of God, a solemn accumulation of predications (59:3), which is followed by the first supplication pleading for help for all kinds of needs and for those in distress. This is followed by a renewed praise of God (60:1), with an attached request for the forgiveness of sins (60:2). Then comes the prayer for peace and general welfare (60:3f) and, finally, an extended intercession for the authorities (61:1f). The whole concludes with a solemn formula of praise and thanksgiving (61:3). — In the form of the prayer, the parallelism and the antithesis of the short links should be noted, as well as the many identical beginnings of the cola and the rhymes and consonances of its endings. The author borrows language for the prayer throughout, and the originality of the whole is not great, which is not surprising. To strike new notes in prayer is given only to the greatest, the rest is carried by the stream of tradition. And the tradition from which our prayer, and the liturgy of the congregation in general, has flowed is rich and old. Christian prayer tradition, the language of the LXX, occasionally also echoes of Christian writings, further contemporary Jewish language of Hellenism can be recognized in the chapters. A clean separation of the individual components is not possible, it is all too intertwined. But the impact of the LXX is strongly felt, and it is unmistakable in a number of places. — The liturgy of the ancient Roman congregation, which can be grasped in 1 Clem. 59–61 and in other places of the letter (20; 33), can also be recognized in later liturgies of the Greek church, where related liturgical tradition is present. Above all, the liturgy in Book VIII of the Apostolic Constitutions comes into consideration again. Fundamental to the questions of the Clementine liturgy is the study by Drews. The liturgy of Book VIII of the Apostolic Constitutions in Lietzmann, *Klementinische Litugie* and the text of the whole book in Funk, *Didascalia*; the ancient liturgies of the Greek church in Swainson, *Greek Liturgies* and Brightman, *Liturgies*; a very useful translation of the Greek liturgy in the *Liturgien*, with introductions by Schermann, see also the abundant literature cited there. On Clement's prayer, see Goltz, *Gebet*, 196–207 as well as Schermann, *Griechische Zauberpapyri*.

59:3 The text of the beginning of the prayer is certain in the textual tradition. Despite the emendations by Bryennios or Lightfoot, neither δὸς ἡμῖν nor κύριε nor any other emendation should be inserted before ἐλπίζειν, nor should the text be improved by changing ἀνοίξας to ἄνοιξον as Hilgenfeld suggests. An anacoluthon is admittedly present, as ἀνοίξας and the second-person pronoun instead of αὐτοῦ or αὐτόν prove. The reason for the anacoluthon is that the text transitions into the prayer and is not freely designed. ἀρχεγόνον has to be paroxytonal because it clearly has an active sense, even though C, the only Greek source for the entire context, reads ἀρχέγονον. The word has been taken over from philosophical and theological language; see above all Pseudo-Aristotle, *De mundo* 6 (Wilamowitz, *Griechisches Lesebuch* 1.2, 195.21): διὰ τὴν πρώτην καὶ ἀρχέγονον αἰτίαν, Papyrus Paris 174 (Wessely, "Griechische Zauberpapyrus," 44–126), line 1459: ἐπικαλοῦμαι χάος ἀρχέγονον ἔρεβος, Damoxenos in Athenaeus III 102a: ἡ φύσις ἀρχέγονον πάσης τέχνης, Irenaeus, *Haer.* I 1 (in the system of the Valentinians): καὶ εἶναι ταύτην πρώτην καὶ ἀρχέγονον Πυθαγορικὴν Τετρακτύν ... καὶ εἶναι ταύτην ἀρχέγονον Ὀγδοάδα, among other sources. God's "name" brought the entire creation into being and Christians hope in this "name"; see Did. 10:3: σὺ δέσποτα παντοκράτορ, ἔκτισας τὰ πάντα ἕνεκεν τοῦ ὀνόματός σου. — ἀνοίξας τοὺς ὀφθαλμοὺς τῆς καρδίας; see above at 36:2, then see Eph 1:18. The image and word ultimately originate from the mystery language, where the initiate's veiled eyes are opened and see the light; Dieterich, *Mithrasliturgie* 10.19: εἶτα ἄνοιξον τοὺς ὀρθαλμοὺς καὶ ὄψει ἀνεῳγυίας τὰς θύρας καὶ τὸν κόσμον τῶν θεῶν ... ὥστε ἀπὸ τῆς τοῦ θεάματος | ἡδονῆς καὶ τῆς χαρᾶς τὸ πνεῦμά σου συντρέχειν καὶ ἀναβαίνειν. The consequence and goal of the enlightenment here is the view of the God of the ecstatic; in our text, which also speaks of spiritual enlightenment, the knowledge of God. On γινώσκειν κτλ., see primarily John 17:3; on ὕψιστον κτλ., the clear *Vorlage* is Isa 57:15: ὁ ὕψιστος ὁ ἐν ὑψηλοῖς κατοικῶν τὸν αἰῶνα, ἅγιος ἐν ἁγίοις ὄνομα αὐτῷ, ὕψιστος ἐν ἁγίοις ἀναπαυόμενος, see further in the Apost. Const. VIII 11.2: κύριε παντοκράτορ, ὕψιστε ὁ ἐν ὑψηλοῖς κατοικῶν, ἅγιε ἐν ἁγίοις ἀναπαυόμενε. The words ἐν ὑψίστοις and ἐν ἁγίοις could be composed in the neuter gender, as ἐν ὑψίστοις in Luke 2:14; they could also be interpreted as masculine and therefore refer to the holy and high angels (cf. 1 Clem. 34:6). On ὕψιστος, see at 1 Clem. 45:7; also in the first berakha of the Shemone-esre, the Eighteen Benedictions (Schürer, *Geschichte*, 2:460–63) God is addressed as אֵל עֶלְיוֹן. (Text in Staerk, *Gebete*; translation of the Jewish worship liturgy in its main components in Fiebig, *Judentum*; the Eighteen Benedictions also in Schürer, *Geschichte*.) The part of the prayer that now follows consists of a series of short, strictly parallel links. On τὸν ταπεινοῦντα κτλ., see Isa 13:11: καὶ ὕβριν ὑπερηφάνων ταπεινώσω, Luke 1:51, berakha 12 in the Eighteen Benedictions: "the one who . . . humbles the arrogant." On τὸν διαλύοντα κτλ., see Ps 32:10: κύριος διασκεδάζει βουλὰς ἐθνῶν ἀθετεῖ δὲ λογισμοὺς λαῶν καὶ ἀθετεῖ βουλὰς ἀρχόντων. On τὸν ποιοῦντα up to ταπεινοῦντα, see Job 5:11: τὸν ποιοῦντα ταπεινοὺς εἰς ὕψος and Isa 10:33: καὶ οἱ ὑψηλοὶ ταπεινωθήσονται, see further Ezek 21:26: ἐταπείνωσας τὸ ὑψηλὸν καὶ ὕψωσας τὸ ταπεινόν, Ezek 17:24; 1 Sam 2:7; Luke 1:52; 14:11; 18:14; Matt 23:12. τὸν πλουτίζοντα καὶ πτωχίζοντα, 1 Sam 2:7: κύριος πλουτίζει καὶ πτωχίζει, Luke 1:53. But Hesiod already says of Zeus: Ῥέα μὲν γὰρ βριάει, ῥέα δὲ βριάοντα χαλέπτει, Ῥεῖα δ' ἀρίζηλον μινύθει καὶ ἄδηλον ἀέξει (*Works and Days* 5f) and in Dieterich, *Papyrus leidensis* VII II, pp. 747f), the following is said of the θεοὶ οὐράνιοι: ὦ τῶν ὑπερεχόντων ὑποτάκται, ὦ τῶν ὑποτεταγμένων ὑψωταί. In the next portion, LS (against HC) insert καὶ σώζοντα before ζῆν, but the well attested addition destroys the dichotomy that runs through the whole section; for the wording, see Deut 32:39: ἐγὼ ἀποκτέννω καὶ ζῆν ποιήσω, also 1 Sam 2:6: κύριος θανατοῖ καὶ ζωογονεῖ and 2 Kgs 5:7: ὁ θεὸς ἐγὼ τοῦ θανατῶσαι καὶ ζωοποιῆσαι; Eighteen Benedictions 2: "who gives life to the dead, . . . who sustains the living with grace, who gives life to the dead with great mercy." μόνον εὐεργέτην κτλ., on this see Num 16:22 and 27:16: θεὸς τῶν πνευμάτων καὶ πάσης σαρκός, also Job 12:10: εἰ μὴ ἐν χειρὶ αὐτοῦ ψυχὴ πάντων ζώντων καὶ πνεῦμα παντὸς ἀνθρώπου and Heb 12:9; Rev 22:6; on εὐεργέτης, see the comments above at 1 Clem. 19:2, and on the entirety see the beginning at 1 Clem. 64. πνεύματα, both in this passage and in other passages, of course, are the angels. On τὸν ἐπιβλέποντα κτλ., see Sir 16:18f: ἄβυσσος καὶ γῆ σαλευθήσονται ἐν τῇ ἐπισκοπῇ αὐτοῦ, ἅμα τὰ ὄρη καὶ τὰ θεμέλια τῆς γῆς ἐν τῷ ἐπιβλέψαι εἰς αὐτὰ τρόπῳ συνσείονται. Psalm 32:13: ἐξ οὐρανοῦ ἐπέβλεψεν ὁ κύριος, Luke 1:48; on the construction with ἐν instead of εἰς, see Blaß-Debrunner, *Grammatik* §218; also Radermacher, *Grammatik*, 116. τὸν ἐπόπτην κτλ., see Esther D 2 (15:5): τὸν πάντων ἐπόπτην θεόν, 2 Macc 7:35: τὸν τοῦ παντοκράτορος ἐπόπτου θεοῦ κρίσιν, as well as 3:39 and 3 Macc 2:21. However, ἐπόπτης also appears on Hellenistic soil in Dieterich, *Papyrus leidensis* VII 26: τὸν προπάτορα θεῶν, πάντων ἐπόπτην καὶ κύριον and Caesar Augustus: Αὐτοκράτορα Καίσαρα θεοῦ υἱὸν θεὸν Σεβαστόν, πάσης γῆς καὶ θαλάσης ἐπόπτην (Fränkel, *Inschriften von Pergamon*, n. 381), see Deißmann, *Licht*, 261, also Schermann, *Griechische Zauberpapyri*, 28f. — τὸν τῶν κινδυνευόντων κτλ., see Jdt 9:11: ταπεινῶν . . . θεός, ἐλαττόνων . . . βοηθός, ἀντιλήμπτωρ ἀσθενούντων, ἀπεγνωσμένων σκεπαστής, ἀπηλπισμένων σωτήρ, Psalms of Solomon 16:4: ὁ σωτὴρ καὶ ἀντιλήμπτωρ μου, Eighteen Benedictions 1: "King, Helper, Savior, and Shield," Acts of Paul and Thecla 37 in a quite liturgical sounding passage: ἀπηλπισμένοις σκέπη, *Passio S. Theodoti Ancyrani* 21 (Ruinart, *Acta Martyrum*, 380): *spes desperatorum*. σωτήρ, the well-known, already often discussed expression of Hellenistic piety, especially of the imperial cult, see Wendland, *Kultur*; Greek index under σωτήρ; and Wendland, "Σωτήρ"; von Harnack, *Reden und Aufsätze*, 1:307–11; von Harnack, *Mission*, 115ff; Lietzmann, *Weltheiland*; among others. The designation σωτήρ only occurs here in this letter. τὸν παντὸς πνεύματος κτλ., see Zech 12:1: πλάσσων πνεῦμα ἀνθρώπου ἐν αὐτῷ, Amos 4:13: κτίζων πνεῦμα, Isa 57:16: πνεῦμα γὰρ παρ᾽ ἐμοῦ ἐξελεύσεται, καὶ πνοὴν πᾶσαν ἐγὼ ἐποίησα, Job 10:12: ἡ δὲ ἐπισκοπή σου ἐφύλαξέν μου τὸ πνεῦμα, Wis. 1:6 (of God): τῆς καρδίας αὐτοῦ (of the blasphemers) ἐπίσκοπος ἀληθής, see also Heb 12:9 and 1 Pet 2:25. Examples of κτίστης and ἐπίσκοπος are in the magical papyri in Schermann, *Griechische Zauberpapyri*, 29 and 31. On τὸν πληθύνοντα κτλ., see Gen 48:16 and also Acts 17:26; the expression is clearly a praise of God, and therefore does not speak against the ἔθνη: gentiles, but universalistic. Christians feel like they have been taken from the multitude of all peoples who inhabit the earth. The thought returns to the beginning of the prayer (cf. 59:2), and therefore complements it. On ἐπαίδευσας, see not only 56:16 and 57:1, but also Titus 2:11f; on ἡγίασας, see John 17:17 as well as 1 Cor 1:2; on ἐτίμησας, see John 12:26 and 1 Pet 2:6f.

    59:4 The solemn, long invocation is followed by the solemn, correspondingly long and also correspondingly stylized supplication; the number of units in vv. 3 and 4 correspond to each other. The content of the individual petitions is summarized in the first unit, which also differs in form from the subsequent ones, and it thus sets the basic tone of the entire section: Help for those in need. On the beginning ἀξιοῦμεν κτλ., see Ps 118:114, as well as Jdt 9:11, where βοηθός and ἀντιλήπτωρ originate. See also Apost. Const. VIII 12.45: ἔτι ἀξιοῦμέν σε ὑπὲρ τῆς πόλεως ταύτης καὶ τῶν ἐνοικούτων ὑπὲρ κτλ. (following are the sick, slaves, banished, outlaws, seafarers, and wanderers)

ὅπως πάντων ἐπίκουρος γένῃ, πάντων βοηθὸς καὶ ἀντιλήπτωρ. On the following, see the first and the second berakha in the Eighteen Benedictions,
which, however, does not have the form of a request, but of praise: "You, O
Lord, are a hero forever, who makes the dead living, who are rich with help,
who upholds the living with grace, who makes the dead alive with great
mercy, upholds those who are falling, and who heals the sick, loosens the
bound, and fulfills his faithfulness to those who sleep in the dust." In *De oratione* 29 Tertullian describes the power of prayer, clearly using expressions
of a liturgy that must be related to ours: *Sola est oratio, quae deum vincit; sed
Christus eam nihil mali voluit operari, omnem illi virtutem de bono contulit.
Itaque nihil novit, nisi defunctorum animas de ipso mortis itinere revocare,
debiles reformare, aegros remediare, daemoniacos expiare, claustra carceris
operire, vincula innocentium solvere. eadem diluit delicta, temptationes rep-
ellit, persecutiones extinguit, pusillanimos consolatur, magnanimos oblectat,
peregrinantes deducit, fluctus mitigat, latrones obstupefacit, alit pauperes,
regit divites, lapsos erigit, cadentes suspendit, stantes continet.* Further, the
Alexandrian liturgy (Markan liturgy) has a passage directly reminiscent of
the Clementine liturgy (Brightman, *Liturgies*, 1:131; Swainson, *Greek Liturgies*, 48): Λύτρωσαι δεσμίους, ἐξέλου τοὺς ἐν ἀνάγκαις, πεινῶντας χόρτασον,
ὀλιγοψυχοῦντας παρακάλεσον, πεπλανημένους ἐπίστρεψον, ἐσκοτισμένους
φωταγώγησον, πεπτωκότας ἔγειρον, σαλευομένους στήριξον, νενοσηκότας
ἴασαι, πάντας ἄγαγε εἰς τὴν ὁδὸν τῆς σωτηρίας, σύναψον καὶ αὐτοὺς τῇ ἁγίᾳ σου
ποίμνῃ· ἡμᾶς δὲ ῥῦσαι ἀπὸ τῶν ἀνομιῶν ἡμῶν, φρουρὸς ἡμῶν καὶ ἀντιλήπτωρ
γενόμενος. Without doubt, the Markan liturgy is related to our passage, but
how the relationship is to be explained is still uncertain. However, 1 Clem.
59:4 was not the direct model for the liturgy of Mark (see Drews, *Liturgies*,
44f). The echoes of the LXX are not as numerous in this part of the prayer as
in the preceding, which is due to the nature of the matter: the solemn des-
ignations for God were taken from the Holy Book, the petitions themselves
come from more recent tradition. The ten petitions are mainly for salvation
from physical distress, although some also take spiritual distress into account.
τοὺς ἐν θλίψει ἡμῶν is to be understood as broadly as possible: the poor, the
afflicted, widows, orphans, etc. On πεπτωκότας, see Ps 144:14: ὑποστηρίζει
κύριος πάντας τοὺς καταπίπτοντας καὶ ἀνορθοῖ πάντας τοὺς κατερραγμένους,
and Ps 146:8: κύριος ἀνορθοῖ κατερραγμένους. The fallen are not the Christians who have fallen spiritually, for whom prayers are said afterward, but
the downcast in general. ἐπιφάνηθι: in the Magical Papyri φαῖνε and φάνηθι
occur frequently (see Schermann, *Griechische Zauberpapyri*, 38). Here, the
ἀσθενεῖς (with LSC against the certainly incorrect ἀσεβεῖς in H) are the sick,
the ἀσθενοῦντες in what follows are the "weak" in a figurative sense; on the
use of ἀσθενεῖς, for instance, in Acts 4:9; 5:15; Luke 10:9, in addition to other

passages. Berakha 8 in the Eighteen Benedictions: "Heal us, Lord, and we will be healed . . . Blessed are you, Eternal One, who heals the sick of his people, Israel." τοὺς πλανωμένους κτλ. refers to the weak, doubting brothers; on the expression, see Ezek 34:16: τὸ πλανώμενον ἐπιστρέψω and berakha 5: "Bring us back, our Father, to your law, and bring us near, our King, to your service, and lead us back in perfect repentance before you." Apostolic Constitutions VIII 10:17: ὑπὲρ τῶν ἔξω ὄντων καὶ πεπλανημένων δεηθῶμεν, ὅπως ὁ κύριος αὐτοὺς ἐπιστρέψῃ. On χόρτασον κτλ., see berakha 9: "fill us with your goodness" as well as Luke 1:53: πεινῶντας ἐνέπλησεν ἀγαθῶν. Regarding the following section, the situation of the Christians under Domitian is to be noted; in Rome and Asia, perhaps also in other provinces, persecutions had taken place, Christians had been imprisoned, banished, and sent to the mines; the church cares for its prisoners and prays for them; see Heb 13:3 and 10:34; from a somewhat later time, see also Ign. *Smyrn.* 6:2; from the second half of the second century. Dionysius of Corinth in Eusebius, *Hist. eccl.* 4.23.10 says: ἐν μετάλλοις δὲ ἀδελφοῖς ὑπάρχουσιν ἐπιχορηγοῦντας δι' ὧν πέμπετε ἀρχῆθεν ἐφοδίων and numerous additional witnesses; see also Apost. Const. VIII 10.15: ὑπὲρ τῶν ἐν μετάλλοις καὶ ἐξορίαις καὶ φυλακαῖς καὶ δεσμοῖς ὄντων διὰ τὸ ὄνομα τοῦ κυρίου δεηθῶμεν. Later liturgies also still retained the petitions for the prisoners and those in exile. On ἐξανάστησον κτλ., παρακάλεσον κτλ., see 1 Thess 5:14; ἀσθενεῖν in a figurative sense occurs frequently, see especially the Pauline Epistles. On γνώτωσαν κτλ., see 1 Kgs 8:60: ὅπως γνῶσιν πάντες οἱ λαοὶ τῆς γῆς ὅτι κύριος ὁ θεὸς αὐτὸς θεὸς καὶ οὐκ ἔστιν ἔτι, 2 Kgs 19:19: γνώσονται πᾶσαι αἱ βασιλεῖαι τῆς γῆς ὅτι σὺ κύριος ὁ θεὸς μόνος, Ezek 36:23: καὶ γνώσονται τὰ ἔθνη ὅτι ἐγώ εἰμι κύριος, see also Isa 37:20 and John 17:3. On Jesus as the παῖς θεοῦ, see 1 Clem. 59:2, 3. On ἡμεῖς λαός κτλ., see Ps 99:3: γνῶτε ὅτι κύριος, αὐτός ἐστιν ὁ θεός, αὐτὸς ἐποίησεν ἡμᾶς καὶ οὐχ ἡμεῖς, [ἡμεῖς δὲ] λαὸς αὐτοῦ καὶ πρόβατα τῆς νομῆς αὐτοῦ. See also Ps 78:13 and 94:7, then 1 Pet 2:25 and the shepherd and the flock in John 10. The prayer returns to the thought with which v. 3 had closed (cf. 1 Clem. 59:3).

60:1 begins with a new invocation to God. The praise is mainly directed to the creator God, but other thoughts are also expressed. The language is again strongly determined by the LXX, but the verbatim citations are not as numerous as in 59:3; there are more echoes and brushes with the LXX than material that has been taken over outright. σὺ (γὰρ LS against HC) τὴν ἀέναον κτλ., on the idea of God revealing himself in creation, see already the excurses and comments at 1 Clem. 20; for individual passages, see Rom 1:20 and Peusdo-Aristotle, *De mundo* 6 (Wilamowitz, *Griechisches Lesebuch II*, 196.11): πάσῃ θνητῇ φύσει γενόμενος ἀθεώρητος ἀπ' αὐτῶν τῶν ἔργων θεωρεῖται. In our passage, it is not directly said that God is seen in the creation, but that the eternal (i.e., the resting, divine existence of the universe) becomes visible through the colorful and changing multiformity of the individual phenomena. The whole thought is much more Platonic-Stoic than early Christian. On the individual passages, see Wis 7:17: αὐτὸς γάρ μοι ἔδωκεν τῶν ὄντων γνῶσιν ἀψευδῆ, εἰδέναι σύστασιν κόσμου καὶ ἐνέργειαν στοιχείων, Plato, *Timaeus* p. 32C: ἡ τοῦ κόσμου ξύστασις, *Timaeus Locrus* 99D: μετὰ δὲ τὰν τῷ κόσμῳ σύστασιν, Diodorus Siculus I 7.1, p. 10: κατὰ τὴν ἐξ ἀρχῆς τοῦ κόσμου σύστασιν . . . . φανεροποιεῖν is a rare and late word. The creator God in the *epiclesis* is also in berakha 1 of the Eighteen Benedictions ("founder of the universe") and in the magical papyri (examples can be found in Schermann, *Griechische Zauberpapyri*, 31). First Clement 60:1 is taken over by the Apost. Const. VIII 22:1: ὁ τὴν τοῦ κόσμου σύστασιν διὰ τῶν ἐνεργουμένων φανεροποιήσας. On σύ, κύριε κτλ., see Ps 88:12f: τὴν οἰκουμένην καὶ τὸ πλήρωμα αὐτῆς σὺ ἐθεμελίωσας, τὴν βορρὰν καὶ θαλάσσας σὺ ἔκτισας. Also the οἰκουμένη and its creation is often mentioned elsewhere in the Psalms. On ὁ πιστὸς κτλ., see Deut 7:9: θεὸς πιστὸς ὁ φυλάσσων διαθήκην καὶ ἔλεος . . . εἰς χιλίας γενεάς and Ps 144:14: πιστὸς κύριος ἐν τοῖς λόγοις αὐτοῦ. On δίκαιος κτλ., see Tobit 3:2: δίκαιος εἶ, κύριε, . . . καὶ κρίσιν ἀληθινὴν καὶ δικαίαν σὺ κρίνεις, Ps 118:137: δίκαιος εἶ, κύριε, καὶ εὐθὺς ἡ κρίσις σου, Ps 144:17: δίκαιος κύριος ἐν πάσαις ταῖς ὁδοῖς αὐτοῦ, etc. See also Dieterich, *Papyrus leidensis* V 31, pp. 803, 831): ὁ μέγας καὶ ἄρρητος καὶ ὅσιος καὶ δίκαιος . . . δαίμων. The connection πιστὸς καὶ δίκαιος also appears in 1 John 1:9. On θαυμαστὸς κτλ., see Sirach 43:29f: φοβερὸς κύριος καὶ σφόδρα μέγας καὶ θαυμαστὴ ἡ δυναστεία αὐτοῦ. On ὁ σοφὸς κτλ., see the well-known praise of creation in Ps 103, then see Ps 146:5: μέγας ὁ κύριος ἡμῶν, καὶ μεγάλη ἡ ἰσχὺς αὐτοῦ, καὶ τῆς συνέσεως αὐτοῦ οὐκ ἔστιν ἀριθμός. On συνετὸς κτλ., see Prov 8:25: πρὸ τοῦ ὄρη ἑδρασθῆναι (likewise in Ps 89:2 in S): on the connection between σοφός and συνετός, but not used of God, see Isa 29:14 and Dan 1:4 LXX. In the following, ὁρωμένοις is now fixed according to all the textual witnesses, and the improvements of the former editors, made when H was the only textual witness available, are now invalid. The sense of the double statement ὁ ἀγαθὸς κτλ. καὶ χρηστὸς κτλ. is: God is good in the visible gifts of his creation and he is gentle and kind in what is not yet visible, but in which his faithful trust. On the thought of visible and invisible gifts, see already 1 Clem. 35:1–3, where the statement is however directed differently than here; then see Heb 11:1. Instead of χρηστός (LSC), read πιστός with H. On ὁρώμενα, see Wis 13:1: ἐκ τῶν ὁρωμένων ἀγαθῶν οὐκ ἴσχυσαν (sc. οἱ ἄνθρωποι) εἰδέναι τὸν ὄντα. On "good" God, see Ps 72:1; 117:1–3; Mark 10:18; ἀγαθὸς θεός is used on pagan ground in a Koic inscription by Nero (Deissmann, *Licht*, 260) and ἀγαθὸς δαίμων in the Magical Papyri (Schermann, *Griechische Zauberpapyri*, 28): ἀγαθὸς θεός and ἀγαθὸς δαίμων have a long prehistory on Greek soil, reaching up far beyond Hellenism: the "gentle" God occurs frequently in the LXX (e.g., Ps 24:8; 99:5; Wis 15:1; see then Luke 6:35; Rom 2:4; 1 Pet 2:3; Eph 2:7; Titus 3:4). The θεοί χρηστοί already occurs in Herodotus, *Hist.* VIII 111. On χρηστὸς κτλ. and the following ἐλεῆμον καὶ οἰκτίρμον, see already Sir 2:10f: ἐμβλέψατε εἰς ἀρχαίας γενεὰς καὶ ἴδετε· τίς ἐνεπίστευσεν κυρίῳ καὶ κατησχύνθη; διότι οἰκτίρμων καὶ ἐλεήμων ὁ κύριος. The connection ἐλεήμων καὶ οἰκτίρμων occurs frequently in the LXX (cf. Ps 85:15; 108:2; 110:4; 111:4; 144:8; Joel 2:13; Jonah 4:2. The actual prayer begins with ἄφες κτλ., which here and in the following implores forgiveness for sins. The merciful and gracious, the good and gentle one forgives sins; in the previously cited passages Sir 2:11 and Ps 102:8, see the connection between God's mercy and the forgiveness of sins. The series ἀνομίας κτλ. descends, going from the serious to the lighter sins; besides the completeness, note the consonances and alliterations within the passage. On the request for forgiveness of sins in other ancient Christian liturgies, see Drews, *Liturgie*, 45.

60:2 The language here again becomes more biblical; certain echoes of our prayer are also found in Luke 1:68–79, which is in the style of the Psalms. δούλων καὶ παιδισκῶν, the detailed and solemn intricateness of the liturgy enumerates both sexes; we stand in the cultically assembled congregations. The negative request for forgiveness of sins is immediately followed by a positive one for sanctification and strength to do the good. Both are closely and intrinsically connected with each other, and recur in the liturgies at all times; see the instruction of Origen, *De oratione* 33 (Lommatzsch, *Origenis Opera*, 17:293; Koetschau, *Origenes Werke*, 2:401), where admittedly the order of the two pieces is reversed: μετὰ δὲ τὴν εὐχαριστίαν φαίνεταί μοι πικρόν τινα δεῖν γινόμενον τῶν ἰδίων ἁμαρτημάτων κατήγορον ἐπὶ θεοῦ, αἰτεῖν πρῶτον μὲν ἴασιν πρὸς τὸ ἀπαλλαγῆναι τῆς τὸ ἁμαρτάνειν ἐπιφερούσης ἕξεως δεύτερον δὲ ἄφεσιν τῶν παρεληλυθότων. On καθάρισον κτλ., see John 17:17 (15:3); the reading καθάρισον attested in the versions is to be preferred against καθαρεῖς in H. On κατεύθυνον κτλ., see Ps 118:133: τὰ διαβήματά μου κατεύθυνον κατὰ τὸ λόγιόν σου as well as Ps 39:3; 36:23; Prov 20:18; Luke 1:79. On ἐν ὁσιότητι κτλ., see 1 Kgs 9:4: καὶ σὺ ἐὰν πορευθῇς ἐνώπιον ἐμοῦ καθὼς ἐπορεύθη Δαυεὶδ ὁ πατήρ σου ἐν ὁσιότητι καρδίας . . . καὶ τοῦ ποιεῖν κατὰ πάντα ἃ ἐνετειλάμην αὐτῷ, see further Luke 1:75. On καλὰ καὶ εὐάρεστα, see already 1 Clem. 21:1 (35:5), then Deut 13:18: ποιεῖν τὸ ἀρεστὸν καὶ τὸ καλὸν ἐναντίον κυρίου τοῦ θεοῦ σου and similarly in 12:15. The ἄρχοντες are not inner-congregational authorities, but the bearers of state power; see below at 1 Clem. 60:4.

60:3f This is followed by the prayer for the welfare and peace for both Christians and the general public. A connection with the Corinthian turmoil was easy to establish here, as in the preceding, with the forgiveness of sins. ἐπίφανον κτλ. is a common LXX expression; see Num 6:25 in the Aaronic blessing; Ps 30:17; 66:1; 80:4, 8, 20; 118:135; Dan 9:17 Theodotion; 3 Macc 6:18; see also ἐπιφάνηθι above at 1 Clem. 59:4. On εἰς ἀγαθά, see Jer 21:10: ἐστήρικα τὸ πρόσωπόν μου ἐπὶ τὴν πόλιν ταύτην εἰς κακὰ καὶ οὐκ εἰς ἀγαθά (cf. also Jer 24:6; Amos 9:4; then on εἰς ἀγαθά, see Gen 50:20; Deut 30:9; etc.). On εἰς τὸ σκεπασθῆναι κτλ., see Isa 51:16: ὑπὸ τὴν σκιὰν τῆς χειρός μου σκεπάσω σε, Wis 5:16: τῇ δεξιᾷ σκεπάσει αὐτούς, καὶ τῷ βραχίονι ὑπερασπιεῖ αὐτῶν (see also 19:8). The connection between χεὶρ κραταιά and βραχίων ὑψηλός is a common LXX expression (cf. Exod 6:1; Deut 4:34; 5:15; 7:19; as well as Jer 39:21; Ezek 20:33f; etc.). On ῥῦσαι κτλ., see Ps 105:10: καὶ ἔσωσεν αὐτοὺς ἐκ χειρῶν μισούντων καὶ ἐλυτρώσατο αὐτοὺς ἐκ χειρὸς ἐχθροῦ, Ps 17:18: ῥύσεταί με ἐξ ἐχθρῶν μου δυνατῶν καὶ ἐκ τῶν μισούντων με, and Luke 1:71. On μισούντων ἀδίκως, see Ps 37:20: οἱ μισοῦντές με ἀδίκως, as well as Justin, 1 Apol. 14.3: ὑπὲρ τῶν ἐχθρῶν εὐχόμενοι καὶ τοὺς ἀδίκως μισοῦντας πείθειν πειρώμενοι. The prayer here is not a prayer for the enemies in the sense of Matt 5:44 (Polycarp, *Phil.* 12:3; Justin, 1 Apol. 14.3; Tertullian, *Apol.* 31: *etiam pro inimicis deum orare et persecuturibus nostris bona precari*), but for protection from one's enemies.

60:4 The prayer for all men, as practiced here, is also demanded or presupposed in 1 Tim 2:1; Polycarp, *Phil.* 12:2f; and very clearly, as here in the general church prayer, Justin, 1 Apol. 65.1 with which *Dial.* 35.8; 96.3; 133.6 should be compared; but in Justin the prayer for peace and welfare of the people does not stand out so much as that for their conversion. The composition ὁμόνοια καὶ εἰρήνη occurs also in 20:10f (liturgical); 61:1; 65:1. The πατέρες are probably not so much the prophets, whose struggles and complaints were recognized from the holy books, as the patriarchs and other great pious individuals of the old covenant, such as Noah, Abraham and Lot, Jacob and his sons, David and Solomon; on πατράσιν ἡμῶν, see the comments on 1 Clem. 4:8; see also 62:2. After αὐτῶν, LSC read ὁσίως, which is omitted in H. The construction, absolute genitive instead of *participium conjunctum*, is familiar in Koine, which likes to give more independence to the participial determiners; see Matt 1:18; 8:1; 9:18; 18:25; Mark 13:1; Luke 12:36; Acts 22:17; 2 Cor 4:18; etc.; from the papyri, Berl. Gr. Urk. IV 1040.19: χαίρω ὅτι μοι ταῦτα ἐποίησας ἐμοῦ μεταμελομένου περὶ μηδενός (much like our passage); see also Radermacher, *Grammatik*, 170; Blaß-Debrunner, *Grammatik*, §423; Moulton, *Sprache*, 114. Also the lack of consistency ὑπηκόους γινομένους, which HLS offer (C is indeterminate), is to be explained from the effort to make the participial clause stand out as much as possible (cf. Acts 26:3); furthermore, with the dative construction a wrong connection with the participle to πατράσιν was not entirely excluded, also a dative immediately follows again. On ἐν πίστει καὶ ἀληθείᾳ, see 1 Tim 2:7. Instead of

παναρέτῳ (H), which is of course one of Clement's favorite words, LSC seem
to read ἐνδόξῳ; on the composition and the adjectival use of παντοκράτωρ,
see Hermas, *Vis.* III 3.5: τοῦ παντοκράτορος καὶ ἐνδόξου ὀνόματος. The words
τοῖς τε ἄρχουσιν καὶ ἡγουμένοις ἡμῶν ἐπὶ τῆς γῆς are to be drawn, as the
newer editors usually do, to the end of 60:4, with LS against HC letting the
new sentence begin with them. It is worth noting that the prayer directly
links obedience to the authorities with obedience to God, but see already
the end of v. 2. The ἄρχοντες and ἡγούμενοι are the emperor and the authorities under him, primarily the legates and proconsuls who administer the
provinces of the empire; see already the ἡγούμενοι in 5:7; then 32:2; 37:2f;
51:5; 55:1. It is not excluded that, besides those mentioned, also the senate is
included among the rulers and leaders, but certainly not, in a Roman letter,
the Roman people; for material on the question, see below.

The prayer for the authorities in 1 Clem. 61 consists of noteworthy
details.

The text is very valuable; it shows us that and how prayers were offered
for the authorities in early Christian congregational worship. This prayer
is also postulated in other approximately contemporaneous passages such
as 1 Tim 2:1f; Polycarp, *Phil.* 12:3. In 1 Clem. 61 we see what it looked
like. These three passages, which testify to the custom of various congregations around the turn of the century, are followed by later testimonies;
see Justin, *1 Apol.* 17.3: βασιλεῖς καὶ ἄρχοντας ἀνθρώπων ὁμολογοῦντες καὶ
εὐχόμενοι μετὰ τῆς βασιλικῆς δυνάμεως καὶ σώφρονα τὸν λογισμὸν ἔχοντας
ὑμᾶς εὑρεθῆναι, and then above all Tertullian, *Apol.* 28–32 and 39; see
especially 30: *precantes sumus semper pro omnibus imperatoribus; vitam
illis prolixam, imperium securum, domum tutam, exercitus fortes, sena-
tum fidelem, populum probum, orbem quietum, quaecumque hominis et
Caesaris vota sunt — haec ab alio orare non possum quam a quo me scio
consecuturum* and 39: *oramus etiam pro imperatoribus, pro ministris eorum
et potestatibus, pro stutu saeculi, pro rerum quiete, pro mora finis;* see also
Tertullian, *Ad Scapulam* 2. "We cannot sacrifice before the images of the
emperor, but we pray for his welfare," is a response that is often found in
the acts and reports of the Christian trials; see *Acts Apollonii* 6; *Acta Cypri-
ani* 1.2 (the texts are in Knopf, *Märtyrerakten* and Gebhardt, *Märtyrerakten*); *Acta Dionysii* in Eusebius, *Hist. eccl.* 7.11.8, among other passages.
Christians rejected the imperial cult in every form, even in the names and
in the everyday sayings; they were clear that all this was service of idols.
To the natural reproach that they were disloyal, violating the reverence
for the emperor and for the majesty of the Roman state, they answered by
pointing out that they prayed for the state and the emperor. Prayer is the
sacrifice of Christians. These prayers, as 1 Clem. 61 and 1 Tim 2:1f show,

go back to the first century. They were probably already a part of the oldest gentile-Christian congregational liturgies, about whose beginnings we know almost nothing (cf. also Rom 13:1ff; Titus 3:1; 1 Pet 2:13–17). The custom of praying for the emperor did not arise among the Christians, but was already prevalent among Jews, who showed the way not to violate the honor of God and yet to show the state the due religious respect. In their synagogues one certainly also interceded for the emperor, and in the temple at Jerusalem two lambs and a bull were sacrificed daily for the emperor and the Roman people, as had been sacrificed before for the Syrian kings; see Lietzmann, *Römer*, at Rom 13:1; Schürer, *Geschichte*, 2:302–4. That also in the mystery cults one prayed for the emperor and the authorities is seen in the services to Isis in Apuleius, *Metamorphosis* XI 17: *tunc ex his unus quem cuncti grammatea dicebunt, pro foribus assistens, coetu pastophorum . . . velut in contionem vacato, indidem de sublimi suggestu de libro de litteris* (the text is not entirely in order) *fausta vota praefatus principi magno senatuique et equiti totoque Romano populo, nauticis navibusque, quae sub imperio mundi nostratis reguntur, renuntiat sermone rituque Graeciensi* τὰ πλοιαφέσια. The words of intercession in 1 Clem. 61, fine and dignified in their attitude, are divided into two groups: v. 1 and v. 2. Each of them links two parts in the arrangement already known to us from the preceding: first the invocation with the praise and glory of God, here of the God who has bestowed rule on men, then the actual supplication, which in the first series pleads for all kinds of great earthly good things, for health, peace, harmony, constancy, which may be granted to the rulers, and which then in the second thought asks that the rulers may use their power well and in a manner pleasing to God. Note then the subtle sub-thought in the first section, which wants to banish and put aside rebellious sentiments that might come to Christians in the face of oppression and persecution; see the anti-state sentiment in Revelation, which was written about the same time. First Clement says Christians should recognize that earthly authority is established by God and submit to God. Clearly the line in Rom 13:1ff and 1 Pet 2:13ff (2:13 διὰ τὸν κύριον; 2:15 θέλημα τοῦ θεοῦ!) is held here. Note further the subtlety that the authorities should desire to walk justly, obediently to God, and in a manner pleasing to him. If they do this, they will of course not persecute Christians, and the church prays the same for itself, paraphrasing once again the request already made: save us from those who hate us unjustly. That the view does not go beyond the Roman world empire—this is the βασιλεία—is self-evident: as in the pagan view, so also in the Christian view, the empire is a realization of the divine purpose of the world, and the barbarians in the south and the north are in view as little as the Parthians in the east. Finally, note that in spite of 59:4, there is no hint of a request like this: "Grant, O Lord, that the authorities may come to the knowledge of the truth and become Christian." This is a thought that remained unattainable for the whole second century. The earthly kingdom and the kingdom of God are still sharply and essentially opposed to each other; the emperor cannot do without the *saeculum*, and Christians cannot be emperors: *et Caesares credidissent super Christo, si aut Caesares non essent necessarii saeculo, aut si et Christiani putuissent esse Caesares* (Tertullian, *Apol.* 21). It is only in the third century that the stories of emperors who were secretly Christians, such as Alexander Severus and Philip the Arab, appear in the east.

61:1 βασιλεία = the earthly kingdom, as it is presented in the Roman empire (cf. above). διὰ τοῦ κράτους σου, it is perhaps significant that διὰ τοῦ ὀνόματός σου is not said: God is glorified through the creation (59:3), but not so much through the Roman empire. εὐστάθεια, a late word, should be understood as the tranquility and permanence of the rule. ἀπροσκόπως "without fail," but perhaps also simply: "without wavering."

61:2 The βασιλεὺς τῶν αἰώνων (1 Tim 1:17; Tob 13:6, 10) opposes the earthly rulers, who are not of divine nature themselves, but are only υἱοὶ τῶν ἀνθρώπων. At the end, ἵλεω κτλ. should not be understand as something like the grace in judgment, but as earthly pardon.

61:3 The phrase ποιεῖν ἀγαθὰ μετά τινος certainly reveals influence from the LXX; see Luke 1:72; 10:37; then 2 Sam 2:6: ποιήσω μεθ᾽ ὑμῶν τὸ ἀγαθὸν τοῦτο, Gen 24:12 ποίησον ἔλεος μετὰ τοῦ κυρίου μου Ἀβραάμ, among other passages. On Jesus Christ as ἀρχιερεύς, see 1 Clem. 36:1. On προστάτης, see 1 Clem. 36:1; in both places, the liturgy is in view.

V. The End of the Letter with a Concluding Admonition and Vows (62:1—65:2)

A. Concluding Exhortations (62–63)

Concluding exhortations are contained within 1 Clem 62–63. Its content is that the Corinthians should obey the admonitions and examples within the detailed letter and return to peace and harmony. Also, the bearers of the letter are certified.

Translation

62:1 About what is proper for our religion, what is inevitably nec-essary for a virtuous life for those who wish to walk piously and righteously, we have written to you in sufficient detail, men and brothers. [2] For we have exhausted the subject of faith and repentance and genuine love and abstinence and moderation and patience, and we have admonished you that you must honorably please almighty God in righteousness and truth and longsuffering; without thinking evil of one another, keep concord in love and peaceableness with persevering gentleness, just as our previously mentioned fathers also lived pleasingly by their humility toward the Father and creator God, and toward all men. [3] And we have reminded you of this all the more gladly, knowing full well that we were writing to faithful and highly respectable men, who have searched out the words of divine teaching.

[63:1] It behooves us, therefore, to turn to the many glorious examples, to bow our necks and be obedient, so that we might abandon the futile quarrel and reach the goal set before us in truth, without any reproach. [2] For you will cause us joy and rejoicing if you obey what is written by us through the Holy Spirit and put away your unjust, jealous anger, according to the admonition we give you about love and harmony in this letter. [3] We also send with you men of faith and understanding, who have walked blamelessly among us from youth to old age, and who also will function as witnesses between you and us. [4] But we do all this so that you may see how all our concern has been and continues to be that you might come quickly to peace.

Textual Notes

62:1 θρησκεία is probably more precise than religion: it is the cult, the worship service (cf. 1 Clem. 45:7; also Acts 26:5; Col 2:18; etc.). The reading ὠφελιμωτάτων εἰς ἐνάρετον βίον κτλ. in H and C should be preferred; L and S smooth out the construction and translate as if it read: τοῖς θέλουσιν ἐνάρετον βίον κτλ. In the accepted reading, διευθύνειν must be taken absolutely, or τὸν βίον must be added to the sense. The assumption that something has fallen out after διευθύνειν (αὐτόν or βίον, or τὴν πορείαν αὐτῶν or τὸν βουλὴν αὐτῶν) is unnecessary. ἐπιστέλλειν means "to write," as in 1 Clem. 7:1. On the self-testimony ἱκανῶς ἐπεστείλαμεν, see already Irenaeus, *Haer.* III 3.3, where our passage is presumably alluded to: ἐπέστειλεν ἡ ἐν Ῥώμῃ ἐκκλησία ἱκανωτάτην γραφὴν τοῖς Κορινθίοις.

62:2 The series of six-members, all with the feminine -ς, has a rhetorical effect, just as the series with three-members which follows it. τόπος means "subject, topic" of the speech and the treatise, as is frequently the case, but it does not mean "passage of the Holy Scripture," as admittedly already C and S translate the passage and newer commentators believe. On ἀμνησικάκως, see 1 Clem. 2:5; reconciliation is also advised to those offended at Corinth. On ἐκτενοῦς ἐπιεικείας, see 1 Clem. 58:2. The πατέρες ἡμῶν are the pious of the OT, as is the case above at 1 Clem. 60:4; see the comments at 1 Clem. 4:8. As an example of humility, they have already been presented, in particular in 1 Clem. 17–19.

62:3 contains an easily understandable, common *captatio.* ἐλλογιμωτάτοις should be read with H; C is doubtful; L has *probatis*; S has *doctis.* On the words, see 58:3. The meaning of "learned," which S uses and which the word can have, would also fit well here. On ἐνκεκυφόσιν, see 40:1; 45:2; 53:1.

63:1 θεμιτόν is a choice word of the written language, which occurs only once in the LXX (Tob 2:13), not at all in the NT, in the rest of early Christian literature only in Justin, *Dial.* 134.3 and Diognetus, *Epistle* 6:10 (if the latter belongs to the older stratum of Christian literature). The word is usually associated with negation; see, however, Sextus Empiricus, *Adv. grammaticos* 81: εἰ θεμιτὸν εἰπεῖν. See also immediately afterward, in v. 2, the similarly rare ἀθέμιτος. On τοιούτοις καὶ τοσούτοις, see 19:1. ὑποθεῖναι τὸν τράχηλον is used differently than in Rom 16:4; see Sir 51:26: τὸν τράχηλον ὑμῶν ὑπόθετε ὑπὸ ζυγόν, καὶ ἐπιδεξάσθω ἡ ψυχὴ ὑμῶν παιδείαν. Also κάμπτειν and σκληρύνειν τὸν τράχηλον occurs in several places within the LXX; Epictetus, *Diss.* IV 1.77: παρέδωκας σαυτὸν δοῦλον, ὑπέθηκας τὸν τράχηλον. The phrase τὸν τῆς ὑπακοῆς τόπον ἀναπληρῶσαι is a marked expression. On τόπος ὑπακοῆς, see 1 Clem. 7:5; on τόπον ἀναπληρῶσαι, see 1 Cor 14:16; on σκοπός, see 1 Clem. 19:2 as well as 6:2.

63:2 διὰ τοῦ ἁγίου πνεύματος can also be connected with ἐκκόψητε; 59:1, however, recommends the connection with γεγραμμένοις.

63:3 The emissaries are mentioned by name in 65:1. Around the year 100 CE, the Roman congregation already had men who belonged to it from youth to old age. On the form γήρους, see Blaß-Debrunner, *Grammatik,* §47.1 and especially Helbing, *Grammatik,* 1:42. μάρτυρες: they should decide whether or not the Corinthians listened to the exhortations of the Romans (cf. 65:1).

B. Two Closing Vows and the Confirmation
of the Emissaries (64–65)

Translation

64:1 Finally, may the all-seeing God, the ruler of the spirits, and the Lord of all flesh, who chose the Lord Jesus Christ and through him made us his own people, grant every soul that calls upon his exalted and holy name faith, reverence, peace, patience and longsuffering, self-restraint, chastity, and temperance, that all might be pleasing to his name through our high priest and patron, Jesus Christ, through whom be glory, majesty, power, might, and honor to him, both now and forever! Amen.

65:1 Send back to us quickly our emissaries, Claudius Ephebus and Valerius Bito, together with Fortunatus, in peace with joy, so that they may report to us as soon as possible about the peace and harmony which we have desired and longed for, so that we too may rejoice as quickly as possible in the good order among you.

65:2 May the grace of our Lord Jesus Christ be with you and with all everywhere who are called by God through him. To him be glory, honor, power, majesty, and eternal dominion from everlasting to everlasting! Amen.

Textual Notes

First Clement 64–65 contains two concluding vows and the certification of the emissaries.

First Clement 64 In the first word of the sentence, ms. A resumes after its lengthy gap. In the vow, we once again hear the language of the liturgy, which we already know from the preceding. On παντεπόπτης, see 1 Clem. 55:6. On δεσπότης τῶν πνευμάτων κτλ., see comments at 59:3: εὐεργέτην πνευμάτων καὶ θεὸν πάσης σαρκός (see Num 16:22). On ἐκλεξάμενον κτλ., see the conclusion of 59:4, then Luke 23:35; 1 En. 40:5; 45:3f; 51:4; 53:6; among other passages (cf. the index in the edition of Flemming and Radermacher) "the chosen one" or "my chosen one" = "the Messiah" the ἐκλεκτός is therefore an older messianic title taken over from Judaism. It is used in the liturgy, even when the Christology is no longer Adoptionistic; see also παῖς θεοῦ in the liturgy. On ἡμᾶς δι' αὐτοῦ, see 1 Cor 8:6; Eph 1:4. On λαὸς περιούσιος, see 29:1f. The expression originates from the LXX (cf. Exod 19:5; 23:22; Deut 7:6; 14:2; 26:18). The infrequent εὐαρέστησις is used in T. Iss. 4. On ἀρχιερεὺς καὶ προστάτης, see 36:1; 61:3.

65:1 The delegation already mentioned in 63:3 is therefore threefold. The names, two double names and one single name, three Latin and two Greek, are in part common and in part (Ephebus and Biton) sufficiently attested. On σὺν καί, see Phil 4:3: μετὰ καὶ Κλήμεντος and *Assumptio Mosis* in Clement of Alexandrian, *Strom.* 6.132.3, p. 806: εἶδεν δὲ Ἰησοῦς τὴν θέαν ταύτην . . . σὺν καὶ τῷ Χαλέβ. That Fortunatus is basically distinguished from the other two by the form of the enumeration, that he is not a Roman but a Corinthian (1 Cor 16:17!) is not very likely with the form of the sentence: the man is sent from Rome with the other two and is also to return to Rome. The Greek-Latin double names of the first two mentioned messengers are to be noted. That they are real Romans is excluded by the form of the names. But the names Claudius and Valerius indicate a relation to the famous *gentes*: the imperial (Claudia) and Valeria, which was connected with Claudia in the marriage of Claudius and Messalina. Among the freedman of Claudius and his successors, the names Claudius/Claudia and Valerius/Valeria are found frequently, more often on stone. The two emissaries would have been imperial freedmen, and since they were Christians from their youth (63:3), they may have belonged already to those of the emperor's household who send their greetings in Phil 4:22 (cf. Lightfoot, *Clement I*, 27f and Knopf, *Nachapostolisches Zeitalter*, 76f). Note the clustering ἐν τάχει . . . θᾶττον . . . τάχιον. θᾶττον in addition to τάχιον, which only occurs in Koine, is very striking (but cf. Mart. Poly. 13:1f); ὅπως θᾶττον is choice, literary Greek, and is next to εἰς τὸ τάχιον, which is colloquial; also, εὐκταῖος is a fine word used in the written language.

65:5 Note θρόνος αἰώνιος (imitated in *Mart. Poly.* 21), unusual in doxologies, and the heavy cluster αἰώνιος . . . αἰώνων . . . αἰώνων with the long syllables.

Second Clement

Introduction

Transmission

This text is preserved only together with 1 Clem., namely in Greek in Codex Alexandrinus (A), whose text unfortunately breaks off at 2 Clem. 12:5, then in the Jerusalem manuscript (H), and translated into Syriac in the Cambridge manuscript (S); see the introduction to 1 Clem. The Latin and Coptic tradition of 1 Clem. does not contain 2 Clem. The designation of the letter as the Second Letter of Clement (to the Corinthians) can be traced back far. It was certainly already present in the second century, probably around 200. This is proven by the agreement of the manuscript tradition concerning the title (cf. before 1:1 and after 20:5) and the testimony of Eusebius in *Hist. eccl.* 3.38.4: ἰστέον δ' ὡς καὶ δευτέρα τις εἶναι λέγεται τοῦ Κλήμεντος ἐπιστολή· οὐ μην ἐθ' ὁμοίως τῇ προτέρᾳ καὶ ταύτην γνώριμον ἐπιστάμεθα, ὅτι μηδὲ τοὺς ἀρχαίους αὐτῇ κεχρημένους ἴσμεν (the oldest *testimonium* for 2 Clememt, which Eusebius himself does not seem to have read). In truth, it is entirely excluded that 1 and 2 Clem. are written by the same author. However, the designation of the writing as 2 Clem. and its connection with 1 Clem., which certainly goes from Rome to Corinth, poses a number of problems.

Literary Character and Outline

Second Clement is not a letter, not even a fictious letter (epistle), but a sermon, as 17:3 and 19:1 prove most clearly (cf. also 15:1). It is the oldest Christian homily we have. Its content is as follows:

I. The surpassing greatness of the beneficence of Christ who called the gentiles (1:1—2:7).

II. The return payment we can offer him, for this is the confession of him, not by word but by deed (3:1—4:5).

III. This confession by deed consists in the fact that we fear God more than men, hold the world in low esteem, and do not shun martyrdom (5:1—6:9).

IV. The toil of the struggle is great, but the reward is glorious; the baptismal grace we have experienced also imposes a sacred obligation, namely, to repent and keep the flesh pure (7:1—8:6).

V. Here, following up on the keyword (*Stichwort*) σάρξ in 8:4, the author turns against the gnostic denial of the resurrection of the flesh; but the polemic is interwoven with all sorts of paraenesis (doing penance) (9:1—12:6).

VI. This section once again takes up the exhortation to repentance and holds it until the end of the sermon. The call to repentance clearly applies also to the already converted congregation (13:1—18:2).

VII. Conclusion: the author again refers to repentance, emphasizes the necessity of suffering but also the greatness of one's own future glory, and concludes the homily with a solemn doxology (19:1—20:5).

Author, Provenance, and Date of the Sermon

We do not know who the author was nor is it likely that we will ever know. From 17:3 and 19:1, as well as from the whole homily, it can be concluded that he belongs to the leaders of the congregation, that is to the clergy, the presbyters, who are responsible for exhorting the congregation. Regarding the place of origin, the early connection of 2 Clem. with 1 Clem. provides a hint. The congregation in which the sermon was preached may be Rome or Corinth. Which of the two congregations is to be preferred cannot be decided with certainty. The image of the games of chance used in 7:1 could speak in favor of Corinth; however, see the explanation of the passage at the comments on 7:1. Speaking in favor of an origin in Rome is 11:2-4, where, independent of 1 Clem. 23:3f, the same apocryphal text is used (cf. the explanation of the passage). However, knowledge of the relevant apocryphon is also possible in Corinth. And yet, the Roman church which composed the Shepherd of Hermas with its exhortation to repentance and its eschatological paraenesis may very well have composed 2 Clem., which is closely related to Hermas in mood and thought. (On the attempt to date 2 Clem. from Alexandria, cf. Bartlet, "Origin," 123–35.) Also, the time of writing must be about the same as that of the Hermas. The homily must have been written before ca. 150. This is demonstrated by the use of apocryphal gospel quotations (4:5; 5:2–4; 8:5; 12:2), the oft-repeated reference to the nearness of the end, the undeveloped, and strongly mythologizing speculation (2 Clem. 14). Also, Justin, *1 Apol.* 53.5f shows familiarity with 2 Clem. 2. On the other hand, the congregation must be warned against too much worldliness, as well as against doubts about the resurrection of the body. The author also recommends martyrdom (5:1), often opposes gnostic teaching and attitude to life (2 Clem. 5; 9:1—12:6), and (an important observation) cites sacred writings of Christian origin alongside the canon of the LXX (cf. 2:4; 14:2; and the explanations of it). An approach to preaching ca. 120–50 best corresponds to the observations cited.

Editions

The first complete edition, according to the discovery of H, is by P. Bryennios, *Τοῦ ἐν ἁγίοις πατρὸς ἡμῶν Κλήμεντος ἐπισκόπου Ῥώμης αἱ δύο πρὸς Κορινθίους ἐπιστολαί* (Constantinople, 1875) — Oscar von Gebhardt et al., *Patrum apostolicorum opera I*, vol. 1, 2nd ed. (Leipzig: Hinrichs, 1876). — Oscar von Gebhardt et al., *Patrum apostolicorum opera*, editio minor, 5th ed. (Leipzig: Hinrichs, 1906). — A. Hilgenfeld, *Novum Testamentum extra canonem receptum*, 2nd ed. (Leipzig: Hinrichs, 1876). — J. B. Lightfoot, *The Apostolic Fathers: S. Clement of Rome*, 2 vols. (London: Macmillan, 1890). — J. B. Lightfoot, *The Apostolic Fathers: Revised Texts with Short Introductions and English Translations*, ed. and completed by J. R. Harmer (London: Macmillan, 1891). — F. X. Funk, *Patres Apostolici I* (Tübingen: Laupp, 1901). — F. X. Funk, *Die apostolischen Väter*, 2nd ed. (Tübingen: Mohr, 1907). — Translation and short explanations by H. von Schubert, "Der sogenannte zweite Clemensbrief, eine Gemeindepredigt," in *Neutestamentliche Apokryphen*, ed. E. Hennecke (Tübingen: Mohr, 1904), 172–79. — H. von Schubert, "Der sogenannte 2. Clemensbrief, eine Gemeindepredigt," in *Handbuch zu den neutestamentlichen Apokryphen*, ed. E. Hennecke (Tübingen: Mohr, 1904), 248–55.

Literature

The relevant sections in the accounts of ancient Christian literature by A. von Harnack, *Geschichte der altchristlichen Literatur bis Eusebius. Teil I (Die Ueberlieferung und der Bestand)* (Leipzig: Mohr, 1893), 47–49; A. von Harnack, *Geschichte der altchristlichen Literatur bis Eusebius. Teil II (Die Chronologie),* vol. I (Leipzig: Mohr, 1897), 438–50. — G. Krüger, *Geschichte der altchrist-lichen Literatur*, 2nd ed. (Freiburg im Breisgau: Mohr, 1898), 39f. — H. Jordan, *Geschichte der altchristlichen Literatur* (Leipzig: Quelle & Meyer, 1911), 188f. — O. Bardenhewer, *Geschichte der altkirchlichen Literatur*. Vol. 1: *Vom Ausgang der apostolischen Zeitalters bis zum Ende des 2. Jahrhunderts*, 2nd ed. (Freiburg im Breisgau: Herder, 1913), 487–90.

Individual Studies

H. Hagemann, "Ueber den zweiten Brief des Klemens von Rom," *Quartalschrift* 43 (1861) 509–31. — A. von Harnack, "Ueber den sogenannten zweiten Brief des Clemens an die Korinther," *Zeitschrift für Kirchengeschichte* 1 (1877) 264–83, 329–64. — T. M. Wehofer, "Untersuchungen zur altchristlichen Epistolographie," *Sitzungsberichte der Wiener Akademie, philosophisch-historische Klasse* 143.17 (1901) 102–37. — C. Taylor, "The Homily of Pseudo-Clement," *Journal of Philology* 28 (1901) 195–208. — F. X. Funk, "Der sogenannte zweite Clemensbrief," *Kirchengeschichtle Abhandlungen und Untersuchungen* 3 (1907) 261–75; see also F. X. Funk, "Der sogenannte zweite Clemensbrief," *Theologische Quartalschrift* 84 (1902) 349–64. — R. Knopf, "Die Anagnose zum zweiten Clemensbriefe," *Zeitschrift für die Neutestamentliche Wissenschaft* 3 (1902) 266–79. — A. F. di Pauli, "Zum sogenannte zweiten Korintherbrief des Clemens Romanus," *Zeitschrift für die Neutestamentliche Wissenschaft* 4 (1903) 321–29. — A. von Harnack, "Zum Ursprung des sogenannte zweiten Clemensbriefes," *Zeitschrift für die Neutestamentliche Wissenschaft* 6 (1905) 67–71. — V. Bartlet, "The Origin and Date of 2 Clement," *Zeitschrift für die Neutestamentliche Wissenschaft* 7 (1906) 123–35. — W. Schüßler, "Ist der zweite Clemensbrief ein einheitliches Ganzes?" *Zeitschrift für Kirchengeschichte* 28 (1907) 1–13. — D. Völter, *Die apostolischen Väter neu untersucht, Teil 2.1: Die älteste Predigt aus Rom (der sogenannte zweite Clemensbrief)* (Leiden: Brill, 1908). — H. Windisch, *Taufe und Sünde im ältesten Christentum* (Tübingen: Mohr, 1908), 329–40. — W. Praetorius, "Die Bedeutung der beiden Klemensbriefe für die älteste Geschichte der kirchlichen Praxis," *Zeitschrift für Kirchengeschichte* 33 (1912) 347–63, 501–28.

Superscriptions

A places 2 Clem. after 1 Clem. without its own superscription, but in the ancient table of contents at the beginning of the manuscript it appears as Κλήμεντος ἐπιστολὴ β΄. H has the superscription: Κλήμεντος πρὸς Κορινθίους β. S reads "The same (i.e., Clement, whose name was mentioned immediately before in the superscription for 1 Clem.) Second Letter to the Corinthians."

I. The Surpassing Greatness of the Beneficence of Christ Who Called the Gentiles (1:1—2:7)

Those in Christ are to be thankful for the salvation they have obtained in Christ and not to think lightly of the sufferings he undertook on their behalf. Sinning is an outworking of thinking lightly of this salvation, of not recognizing one's calling. Instead, those saved through Christ are to confess Christ, not with their mouths but with their actions.[1]

Translation

[1:1] Brothers, we must think about Jesus Christ as [we think] about God, as [we think] of the judge of the living and the dead; and we are not to think lightly of our salvation. [2] For if we think lightly of him, we expect little from him; and those who listen as if these things are little sin, and we sin because we do not know from where we are called and from whom, and for what place, and all that Jesus Christ took upon himself to suffer for our sakes. [3] Now what will we give him? Or what fruit, worthy of what he himself has given us? How much holy thanks do we owe him? [4] For he has given us the light; like a father he has addressed us as sons; when we were perishing, he saved us. [5] Now what praise will we give him, or what return for what we have received? [6] We were blind in understanding, worshipping stones and wood and gold and silver and brass, works of men, and all our life was nothing but death. Now, when we were in darkness, and such a great mist filled our faces, we saw, because by his will we cast off the cloud that surrounded us. [7] For he had mercy on us and saved us with compassion, because he saw in us great error and ruin, and that we held no hope of salvation except if it came from him. [8] For he called us when we were not, and from non-existence he wished us to be. [2:1] "Rejoice, barren one, you who do not give birth, break forth and rejoice, you who are not in labor; for numerous are the children of the lonely one, more than she who has a husband. When it is said, "Rejoice, barren woman, you who do not give birth," it is said of

---

1. TN: This paragraph is not present within the original German text but has been added for the sake of unity and clarity in the newly formatted English edition.

us: for our church was barren before children were given to her.
² When it is said, "Rejoice, you who are not in labor," it means
this: carry our prayers up to God with simplicity, so that we do
not become feeble like a woman in labor. ³ When it says, "For
numerous are the children of the lonely one, more than the one
who has a husband," (this is said) because our people seemed to
be forsaken by God, but now that we have believed, we have become more numerous than those who seem to have God. ⁴ And
another Scripture says, "I did not come to call the righteous, but
sinners." ⁵ That is to say: he had to save those who were perishing. ⁶ For this is great and admirable not to set upright what is
already standing, but that which is falling. ⁷ In the same way,
Christ wanted to save what was perishing, and he saved many,
because he came and called us right when we were perishing.

Textual Notes

1:1 The form of address ἀδελφοί, occasionally extended by μου, runs
throughout the homily. Only in 19:1 and 20:2 is the female part of the
audience also considered. On the *theologia Christi* of the introduction and
the entire homily, see von Harnack, *Dogmengeschichte*, 206–10, as well
as Bousset, *Kyrios Christos*, 303f. For religious and practical-cultic motives, the preaching of Christ unhesitatingly makes the highest statements,
namely in the opening chapters Christ belongs for them in the divine
sphere without any reduction. The religious commitments with respect
to Christ are the same as those with respect to God. Second Clement 1
also shows very clearly what the *theologia Christi* is based on for the faithful: Christ is the judge of the world and the great king; his gifts of grace
surpass all imaginable benefits, his reward to the faithful at the end of
the world, salvation, is certain and unspeakably high. Therefore, one must
not think less of him than of God. On κριτοῦ ζώντων καὶ νεκρῶν, see Acts
10:42; 2 Tim 4:1; the *Symbolum Apostolicum*; 1 Pet 4:5; as well as Rom 14:9
and 1 Thess 4:15–17; etc. The words intensify θεοῦ, see also Barn. 7:2 and
note, in addition to this climax, the fourfold consonance with -οῦ, as well
as the weighted syllables in ζώντων καὶ νεκρῶν. The σωτηρία is not only
eschatological; see v. 4 and 2:7: the calling, the enlightenment, the forgiveness of sins, etc. belong to it; but the preservation to the future glory is, of
course, the crowning conclusion of the σωτηρία.

1:2 Therefore, right at v. 2 there is the eschatological phrase, which occupies so much space in the paraenesis of the whole sermon. The reading
followed in the translation is that of S: . . . μικρῶν ἁμαρτάνουσιν καὶ ἡμεῖς

ἁμαρτάνομεν, where A and H simply read μικρῶν ἁμαρτάνομεν. Timotheos Ailuros and Severus of Antioch (cf. below) admittedly also seem to have read the text as in AH, but the reading has its difficulties. In the textual form of S, the ἀκούονες must be the catechumens and guests opposed to the ἡμεῖς, the congregation. Second Clement 1:1f is cited twice in the Syriac tradition within the christological controversies of the fifth and sixth centuries in the extant tradition. In Timotheos Ailuros and in Severus of Antioch, the passages are fragments contained in two Syriac manuscripts of the British Museum, and are printed in Lightfoot, *Clement*, 180f and 182f (from Cureton, *Corpus Ignatiamim*, 212, 244, and 215, 246; cf. also Pitra, *Analecta Sacra*, 4:276). Whether, by the way, the Christology of the opening sentences contains a point against heresy—this would then be an "Ebionite" heresy—is by no means certain, but note the polemic against the Jews in ch. 2. Note also the view that emerges in v. 2: false Christology leads to sin.

1:3 ἀντιμισθία, which occurs several more times in what follows, is distinctly Koine, which loves intensification by ἀντί (cf. Rom 1:27; 2 Cor 6:13; Theophilus, *Ad Autol.* II 9). The word strikes a motif of the paraenesis, which then recurs several times in what follows; see vv. 3–4, where it is elaborated what is our reward in return. The three questions of v. 3 correspond to three answers in v. 4; note the rhetoric. In τίνα καρπὸν ἄξον there is an echo of the word of the Baptist in Matt 3:8. ὅσια: The LXX readily translates the adjective *chasid* with ὅσιος, and once Isa 55:3 also translates the noun *chêsêd* with τὸ ὅσιον. Following this observation, the commentators on 2 Clem. conceive of ὅσια as mercies or gifts of grace. However, since this use of ὅσια is quite isolated, it is better to stick to the prevailing Greek usage, according to which ὅσιον is that which refers to the gods, which one owes them, the service of God, the religious and cultic duty (contrast δίκαιον, the duty with respect to men); here in the figurative sense of the believer's reward in return. This sense fits very well with ὀφείλομεν and the broader context. ὅσια parallels ἀντιμισθία and καρπός.

1:4 φῶς appears only here in the homily. The sense of the ambiguous term, which is used broadly and has a long history (cf. Wetter, *Phōs*), is determined in v. 6, where it includes primarily the true knowledge of God. On πατὴρ υἱούς, see 9:10, where the same statement is made by God; see further Hos 1:10, Rom 9:26, and 2 Cor 6:18.

1:5 δώσωμεν in A; δώσομεν in H. On the confusion between ο and ω in the verbal forms and on the resulting appearance of a future subjunctive, see Blaß-Debrunner, *Grammatik*, §28. The increased μισθὸν ἀντιμισθίας is meant to be rhetorical, but is already stilted.

1:6 The congregation of the audience is, if not exclusively, then quite predominantly gentile Christian (cf. 2 Clem. 2). The series λίθους ξύλα κτλ.

is common (cf. Rev 9:20; then Ps 113:2; 134:15; Dan 5:23; Wis 13:10–19; etc. The polemic of Jewish-Hellenism against images, which was taken over by Christians, goes back to the philosophy of enlightenment of the Greeks, especially the Stoa, but also their predecessors, the Eleatics (Xeno, *Fragmente* 14–16 in Diels, *Vorsokratiker I*, 60f) and already in Heraclitus; see Heraclitus 5 in Diels, *Vorsokratiker I*, 78: " . . . and they also pray to these images of the gods, as if one wanted to converse with buildings." See also below at 3:1 the discussion of νεκροὶ θεοί. — βίος . . . θάνατος, the thought and rhetorical figure occur frequently and in many variations (cf. 2 Clem. 3:1; 2 Cor 6:9; 1 Tim 5:6; Ign. *Eph.* 7:2; etc.); but also see Heraclitus, *Fragm.* 62 in Diels, *Vorsokratiker I*, 89: . . . ἀθάνατοι θνητοί, θνητοὶ ἀθάνατοι, ζῶντες τὸν ἐκείνων θάνατον, τὸν δὲ ἐκείνων βίον τεθνεῶτες and the famous Euripides fragment from Polyeidos (*Fragm.* 639 in Nauck, *Tragoediae*): Τίς δ' οἶδεν εἰ τὸ ζῆν μέν ἐστι κατθανεῖν, Τὸ κατθανεῖν δὲ ζῆν κάτω νομίζεται; see also *Fragm.* 830: Τίς δ' οἶδεν εἰ ζῆν τοῦθ' ὃ κέκληται θανεῖν, Τὸ ζῆν δὲ θνήσκειν ἐστί; Augustine, *Confessions* I 6.7: *in istam dico vitam mortalem an mortem vitalem nescio.* Note still βίος not ζωή, which is used for the designation of life in the higher sense. In the following, ἀνεβλέψαμεν κτλ., the wording and the image of Heb 12:1 must have intervened, though the thoughts here and there are quite different. On the construction περικεῖσθαί τι, see Acts 28:20; Heb 5:2; and τιάρας περικείμενοι in Strabo, *Geogr.* XV 3.15, p. 733; στεφάνους περικείμενος in Plutarch, *Arat.* 17; etc.

1:7 καὶ μηδεμίαν ἐλπίδα κτλ. can also be dependent upon ἔσωσεν, but this option is not recommended.

1:8 κλῆσις in 2 Clem. is not, of course, the predestination calling κατὰ πρόθεσιν of God in the sense of Rom 8:28–30, but the leading of Christ or God which has brought the believer into the church. Within the church, meanwhile, he is by no means yet secure in life, as the whole penitential nature of the homily proves. The calling of which the homily often speaks takes place mostly through Christ (cf. 1:2, 8; 2:4, 7; 5:1; 9:5), though occasionally also through God (10:1 and 16:1). οὐκ ὄντας . . . ἐκ μὴ ὄντος, the state of unbelief is that of non-being; see θάνατος above at v. 6. On the wording of the whole sentence, see Rom 4:17: καλοῦντος τὰ μὴ ὄντα ὡς ὄντα and Philo, *Spec.* IV 187 (ed. Mangey, 367): τὰ γὰρ μὴ ὄντα ἐκάλεσεν εἰς τὸ εἶναι. The shift between οὐκ and μή is not easy to explain. τὸ μὴ ὄν is the more common expression for "that which is not" and it can be traced from the Ionic natural philosophers to the Neoplatonists; see Xeno in [Aristotle] *De Melisso*, Xenophanes, *Gorgia* 977b (Diels, *Vorsokratiker I*, 46): ἄπειρον μὲν <γὰρ> τὸ μὴ ὂν εἶναι . . . , οἷον δὲ τὸ μὴ ὄν, οὐκ ἂν εἶναι τὸ ὄν, Parmenides (*Fragment* 8.9f, in Diels, *Vorsokratiker I*, 155): Οὐδέ ποτ' ἐκ μὴ ἐόντος ἐφήσει πίστιος ἰσχύς Γίγνεσθαί τι παρ' αὐτό; on the other hand, Plotinus, *Ennead.* I 8.3: μὰ ὂν δὲ οὔτι τὸ παντελῶς μὴ ὄν, ἀλλ' ἕτερον μόνον τοῦ ὄντος, οὐχ οὕτω δὲ μὴ ὄν, ὡς κίνησις καὶ στάσις ἡ περὶ τὸ ὄν, ἀλλ᾿ ὡς εἰκὼν τοῦ ὄντος ἢ καὶ ἔτι μᾶλλον μὴ ὄν. Now, since later in Koine μή is used with all moods except the indicative, οὐκ ὄντας is doubly conspicuous. The reason for its use is probably, on the one hand, rhetoric, which loves the change of expression, but, on the other hand, οὐκ emphasizes more strongly the non-factuality of the expression; see 1 Pet 1:8: ὃν οὐκ ἰδόντες ἀγαπᾶτε, εἰς ὃν ἄρτι μὴ ὁρῶντες . . . ἀγαλλιᾶσθε.

Second Clement 2 introduces a quotation from Isa 54:1 and cites it verbatim; Gal 4:21 and Justin, *1 Apol.* 53.5 use it in the same way. The way in which the passage is introduced without a citation formula, as it were a matter of course, yet carefully interpreted, is best explained if the congregation had just heard it in the passage of Scripture that had been read before the sermon (cf. 19:1). The other possibility is that the passage is assumed to be very well known and therefore can be used without a quotation formula. The interpretation is of course held in the sense and taste as well as the method of ancient Jewish/Christian exegesis and is accordingly very forceful. ἐκκλησία: The assumption here and in what follows is that the church is a preexistent, heavenly being (cf. 2 Clem. 14). The ἐκκλησία ἡμῶν is the church *par excellence*, not merely the gentile Christian church; for the church is one. In fact, however, for the preacher it is gentile Christian according to its overwhelming majority (see already 1:6). The church as a woman, the believers as her children is probably an idea taken directly from Judaism; see Gal 4:20; 4 Esd 10:7: Zion, mother of us all; and then in the prophets Israel is called a woman and a mother (Hos 2:2–17; Isa 50:1; Ezra 23; etc.).

2:2 is particularly forceful in interpretation. βοᾶν from the call to prayer in Luke 18:7; 1 Clem. 34:7; and frequently in the LXX, Hos 7:14; Jonah 1:5; Isa 58:9; Neh 9:4; Tob 6:18; etc. Sophocles, *Electra* 630f: ὑπ᾿ εὐφήμου βοῆς θῦσαι . . . . On ἐγκακῶμεν, add ἀναφέροντες κτλ.

2:3 ἔρημος ἀπό is Koine usage; the genitive in its various meanings (partitive genitive, genitive with verbs or adjectives of touching, grasping, appreciating, genitive of separation, of fullness and of lack, etc.) is readily replaced with prepositions. The genitive when used with adjectives is especially restricted when compared with classical Greek; see Rademacher, *Grammatik*, 102f; Blaß-Debrunner, *Grammatik*, in the index under ἐξ, ἀπό, ἐν, κατά, and on the genitive with adjectives at §182. It is recommended to understand ἔρημος as an adjective of separation; see Jer 51:2: ἔρημος ἀπὸ ἐνοίκων, 40:10: ἔρημος ἀπὸ ἀνθρώπων . . . . ὁ λαὸς ἡμῶν is the *tertium genus*, the people of Christ, gathered together from among the nations; δοκοῦντες ἔχειν θεόν are the Jews; see the kerygma of Peter in Clement of Alexandria, *Strom.* 6.5.41 (Klostermann, *Apocrypha I*, 15; Preuschen, *Antilegomena*, 90): μηδὲ κατὰ Ἰουδαίους σέβεσθε· καὶ γὰρ ἐκεῖνοι μόνοι οἰόμενοι τὸν θεὸν γινώσκειν οὐκ ἐπίστανται λατρεύοντες ἀγγέλοις καὶ ἀρχαγγέλοις, μηνὶ καὶ σελήνῃ, see also Diogentus 3:2.

2:4 ἑτέρα γραφή, what follows is a word of the Lord (see Mark 2:17; Matt 9:13): The Gospel tradition is described as γραφή next to and behind the Old Testament word of God, a very significant fact for the history of the canon; for parallels before Justin, see 2 Clem 14:2; Barn. 4:14; Pol. *Phil.* 12:1; for the configuration of this observation in the history of the canon, see Zahn, *Grundriß*, §4; Jülicher, *Einleitung*, §35; Leipoldt, *Geschichte*, 1:125f; Knopf et al., *Einführung*, 145f.

2:6 On the formula μέγα καὶ θαυμαστόν, see 1 Clem. 26:1; 50:1; 53:3. It also occurs in the LXX; see Deut 28:59; Job 42:3; Tob 12:22; Dan 9:4 (Theodotion).

2:7 On the conception of Jesus as the savior of sinners, of the rejected, and its proximity to the gentile church, see Luke 19:10; 1 Tim 1:15; and especially clearly Barn. 5:9, where the word of the Lord from 2 Clem. 2:4 is cited, as well as in Barn. 14:5. The words καὶ καλέσας κτλ. incidentally form a pentameter.

II. The Return Payment We Can Offer Him: Not Word but Deed (3:1—4:5)

Second Clement 3–4 argues that our recompense for Christ's good deed is confession to him, not by word, but by deed.

In the series of motives and quietives which the preacher puts forward to move his audience to good and to warn them against evil, he prefixes the consideration of the ἀντιμισθία. Second Clement 1:3–5 already sounded it clearly; here the author elaborates upon it. The motif is beautiful, though the piety of 2 Clem. stands far apart from the Johannine, "Let us love, for he first loved us."

Translation

3:1 Since he has shown us such great mercy, to start with we, the living, do not sacrifice to dead gods or worship them, but through him we have known the Father of truth. What else is the knowledge directed to him than this, not to deny him through whom we have come to know him. 2 He himself says, "Whoever confesses me before men, I will confess him before my Father. 3 This, then, is our reward for confessing him through whom we are saved. 4 But how do we confess him?

By doing what he says and not disobeying his commandments and honoring him not only with our lips, but with all our heart and mind. ⁵ He also says in Isaiah, "This people honors me with their lips, but their heart is far from me."

⁴:¹ Therefore, we should not only call him Lord, for this will not save us. ² For he says, "Not everyone who says to me 'Lord, Lord' will be saved, but whoever does righteousness." ³ Therefore, brothers, let us now confess him with our deeds, by loving one another, by not committing adultery, by not slandering one another or being envious of one another, but by being abstinent, merciful, and kind. We should also be sympathetic toward one another and not stingy. By these deeds we confess him and not by their opposites. ⁴ And let us not fear people, but God. ⁵ For this reason, when you do these things, the Lord says, "If you are united with me at my bosom and do not do my commandments, I will cast you away and say to you, 'Go away from me. I do not know you, where you are from, you who do lawlessness.'"

Textual Notes

3:1 On ἔλεος, see 1:7. In what follows there is an anacoluthon, with which πρῶτον μέν corresponds to nothing further. The preacher goes back to what has already been said (cf. 1:6). On νεκροῖς θεοῖς, see Wis 15:17: θνητὸς δὲ ὢν νεκρὸν ἐργάζεται χερσὶν ἀνόμοις· κρείττων γάρ ἐστιν τῶν σεβασμάτων αὐτοῦ, ὧν αὐτὸς μὲν ἔζησεν, ἐκεῖνα δὲ οὐδέποτε, then see Acts of Carpi 12 (Knopf, *Märtyreracten*, 11; Gebhardt, *Märtyreracten*, 14): οἱ ζῶντες τοῖς νεκροῖς οὐ θύουσιν. On πατὴρ τῆς ἀληθείας, see 19:1: θεὸς τῆς ἀληθείας, then John 15:26 and 8:44. The entire construction sounds Johannine (cf. John 17:3). But we cannot bring in the Johannine concept of "knowledge" here. The *gnosis* of God, which 2 Clem. has in mind, is monotheism. The logic of τίς ἡ γνῶσις κτλ. is somewhat forceful. But the statement that the true knowledge of God consists in the confession of Christ has its meaning in the fact that Christ alone conveys this knowledge. The ἀρνεῖσθαι of Christ also occurs in Matt 10:33; Luke 12:9; Acts 3:13f; 1 John 2:22; Jude 4; 2 Pet 2:1; and then quite frequently in Hermas.

3:2 Note how here and in the preceding αὐτός sometimes means God and sometimes means Christ. This, too, is a "naïve modalism." In λέγει δὲ καὶ αὐτός, an αὐτὸς ἔφα sounds through: one could only speak in this manner if they were accustomed to speak of Christ simply as αὐτός. On the citation, see Matt 10:32; Luke 12:8. The wording is closer to Matthew than it is to Luke, but does not seem to be taken directly from Matthew either, especially if the words ἐνώπιον τῶν ἀνθρώπων are omitted in agreement with S. The phrases τὸν ὁμολογήσαντα up to πατρός μου and then in the following ἐν τίνι up to τῶν ἐντολῶν are cited by a later scribe, Nikon of Rhaithos (eleventh cent.).

3:3 μισθός: here, then is the answer to the questions in 1:3, 5. After ἐάν, A reads οὖν, which, however, is difficult to bear, especially after the immediately preceding οὖν.

3:4 ἐξ ὅλης καρδίας καὶ ἐξ ὅλης τῆς διανοίας is an allusion to Deut 6:5: ἐξ ὅλης τῆς διανοίας [AF καρδίας] σου καὶ ἐξ ὅλης τῆς ψυχῆς σου καὶ ἐξ ὅλης τῆς δυνάμεώς σου. Second Clement probably has Mark 12:30 (Matt 22:37; Luke 10:27) in mind, however, since there διάνοια and καρδία appear side-by-side, not in place of one another as in the LXX.

3:5 In the word of the prophet (Isa 29:13), the pre-existent heavenly Christ speaks, especially since the Christ on earth also used this word (cf. Mark 7:6; Matt 15:8). As the form of the quotation shows, 2 Clem. quotes from the Gospel tradition and not directly from the LXX (ἐγγίζει μοι ὁ λαὸς οὗτος ἐν τῷ στόματι αὐτοῦ καὶ ἐν τοῖς χείλεσιν τιμῶσίν με. ἡ δὲ καρδία αὐτῶν πόρρω ἀπέχει ἀπ' ἐμοῦ); see also 1 Clem. 15:2, where also ἄπεστιν (Synoptics) is read and not ἀπέχει (LXX).

Second Clement 4 has a tight connection with what precedes. The treatment of the previous topic continues without interruption.

4:2 The short quotation clearly deviates from Matt 7:21, even more from the parallel in Luke 6:46. The fact that the preacher had the Matthean text in mind, but freely transformed it, can hardly be assumed since the motives for the transformation cannot be discerned. And it is unlikely to have been a mistake in memory since the quotation is too short. The remaining option is that he likely drew it from a different tradition, be it written or oral. Extra-canonical tradition appears immediately afterward.

4:3 The ἔργα are unfolded in short, antithetical moral catechisms. ἀγαπᾶν precedes, then come three negative and three positive components, each corresponding to the other, and an antithetical double component concludes the list. Sensuality and neglect of brotherly love are the chief evils combated (cf. already Paul in 1 Thess 4:3-10). On καταλαλεῖν, see Jas 4:11; 1 Clem. 30:3; Hermas, Mand. II 2f; Sim. IX 23.3f; and other passages in Hermas). Blaspheming and slandering was a great vice among the Greeks and those from the east who composed the ancient congregations. Related to these is ζῆλος, fighting over positions and jealousy within the congregation (cf. especially 1 Clem. 3-6; 14:1; etc.; also Hermas, Sim. VIII 7.4). On the ideal of the ἐρκράτει, see the remarks in 2 Clem. 8:4; 12:5; etc. ἀγαθός occurs frequently; see also Titus 2:5; 1 Pet 2:18.

4:4 See Acts 4:19; 5:29; and the comments at 1 Clem. 14:1. The admonition, in itself very general, already leads over to a certain great admonition of the following, namely, that of not shunning martyrdom (cf. 2 Clem. 5). — μᾶλλον ἀλλά is a casual construction, two constructions are mixed together: οὐ . . . ἀλλά and μᾶλλον . . . ἤ.

4:5 Even ταῦτα is casual and is not artful; for it refers not only to what was mentioned last, the fear of man, but, as ἐντολάς proves in the citation, it reaches beyond it to all the ugly conduct which was mentioned in the preceding clauses. Likewise, διὰ τοῦτο is blurry. The quotation is the first undoubtedly apocryphal text in the series of non-canonical sayings of the Lord which 2 Clem. uses, and for which at least one apocryphal gospel writing must have been available to him. Echoes of our word in the synoptic tradition are unmistakable; see Luke 13:27: καὶ ἐρεῖ· λέγω ὑμῖν, οὐκ οἶδα πόθεν ἐστέ· ἀπόστητε ἀπ᾽ ἐμοῦ πάντες ἐργάται ἀδικίας and Matt 7:23 (not so close in spite of ἀνομίαν): καὶ τότε ὁμολογήσω αὐτοῖς ὅτι οὐδέποτε ἔγνων ὑμᾶς· ἀποχωρεῖτε ἀπ᾽ ἐμοῦ οἱ ἐργαζόμενοι τὴν ἀνομίαν. But of course the word cannot be derived from the synoptic tradition, which in turn echoes Ps 6:9: ἀπόστητε ἀπ᾽ ἐμοῦ πάντες οἱ ἐργαζόμενοι τὴν ἀνομίαν. Justin uses this threatening word twice with the synoptic introduction, namely in 1 Apol. 16.11: ἀποχωρεῖτε ἀπ᾽ ἐμοῦ ἐργάται τῆς ἀνομίας and Dial. 76.5: καὶ ἐρῶ αὐτοῖς ἀναχωρεῖτε ἀπ᾽ ἐμοῦ. — In συνηγμένοι ἐν τῷ κόλπῳ μου the image of the shepherd can be present, with an allusion to Isa 40:11: ὡς ποιμὴν ποιμανεῖ τὸ ποίμνιον αὐτοῦ καὶ τῷ βραχίονι αὐτοῦ συνάξει ἄρνας (on the image of the flock like the quotation, cf. 5:2), however, it can also have in mind the image of the banquet like in Luke 13:26: ἐφάγομεν ἐνώπιόν σου, see the bosom of Abraham in Luke 16:22f. The quotation once again stresses doing Christ's commandments, which is what the whole context is about.

III. Implications of Confessing God with Deeds (5:1—6:9)

Second Clement 5–6 supplies the justification for the demand to abandon this world with the original Christian-Jewish doctrine of the two eons and the words of Jesus about two masters.

Translation

5:1 Therefore, brothers, let us give up life as sojourners in this world and do the will of him who called us, and let us not be afraid to go out of this world. 2 For the Lord says, "You will be like sheep in the midst of wolves." 3 Peter answered him, "What if the wolves tear apart the sheep?" ⁴ Jesus said to Peter, "Let the sheep not fear the wolves after they are dead; nor fear those who kill you, and can do nothing else to hurt you; but fear him who, after your death, has power over soul and body, to cast them into the fire of hell." ⁵ And know, brothers, that the sojourn of this flesh in this world is small and of short duration, but the promise of Christ is great and admirable, namely, rest in the future kingdom and eternal life. ⁶ What must we do to attain such things, if not walk in a holy and righteous manner, and regard worldly matters as foreign and not desire them. ⁷ For if we desire to possess them, we fall from the righteous path.

⁶:¹ But the Lord says, "No servant can serve two masters." If we wish to serve God as well as Mammon, there is no advantage for us. "What use is it then if someone gains the whole world but loses their soul?" ³ But this age and the future age are two enemies. ⁴ The former proclaims adultery and profanity and covetousness and deceit, while the latter says goodbye to these things. ⁵ So we cannot be friends of the two; instead, we must say goodbye to this age and cling to the one to come. ⁶ We believe that it is better to hate the things of this age, because they are small and short-lived and perishable, but to love those things, the imperishable goods. ⁷ For if we do the will of Christ, we will find rest; but if not, nothing will save us from eternal punishment for disobeying his commandments. ⁸ For Scripture also says in Ezekiel, "If Noah and Job and Daniel arise, they will not save their children" who are in captivity. ⁹ If, however, even such righteous ones cannot save their children with their righteous deeds, with what confidence will we, if we do not preserve our baptism pure and undefiled, enter the kingdom of God? Or who will be our advocate if we are not found in possession of holy and righteous works.

Textual Notes

5:1 Christians are strangers and guests, παροικοῦντες and ἐπιδημοῦντες (5:5 ἐπιδημία), in this world. Their true citizenship is in another world (cf. the prescript in 1 Clem.). For justification of the moral demand from the Great One who has given every good thing, see Heb 11:14ff; 12:21–28; 13:14; Col 3:1f; very clearly in the first parable of Hermas, etc. Receiving good things from heaven obligates one to holy living and to the greatest sacrifices. Here, as 4:4 already subtlety indicated, martyrdom is clearly demanded, although the instruction to go out of the world is by no means limited to martyrdom (cf. 5:6; 6:1ff). The encouragement to martyrdom can also be prompted by the polemic against *gnosis*, which is clear in various places in the sermon. The gnostics who deny the resurrection of the flesh also reject martyrdom; see Basilides' words from Agrippa Castor (Eusebius, *Hist. eccl.* 4.7.7): ... ἀδιαφορεῖν εἰδωλοθύτων ἀπογευομένους καὶ ἐξομνυμένους ἀπαραφυλάκτως τὴν πίστιν κατὰ τοὺς τῶν διωγμῶν καιρούς .... See also Iren. *Haer.* III 18.5 and Tertullian's tractate *Scorpiace*. καλέσας is probably Christ due to the connection.

5:2f The second certain citation of an apocryphal gospel follows. Here also contact with the synoptic tradition can be assumed. For v. 2, see Luke 10:3; Matt 10:16: ἰδοὺ ἐγὼ ἀποστέλλω ὑμᾶς ὡς ἄρνας (Matt πρόβατα) ἐν μέσῳ λύκων. For v. 3, see Luke 12:4f: μὴ φοβηθῆτε ἀπὸ τῶν ἀποκτεννόντων τὸ σῶμα καὶ μετὰ ταῦτα μὴ ἐχόντων περισσοτερόν τι ποιῆσαι . . . φοβήθητε τὸν μετὰ τὸ ἀποκτεῖναι ἔχοντα ἐξουσίαν ἐμβαλεῖν εἰς τὴν γέενναν and Matt 10:28: καὶ μὴ φοβεῖσθε ἀπὸ τῶν ἀποκτεννόντων τὸ σῶμα τὴν δὲ ψυχὴν μὴ δυναμένων ἀποκτεῖναι· φοβεῖσθε δὲ μᾶλλον τὸν δυνάμενον καὶ ψυχὴν καὶ σῶμα ἀπολέσαι ἐν γεέννῃ. Second Clement evidences closer contact with the Lukan form of the tradition than the Matthean form. See still the quotation in Justin, *1 Apol.* 19.7, which is again different from the Synoptics and shows a kinship with 2 Clem.: μὴ φοβεῖσθε τοὺς ἀναιροῦντας ὑμᾶς καὶ μετὰ ταῦτα μὴ δυναμένους τι ποιῆσαι, εἶπε, φοβήθητε δὲ τὸν μετὰ τὸ ἀποθανεῖν δυνάμενον καὶ ψυχὴν καὶ σῶμα εἰς γέενναν ἐμβαλεῖν. Finally, see the citations from Clement of Alexadria, *Excerpta ex Theod.* 14.3 and 51.3; Iren. *Haer.* III 18.5. But what none of the synoptic texts and the texts which follow show is the form of the dialogue between Jesus and Peter, and this observation is decisive for the conclusion that 2 Clem. follows an apocryphal model, which then also includes that which goes beyond the Synoptics: Peter's question as well as Jesus' answer to it: μὴ φοβείσθωσαν . . . up to ἀποθανεῖν αὐτά. From which apocryphal text it originates cannot be said with any certainty (see 2 Clem. 12:2). In the dialogue, 5:2–4 is undoubtedly connected with 12:2; if 2 Clem. 4:5 and 5:2–4, like 12:2 come from an Egyptian gospel, then this saying must have had familiarity with it, in addition to very strong deviations from the synoptic model.

5:5 See 2 Clem. 6:6 where μικρὰ καὶ ὀλιγοχρόνια also appears; see further 1 John 2:17 among other passages. On μεγάλη καὶ θαυμαστή, see the comments at 2 Clem. 2:6. καί before ἀνάπαυσις is explanatory (epexegetical καί), as also in John 1:16: καὶ χάριν ἀντὶ χάριτος, Gal 6:16: καὶ ἐπὶ τὸν Ἰσραὴλ τοῦ θεοῦ; see Blaß-Debrunner, *Grammatik*, §442.9; 471.3. On ἀνάπαυσις, see 2 Clem. 6:7 (Matt 11:28), then Rev 14:13, and above all κατάπαυσις in Heb 3f, especially 4:8–11.

5:6 Here, martyrdom is no longer demanded, but a righteous way of life, as in v. 4. ὁσίως καὶ δικαίως, righteous before God and people (cf. 1:3); the same connection also afterward in 2 Clem. 6:9; 1 Thess 2:10; etc. On τὰ κοσμικὰ ὡς ἀλλότρια ἡγεῖσθαι, see 1 Cor 7:29–31 and above all Herm. *Sim.* I. The construction of the clause in the second part is loose; the accusative εἰ μὴ τὸ . . . ἀναστρέφεσθαι κτλ. answers the question τί ποιήσαντας. It would have been better formulated with εἰ μὴ . . . ἀναστρεφομένους κτλ. The correction τῷ for τό, however, is entirely unnecessary.

5:7 ἀποπίπτειν with the genitive in its figurative sense is especially popular in Koine Greek.

6:1 Jesus' admonition concerning the service of two masters is interwoven into the paraenesis, which before and after seeks to achieve its effect with the doctrine of the two eons. The quotation comes from Luke 16:13 verbatim; Matt 6:24 lacks οἰκέτης, and the allusion θεῷ μαμωνᾷ also comes from Luke. On the warning against service of Mammon, see the warning against covetousness in 2 Clem. 4:3 and 6:4.

6:2 The citation comes closest to Matt 16:26: τί γὰρ ὠφεληθήσεται ἄνθρωπος, ἐὰν τὸν κόσμον ὅλον κερδήσῃ, τὴν δὲ ψυχὴν αὐτοῦ ζημιωθῇ, at a greater distance are Mark 8:36 and Luke 9:25; see also Justin, *1 Apol.* 15.12: τί γὰρ ὠφελεῖται ἄνθρωπος ἂν τὸν κόσμον ὅλον κερδήδῃ, τὴν δὲ ψυχὴν αὐτοῦ ἀπολέσῃ.

6:3 αἰὼν οὗτος and αἰὼν μέλλων appear only here within the sermon; before and afterward κόσμος, κόσμος οὗτος, the βασιλεία, etc. appear. On this matter see Gal 1:4; 2 Cor 4:4; Jas 4:4; 1 John 5:19; Hermas, *Sim.* I, among other places; 4 Esd 7:50: *non fecit Altissimus unum saeculum, sed duo*; 8:1f; Apocalypse of Baruch 44:9, 12; among other places; Bousset, *Religion*, 278–86.

6:4 On the catalog of vices (*Lasterliste*): fornication, avarice, fraud, see already above at 4:3. φθορά does not have the general meaning it might otherwise have, but should be interpreted as sexual vice since μοιχεία is next to it.

6:5 On χρᾶσθαι instead of χρῆσθαι, see Blaß-Debrunner, *Grammatik*, §88; Helbing, *Grammatik*, 110; as well as Lobeck, *Eclogæ*, 61.

6:6 On μικρὰ καὶ ὀλιγοχρόνια see 2 Clem. 5:5 and likewise also ἀνάπαυσις in v. 7.

6:7 The double conditional clause is pleonastic: εἰ δὲ μήγε . . . ἐὰν παρακούσωμεν. However, it contains on account of εἰ, ἐάν different shades; see εἰ . . . ἐάν immediately afterward in v. 9 and then John 13:17: in these instances, εἰ presents the condition as real and present, ἐάν lets the act depend on the circumstances. On αἰώνιος κόλασις, see Matt 25:46.

6:8 The citation is pieced together from Ezek 14:14: καὶ ἐὰν ὦσιν οἱ τρεῖς ἄνδρες οὗτοι ἐν μεσῳ αὐτῆς (sc. τῆς γῆς), Νῶε καὶ Δανιἠλ καὶ Ἰώβ, αὐτοὶ ἐν τῇ δικαιοσύνῃ αὐτῶν σωθήσονται, v. 16 καὶ οἱ τρεῖς ἄνδρες οὗτοι ἐν μέσῳ αὐτῆς ὦσι, ζῶ ἐγώ, λέγει κύριος, εἰ υἱοὶ ἢ θυγατέρες σωθήσονται, ἀλλ᾽ ἢ αὐτοὶ μόνοι σωθήσοντια, v. 18 καὶ οἱ τρεῖς οὗτοι ἄνδρες ἐν μέσῳ αὐτῆς, ζῶ ἐγώ, λέγει κύριος, οὐ μὴ ῥύσωνται υἱοὺς οὐδὲ θυγατέρας, αὐτοὶ μόνοι σωθήσονται. Note from the *Vorlage* the change Noah, Job, Daniel (also in Apost. Const. II 14.4), which is probably intended to be chronological. Note also the addition of ἐν τῇ αἰχμαλωσίᾳ, which is found often in the LXX.

6:9 δικαιοσύναι are righteous deeds, as is how the terms is used frequently in the LXX: Ezek 3:20; 33:13; Dan 9:18 (also in Theodotion), etc. A new motif is introduced into the paraenesis with τηρήσωμεν κτλ.: the obligation to keep the seal of baptism pure; see the repetition of the exhortation in 7:6 and 8:6. On τηρήσωμεν τὸ βάπτισμα, see the Acts of Paul and Thecla 6: μακάριοι οἱ τὸ βάπτισμα τηρήσαντες.

In our passage and these two closely related ones, the preacher gives some hints about what the sacrament of *baptism* means to him. Twice he calls it a seal, which is an expression Hermas uses in *Sim.* VIII 2.2, 4; IX 16.3–7; IX 17.4; IX 31.1, 4; see also Acts of Paul: Martyrdom of Paul 5 (Bonnet, *Acta*, 1:105–17): ἐκεῖνοι ὑμῖν δώσουσιν τὴν ἐν κυρίῳ σφραγῖδα and likewise in 7. The name is borrowed from the piety of Hellenism and indicates a mysterious sign placed on the initiated. Through the seal, they become the property of the god to whom they have surrendered, receiving from him—because he recognizes them as his own—protection and strength against the strong, hostile forces that surround humanity, especially when they need protection the most, namely in the hour after death, when the freed soul must travel through the territories of the demons to reach its god in the region of light of the upper world. The seal itself could be very different: a carved letter or a name, or otherwise a torn or burned sign, a scar in a certain place, etc. But it could also be understood as an invisible sign, which consisted in a washing or anointing or sprinkling, or even only in the naming of special mysterious names, especially that of the god himself, and in the utterance of mysterious formulas and were thus disclosed. Circumcision was also understood as a seal (cf. Rom 4); see also the sign probably burned on with a red-hot iron, with which "Mithras marked his soldiers on the forehead" (Tertullian, *Praescr.* 40), the hymn of the Nazarenes (Hippolytus, *Haer.* V 10) where Jesus says: σφραγῖδας ἔχων καταβήσομαι, among other examples (cf. Bousset, *Kyrios Christos*, 278ff; Dölger, *Sphragis*, esp. 39ff). — Christians seem to have spoken of seals rather early either in a figurative or in a very real way. In 2 Cor 1:22 Paul already speaks of the sealing of the Christians; see also the Pauline school in Eph 1:13; 4:30, and also Rev 7:2f; 3:12; 14:1;

13:16f; 22:4 (also Gal 6:17). In 2 Cor 1:22 Paul understands the seal which is put on the Christians to be the Spirit, the great assurance, the deposit for the believers. From then on it was only a small step to understand baptism as a seal, because the *pneuma* descended at baptism, because in it the powerful and mysterious name of Jesus was mentioned, and because it had the merit of being an outward act with naming and immersion, which could very easily be paralleled with the pagan sealings; on the whole question, see Anrich, *Myserienwesen*, 120–25; Wobbermin, *Mysterienwesen*, 144–54; Heitmüller, *Im Namen Jesu*, 333f; Bousset, *Kyrios Christos*, 278–81; Gruppe, *Griechische Mythologie*, 1616f; Heitmüller, "Sphragis," 40ff; and above all Dölger, *Sphragis*. — It can be safely assumed for 2 Clem. that he imagines that the new convert receives an invisible sign as a seal at baptism, probably on the head. Through sins, especially through the sins of the flesh, it loses its luster; according to the state of one's seal, the person receives their judgment. — The views of baptism and its obligation are strangely strict and ancient here. The sins of the unconverted are done away with; now it is necessary to remain faithful and pure until the new eon comes. Christians must sin no more. The explanations of 2 Clem. 6:9—7:6, also in 8:6, are clear, serious, and emphatic. The fact that the preacher during his era could no longer hold on to these ideas, however, is clearly seen in later remarks; see the call to repentance in 2 Clem. 8; 16f; 18:2. See also Windisch, *Taufe und Sünde*, 331ff.

βασίλειον is actually a royal palace, and this meaning would fit quite well here. If this is accurate, perhaps we can assume an allusion to Matt 22:11f. However, in 17:5 βασίλειον clearly means βασιλεία, and the word is used with this sense elsewhere (cf. T. Jud. 17; 22f; Gaius in Eusebius, *Hist. eccl.* 3.28.2; 7.17.2; etc.). The use of the simple word παράκλητος (cf. Did. 5:2, and for the meaning of the word, see the explanation in Bisping, *Johannes*, at John 14:16), which also belongs to everyday life, is not sufficient to establish contact with Johannine usage and thought. On the personification of good works and their role in the judgment, see also 1 Tim 5:24f, where the works precede or follow, and also Rev 14:13; for more on this originally, likely Persian conception, see Weiß, *Korintherbrief*, 83 at 1 Cor 3:14f.

IV. The Toil of the Struggle Is Great, but the Reward Is Glorious (7:1—8:6)

Second Clement 7–8 contains the paraenesis on baptism. The admonitions of the two chapters are held together by the reference to baptismal grace and obligation (cf. 6:9 along with 7:6 and 8:6); τηρεῖν τὸ βάπτισμα ἁγνόν is the keyword (*Stichwort*).

Translation

⁷:¹ So now, my brothers, let us fight, knowing that the competition is ready and that many go to the earthly competitions, but not all will receive crowns, but only those who have labored much and fought well. ² Now let us fight so that we might receive a crown. ³ So let us run the straight course, the imperishable competition, and let us go to it in great numbers and fight where we can, so that we may also receive a crown. And if we cannot all receive a crown, then let us come as close as possible to it. ⁴ We must know that whoever is caught cheating in an earthly competition, he will be lashed, taken away, and thrown out of the stadium. ⁵ What do you think? What will the one who cheats in an imperishable battle suffer? ⁶ Of those who do not keep the seal, it is said, "their worm will not die and their fire will not go out, and they will be a spectacle to all flesh."

⁸:¹ For as long as we are on earth, we should repent. ² For we are clay in the hand of the craftsman. As it is with the potter, when he makes a vessel and it is misshaped or broken in his hands, he fashions it anew, but if he had put it into the kiln, he is not able to improve upon it—so too with us: as long as we are in this world, let us repent with our whole hearts for what we have done in the flesh so that we might be saved by the Lord, as long as we still have time to repent. ³ For when we depart from the world, we are no longer able to confess our sins or repent. ⁴ Therefore, brothers, if we have done the will of the Father and have kept the flesh pure and have heeded the commandments, we will receive eternal life. ⁵ For the Lord says in the gospel, "If you have not kept the small thing, who will give what is greater to you? For I say to you that whoever is faithful with the smallest matter is faithful with many things." ⁶ Thus, he is saying this: keep the flesh pure and the seal unstained, so that we will receive eternal life.

Textual Notes

Second Clement 7: The image of the games of combat is extremely popular in contemporary philosophical-ethical popular literature. "The diatribe parallels constantly compare the exercise of virtue with athletics"; see Wendland, *Kultur*, 358, both the note and the literature listed there. Paul, too, in 1 Cor 9:24–27, a passage that 2 Clem. seems to draw upon, uses a generally popular image, but not one that was suggested to him precisely by the Corinthian

(Isthmian) games. ἐν χερσίν = πρόχειρος. The word καταπλεῖν simply means "from the high seas to the land" and not "to sail to us by sea," and the words need not be intended for an audience living in a place where famous competitions are held and to which one travels by sea. The great *agone* of the time are the four ancient ones at Olympia, Corinth, Delphi, and Nemea, but also newer games had won high reputation, the Eurycles in Sparta, the Athenian Panhellenia and Panathenaea, the Capitoline games at Rome; on the nature of the games and the rather outstanding appreciation of the victories portrayed on the Greek stage during the imperial age, as well as the Roman reluctance against it, see Mommsen, *Römische Geschichte*, 5:264–66, Friedländer, *Sittengeschichte* II/8, 483–504. On κοπιάσαντες καὶ ἀγωνισάμενοι, see 1 Tim 4:10. κοπιᾶν can apply to the effort on the day of battle, but also to the preparation (1 Cor 9:25). On καλῶς, see v. 4 φθείρων.

7:2f For Christians, the image of the victory wreath is naturally connected with the idea of the heavenly halo, the wreath of life (cf. Rev 2:10; 4:4; etc.; Jas 1:12; 1 Pet 5:4; 2 Tim 4:8; Herm. *Sim.* VIII 2:1; 3:6; etc.).

7:3 θέωμεν should be read with S instead of the reading in AH (θῶμεν). εὐθεία ὁδός speaks of the racetrack, but deliberately sounds like "the straight path (of the Lord)" (cf. Acts 13:10; 2 Pet 2:15). θέω with the accusative, similar to Herodotus, *Hist.* VIII 74: δρόμον θεῖν. — κἂν ἐγγὺς τοῦ στεφάνου: second and third place may also receive honorary prizes; Josephus, *J. W.* I 21.8, 415: "Herod established fighting games every fifth year in honor of the emperor πρῶτος αὐτὸς ἆθλα μέγιστα προθείς . . . ἐν οἷς οὐ μόνον οἱ νικῶντες ἀλλὰ καὶ οἱ μετ' αὐτοὺς καὶ οἱ τρίτοι τοῦ βασιλικοῦ πλούτου μετελάμβανον; see however already the distribution of prizes in the combat games in honor of the fallen Patroclus, II 23. Allusion to our passage in Dorotheus Archimandrita (ca. 600): ὡς λέγει καὶ ὁ ἅγιος Κλήμης· κἂν μὴ στεφανῶταί τις, ἀλλὰ σπουδάσῃ μὴ μακρὰν εὑρεθῆναι τῶν στεφανουμένων (Doctrina 23, Migne PG 88, p. 1836).

7:4f φθαρτόν . . . φθείρων . . . ἀφθαρσίας . . . φθείρων is a wordplay. ἀγῶνα φθείρειν is a technical term for deceitful violation of the rules of combat in betting. The punishment for this is flogging by μαστιγοφόροι (or ῥαβοοῦχοι) and exclusion from the track; see Epiphanius, *Haer.* 61.7: παραφθείρας ἀγῶνα ὁ ἀθλητὴς μαστιχθεὶς ἐκβάλλεται τοῦ ἀγῶνος; on the image, see still 2 Tim 2:5. The future παθεῖται is a vulgarization and probably originated by analogy from ἔκβαλον βαλῶ; on εἷλον ἑλῶ see Blaß-Debrunner, *Grammatik*, §74.3.

7:6 On the baptism paraenesis, see the comments above at 6:9. The citation of the final verse of Isaiah (Isa 66:24) is verbatim (cf. still Mark 9:44, 46, 48).

Second Clement 8: An exhortation to repentance is woven into the baptism paraenesis, and the conclusion of the chapter returns to the sermon on baptism.

8:1 The sermon brings forth the first call to repentance. As what follows shows, there is time for repentance as long as man is alive. That this assumption contradicts the baptismal obligation as formulated in 6:9, 7:6, and 8:6 is immediately clear; the Christian has obtained forgiveness of sins and he has to keep his seal pure from baptism on. Since one does not like to suppose that the two views, so strongly contradictory, stand immediately side by side (8:1f right after 7:6), it is advisable to take μετανοήσωμεν (and correspondingly 9:7f) as broadly as possible, such that it applies to all humanity and not to Christians: that the unbaptized, catechumens, and guests were accepted among the hearers is certain (cf. already the comments at 2 Clem. 1:2). But a separation throughout the letter cannot be made: from 2 Clem. 13:1 on, the exhortation to repent is clearly directed toward all Christians (cf. 15:1; 16:1, 4; 17:1f; 19:1; and especially 18:2). Second Clement thus links two exhortations together, the ancient Christian baptism paraenesis and the ecclesiastical call to repentance. — ὡς = "as long as" (cf. also 2 Clem. 9:7; Gal 6:10; etc.).

8:2 A parable is used, but it has faint allegorical features. The image of the potter and his vessels in Jer 18:4–6 (cf. Rom 9:21) may be suggested, but the application does not coincide; see also T. Naph. 2; Athenagoras 15; and especially Theophilus, *Autol.* II 26: οὐ μὴν ἀλλὰ καὶ καθάπερ σκεῦός τι, ἐπὰν πλασθὲν αἰτίαν τινὰ σχῇ ἀναχωνεύεται ἢ ἀναπλάσσεται εἰς τὸ γενέσθαι καινὸν καὶ ὁλόκληρον. οὕτως γίνεται καὶ τῷ ἀνθρώπῳ διὰ θανάτου, see also the note in von Otto, *Corpus Apologetarum*, vol. 8. εἰς τὴν χειρα = ἐν τῇ χειρί, see Radermacher, *Grammatik*, 10 and 116; Blaß-Debrunner, *Grammatik*, §205. καὶ ἐν ταῖς χερσὶν αὐτοῦ διαστραφῇ should be read in agreement with A, against the reading in HS which is ἐν ταῖς χερσὶν αὐτοῦ καὶ διαστραφῇ. κάμινον τοῦ πυρὸς . . . βοηθήσει is faintly allegorical; behind the potter, the judge of the world looks out, who puts the sinner into the hellish fire, which is rather similar to Mark 4:29 (cf. also Matt 3:12). In the rest of the image, the potter should not be read as equal to God, otherwise the meaning becomes something the author surely did not intend: God is responsible, because only he affects repentance (cf. Rom 9:19). ἐν τῇ σαρκί can also be connected with μετανοήσωμεν if needed; before ἅ add ἀπὸ (or ἐκ) τούτων.

8:3 *Exhomologesis* is mentioned only here in the letter; what is surely meant is the public confession that is made once before baptism and then constantly by the believers in the worship service (cf. Did. 14:1).

8:4 ἀδελφοί clearly addresses the faithful, not the guests. Between the general exhortations ποιήσαντες κτλ. and φυλάξαντες κτλ., pointing to the two pre-eminent instances, the Father and the Lord, stands the definite single exhortation τὴν σάρκα ἁγνὴν τηρήσαντες. τηρεῖν takes up the cue of the baptism paraenesis (cf. 6:9; 7:6), and the whole expression, which recurs in 8:6, can hardly be interpreted other than as a reference to the requirement of perfect asceticism, which also excludes conjugal intercourse (cf. the comments at 2 Clem. 12:5; 14:3; 15:1). On the expression, see the Acts of Paul and Thecla 5: μακάριοι οἱ ἁγνὴν τὴν σάρκα τηρήσαντες, ὅτι αὐτοὶ ναὸς θεοῦ γενήσονται (and the makarisms that follow there, e.g., μακάριοι οἱ ἔχοντες γυναῖκας ὡς μὴ ἔχοντες . . .) and 12: ἄλλως ἀνάστασις ὑμῖν οὐκ ἔστιν, ἐὰν μὴ ἁγνοὶ μείνητε καὶ τὴν σάρκα μὴ μολύνητε ἀλλὰ τηρήσητε ἁγνήν. To live completely abstemiously is the ideal in 2 Clem. as elsewhere. Certainly here, as before and as follows, polemics against certain gnostic trends that teach the παραχρῆσθαι τῇ σαρκί can be discerned; see Hermas, Sim. V 7.1f, then the Nicolaitans in Rev 2f and the heretics of Jude, as well as the gnostic word of gold, which does not lose its beauty and proper nature, even when thrown into the dirt, in Irenaeus, Haer. I 6.2, among other passages.

8:5 ἐν τῷ εὐαγγελίῳ, according to the well-known, ancient usage: the gospel is one. The word itself comes from an apocryphal tradition; Luke 16:10f is closely related to our passage but cannot be the direct Vorlage. Irenaeus seems to know the framing of the logion; Irenaeus, Haer. II 34.3: Et ideo dominus dicebat ingratis existentibus in eum: si in modico fideles non fuistis, quod magnum est quis dabit vobis? significans quoniam qui in modica temporali vita ingrati exstiterunt ei qui eam praestitit, iuste non percipient ab eo in saeculum saeculi longitudinem dierum; see then also Hippolytus, Refutatio X 33.7: ὑπάκουε τῷ πεποιηκότι καὶ μὴ ἀντίβαινε νῦν, ἵνα ἐπὶ τῷ μικρῷ πιστὸς εὑρεθεὶς καὶ τὸ μέγα πιστευθῆναι δυνηθῇς. For 2 Clem. τὸ μικρὸν τηρεῖν = τὴν σάρκα ἁγνὴν τηρεῖν and μέγα is the ζωὴ αἰώνιος.

8:6 See comments at 2 Clem. 6:9. ἄσπιλον τηρεῖν, also in 1 Tim 6:14; Jas 1:27. On the aorist imperative τηρήσατε, see Blaß-Debrunner, Grammatik, §337.1

V. The Resurrection and Assorted Paraenesis (9:1—12:6)

Second Clement 9–12 is written against the doubters. The polemic is occasionally interwoven with paraenesis but is otherwise clear and coherent. The gnostic denial of eschatology is opposed, first by addressing those who deny the resurrection of the flesh in 2 Clem. 9:1–5.

Translation

⁹:¹ And none of you should say that this flesh will not be judged and will not be resurrected. ² Know [this]: wherein were you saved, wherein were you made to see, if not while dwelling in this flesh? ³ Therefore, we must keep the flesh as a temple of God. ⁴ For as you were called in the flesh, so also you will come in the flesh. ⁵ If Christ, the Lord, who saved us was at first a spirit, then became flesh, and called us in this way, then we also will receive the reward in the flesh. ⁶ Therefore, let us love one another, so that we all might enter the kingdom of God. ⁷ As long as we still have time to be healed, let us give ourselves to God who can heal us, repaying him what is owed. ⁸ What then is that? To repent from a sincere heart. ⁹ For he knows all things beforehand and knows what is in our hearts. ¹⁰ Therefore, let us praise him, not with the mouth alone, but also from the heart, so that he might accept us as sons. ¹¹ For the Lord has said, "My brothers are those who do the will of my Father."

¹⁰:¹ Therefore, my brothers, let us do the will of the Father who called us so that we may live, and let us pursue virtue all the more, leaving wickedness as the forerunner of our sins, and let us flee ungodliness so that evil may not seize us. ² For if we make haste to do good, peace will come to us. ³ For this reason, peace can find no one, namely because they all let the fear of others flow in, because they prefer pleasure instead of the future promise. ⁴ For they do not know what torment the pleasure of this world brings and what delight the future promise brings. ⁵ And if they only did that, then it would be bearable; but they persist in bringing bad teachings to innocent souls, without considering that they will receive double judgment, judgment of both themselves and those who listen to them.

¹¹:¹ Now, let us serve God with pure hearts, and we will be righteous. But if we do not serve him, because we do not believe God's promise, then we will be miserable. ² For the prophetic word says, "Miserable are the doubters who are double-minded in their hearts, who say, 'We have heard these things long ago, even at the time of our fathers, but we waited day after day and saw none of them happen.' ³ You fools, compare yourselves to the trees, take the vine; first the leaves fall off, then a sapling grows, after that a sour grape, and then a ripe grape. ⁴ So also my people have had troubles and tribulations, but afterward they will receive good." ⁵ So, my brothers, let us not doubt, but stand firm full of good confidence that we might also reap the reward.

⁶ For the one who has made the promise is trustworthy to give everyone the reward according to their works. ⁷ Now, if we do righteousness before God, we will enter into his kingdom and receive the promises which "ear has not heard, nor eye seen, nor have entered into the heart of man."

¹²:¹ Therefore, let us constantly await the kingdom of God in love and righteousness, since we do not know the day of the appearance of God. ² For when the Lord himself was asked by someone, when the kingdom would come, he said, "When the two are one, and when the outside is like the inside, and when the male with the female is no longer male or female." ³ Now, "the two are one" when we speak the truth to one another and there is one soul in two bodies without hypocrisy. ⁴ "And the outside is like the inside," means this: he calls the soul the inside and the body the outside. Now, as your body is visible, so also should your soul be visible in your good deeds. ⁵ "And the male with the female, neither male nor female," means this: when a brother looks at a sister, he does not think of her as a woman, nor does she think of him as a man. ⁶ "When you do this," he says, "the kingdom of my Father will come."

Textual Notes

9:1 The keyword (*Stichwort*) which drives v. 1 is σάρξ. Doubts about the resurrection of the flesh are as old in the gentile church as the church itself (cf. already 1 Cor 15). These doubts were deepened in the gnostic movement. As in earlier passages of the letter, we can see here polemics against *gnosis*. On the rejection of the resurrection by *gnosis*, see 2 Tim 2:18; Polycarp, *Phil.* 7; Justin, *Dial.* 80.4 (λέγουσι μὴ εἶναι νεκρῶν ἀνάστασιν, ἀλλὰ ἅμα τῷ ἀποθνήσκειν τὰς ψυχὰς αὐτῶν ἀναλαμβάνεσθαι εἰς τὸν οὐρανόν); Iren. *Haer.* I 23.3; II 31.2 (*esse resurrectionem a mortuis agnitionem eius, quae ab iis dicitur, veritatis*); IV 31.1; Tertullian, *Res.* 19; etc. — The entirety of 2 Clem. 9:1–5 is preserved in an anonymous Syriac fragment; see Lightfoot, *Clement,* 1:184–85. Also, a Syriac fragment of Timothy of Alexandria contains the christological phrase εἰ Χριστὸς . . . ἐκάλεσεν after the citation of 1:1f; see the comments above at 2 Clem. 1:2 as well as Lightfoot, *Clement,* 1:181f.

9:2 On ἀνεβλέψατε, see above τοιαύτης ἀχλύος γέμοντες ἐν τῇ ὁράσει ἀνεβλέψαμεν κτλ.

9:3 On ναὸν θεοῦ, see Ign. *Phld.* 7:2: τὴν σάρκα ὑμῶν ὡς ναὸν θεοῦ τηρεῖτε, *Eph.* 15:3: ἵνα ὦμεν αὐτοῦ ναοί, 1 Cor 6:19, and expressed somewhat differently in 1 Cor 3:16f and 2 Cor 6:16.

9:4 ἐλεύσεσθε, namely into judgment, as the preceding and immediately following demonstrate; possibly also with reference to the supplement εἰς τὴν βασιλείαν τοῦ θεοῦ in v. 6.

9:5 AHS and Timotheus (cf. 9:1) read εἷς Χριστός. The correct reading is preserved in the Syriac fragment. On Christology, see 2 Clem. 14:2–4, then Hermas, *Sim.* IX 1.1: ἐκεῖνο γὰρ τὸ πνεῦμα ὁ υἱὸς τοῦ θεοῦ ἐστιν and *Sim.* V 6.5–7, Theophilus *Autol.* II 10: οὗτος οὖν (sc. ὁ λόγος) ὢν πνεῦμα θεοῦ . . . κατήρχετο εἰς τοὺς προφήτας, Tertullian, *Adv., Marc.* III 16: *spiritus creatoris qui est Christus*. On *pneumatic* Christology, see von Harnack, *Dogmengeschichte*, 1:211–20; Seeberg, *Dogmengeschichte*, 1:95f; Loofs, *Dogmengeschichte*, 93–98.

9:6 In v. 6 the paraenesis resumes. It deals with the same general exhortations that have already been sounded before: Repent, do the will of God, do good, pursue virtue. A specific demand is only made in 9:6: let us love one another (on this, see already 4:3, then again in 13:4, as well as 12:1 and 15:2). The paraenesis ends in 10:4 with a clear polemic against the false teachers and their seduction.

9:7f The second exhortation to repentance is also still rather vague (cf. 8:1). On ἀντιμισθία see 1:3, 5; 3:3; 15:2. Here, the repentance is the ἀντιμισθία.

9:9 προγνώστης does not occur in the NT; in the Apostolic Fathers, it only occurs here; however, see Justin, *1 Apol.* 44.11: προγνώστου τοῦ θεοῦ ὄντος, similarly in *Dial.* 16.3; *Dial.* 23.2: φιλάνθρωπον καὶ προγνώστην καὶ ἀνενδεῆ καὶ δίκαιον καὶ ἀγαθόν, see also 92.2; Tatian 19.3; Theophilus, *Autol.* II 15: ὁ θεὸς προγνώστης ὤν. The word essentially belongs to Christian usage. τὰ ἐνκάρδια in H (A has ταενκάρδια; the *iota* subscript is always missing, as in the other majuscules) is a very uncommon word. Perhaps it would be better to read τὰ ἐν καρδίᾳ, a frequently recurring phrase in the LXX (e.g., Deut 8:2).

9:10 ἀπὸ καρδίας resumes ἐξ εἰλικρινοῦς καρδίας. The praise of the heart consists in doing. υἱούς as above in 1:4.

9:11 Since Christ is the Son of God, Christians are his brothers. The quotation does not agree in wording or in arrangement with Matt 12:50 (ὅστις γὰρ ἂν ποιήσῃ τὸ θέλημα τοῦ πατρός μου τοῦ ἐν οὐρανοῖς, αὐτός μου ἀδελφὸς καὶ ἀδελφὴ καὶ μήτηρ ἐστιν) nor with Luke 8:21 (μήτηρ μου καὶ ἀδελφοί μου οὗτοί εἰσιν οἱ τὸν λόγον τοῦ θεοῦ ἀκούοντες καὶ ποιοῦντες); Mark 3:35 is even further removed; Clement of Alexandria, *Ecl.* 20 has ἀδελφοί μου γάρ, φησὶν ὁ κύριος, καὶ συνκληρονόμοι οἱ ποιοῦντες τὸ θέλημα τοῦ πατρός μου. This is, if one omits καὶ συνκληρονόμοι (which Clement of Alexandria must have had in his *Vorlage*, as the context proves), pretty much the wording of 2 Clem. Epiphanius, *Haer.* 30.14 has: οὗτοί εἰσιν οἱ ἀδελφοί μου καὶ ἡ μήτηρ καὶ ἀδελφαὶ οἱ ποιοῦντες τὰ θελήματα τοῦ πατρός μου. As the context suggests, he perhaps cites from a Judaeo-Christian gospel. Second Clement therefore neither quotes Matthew nor Luke freely, but again follows an extra-canonical source. See Resch, *Agrapha*, num. 89, p. 129f and Ropes, *Sprüche Jesu*, 27ff.

10:1 is closely related to the quotation just given (cf. 8:4; 5:1; etc.). The call here is done by God (cf. 1:8). ἵνα ζήσωμεν is dependent on ποιήσωμεν and not καλέσαντος, and καὶ διώξωμεν belongs in the main clause and not the purpose clause. ἀρετή is an uncommon word in ancient Christian ethics; however, see Phil 4:8; 2 Pet 1:3–5; Hermas, *Mand.* I 2; VI 2.3; XII 3.1; *Sim.* VI 1.4; VIII 10.3; in the LXX, significantly, ἀρετή occurs in Wisdom of Solomon and then in the books of the Maccabees, especially 4 Maccabees. κακία quite generally means a bad mindset; from this mindset, then, individual sins in deed emerge (cf. Jas 1:14f). προοδοιπόρος is an uncommon and later word; see Schmidt, *Hesychii*, s.v. ὁδουρός, who explains this word among others with ὁδοῦ κατάρχων. The verb προοδοιπορεῖν is also late; see Josephus, *Ant.* III 1.1 §2: τῆς προωδοιπορημένης and Lucian, *Hermotimus* 27: τοῖς προωδοιπορηκόσιν . . . πιστεύσας οὐκ ἂν σφαλείης. On καταλάβῃ, see Barn. 4:1.

10:2 ἀγαθοποιεῖν occurs again alone; on διώξεται ἡμᾶς εἰρήνη, see Ps 33:15: ζήτησον εἰρήνην καὶ δίωξον αὐτήν.

10:3 διὰ ταύτην γὰρ τὴν αἰτίαν, namely because only the good doers are reached by peace. εὑρεῖν ἄνθρωπον, οἵτινες is not exactly smooth and simple; since in the foregoing we spoke of pursuing, catching up to peace—the whole paraenesis in 10:1–3 exists in the image of going before and after, catching up to, reaching peace—it is best to conceive of αὐτήν (sc. εἰρήνην) as subject and ἄνθρωπον as object. However, the construction can also be reversed, making ἄνθρωπον the subject and εἰρήνην the object. Perhaps, however, there is an error in the text in εὑρεῖν, which should be improved, though not in favor of Lightfoot's preferred reading of εὐημερεῖν but rather with εἰρηνεύειν or εἰρηνεῖν. The construction ἄνθρωπον οἵτινες is tolerable, οἵτινες is explanatory, *quippe qui*. παράγειν means to bring in, instill, teach; see v. 5: κακοδιδασκαλοῦντες τὰς ἀναιτίους ψυχάς, and on the idea, see above at 4:4. προαιρούμενοι or προῃρημένοι is an improvement based on S; AH read προαιρούμεθα. The heretics teach the fear of man and present enjoyment, preaching worldly life and escape from martyrdom (cf. above at 4:4—6:7). ἐπαγγελία here and in v. 4, the subject of the promise (cf. Gal 3:14; Acts 1:4). The eschatological rationale of the paraenesis, which occupies such a large space in the sermon, again emerges strongly here.

10:4 τρυφή is a strong, sensual depiction; on the heritage of Jewish hope for the future, see the many passages in Bousset, *Religion*, 275.

10:5 On the false teachers, see Ignatius, *Eph.* 16:2: ὁ τοιοῦτος, ῥυπαρὸς γενόμενος, εἰς τὸ πῦρ τὸ ἄσβεστον χωρήσει, ὁμοίως καὶ ὁ ἀκούων αὐτοῦ. — ἀνεκτὸν ἦν = ἀνεκτὸν ἂν ἦν. The ἄν in the apodosis of the *unrealis*, hypothetical clause is not always present in Koine (cf. Blaß-Debrunner, *Grammatik*, §360); see John 15:22: εἰ μὴ ἦλθον . . . , ἁμαρτίαν οὐκ εἴχοσαν (similarly in v. 24); Oxyrhynchus Papyri, vol. 3, number 530 (second cent. CE): εἰ πλεῖον δέ μοι παρέκειτο, πάλιν σοι ἀπεστάλκειν. — On κακοδιδασκαλεῖν, see Ign. *Phld.* 2:1 (κακοδιδασκαλία); see also Titus 2:3; 1 Tim 1:3; 6:3; Ign. *Poly* 3:1. On δισσὴ κρίσις, see Apost. Const. V 6.5: καὶ ἑτέροις αἴτιοι ἀπωλείας γενησόμεθα καὶ διπλοτέραν ὑποίσομεν τὴν κρίσιν. The ἀναίτιοι ψυχαί are of course to be sought in the circles close to the congregation: simple believers and catechumens.

Second Clement 11: The connection with the preceding is tight and good; the fight against the doubters continues. The piety that is expressed here is strongly rationalistic and moralistic. To a certain degree it belongs to a Jewish stratum. God has given a great and glorious promise. One must believe in it and walk righteously in view of it. The righteous one who has fulfilled the will of God then carries away his reward in the future participation in the promise.

11:1 δίκαιοι applies—as the future ἐσόμεθα and the antithesis ταλαίπωροι ἐσόμεθα attest—to the day of judgment. On ἐπαγγελία, see 10:3f; 11:6f.

11:2 On προφητικὸς λόγος, see 2 Pet 1:19.

11:2–4 The citation in 2–4 comes from a Jewish apocryphon, as the citation formula already indicates. The book itself is unknown to us and the conjectures about its title (the Book of Eldad and Modad?) are entirely uncertain. The citation is also used in 1 Clem. 23f; see the explanation there. Second Clement deviates in several places from the form of the quotation given in 1 Clem., and also adds an entire sentence in v. 4, which indicates that he himself still knew the apocryphon in question, even if his choice of the quotation itself might have been determined by 1 Clem. Immediately after v.7, he alludes to a text, which 1 Clem. 34:8 explicitly cites: τῇ καρδίᾳ instead of τῇ ψυχῇ; πάλαι is missing in 1 Clem.; instead of ἡμεῖς . . . up to ἑωράκαμεν, 1 Clem. has καὶ ἰδοὺ γεγηράκαμεν καὶ οὐδὲν ἡμῖν τούτων συνβέβηκεν; before ἀνόητοι, 1 Clem. has ὦ; after γίνεται, it reads εἶτα φύλλον, εἶτα ἄνθος καὶ; 2 Clem. 11:4 is missing in 1 Clem. On ἡμέραν ἐξ ἡμέρας, see Gen 39:10; Num 30:15; Ps 95:2; Jer 52:34; 2 Pet 2:8; the phrase is good Greek (Hebraism is 2 Cor 4:16: ἡμέρᾳ καὶ ἡμέρᾳ); see Euripides, *Rhesus* 445f: ἡμέραν δ’ ἐξ ἡμέρας Ῥίπτεις κυβεύων τὸν πρὸς Ἀργείους Ἄρην and Heniochus (author of comedies from the fourth cent.) in Kock, *Comicorum*, 2:434: ἠδιέφθορεν αὐτὰς . . . ξενίζουσ’ ἡμέραν ἐξ ἡμέρας ἀβουλία . . . .

11:6 See Heb 10:23: πιστὸς γὰρ ὁ ἐπαγγειλάμενος. The preacher probably knowns the letter (cf. 1:6). ἀποδιδόναι ἑκάστῳ κτλ., on this good Jewish norm of judicial retribution, see Matt 16:27; Rom 2:6; 2 Tim 4:14; Rev 22:12; 1 Clem 34:3; as well as Rom 14:12; 2 Cor 5:10; Heb 9:27; 1 Pet 1:17; etc.

11:7 For the allusion at the end, see 1 Cor 2:9 and the comment on 1 Clem. 34:8; see also below at 14:5.

Second Clement 12 deals with the "when" of the kingdom of God.

12:1 καθ' ὥραν can also be interpreted differently than in the translation provided, namely "at its appointed, crucial hour." But the reason ἐπειδὴ κτλ. fits better with the proposed view. From the remarks which follow immediately after, of course, it is evident that the coming of the Lord is not felt to be immediately near: first, the ideal of asceticism must be realized. The parousia is here designated as ἐπιφάνεια τοῦ θεοῦ; not only Christ, but also God appears with his kingdom. The expression itself is purely Hellenistic, and there are many phrases that support this; see Dibelius, *Briefe des Apostels Paulus*, at 2 Tim 1:10 and Titus 2:13. For 2 Clem., see 17:4.

12:2 In the introductory formula, the kingdom is called the βασιλεία of the κύριος. The designation of Christ as the king in the kingdom of God is rare; on βασιλεία τοῦ Χριστοῦ in the post-apostolic literature, however, see Col 1:13; Eph 5:5; Heb 1:8; 2 Tim 4:1, 18; 2 Pet 1:11. The quotation itself is from the Gospel of the Egyptians, and the person asking the question there was Salome; see the citation in Clement of Alexandria, *Strom.* 3.13.92 (p. 552 P): . . . διὰ τοῦτό τοι ὁ Κασσιανός φησι· πυνθανομένης τῆς Σαλώμης πότε γνωσθήσεται τὰ περὶ ὧν ἤρετο, ἔφη ὁ κύριος· ὅταν τὸ τῆς αἰσχύνης ἔνδυμα πατήσητε καὶ ὅταν γένηται τὰ δύο ἓν καὶ τὸ ἄρρεν μετὰ τῆς θηλείας οὔτε ἄρρεν οὔτε θῆλυ (reprint of the few preserved fragments of the Gospel of the Egyptians in Klostermann, *Apocrypha II*; Preuschen, *Antilegomena*, num. II, there, also the translation; for a translation and explanation, as well as the treatment of relevant questions and bibliography, see Hennecke, *Apokryphren*, 21–23 and *Handbuch*, 38–42). Since the gospel citation in 2 Clem. 12:2 certainly comes from the Gospel of the Egyptians, it can be assumed that the other gospel citations within the sermon are also taken from there, especially those in 4:5 and 5:2–4, but perhaps also others, which are close to the synoptic versions but which do not match them exactly. The attitude preserved in the Gospel of the Egyptians is strictly encratic. Also, our preacher reads asceticism out of the end of the citation.

12:3–5 On the exegetical method, including the formulas used, see 2:1–3.

12:3 ἑαυτοῖς = ἀλλήλοις, see Blaß-Debrunner, *Grammatik*, §287. Noteworthy is the optative εἴη after the subjunctive λαλῶμεν.

12:4 If the moralizing interpretation presented by the preacher here were correct, then the text would have to say at least καὶ τὸ ἔσω ὡς τὸ ἔξω.

12:5 τοῦτο is the last word preserved in A, the rest is missing; from here on only H and S serve as textual witnesses. οὐδέν instead of μηδέν is striking. μηδὲ φρονῇ is the reading in C; S inserts the additional phrase "if a sister sees a brother." Von Gebhardt and von Harnack have relieved the almost unbearable breviloquy of C by inserting ἤδε after μηδ'. Even then the ellipsis is to be filled with the sense ἀδελφὸν ἰδοῦσα.

12:6 still clearly belongs to the quotation according to its form, as is proven especially by πατρός μου. But whether 2 Clem. really still read these words in the Gospel of the Egyptians is questionable. He can draw the conclusion from the form of the citation himself. φησίν = "he means"; on this usage of φησίν, see Barn. 7:11; as well as Barn. 6:9; 10:3, 4, 5, 7; 11:8, 11; 12:2; etc. — The demand of 12:5—in light of which 8:4, 6 (τηρεῖν τὴν σάρκα ἀγνήν), as well as ch. 14 and 15:1 are to be considered—is striking and very strange. For the whole congregation the ideal of asceticism is established here, when, according to other demands and intimations of the sermon, the congregation has by no means outgrown the necessity of the fundamental admonition of the call to repentance. But the words of the homilist are sufficiently clear and do not bear any weakening in the sense that it is merely a question of the prohibition of fornication in deed, word, or thought. The ideal is perfect, sexual abstinence, just as Did. 6:1f presents it as the ideal of perfection. The demand in 2 Clem. is related to eschatology: the end will come when the entire congregation fulfills this ideal. Thus the end is postponed, and it is made dependent on the behavior of humanity, not on the will of God. Similar lines of thought can be traced within Judaism, especially, as here, in connection with the call to repentance. The end did not come, all calculations are deceptive. Then they said that all the dates have expired, now the matter depends only on repentance; or that the Messiah will come when all Israel repents together for one day. On the postponement of the end of the world, see Bousset, *Religion*, 284f and the citations from the rabbinic literature in Weber, *Jüdische Theologie*, 2:348f.

VI. Exhortation to Repentance (13:1—18:2)

Second Clement 13–18 contains exhortations to repentance. The demand to repent to finally fulfill the will of God, is taken up again for the third time and is held until the end of the sermon. From here on it is perfectly clear that the call to repentance does not only apply to the unconverted, but also to those who have been baptized and to the believers: they also are full of foolishness and wickedness (13:1), and they must be spoken to as well as the unconverted.

Translation

13:1 Therefore, brothers, let us finally repent and let us be sober to do good, for we are full of great foolishness and wickedness. Let us wipe away from us the former sins, and, repenting from our hearts, be delivered. And let us not be pleasing to others nor to one another, but also, as it corresponds to righteousness, let us be pleasing among those outside, so that the Name might not be blasphemed on our account. 2 For the Lord says, "My Name is constantly being blasphemed among the gentiles" and "Woe to the one on whose account my Name is blasphemed." "How is it blasphemed? Because you do not do what I want." 3 For if the gentiles hear the word of God from our mouths, they marvel at them as magnificent and great. But afterward, when they discover that our works are not worthy of the words we speak, they turn from there to blasphemy, saying it is a fable and a lie. 4 For if they hear from us that God says, "It is not grace when you love those who love you, but it is grace when you love your enemies and those who hate you"—when they hear this, they are amazed at the excessive goodness. But if they see that not only do we not love those who hate us, but we even do not love those who love (us), they laugh at us and the Name is blasphemed.

14:1 Therefore, brothers, if we do the will of our Father, God, we will be a part of the first church, the pneumatic church, which was established before the sun and the moon; but if you do not do the will of the Lord, we will be like the one of whom the Scripture says, "My house has become a den of thieves." Therefore, let us choose to belong to the church of life, so that we might be saved. 2 Now, I do not believe that you are ignorant that the living church is the body of Christ. For the Scripture says, "God created mankind male and female"; the male is Christ, and the woman is the church. Furthermore, the books of the Prophets and the Apostles say that the church did not only just come into existence but was there in the beginning. For it was spiritual, just as our Jesus (was); but in the last days he was revealed so that he could deliver us. 3 However, the church, which was spiritual, was revealed in the flesh of Christ, signifying to us that if any of us keep it in the flesh and do not stain it, he will receive it in the Holy Spirit. For this flesh is the antitype of the Spirit. Therefore, no one who stains the antitype will receive the archetype. Now, this is what is meant, brothers: Protect the flesh so that you might receive a portion in the Spirit. [4] But if we say that the flesh is the church and the Spirit is Christ, then whoever transgresses against the flesh has transgressed against the Church. Such a person will not have a portion in the Spirit, which is Christ. [5] The flesh can receive such a glorious and imperishable life, when the Spirit holds on tight to it: no one can testify to nor say what the Lord has prepared for his chosen ones.

[15:1] I do not believe that I have given poor advice about abstinence; whoever keeps it will not regret it, but will deliver not only himself but also me, who gave the advice. For it is no small reward to turn an erring and perishing soul to salvation. [2] For we are able to repay this reward to God who created us, if he who speaks and he who hears both speaks and hears with faith and love. [3] Now, let us remain righteous and holy in that which we have believed, so we can entreat God with confidence, who says, "Even while you are still speaking, I will say, 'See, I am here.'" [4] For this word is a sign of a great promise; for the Lord says that he is more ready to give than the supplicant (to ask). [5] Now, since we have a portion in such a great leniency, let us not envy one another, when we are partakers of such great good things. For as great a delight as these words bring to those who have done them, so great a condemnation do they bring to the disobedient.

[16:1] Therefore, brothers, since we have received no meager opportunity for repentance, let us, while we still have time, return to God, the one who called us, as long as we still possess the one who accepts us. [2] For if we say goodbye to these pleasures and conquer our souls, by not doing its evil desires, then we will be partakers of Jesus' mercy. [3] Recognize, however, that the day of judgment is already coming "like a burning oven and some of the heavens will melt" along with the entire earth like lead, which melts in the fire; and then the deeds of mankind done in secret and in public will be revealed. [4] Now, charity is as good as repentance over sins; "Love, however, covers a multitude of sins," prayer from a pure conscience delivers from death. Blessed is everyone who is found full of these things, for charity is a relief from sin. [17:1] Therefore, let us repent from our whole heart, so that not one of us perishes. For if we have commandments that we should also do this, to depart from idols and give instruction to catechumens, how much less may a soul that already knows

God perish? [2] Thus, let us help one another to bring even the weak to the good, so that we may all be saved, and let us convert and admonish one another. [3] And let us not only just now, when we are admonished by the presbyters, pretend to believe and be attentive, but also when we have gone home, let us remember the commandments of the Lord and not let earthly desires pull us away in the opposite direction, but let us come together more often and try to advance in the commandments of God, so that we may be gathered together with one mind for life. [4] For the Lord said, "I am coming to gather all nations, tribes, and tongues." With this he means the day of his appearance, when he comes to deliver us, each according to his works. [5] And the unbelievers will see his glory and his power and will be dismayed when they see his rule over the world with Jesus and will say, "Woe to us, that you were here and we did not know it and did not believe it and did not follow the presbyters, who preached to us of our salvation. "And their worm will not cease, and their fire will not be extinguished, and they will be a spectacle for all flesh." [6] With this he means on that day of judgment, when they will see those who were godless among us and who played a devious game with the commandments of Jesus Christ. [7] However, those who are righteous, who have acted well, who have withstood torments, and who have had little regard for the passions will praise their God when they see how those who have strayed and have denied Jesus by words or works will be tortured with terrible torments in eternal fire and will say, "There is hope for the one who has served God from his whole heart.

[18:1] And now let us belong to those who are thankful, to those who have served God and not to the godless, who will be judged. [2] For even I, who am a very poor sinner and have by no means escaped temptation, but am still in the midst of the devil's instruments, nevertheless strive to pursue righteousness so that I might be able to at least come close to it, because I fear the coming judgment.

Textual Notes

In 2 Clem. 13 the exhortation to repent is supported here by reference to the honor of the congregation.

13:1 οὖν in H, which is not translated in S, is rather noteworthy in its position after the vocative. It may have originated from the corruption of the word μου. τέκνα οὖν φωτὸς ἀληθείας in Ign. *Phld.* 2:1 is not a precise parallel, nor is ὑμεῖς οὖν τέκνα μου, which occurs frequently in the Testaments of the Twelve Patriarchs (cf. T. Zeb. 8:1; T. Asher 3:1; T. Jos. 11:1; T. Benj. 8:1). νήφειν in its figurative sense is explained by Hesychius with σωφρονεῖν βίῳ; see 1 Thess 5:6, 8; 2 Tim 4:5; 1 Pet 1:13; 4:7; 5:8; Ign. *Poly.* 2:3; Polycarp, *Phil.* 7:2; then the *Corpus Hermeticum* I 27 (Reitzenstein, *Poimandres*, 337): ὦ λαοί, ἄνδρες γηγενεῖς, οἱ μέθῃ καὶ ὕπνῳ ἑαυτοὺς ἐκδεδωκότες καὶ τῇ ἀγνωσίᾳ τοῦ θεοῦ, νήψατε, παύσασθε δὲ κραιπαλῶντες, θελγόμενοι ὕπνῳ ἀλόγῳ, but Epicharmos already has: νᾶφε καὶ μέμνασ᾽ ἀπιστεῖν (Diels, *Vorsokratiker I*, 123). On ἐξαλείψωμεν, see Acts 3:19 as well as Col 2:14. ἀνθρωπάρεσκοι is probably biblical Greek; see Ps 52:6: ὁ θεὸς διεσκόρπισεν ὀστᾶ ἀνθρωπαρέσκων, Ps. Sol. 4:8, 10, 21; Eph 6:6; Col 3:22; Apost. Const. II 21.1. Christians are servants of men when they live dissolutely and worldly lives, but how they are to be pleasing to the gentiles as true Christians is shown in what follows. ἑαυτοῖς = ἀλλήλοις as above in 12:3. On οἱ ἔξω, see 1 Cor 5:12f; 1 Thess 4:12; Col 4:5; 1 Clem. 47:7; etc. The term seems to have originated in Judaism, wherein the gentiles were labelled with it. The prologue to Sirach 5 says: οἱ ἐκτός, Josephus, *Ant.* XV 9.2 §316: οἱ ἔξωθεν (for an analogous usage in the Aristotelian language, cf. Gellius, *Noctes Atticae* XX 5.1). On the motif of community honor introduced here, see 1 Clem. 47:7. The ὄνομα is to be understood as the name of Christ, as is evident from the following citation. S has "the name of the Lord." How he is blasphemed is shown by the remarks that follow. On ὄνομα *par excellence*, without an addition, see Jas 2:7; Ign. *Eph.* 3:1; Tertullian, *Idol.* 14: *ne nomen blasphemetur*; etc.

13:2 The first citation comes from Isa 52:5: δι᾽ ὑμᾶς διὰ παντὸς τὸ ὄνομά μου βλασφημεῖται ἐν τοῖς ἔθνεσιν (cf. also Ezek 36:20, 23). The second citation, which extends all the way to βούλομαι and not just to ὄνομά μου, comes from an unknown source; see Ign. *Trall.* 8:2; Polycarp, *Phil.* 10:3; Apost. Const. I 10.1; III 5.6. At the beginning, οὐαὶ δι᾽ ὄν should be read in agreement with S, against the simple διό attested in H.

13:3 New Testament words, a saying of Jesus (13:4) is marked with the solemn designation λόγια τοῦ θεοῦ, otherwise used for Old Testament citations (Rom 3:2; Heb 5:12; 1 Clem. 19:1; 53:1); see also below at v. 4 (λέγει ὁ θεός) and 2 Clem. 2:4, where a word of the Lord is called γραφή.

13:4 The citation comes close to Luke 6:32, 35, but whether the preacher gets the saying from there is uncertain; see Did. 1:3: ποία γὰρ χάρις, ἐὰν ἀγαπᾶτε τοὺς ἀγαπῶντας ὑμᾶς . . . ὑμεῖς δὲ ἀγαπᾶτε τοὺς μισοῦντας ὑμᾶς καὶ οὐχ ἕξετε ἐχθρόν, also Justin, *1 Apol.* 15.9 has: ἀγαπᾶτε τοὺς μισοῦντας ὑμᾶς. — ἀγαθότης = χρηστότης, see 4:3: ἀγαθούς.

Second Clement 14: Woven into the speech about repentance and tightly connected to it is the theme of ἐγκράτεια, to keep the flesh pure, and it is grounded with peculiar speculations about Christ and the church. The speculations are not of the preacher's own creation but have come down to him from tradition; see οὐκ οἴομαι δὲ ὑμᾶς ἀγνοεῖν in v. 2. His own material is only the far-reaching, confusing assemblage of related, but still different, ideas and circles of ideas, and their enclosure in his reasoning which is directed at the justification of asceticism. The preacher shows that he is not very speculative, which does not prevent him from being proud of what he presents (cf. 15:1). In Paul and in the circle of the mysticism of the Pauline school (Ephesians), who followed after Paul, we can recognize the age and the spread of the ideas brought here. On the whole, see also the very opaque hints of Did. 11:11 and the explanation there.

14:1 ποιοῦντες τὸ θέλημα κτλ., on this preferred expression of the author, see 5:1; 6:7; 8:4; 9:11; 10:1. The church in mind here is the primitive church (πρώτη), pneumatic, pre-existent, the ἐκκλησία τῆς ζωῆς or ζῶσα (v. 2). It is therefore an invisible, illustrious, celestial entity, which came into being before the creation of the world. On this speculation, see already 2 Clem. 2:1: στεῖρα κτλ., see further the ἐκκλησία in Ephesians; Herm. Vis. I 1.6; 3.4; II 4.1; and Papias' interpretation, who interpreted the whole account of creation to Christ and the church according to the indication of Anastasius Sinaita; see Papias, *Frag.* 6 in the editions of the Apostolic Fathers by von Gebhardt and von Harnack-Zahn, and by Funk. The eon Ἐκκλησία of Valentine, which belongs to the first Ogdoas (Irenaeus, *Haer.* I 11.1) should also be mentioned here. On πνευματικῆς, imbued with divine *pneuma* and divine holiness, see vv. 2–3 and the κατοικτήριον τοῦ θεοῦ ἐν πνεύματι in Eph 2:22. ἐκκλησία τῆς ζωῆς, because it has life and imparts life. On ἐγενήθη κτλ., see Jer 7:11: μὴ σπήλαιον λῃστῶν ὁ οἶκός μου; (Mark 11:17 par.). The phrase ἐσόμεθα ἐκ τῆς γραφῆς κτλ. is an abbreviation for ἐσόμεθα ἐκ τούτων, περὶ ὧν λέγει ἡ γραφή.

14:2 From here on, the heavenly invisible church and also the visible church are placed in relation to Christ, the heavenly and visible one. ζῶσα is explained by ζωῆς; see also θεὸς ζῶν, λόγος ζῶν, λόγια ζῶντα, ὕδωρ ζῶν (John 4), etc. The image of the church as the body of Christ, which grew on the soil of mysticism, is already found in Paul (cf. Rom 12:5; 1 Cor 10:16f; 12:27; Col 1:18, 24; 2:19; 3:15) and is then further depicted and passed on in Ephesians (1:23; 2:16; 4:4, 12–16; 5:30). This is based on the mystical experience that in the experience of Christ one's own small being is united with the larger one of the church and is flooded by the all-pulsating stream of divine life. Immediately the preacher inserts another conception, that of the heavenly syzygy of the preexistent Christ with the preexistent church and the interpretation of the creation account in Gen 1:21 in light of this syzygy; see here especially Eph 5:30–32 (σῶμα and syzygy; the connecting factor is probably this: the

woman is the body of the man, they become one flesh in the union of love);
Did. 11:11, furthermore the syzygy of Valentinius in Irenaeus, *Haer.* I 11.1:
Ἄνθρωπος (the heavenly man) καὶ Ἐκκλησία; at last the above-mentioned
interpretation of the hexaemeron on Christ and the church as presented
by Papias; see then the notions, not mystical or gnostic but eschatologically
determined, of the church as the bride of the Messiah, the day of the parousia as the wedding day (cf. Rev 19:7, 9; 21:2, 9; 22:17; John 3:29; and in the
Lord's discourses at Mark 2:19; Matt 22:1–10; 25:1–13; Luke 12:36). In the
following, the text fluctuates: H has ὅτι, S has ἔτι, after βιβλία S adds "of the
prophets"; since the predicate is missing in the sentence, λέγουσιν needs to
be added at the end with S. τὰ βιβλία καὶ οἱ ἀπόστολοι is an important phrase
in the history of the canon. The books (of the prophets) are the Old Testament authorities, to which then still, namely with the reading βιβλία without
any other qualification, the gospels are added, in which the Lord speaks (cf.
2 Clem. 2:4). On the other hand, the apostles do not exist yet among the holy
"books." For passages of the OT which the preacher might have in mind, in
addition to Gen 1f, see Ps 44, the wedding song, which Justin, *Dial.* 63.4f
already interprets with reference to Christ and the church. Among the "apostles" especially the above-mentioned passages from Ephesians and Revelation
come into consideration. ἄνωθεν = from the beginning on; see Luke 1:3 and
Acts 26:5. ἐφανεφώθη δέ κτλ. can also be translated: "but it was revealed . . . ,"
"so it might save us," and the sentence structure speaks in favor of this at first.
But otherwise the preacher always says σώζειν of Christ, and hereafter he only
seems to speak of the φανεῖσθαι of the church: ἡ ἐκκλησία . . . ἐφανερώθη. . . .
On ἐπ' ἐσχάτων τῶν ἡμερῶν, see Gen 49:1; Deut 4:30; Dan 2:28 (LXX and
Theodotion); 10:14 (Theodotion); Hos 3:5; Mic 4:1; as well as 2 Pet 3:3.

14:3 The church appears in the flesh of Christ, because the earthly
church is the σῶμα of Christ. This seems to interpret the strange statement,
which is immediately turned ascetic-practical; on τηρεῖν κτλ., see 8:4; 12:5.
One preserves the church in the flesh by keeping one's own flesh pure. The
possession of the Spirit here and in the following is conceived of as future; it
is the result and reward of asceticism, see Weinel, *Wirkungen*, 146f, 224–26.
ἀπολήψεται αὐτήν means: he will be received in it at the future consumma-
tion. ἀντίτυπος and αὐθεντικόν mean "copy" and "autograph" respectively.
The view Platonizes to some extent, but only on the surface. That the flesh
is the antitype of the Spirit is a very strange view, but see 2 Clem. 14:4 and
1 Cor 6:18–20. On ἀντίτυπος, see Heb 9:24; 1 Pet 3:21. On αὐθεντικόν, Passow, *Handwörterbuch* does not record the meaning given here; see Georges,
Handwörterbuch, under *authenticus*; Tert. *De Monogamia* 11: *sciamus plane
non sic esse in Graeco authentico*; Digesta XXVIII 3.12: *exemplo* (copy)
quidem aperto nondum apertum est testamentum; quod si authenticum

(original) *patefactum est totum, apertum*; Pseudo-Ignatius, *Phild.* 8:2: αὐθέντικον . . . ἀρχεῖον (in a part of the tradition).

14:4 Here it becomes somewhat clear why the σάρξ is spoken of so highly; on the matter, see above at 14:2. The confusion in thought is significant here. As to the interposition of Christ and the *pneuma*, see already 2 Cor 3:11 and above at 2 Clem. 9:5.

14:5 ἃ ἡτοίμασεν κτλ. is an allusion to 1 Cor 2:9; see above at 11:7.

15:1 Note the preacher's pride in his counsel; he wishes to save errant and lost souls. ἥν by itself can also be related to συμβουλία, but ποιεῖν, which is next to both accusatives, would then take on a double meaning: to give counsel and to take counsel. On ἑαυτὸν σώσει κἀμέ, see 19:1; 1 Tim 4:16; Ezek 3:21: σὺ δὲ ἐὰν διαστείλῃ τῷ δικαίῳ τοῦ μὴ ἁμαρτεῖν καὶ αὐτὸς μὴ ἁμάρτῃ, ὁ δίκαιος ζωῇ ζήσεται, ὅτι διεστείλω αὐτῷ· καὶ σὺ τὴν σεαυτοῦ ψυχὴν ῥύσῃ. Hippolytus, *Antichr.* 2 (ed. Achelis, *Hippolytus*, 5): ὅπως γένηται ἀμφοτέροις κοινὴ ὠφέλεια, τῷ μὲν λέγοντι τὸ διὰ μνήμης κρατήσαντι ὀρθῶς ἐκθέσθαι τὰ προκείμενα, τῷ δὲ ἀκούοντι τὸ ἐπιστῆσαι τὸν νοῦν πρὸς τὰ λεγόμενα. On μισθὸς γὰρ οὐκ ἔστι κτλ., see Jas 5:20.

15:2 ἀντιμισθία and μισθός to God or to Christ (cf. 1:3, 5; 3:3; 9:7f). It is striking that it is not God as savior who is mentioned here, but rather God as creator. λέγων καὶ ἀκούων, it is a sermon and even when it is repeated it is read aloud; see 17:3; 19:1; as well as Rev 1:3 and Dionysius of Corinth in Eusebius, *Hist. eccl.* 4.23.11. πίστις καὶ ἀγάπη, mutual trust and love must prevail if the word is to work.

15:3 ἐμμείνωμεν κτλ., after that, only the preservation of the grace already received would be necessary, but not repentance; see τηρεῖν τὴν σφραγῖδα in 8:6. The preacher wavers in his assessment; see Windisch, *Taufe und Sünde*, 334f. On δίκαιοι καὶ ὅσιοι, see 5:6, also the comments at 1:3. The quotation comes from Isa 58:9: ἔτι λαλοῦντός σου ἐρεῖ· ἰδοὺ πάρειμι, see also Isa 65:24: ἔτι λαλούντων αὐτῶν ἐρῶ· τί ἐστιν, see also Barn. 3:5.

15:5 ἑαυτοῖς = ἀλλήλοις, as in 12:3; 13:1; 17:2; etc.

16:1 On the exhortation to repent while time remains, see 8:1–3; 9:7. On οὐ μικράν, see 15:1. On ἀφορμὴν λαβόντες, see Rom 7:8, 11. God is the one who calls, as in 11:1.

16:2 On the rare and on the whole, late word ἡδυπάθεια, see 2 Clem. 17:7, as well as Xenophon, *Cyr.* VII 5.74: εἰ μὲν τρεψόμεθα ἐπὶ ῥᾳδιουργίαν καὶ τὴν τῶν κακῶν ἀνθρώπων ἡδυπάθειαν, οἳ νομίζουσι τὸ μὲν πονεῖν ἀθλιώτατον, τὸ δὲ ἀπόνως βιοτεύειν ἡδυπάθειαν, 4 Macc 2:2, 4: διανοίᾳ περιεκράτησεν τῆς ἡδυπαθείας and τὴν τῆς ἡδυπαθείας οἰστρηλασιαν ἐπικρατεῖν, as well as Marcus Aurelius, *In semet ipsum* X 33: οἷόν ἐστι τοῖς ἡδυπαθοῦσιν ἡ τρυφή.

16:3 Malachi 4:1: διότι ἰδοὺ ἡμέρα ἔρχεται καιομένη ὡς κλίβανος καὶ φλέξει αὐτούς. On the teaching of the burning of the world, see the excursus at 2 Pet 3:10 in Knopf, *Briefe Petri und Judä*, as well as the comments at 2 Pet 3:7). That only some of the heavens will burn, then of course the lower ones, cannot be proven with parallels. Lightfoot would like to read [αἱ] δυνάμεις instead of τινες, with reference to Isa 34:4: καὶ τακήσονται πᾶσαι αἱ δυνάμεις τῶν οὐρανῶν. The form μόλιβος instead of μόλυβδος is Hellenistic and Byzantine (cf. Exod 15:10; Num 31:22; Job 19:24; etc.). In a number of passages in the LXX, the tradition fluctuates between μόλιβος, μόλυβος, μόλιβδος, and μόλυβδος (cf. also Sophocles, *Greek Lexicon*, s.v.). In modern Greek, μολίβι is the vernacular, whereas μόλυβδος is the artificially archaic form of the written language.

16:4 links up with ἔργα from the preceding: the "good works" are enumerated. Prayer, fasting, almsgiving are the good works of Judaism, the pillars of its piety, morality, and congregationalism; see Bousset, *Religion*, 202–9 and on the preferential position of almsgiving also pp. 162f; see further Bauer, *Die Evangelien*, at Matt 6:1–18. The preacher has Tob 12:8f in mind: ἀγαθὸν προσευχὴ μετὰ νηστείας καὶ ἐλεημοσύνης καὶ δικαιοσύνης . . . καλὸν ποιῆσαι ἐλεημοσύνην ἢ θησαυρίσαι χρυσίον. ⁹ ἐλεημοσύνη ἐκ θανάτου ῥύεται καὶ αὕτη ἀποκαθαριεῖ πᾶσαν ἁμαρτίαν. On ἀγάπη δὲ καλύπτει πλῆθος ἁμαρτιῶν, see 1 Pet 4:8 and the comments at 1 Clem. 49:4. Second Clement, like 1 Peter, understands the word as closely related to the sin-redeeming power of almsgiving, in the sense of Jewish and early Christian piety. On καλύπτει πλῆθος ἁμαρτιῶν, see Jas 5:20. On ἐκ καλῆς συνειδήσεως see Heb 13:18, and on praying with a good conscience see Did. 4:14; Barn. 19:12; and also 1 Clem. 34:7; 41:1. It is striking, and stands in contradiction to the foregoing, that greater success is attributed to prayer than to alms; the former only covers a multitude of sins, whereas the latter saves from death. On κούφισμα ἁμαρτίας, see 1 Esd 8:83: σύ, κύριε, ὁ κουφίσας τὰς ἁμαρτίας ἡμῶν.

Second Clement 17f continues the call to repentance. The author expresses the realization that even Christians are still sinners with great clarity.

17:1 On μετανοήσωμεν ἐξ ὅλης καρδίας, see 8:2; 19:1; as well as 9:8. παραπόλλυσθαι already appears in Aristophanes, *Vesp.* 1228: τουτὶ σὺ δράσεις; παραπολεῖ βοώμενος, then frequently in the authors of the Hellenistic age; see Lucian, *Nigr.* 13: δέδοικε μὴ παραπόληται μεταξὺ λουόμενος. The words ἐντολὰς ἔχομεν can be related to the gospel tradition such as Matt 28:19f or Mark 16:15. However, ἀπὸ τῶν εἰδώλων ἀποσπᾶν and κατηχεῖν do not appear there. The early Christian text which most clearly articulates these commandments is the *Kerygma Petri* (Klostermann, *Apocrypha*; Preuschen, *Antilegomena*; Henecke, *Apokryphen*). ἵνα . . . πράσσωμεν is the reading in S; H simply has πράσσομεν. If H is followed, then it would be best to place the words καὶ τοῦτο πράσσομεν in parentheses.

17:2 ἑαυτοῖς = ἀλλήλοις, as already often in the preceding (cf. 15:5; etc.). Immediately afterward comes ἐπιστρέψωμεν ἀλλήλους. The ἀσθενοῦντες are of course members of the congregation, souls which already recognize God. On σωθῶμεν ἅπαντες, see 1 Clem. 2:4. ἐπιστρέψωμεν and νουθετήσωμεν can of course also be dependent on ὅπως, though not well.

17:3 We get a glimpse into the ancient Christian worship service; in the gathering of the congregation on Sunday, the sermon is held (cf. 15:1f and 19:1). On νουθετεῖσθαι ἡμᾶς ὑπὸ τῶν πρεσβυτέρων, see Justin, *1 Apol.* 67.4: ὁ προεστὼς διὰ λόγου τὴν νουθεσίαν καὶ πρόκλησιν τῆς τῶν καλῶν τούτων μιμήσεων ποιεῖται. The πρεσβύτεροι appear only here and in v. 5 within the homily; both pieces of data show the same thing: The presbyters are responsible for the proclamation, especially for the worship service; the homily, however, does not mention the other responsibilities they might have. The author himself belongs to the presbyters, despite the hortatory subjunctive in this passage. Otherwise, he must have been a teacher or a lector within the congregation. ἀντιπαρέλκεσθαι does not appear as of yet in the lexica; it seems to be a *hapaxlegomenon.* On κοσμικῶν ἐπιθυμιῶν, see Titus 2:12; in the life of the home and everyday life, the lure of the world entices Christians, and ἐπιθυμίαι by no means refers only to the field of sensuality. On the exhortation to come into the worship service of the congregation, see Ignatius, *Eph.* 13:1: σπουδάζετε οὖν πυκνότερον συνέρχεσθαι εἰς εὐχαριστίαν θεοῦ καὶ εἰς δόξαν. ὅταν γὰρ πυκνῶς ἐπὶ τὸ αὐτὸ γίνεσθε, καθαιροῦνται αἱ δυνάμεις τοῦ σατανᾶ, καὶ λύεται ὁ ὄλεθρος αὐτοῦ ἐν τῇ ὁμοίᾳ ὑμῶν τῆς πίστεως κτλ. Ignatius, *Poly.* 4:2: πυκνότερον συναγωγαὶ γινέσθωσαν· ἐξ ὀνόματος πάντας ζήτει. See also Heb 10:25; Barn. 4:10; Herm. *Sim.* IX 26.3; Apost. Const. II 59 and 60. πυκνότερον is not about increasing congregational meetings, but about having the members of the church come to the appointed meetings in as large numbers as possible. On προσερχόμενοι (S has προσευχόμενοι), supplement with something like τῇ συναγωγῇ ἡμῶν, and note the alliteration. On τὸ αὐτὸ φρονοῦντες, see the above-mentioned passage at Ign. *Eph.* 13 with its praise of the power that lies in the unanimously gathered church.

17:4 Both in 17:3 and here in v. 4, κύριος can refer to God or Christ. The preexistent Christ can speak in the prophet (3:5); on the other hand, the ἐπιφάνεια of God is also spoken of in 12:1. The following also does not yield a decision, since it is not clear whether ἐν τῷ Ἰησοῦ in v. 5 introduces a new person. The citation in v. 4 comes from Isa 66:18: ἔρχομαι συναγαγεῖν πάντα τὰ ἔθνη καὶ τὰς γλώσσας, the φυλαὶ καὶ γλῶσσαι come from Daniel, where they appear frequently; see also Dan 3:2 (LXX): ἐπισυναγαγεῖν πάντα τὰ ἔθνη καὶ φυλὰς καὶ γλώσσας (cf. also Rev 11:9; 14:6). On the content, see also Matt 24:30f; 25:32. On the interpretive formula τοῦτο δὲ λέγει, see 8:6; on ἐπιφάνεια, see 12:1. λυτρώσεται fits poorly in the context. A word like κρινεῖ would be expected; see after all Eph 4:30; Luke 21:28; Rom 8:23. On ἕκαστον κατὰ τὰ ἔργα αὐτοῦ, the familiar Jewish norm of retribution on the day of judgment, see Ps 61:13; Prov 24:12; as well as Job 34:11; Jer 17:10; 39:19; Rom 2:6; Matt 16:27.

17:5 καὶ ὄψονται τὴν δόξαν αὐτοῦ comes from the above-cited Isa 66:18, where following γλώσσας is καὶ ἥξουσιν καὶ ὄψονται τὴν δόξαν μου (cf. then Matt 24:30; 25:31; Rev 1:7). On ξενισθήσονται, see 1 Pet 4:4, 12; on βασίλειον above, see 6:9. The statement does not refer to unbelieving pagans, but to the unfaithful, unbelieving Christians who heard the presbyters' preaching but did not believe it; see 17:6: τοὺς ἐν ἡμῖν ἀσεβήσαντας κτλ. — ἐν τῷ Ἰησοῦ = in the hand of Jesus. On σὺ ἧς, see the absolute I saying ἐγώ εἰμι in John 8:24, 28; 18:5–8. On the presbyters and their sermon, see the comments at 2 Clem. 17:3. ὁ σκώληξ αὐτῶν κτλ. comes from Isa 66:24; the passage is cited without an introductory formula because it was already quoted above at 7:6 (cf. also Mark 9:44–48).

17:6 τὴν ἡμέραν reaches back to τὴν ἡμέραν in v. 4. On ὄψονται, the subject should be taken as generally as possible: man, all men. S reads ἡμῖν; H has ὑμῖν. On παραλογίζεται "cheat," see Jas 1:22; Col 2:4.

17:7 εὐπραγεῖν means "act well," and not "be happy"; this meaning required here is not recorded in the lexica; see, however, εὐπραγία in Passow, *Handwörterbuch*. On ὑπομείναντες τὰς βασάνους, see Heb 10:32f; on ἡδυπαθείας, see above at 16:2. The ἀστοχήσαντας, as what follows immediately shows, were once Christians; on the word, see 1 Tim 1:6; 6:21; 2 Tim 2:18; Did. 15:3; it means "to miss the mark"; see also Plutarch, *Galba* 16: βουλόμενος δὲ τῆς περὶ τὰς δωρεὰς ἀμετρίας καὶ πολυτελείας τοῦ Νέρωνος ἀποδεικνύναι μεγάλην μεταβολὴν ἀστοχεῖν ἐδόκει τοῦ πρέποντος. On ἀρνησαμένους, which presupposes the oppression of Christians, see 5:1ff as well as 3:2f and 4:1f. On πυρὶ ἀσβέστῳ, see Matt 3:12 and Mark 9:43; on δόξαν διδόναι, see Rev 4:9; 11:13; 14:7; etc. S reads διδόντες; H δόντες. — The description of the day of judgment and the consternation of the wicked, the triumph of the righteous, with citation of the speeches of the one and the other, has been at all times a favorite τόπος of congregational paraenesis. On 2 Clem. 17:5ff see especially Wis 5:1–5: τότε στήσεται ἐν παρρησίᾳ πολλῇ ὁ δίκαιος κατὰ πρόσωπον τῶν θλιψάντων αὐτὸν καὶ τῶν ἀθετούντων τοὺς πόνους αὐτοῦ. ἰδόντες ταραχθήσονται φόβῳ δεινῷ, καὶ ἐκστήσονται ἐπὶ τῷ παραδόξῳ τῆς σωτηρίας. ἐροῦσιν ἐν ἑαυτοῖς μετανοοῦντες καὶ διὰ στενοχωρίαν πνεύματος στενάξουσιν. Οὗτος ἦν ὃν ἔσχομέν ποτε εἰς γέλωτα καὶ εἰς παραβολὴν ὀνειδισμοῦ, οἱ ἄφρονες· τὸν βίον αὐτοῦ ἐλογισάμεθα μανίαν καὶ τὴν τελευτὴν αὐτοῦ ἄτιμον· πῶς κατελογίσθη ἐν υἱοῖς θεοῦ, καὶ ἐν ἁγίοις ὁ κλῆρος αὐτοῦ ἐστιν; κτλ. Barnabas 7:9: . . . ὄψονται αὐτὸν τότε τῇ ἡμέρᾳ . . . καὶ ἐροῦσιν· Οὐχ οὗτός ἐστιν ὅν ποτε ἡμεῖς ἐσταυρώσαμεν ἐξουθενήσαντες καὶ κατακεντήσαντες καὶ ἐμπτύσαντες; ἀληθῶς οὗτος ἦν ὁ τότε λέγων ἑαυτὸν υἱὸν τοῦ θεοῦ εἶναι. And especially passionate is Tertullian, *Spect.* 30: *Quale autem spectaculum in proximo est adventus domini iam indubitati iam superbi, iam triumphantis! . . . Quae tunc spectaculi latitudo! quid admirer? quid rideam? ubi gaudeam? ubi exultem . . . malim ad eos potius conspectum insatiabilem conferre, qui in dominum desaevierunt. Hic est ille, dicam, fabri aut quaestuariae filius, sabbathi destructor, Samarites et daemonium habens. hic est, quem a Juda redimistis . . . hic est, quem clam discentes subripuerunt, ut resurrexisse dicatur* etc.

18:1 εὐχαριστούντων takes δόξαν διδόντες up again; δεδουλευκότων τῷ θεῷ the τῷ δεδουλευκότι θεῷ of the preceding. The κρινόμενοι ἀσεβεῖς are, according to the preceding, false Christians.

18:2 The preacher's confession of sin is strong and striking, but not too surprising after the preceding exhortations to repentance, all of which were addressed to believers and to the baptized. "He makes a personal confession of his own imperfection; in him they shall now learn how a poor sinner must be in mind and be tuned"[2] (Windisch, *Taufe und Sünde*, 337). πανθαμάρτωλος (missing in most of the lexica) describes the one who is entirely and only a sinner, and nothing more. Instead of γεύγων in H, S has φυγών. The word ὄργανον "tool" also denotes machines, especially war machines, which would fit well here in context. On δικαιοσύνην διώκειν, see 1 Tim 6:11; 2 Tim 2:22. On κἄν "if at all possible, in any case," see Ign. *Eph* 10:1: κἄν ἐκ τῶν ἔργων. On ἐγγὺς αὐτῆς γενέσθαι, see 7:3 as well as Phil 3:12.

VII. Conclusion: Repentance, Suffering, Future Glory, and a Doxology (19:1—20:5)

Second Clement 19–20 contains the conclusion of the work. The author again refers to what has preceded (chs. 13–18), repentance (19:1–3), emphasizes the necessity of suffering for the righteous one but also one's own future glory (19:3—20:4), and then concludes the book with a doxology. On the attempt to distinguish chs. 19 and 20 from what precedes them, see Pauli, "Zweiten," 321–29 and more determined still Schüßler, "Zweiten," 1–13.

---

2. TN: The German "und gestimmt sein muß" is figurative language meaning "brough into tune" like an instrument before a concert.

Translation

^{19:1} So then, brothers and sisters, after the God of truth has spoken, I am reading to you an exhortation that you pay attention to what is written, so that you may save both yourselves and the one who reads in your midst. For as a reward I ask of you that you might repent with all your heart and thus obtain salvation and life. For if we do that, we will set a goal for all the younger ones who want to strive for piety and for the goodness of God. ² And let us not like fools consider it evil and be angry when someone admonishes us and turns away from unrighteousness to righteousness. For sometimes we do not even know that we are doing evil, because of the doubt and unbelief that is in our soul, and we are darkened in mind by empty desires. ³ So then let us do righteousness, that we may be saved for the end. Blessed are those who obey these commandments. Even if they suffer evil in this world for a short time, they will reap the immortal fruit of the resurrection. ⁴ So then may the pious one not be grieved if he endures pain in the present: a blessed time awaits him. He will have bliss above with the fathers until sorrowless eternity.

^{20:1} But also do not let this distress your minds, that we see how the unrighteous are rich and the servants of God are oppressed. ² Let us believe, then, brothers and sisters, that we pass the test of the living God in the contest, and we exercise ourselves in the present life, that we may be crowned in the life to come. ³ None of the righteous has obtained the fruit quickly but waits for it. ⁴ For if God repaid the wages of the righteous instantly, we would immediately engage in commerce and not godliness. For we would have only the appearance of the righteous one, whereas we would not pursue what is godly but what is profitable. For this reason, divine judgment harms the spirit that is not upright and weighs it down with chains. ⁵ To the only invisible God, the Father of truth, who sent to us from himself the savior and guide of immortality, through whom he also made known to us the truth and heavenly life, to him be the glory forever and ever. Amen.

Textual Notes

19:1 The form of address ἀδελφοὶ καὶ ἀδελφαί only occurs again in 20:2. On θεὸς τῆς ἀληθείας, see 3:1; 20:5. The God of truth has spoken in the scriptural reading which the congregation heard before the sermon, and with which the sermon ties in (εἰς τὸ προσέχειν τοῖς γεγραμμένοις). It is read from the manuscript. The natural linking of Scripture reading and the sermon was adopted by the church from the synagogue (Schürer, *Geschichte*, 2:451–56; Luke 4:20f; Acts 13:15). It was certainly in use in the churches of the apostolic era, although we lack explicit source material. First Corinthians 14:26 does not fully enumerate the parts of the worship service. For the later churches, see 1 Tim 4:13: πρόσεχε τῇ ἀναγνώσει, τῇ παρακλήσει, τῇ διδασκαλίᾳ, Justin, *1 Apol.* 67.3f: καὶ τῇ τοῦ ἡλίου λεγομένῃ ἡμέρᾳ πάντων κατὰ πόλεις ἢ ἀγροὺς μενόντων ἐπὶ τὸ αὐτὸ συνέλευσις γίνεται, καὶ τὰ ἀπομνημονεύματα τῶν ἀποστόλων ἢ τὰ συγγράμματα τῶν προφητῶν ἀναγινώσκεται, μέχρις ἐγχωρεῖ. εἶτα παυσαμένου τοῦ ἀναγινώσκοντος ὁ προεστὼς διὰ λόγου τὴν νουθεσίαν καὶ πρόκλησιν τῆς τῶν καλῶν τούτων μιμήσεως ποιεῖται, quite similarly in *Apost. Const.* II 54.1: μετὰ τὴν ἀνάγνωσιν καὶ τὴν ψαλμῳδίαν καὶ τὴν ἐπὶ ταῖς γραφαῖς διδασκαλίαν. See also Tertullian, *Apol.* 39 and *An.* 9. On an attempt to determine the Scripture lesson preceding our sermon (Isa 54–66), see Knopf, "Anagnose," 266–79 and on the other hand Schüßler, "Zweiten," 1–13. The sermon was read out, not extemporaneously delivered, which is different than Origen according to Eusebius, *Hist. eccl.* 6.36.1. On ἵνα καὶ ἑαυτοὺς σώσητε κτλ., see 15:1f. Instead of σκοπόν (S), which is generally assumed by the editors, and which von Gebhardt already conjected, read κόπον with H. On the content, see *Apost. Const.* II 6.7: σκοποὺς γὰρ εἶναι δεῖ ὑμᾶς τῷ τοὺς ἐπισκόπους, ὅτι καὶ ὑμεῖς σκοπὸν ἔχετε τὸν Χριστόν. καὶ ὑμεῖς οὖν γίνεσθε σκοποὶ ἀγαθοὶ τῷ λαῷ τοῦ θεοῦ, Polybius VII 8.9: σκοπὸν προέθηκε κάλλιστον. The νέοι are not the catechumen, but the newly converted and the congregational members who are young in years; see 1 Clem. 1:3; 21:6; *Apost. Const.* II 10.1: The unworthy bishop is αἴτιος σκανδάλου πολλοῖς νεοφύτοις καὶ κατηχουμένοις . . . ἔτι δὲ νέοις καὶ νέαις τῇ ἡλικίᾳ.

19:2 On ἀγανακτῶμεν κτλ., see 1 Clem. 56:2. The article before ἄσοφοι as above at 1:2, if one follows the reading of AH and Wis 5:4, if one interpolates οἱ ἄφρονες, τὸν βίον αὐτοῦ ἐλογισάμεθα μανίαν, Origen, *Or.* 5: ἀπολειπόμεθα οἱ ἄνθρωποι πλεῖον τοῦ θεοῦ. Instead of ἐνίοτε in S, read ἔνια attested in H. On διψυχίαν καὶ ἀπιστίαν, see the statements in 2 Clem. 11 and then 17:5, where the ἄπιστοι are the baptized. The tireless fighter against διψυχία within the congregation is Hermas. Doubtfulness and unbelief dull the conscience just as much as giving in to idle desires. On ἐσκοτίσμεθα τὴν διάνοιαν, see Rom 1:21: ἐσκοτίσθη ἡ ἀσύνετος αὐτῶν καρδία and especially Eph 4:18: ἐσκοτωμένοι τῇ διανοίᾳ, see further 1 Clem. 36:2 and 2 Clem. 1:6.

19:3–4 κἂν . . . κακοπαθήσωσιν ἐν τῷ κόσμῳ τούτῳ in v. 3 and ἐὰν ἐπὶ τοῖς νῦν χρόνοις ταλαιπωρῇ in v. 4: The construction of these clauses deals with the sufferings of persecution and oppression, which affect the Christians as such. On these sufferings, which can extend to the point of martyrdom, see above at 4:4 and 5f. Here, as there, consolation is found in reference to the blessed future which awaits the faithful and the proven.

19:3 On ὀλίγον χρόνον, see 1 Pet 1:6: ὀλίγον ἄρτι, εἰ δέον, λυπηθέντες and 5:10: ὀλίγον παθόντας. Pseudo-Ignatius, *Mar. Cassob.* 4.3: ὁ γὰρ παρὼν πόνος ὀλίγος, ὁ δὲ προσδοκώμενος μισθὸς πολύς. On καρπὸν τρυγήσουσι, see Hos 10:12: σπείρατε ἑαυτοῖς εἰς δικαιοσύνην, τρυγήσατε εἰς καρπὸν ζωῆς. The image of the fruit is used differently here and in 20:3 than it is in 1:3: there it is the good deed that is offered by man worthy of repentance; here, how-ever, it is eschatologically the final yield of the pious life, offered by God to the person for their enjoyment. On the epithet ἀθάνατος, which is rare in early Christian texts and in the LXX, see 1 Clem. 36:2: ἀθανάτου γνώσεως, Wis 1:15: δικαιοσύνη γὰρ ἀθάνατός ἐστιν.

19:4 ἄνω, above in heaven, comes from a different eschatology than the ἀνάστασις just used. Here, the πατέρες are, nevertheless, the OT pious, although at the time of our sermon several generations of Christians had already passed away. ἀλύπητος is a reference back to λυπείσθω; the word, which is not frequent, certainly has a passive sense here, and is stronger than ἄλυπος: "without grief," not affected by sorrow; see Sophocles, *Trach.* 168: τὸ λοιπὸν ἤδη ζῆν ἀλυπήτῳ βίῳ. Second Clement 19:4 is tacitly used by Hippoly-tus in *Univ.*; de Lagarde, *Clementia*, p. 69, line 10ff: ἡ τῶν πατέρων δικαίων τε ὁρωμένη ὄψις πάντοτε μειδᾷ, ἀναμενόντων τὴν μετὰ τοῦτο τὸ χωρίον ἀνάπαυσιν καὶ αἰωνίαν ἀναβίωσιν ἐν οὐρανῷ ... line 22ff (of the unjust) ἀλλὰ καὶ οὗτοι τὸν τῶν πατέρων χορὸν καὶ τοὺς δικαίους ὁρῶσι, καὶ ἐπ' αὐτῷ τούτῳ κολαζόμενοι ... p. 70, line 4ff: μὴ ἀπιστήσητε ὡς καὶ τὸ σῶμα ἐκ τῶν αὐτῶν στοιχείων σύνθετον γενόμενον δυνατὸς ὁ θεὸς ἀναβιώσας ἀθάνατον ποιεῖν.

Second Clement 20 is closely related to what we have just discussed, the suffering of Christians for the sake of their faith. But the problem broadens: it is the sufferings of the righteous in general, more precisely the depressed social position of the righteous in relation to the rich wicked. The question of theodicy, which arises in the face of the disproportion of external conditions and moral worthiness, is already present in the religion of the prophets (cf. Ps 72). In post-exilic Judaism, the poor are often those who please God and the rich are the ones hated by him, although on the other hand Israel at all times of its history tended to consider wealth as a gift and a reward from God (cf. Ps 36). Even the book of Job ends with the suffering righteous becoming rich again. Very early and very acutely formulated, as it is here, the question appears again in Greek literature; see Solon, *Frag.* 15 in Bergk, *Poetae*: πολλοὶ γὰρ πλουτεῦσι κακοί, ἀγαθοὶ δὲ πένονται and much more passionately in Theognis (Bergk, *Poetae*) 743–52: καὶ τοῦτ', ἀθανάτων βασιλεῦ, πῶς ἐστι δίκαιον, Ἔργων ὅστις ἀνὴρ ἐκτὸς ἐὼς ἀδίκων, Μή τιν' ὑπερβασίην κατέχων μηδ' ὅρκον ἀλιτρόν, Ἀλλὰ δίκαιος ἐών, μὴ τὰ δίκαια πάθῃ; Τίς δή κεν βροτὸς ἄλλος, ὁρῶν πρὸς τοῦτον, ἔπειτα Ἄζοιτ' ἀθανάτους, καὶ τίνα θυμὸν ἔχων, Ὁππότ' ἀνὴρ ἄδικος καὶ ἀτάσθαλος, οὔτε τευ ἀνδρός Οὔτε τευ ἀθανάτων μῆνιν ἀλευόμενος Ὑβρίζῃ πλούτῳ κεκορημένος, οἱ δὲ δίκαιοι Τρύχονται χαλεπῇ τειρόμενοι πενίῃ; — The Stoics had already dealt with the problem since the time of Chrysippus; for an example see the younger Stoics such as Seneca's *De providentia* and Epictetus' *Dissert.* II 17 (περὶ προνοίας) with the formulation of the problem thus: ὁ ἄδικος πλέον ἔχει. The congregation for whom the sermon is intended must have been composed very largely of members of the lower classes; see Knopf, *Nachapostolisches Zeitalter*, 64–70; Deissmann, *Urchristentum*. — Second Clement 20:1, 3, 4 is cited in the *Sacra Parallela*, with minor variants; for the text, see Lightfoot, *Clement*, 1:193f; Holl, *Epiphanius*, 2.

20:2 The preacher solves the question with images and thoughts taken from the Stoics and with the Judeo-Christian transcendental belief in retribution. Christian is the θεὸς ζῶν and the βίος μέλλων. Stoic is the image of competition and gymnastics (cf. above at 7:1). Stoic, however, is also the thought that sufferings possess an educating and strengthening power and thus fit into the divine plan of the world. God is a father who will not spare his sons labor, toil, sweat, and pain in order to educate them, for in the midst of struggle the virtue of the wise man proves itself; see Seneca, *Prov.* 2; *Ep.* 64.4; Marcus Aurelius IV 49; Epictetus, *Diat.* I 6.30–43; 24.1 (αἱ περιστάσεις εἰσὶν αἱ τοὺς ἄνδρας δεικνύουσαι. λοιπὸν ὅταν ἐμπέσῃ περίστασις, μέμνησο ὅτι ὁ θεὸς ὡς ἀλείπτης τραχεῖ νεανίσκῳ συνβέβληκεν. — Ἰνατί; φησιν. — Ἵνα Ὀλυμπιονίκης γένῃ· δίχα δ' ἱδρῶτος οὐ γίνεται). On the connection between πεῖραν ἀθλεῖν and the transitive use of ἀθλεῖν, see Plutarch, *Demetr.* 5 (on Ptolemaios I): ἀνδρὶ ... ἐκ τῆς Ἀλεξάνδρου παλαίστρας ἠθληκότι πολλοὺς καὶ μεγάλους καθ' αὑτὸν ἀγῶνος.

20:4 On ἐμπορίαν, see 1 Tim 6:5: πορισμὸν εἶναι τὴν εὐσέβειαν, Did. 12:5: χριστέμπορος, Augustine, *Civ.* I 8: *si omnibus eas petentibus daret* (sc. *deus res secundas) non nisi propter talia praemia serriendum illi esse arbitraremur, nec pios nos faceret talis servitus sed potius cupidos et araros.* — On the seldom used θεοσέβεια in early Christian literature, see 1 Tim 2:10; Diog. 1:1; 3:3; 4:5f; 6:4; as well as Gen 20:11; Sir 1:25; 4 Macc 7:6, 22; 15:28; 17:15. ἔβλαψε: βλάπτειν is often used of divine punishment, revenge, and harm; see Homer, *Il.* 9.507: (ἄτη) βλάπτουσ' ἀνθρώπους, *Od.* 1.195: ἀλλά νυ τόν γε θεοὶ βλάπτουσι κελεύθου, Plutarch, *Caesar* 45 (of Pompey during the battle of Pharsalos): οὐκέτι ἦν ὁ αὐτὸς οὐδ' ἐμέμνητο Πομπήϊος ὢν Μάγνος ἀλλὰ ὑπὸ θεοῦ μάλιστα βλαπτομένῳ τὴν γνώμην ἐοικώς. Instead of δεσμοῖς in S, read δεσμός with H. On the entire clause, see Jude 6: ἀγγέλους τε τοὺς μὴ τηρήσαντας τὴν ἑαυτῶν ἀρχήν ... εἰς κρίσιν μεγάλης ἡμέρας δεσμοῖς ἀϊδίοις ὑπὸ ζόφον τετήρηκεν. The interpretation of διὰ τοῦτο θεία κρίσις κτλ., how-ever, cannot be decided by an appeal to Jude 6, but presents all sorts of difficulties that cannot be resolved with certainty. The different possibilities are: (1) the aorist ἔβλαψε and ἐβάρυνε are gnomic; then a generally valid rule is pronounced; πνεῦμα is not a superhuman spiritual entity, but instead the word denotes, in popular usage, the inner part of man, his "soul," his "spirit" (cf. Mark 14:38; Luke 8:55; 2 Cor 7:1; Gen 6:17; 7:15; Jude 15, 19; 1 Sam 30:12; 1 Kgs 20:5; Sir 9:9; etc.): God's judgment strikes the unrigh-teous souls because of calculating, hypocritical piety and weighs them down with fetters. But the gnomic aorist is very rare in popular Hellenistic speech, if it has not dwindled altogether. Furthermore δεσμοῖς (or δεσμός) sounds very definite and is difficult to rhyme with a general statement about divine punishment. (2) The aorist is a real aorist and applies to a specific example of divine punishment: (a) the bondage of Satan, perhaps of his comrades in primeval times (like Jude 6); there is great difficulty with this assumption, which the wording suggests, because of the necessity of having to assume that Satan's punishment on account of hypocritical, acquisitive piety; we hear of this nowhere else. (b) The preacher alludes to an incident in the con-gregation; the allusion was effortlessly understood by the audience, while it remains obscure to us. In an affliction, perhaps an illness, which has struck an unworthy member of the congregation, divine judgment is recognized. In this interpretation, which is the most likely in view of the other options, only πνεῦμα is difficult, or rather at least striking.

20:5 On τῷ μόνῳ θεῷ ἀοράτῳ, see 1 Tim 1:17: ἀοράτῳ μόνῳ θεῷ, as well as Rom 16:27: μόνῳ σοφῷ θεῷ and Jude 25: μόνῳ θεῷ. On πατρὶ τῆς ἀληθείας, see above at 2 Clem. 3:1 and 19:1. ἐξαποστείλαντι sounds like Gal 4:4: ἐξαπέστειλεν ὁ θεὸς τὸν υἱὸν αὐτοῦ. On σωτῆρα καὶ ἀρχηγόν, see Acts 5:31: ἀρχηγὸν καὶ σωτῆρα, as well as Heb 2:10: τὸν ἀρχηγὸν τῆς σωτηρίας, 12:2: τὸν τῆς πίστεως ἀρχηγόν and on ἀρχηγὸν τῆς ἀφθαρσίας, see Acts 3:15: ἀρχηγὸν τῆς ζωῆς and the martyrdom in Lyon in Eusebius, *Hist. eccl.* 5.2.3: ἀρχηγῷ τῆς ζωῆς τοῦ θεοῦ. ἀρχηγός and ἀρχηγέτης is the progenitor and an-cestor of a new lineage, the heroes with whom a new line of life begins, also the builder of a new city and founder of a new state. — S has the postscript: *This Ends the Second Letter of Clement to the Corinthians.* H provides only the stichoi and word count.

Bibliography

Ábel, Jenő, ed. *Orphica*. Bibliotheca scriptorum Gracorum et Romanorum Teubneriana. Lipsiae: Pragae, 1885.

Achelis, Hans. *Die ältesten Quellen des orientalischen Kirchenrechtes*. Texte und Untersuchungen zur Geschichte der altchristlichen Literatur 6. Leipzig: Hinrichs, 1891.

———, ed. *Hippolytus Werke*. Leipzig: Hinrichs, 1897–1929.

———. *Virgines subintroductae*. Leipzig: Hinrichs, 1902.

Aland, Kurt. *Glanz und Niedergang der deutschen Universität. 50 Jahre deutscher Wissenschaftsgeschichte in Briefen an und von Hans Lietzmann (1892–1942). Mit einer einführenden Darstellung herausgegeben von Kurt Aland*. Berlin: de Gruyter, 1979.

Anrich, Gustav. *Das antike Mysterienwesen in seinem Einfluss auf das Christentum*. Göttingen: Vandenhoeck, 1894.

Bardenhewer, Otto. *Geschichte der altchristlichen Literatur*. 2nd ed. Freiburg: Herdersche Verlagshandlung, 1913.

———. *Geschichte der altkirchlichen Literatur*. Vol. 1, *Vom Ausgang der apostolischen Zeitalters bis zum Ende des 2. Jahrhunderts*. 2nd ed. Freiburg: Herder, 1913.

Barker, Edmund Henry. Ἀρκαδίου περὶ τονων. Leipzig: N.p., 1820.

Bartlet, Vernon. "The Origin and Date of 2 Clement." *Zeitschrift für die Neutestamentliche Wissenschaft* 7 (1906) 123–35.

Batiffol, Pierre. *Studia patristica*. Paris: Leroux, 1890.

Bauer, Adolf. "Die Legende von dem Martyrium des Petrus und Paulus in Rom." *Wiener Studien* 38 (1916) 270–307.

Bauer, Walter. *Die Evangelien*. Handbuch zum Neuen Testament 2. Tübingen: Mohr, 1919.

Baumstark, Anton. *Liturgische Text III. Die Konstantinopolitanische* Messliturgie *vor dem IX. Jahrhundert. Übersichtliche Zusammenstellung des wichtigsten Quellenmaterials*. Kleine Texte für Vorlesungen und Übungen 35. Bonn: Marcus und Weber, 1909.

Beckh, Hermann. *Buddhismus (Buddha und seine Lehre)*. Berlin: Göschen, 1916.

Beer, Bernhard. *Leben Abrahams nach Auffassung der jüdischen Sage*. Leipzig: O. Leiner, 1859.

Bekker, Immanuel. *Anecdota Graeca*. Vol. 1. Granz: Berolini: Apud G. C. Nauckium, 1814.

Bensly, Robert Lubbock. *The Epistles of S. Clement to the Corinthians in Syriac.* Cambridge: Cambridge University Press, 1899.

Bergh van Eysinga, Gustav Adolf van den. *Onderzoek naar de echtheid van Clemens eerste brief aan de Corinthiërs.* Leiden: Brill, 1908.

Bergk, Theodor. *Poetae lyrici Graeci.* Vol. 2. 4th ed. Leipzig: Teubner, 1915.

Bertholet, Alfred, and Wilhelm Grube. *Religionsgeschichtliches Lesebuch.* Tübingen: Mohr, 1908.

Bisping, Aug. *Erklärung der Briefe an die Epheser, Philipper und Kolosser.* Handbuch zum Neuen Testament 6.2. Münster: Aschendorff, 1866.

———. *Erklärung des Evangeliums nach Johannes.* Handbuch zum Neuen Testament 3. Münster: Aschendorff, 1869.

Blass, Frederich, and Albert Debrunner. *Grammatik des neutestamentlichen Griechisch.* 4th ed. Göttingen: Vandenhoeck & Ruprecht, 1913.

Bonhöffer, Adolf Friedrich. *Epictet und die Stoa: Untersuchungen zur stoischen Philosophie.* Stuttgart: F. Enke, 1890.

Bonnet, Max. *Acta apostolorum apocrypha.* Vol. 2.1. Leipzig: Mendelssohn, 1898.

Bonwetsch, Nathanael, and Hans Achelis. *Hippolytus Werke.* Vol. 1.2, *Exegetische und homiletische Schriften: Hälfte, Kleinere exegetische und homiletische Schriften.* Leipzig: Hinrichs, 1897.

Bousset, Wilhelm. *Der Antichrist in der Ueberlieferung: Des Judentums, des neuen Testaments und der alten Kirche.* Goettingen: Vandenhoeck & Ruprecht, 1895.

———. *Die Religion des Judentums im neutestamentlichen Zeitalter.* 3rd ed. Berlin: Reuther & Reichard, 1903.

———. *Kyrios Christos: Geschichte des Christusglaubens von den Anfängen des Christentums bis Irenaeus.* 2nd ed. Göttingen: Vandenhoeck & Ruprecht, 1921.

Brandt, A. J. H. W. *Die mandäische Religion, ihre Entwickelung und geschichtliche Bedeutung erforscht, dargestellt und beleuchtet.* Leipzig: Hinrichs, 1889.

Brightman, F. E. *Liturgies Eastern and Western.* Oxford: Clarendon, 1896.

Bryennios, Philotheos. *Διδαχὴ τῶν δώδεκα ἀποστόλων.* N.p.: Constantinople, 1883.

———. *Τοῦ ἐν ἁγίοις πατρὸς ἡμῶν Κλήμεντος ἐπισκόπου Ῥώμης αἱ δύο πρὸς Κορινθίους ἐπιστολαί.* N.p.: Constantinople, 1875.

Bultmann, Rudolf. "Review of R. Knopf's Einführung in das Neue Testament." *Deutsche Literturzeitung* 42 (1921) 254–55.

———. "Review of R. Knopf, H. Weinel, and H. Lietzmann's Einführung in das Neue Testament." *Theologische Literaturzeitung* 48 (1923) 394–96.

Cotelier, Jean-Baptiste. *SS. Patrum qui temporibus apostolicis floruerunt.* Antwerpiae: Clericus, 1689.

Cumont, Franz. *Die Mysterien des Mithras: Ein Beitrag zur Religionsgeschichte der römischen Kaiserzeit.* Leipzig: Teubner, 1903.

———. *Die orientalischen Religionen im römischen Heidentum: Vorlesungen.* 2nd ed. Leipzig: Hinrichs, 1914.

———. *Textes et monuments figurés relatifs aux mystères de Mithra.* Vol. 1. Bruxelles: Lamertin, 1899.

Cureton, William, ed. *Corpus Ignatianum: A Complete Collection of the Ignatian Epistles, Geniune, Interpolated, and Spurious; Together with Numerous Extracts from Them, as Quoted by Ecclesiastical Writers Down to the Tenth Century; in Syriac, Greek, and Latin: an English Translation of the Syriac Text, Copious Notes, and Introduction.* London: Rivington, 1849.

Curtis, Samuel Ives. *Ursemitische Religion im Volksleben des heutigen Orients.* Leipzig: N.p., 1903.

Deissmann, Adolf. *Bibelstudien: Beiträge, zumeist aus den Papyri und Inschriften, zur Geschichte der Sprache, des Schrifttums und der Religion des hellenistischen Judentums und des Urchristentums.* Marburg: Elwert, 1895.

———. *Das Urchristentum und die unteren Schichten.* 2nd ed. Göttingen: Vandenhoeck & Ruprecht, 1908.

———. *Licht vom Osten.* 2nd ed. Tübingen: Mohr, 1909.

De Jonge, H. J. "On the Origin of the Term 'Apostolic Fathers.'" *The Journal of Theological Studies* 29 (1978) 503–5.

De Lagarde, Paul. *Clementia.* Leipzig: Brockhaus, 1865.

Diels, Hermann. *Die Fragmente der Vorsokratiker: Griechisch und Deutsch.* 3rd ed. Berlin: Weidmann, 1912.

———. *Doxographi Graeci.* Berlin: Typis et impensis G. Reimeri, 1879.

Dieterich, Albrecht. *Abraxas: Studien zur Religionsgeschichte des später Altertums.* Leipzig: Teubner, 1891.

———. *Papyrus leidensis.* Jahrbücher für klassische Philologie 16. Supplementband. Leipzig: N.p., 1888.

Di Pauli, Andreas Freiherrn. "Zum sogenannte zweiten Korintherbrief des Clemens Romanus." *Zeitschrift für die Neutestamentliche Wissenschaft* 4 (1903) 321–29.

Dittenberger, Wilhelm, and Friedrich Hiller von Gaertringen. *Sylloge inscriptionum Graecarum.* 2nd ed. Leipzig: Hirzel, 1915–24.

Dölger, Franz Jos. *Sphragis: Eine altchristliche Taufbezeichnung in ihren Beziehunbgen zur profanen und religiösen Kultur des Alterums.* Studien zur Geschichte und Kultur des Altertums 5. Paderborn: Ferdinand Schöningh, 1911.

Draper, Jonathan A. "Die Didache." In *Die Apostolischen Väter. Eine Einleitung,* edited by Wilhelm Pratscher, 17–38. Uni-Taschenbücher 3272. Göttingen: Vandenhoeck & Ruprecht, 2009.

Drews, Paul. "Apostlelehre (Didache)." In *Handbuch zu den neutestamentlichen Apokryphen,* edited by Edgar Hennecke, 256–83. Tübingen: Mohr, 1904.

———. "Die Kirchenordnungen." In *Neutestamentliche Apokryphen,* edited by Edgar Hennecke, 182–94. Tübingen: Mohr, 1904.

———. "Eucharistie." In *Realencyklopädie für protestantische Theologie und Kirche,* 560–72. 3rd ed. Leipzig: Hinrichs, 1898.

———. *Untersuchungen über die sogenannte clementinische Liturgie im VIII. Buch der apostolischen Konstitutionen. I. Die clementinische Liturgie in Rom.* Studien zur Geschichte des Gottesdienstes und des gottesdienstlichen Lebens II und III. Tübingen: Mohr, 1906.

———. "Untersuchungen zur Didache." *Zeitschrift für die neutestamentliche Wissenschaft und die Kunde des Urchristentums* 5 (1904) 53–79.

Drobner, H. R. *Lehrbuch der Patrologie.* Freiburg: Herder, 1994.

Dubowy, Ernst. *Klemens von Rom über die Reise Pauli nach Spanien: Historisch-kritische Untersuchung zu Klemens von Rom: 1. Kor. 5,7.* Biblische Studien 19.3. Freiburg: Herder, 1914.

Eidem, Erling. *Pauli Bildvärld. Athletae et milites Christi.* Lund: N.p., 1913.

Erman, Adolf. *Die aegyptische Religion.* Handbücher der Königlichen Museen zu Berlin. 2nd ed. Berlin: Reimer, 1909.

Euting, Julius. *Qolasta oder Gesänge und Lehren von der Taufe und dem Ausgang der Seele als mandäischer Text mit sämmtlichen Varianten, nach Pariser und Londoner Manuscripten, mit Unterstützung der deutschen morgenländischen Gesellschaft in Leipzig, autographirt und herausgegeben von Dr. J. Euting, Stiftsbibliothekar in Tübingen.* Stuttgart: Schepperlen, 1867.

Fiebig, Paul. *Ausgewählte Mischnatraktate in deutscher Übersetzung.* Tübingen: Mohr, 1912.

———. *Das Judentum von Jesus bis zur Gegenwart.* Tübingen: Mohr, 1916.

Field, Frederick, ed. *Origenis Hexaplorum quae supersunt; Sive veterum interpretum graecorum in totum Vetus Testamentum fragmenta. Post Flaminium Nobilium, Drusium, et Montefalconium, adhibita etiam versione Syro-Hexaplari, concinnavit, emedavit, et multis partibus auxit Fridericus Field.* Oxford: Clarendon, 1875.

Fischer, Joseph A. *Die Apostolischen Väter. Eingeleitet, herausgegeben, übertragen und erläutert.* Schriften des Urchristentums. Erster Teil. Darmstadt: Wissenschaftliche Buchgesellschaft, 1964.

Flemming, Joh, and Hans Achelis. *Die syrische Didaskalia.* Texte und Untersuchungen zur Geschichte der altchristlichen Literatur 10. Leipzig: Hinrichs, 1904.

Fränkel, Max, et al., eds. *Die Inschriften von Pergamon.* Berlin: W. Spermann, 1890–95.

Friedländer, Ludwig. *Darstellungen aus der Sittengeschichte Roms in der Zeit von Augustus bis zum Ausgang der Antonine.* 4 vols. Leipzig: Hirzel, 1910.

Funk, Franz Xaver. "Der sogenannte zweite Clemensbrief." *Kirchengeschichtle Abhandlungen und Untersuchungen* 3 (1907) 261–75.

———. "Der sogenannte zweite Clemensbrief." *Theologische Quartalschrift* 84 (1902) 349–64.

———. *Die apostolischen Väter.* 2nd ed. Tübingen: Mohr, 1907.

———. *Didascalia et Constitutiones Apostolorum.* Paderborn: Schöningh, 1906.

———. *Doctrina duodecim apostolorum, canones apostolorum ecclesiastici ac reliquae doctrinae de duabus viis expositiones veteres.* Tübingen: Laupp, 1887.

———. *Patres Apostolici I.* 2nd ed. Tübingen: Laupp, 1901.

Gaisford, Thomas. *Etymologicon magnum. seu verius lexicon.* Oxonii: E. Typographeo Academico, 1848.

Georges, Karl Ernst. *Lateinisch-Deutsches und Deutsch-Lateinisches Handwörterbuch.* Leipzig, Hahn, 1843.

Goldschmidt, Lazarus, trans. *Der babylonische Talmud.* 12 vols. Berlin: Harz, 1906–25.

Goodspeed, Edgar J., ed. *Die ältesten Apologeten.* Göttingen: Vandenhoeck & Ruprecht, 1914.

———. *Index apologeticus.* Leipzig: Hinrich, 1912.

Gregory, Andrew F., and C. M. Tuckett, eds. *The Reception of the New Testament in the Apostolic Fathers.* Oxford: Oxford University Press, 2005.

———. *Trajectories through the New Testament and the Apostolic Fathers.* Oxford: Oxford University Press, 2005.

Greßman, Hugo, et al. *Altorientalische Texte und Bilder zum Alten Testamente.* Tübingen: Mohr, 1909.

Gruppe, Otto. *Griechische Mythologie und Religionsgeschichte.* Vol. 2. München: Beck, 1906.

Gunkel, Hermann. *Genesis.* Handkommentar zum Alten Testament 1. 4th ed. Göttingen: Vandenhoeck & Ruprecht, 197.

Gunkel, Hermann, and Heinrich Zimmern. *Schöpfung und Chaos in Urzeit und Endzeit: Eine religionsgeschichtliche Untersuchung über Gen 1 und Ap Joh 12*. Göttingen: Vandenhoeck & Ruprecht, 1895.

Hagemann, Hermann. "Ueber den zweiten Brief des Klemens von Rom." *Quartalschrift* 43 (1861) 509–31.

Hammann, Konrad. *Paul Siebeck und sein Verlag*. Tübingen: Mohr Siebeck, 2021.

Harris, J. Rendel. "On an Obscure Quotation in the First Epistle of Clement." *Journal of Biblical Literature* 29 (1910) 190–95.

———. *The Teaching of the Apostles*. London: Clay, 1887.

Hartke, W. *Die Sammlung und die ältesten Ausgaben der Paulusbriefe*. Bonn: Georgi, 1917.

Hauschildt, Hermann. "πρεσβύτεροι in Ägypten im I.–III. Jahrhundert n. Chr." *Zeitschrift für die neutestamentliche Wissenschaft und die Kunde des Urchristentums* 4 (1903) 235–42.

Heitmüller, Wilhelm. *"Im Namen Jesu": Eine sprach und religionsgeschichtliche Untersuchung zum Neuen Testament, speziell zur altchristlichen Taufe*. Göttingen: Vandenhoeck & Ruprecht, 1903.

———. "Sphragis." In *Neutestamentliche Studien: Georg Heinrici zu seinem 70. Geburtstag (14. März 1914)*, edited by Adolf Deißmann and Hans Windisch, 40–59. Leipzig: Heinrici, 1914.

Helbing, Robert. *Grammatik der "Septuaginta," Laut und Wortlehre*. Göttingen: Vandenhoeck & Ruprecht, 1907.

Hengel, Martin, and Anna Maria Schwemer. *Geschichte des frühen Christentums*. Vol. 1, *Jesus und das Judentum*. Tübingen: Mohr Siebeck, 2007.

Hennecke, Edgar. *Handbuch zu den neutestamentlichen Apokryphen*. Tübingen: Mohr, 1904.

———. *Neutestamentliche Apokryphen*. Tübingen: Mohr, 1904.

———. *Neutestamentliche Apokryphen*. 2nd ed. Tübingen: Mohr, 1924.

Henrichsen, R. I. F. *De Phoenicis fabula apud Græcos, Romanos et populos orientales commentationis*. Havniae: Schulzii, 1825–27.

Hense, Otto, ed. *C. Musonii Rufi Reliquiae*. Bibliotheca scriptorum Graecorum et Romanorum Teubneriana. Leipzig: Teubner, 1905.

Hercher, Rudolf. *Epistolographoi hellenikoi: Epistolographi Graeci*. Paris: Didot, 1873.

Hilgenfeld, Adolf. *Novum Testamentum extra canonem receptum*. 2nd ed. Leipzig: Hinrichs, 1876.

Holl, Karl. *Die handschriftliche Überlieferung des Epiphanius*. Texte und Untersuchungen zur Geschichte der altchristlichen Literatur 20. Leipzig: Hinrichs, 1910.

Holtzmann, Oscar. *Der Tosephtatraktat Berakot: Text, Übersetzung und Erklärung*. Giessen: Töpelmann, 1912.

Huggenberger, Alfred. *Dorfgenossen: Neue Erzählungen*. Leipzig: Staackmann, 1914.

Iselin, L. E. *Eine bisher unbekannte Version des ersten Teiles der Apostellehre (Didache)*. Texte und Untersuchungen zur Geschichte der altchristlichen Literatur 13. Leipzig: Hinrich, 1895.

Jefford, Clayton N., ed. *The Didache in Context: Essays on Its Text, History, and Transmission*. Supplements to Novum Testamentum 77. Leiden: Brill, 1995.

Jordan, Hermann. *Geschichte der altchristlichen Literatur*. Leipzig: Quelle & Meyer, 1911.

Jülicher, Adolf. *Einleitung in das Neue Testament*. Grundriss der theologischen Wissenschaften 3.1. 5th and 6th eds. Tübingen: Mohr, 1919.

Klein, Gottlieb. *Der älteste christliche Katechismus und die jüdische Propaganda-Literatur*. Berlin: Reimer, 1909.

———. "Die Gebete in der Didache." *Zeitschrift für die Neutestamentliche Wissenschaft* 9 (1908) 132–46.

Klostermann, Erich. *Apocrypha*. Vol. 1, *Reste des Petrusevangeliums, der Petrusapocalypse und des Kerygma Petri*. Kleine Texte für Vorlesungen und Übungen 3. Bonn: Marcus und Weber, 1903.

———. *Apocrypha*. Vol. 2, *Evangelien*. Kleine Texte für Vorlesungen und Übungen 8. 2nd ed. Bonn: Marcus und Weber, 1910.

Knopf, Rudolf. *Ausgewählte Märtyreracten*. Sammlung ausgewählter kirchen und dogmengeschichtlicher Quellenschriften 2. 2nd ed. Tübingen: Mohr, 1901.

———. "Clemens an die Korinther." In *Handbuch zu den neutestamentlichen Apokryphen*, edited by Edgar Hennecke, 173–90. Tübingen: Mohr, 1904.

———. "Clemens an die Korinther." In *Neutestamentliche Apokryphen*, edited by Edgar Hennecke, 84–112. Tübingen: Mohr, 1904.

———. *Das Nachapostolische Zeitalter. Geschichte der christlichen Gemeinden. Vom Beginn der Flavierdynastie bis zum Ende Hadrians*. Tübingen: Mohr, 1905.

———. *Der Erste Clemensbrief*. Texte und Untersuchungen 20.1. Leipzig: Hinrichs, 1899.

———. "Die Anagnose zum zweiten Clemensbriefe." *Zeitschrift für die Neutestamentliche Wissenschaft* 3 (1902) 266–79.

———. *Die Briefe Petri und Judä*. Meyers kritisch-exegetischer Kommentar über das Neue Testament 12. 7th ed. Göttingen: Vandenhoeck & Ruprecht, 1912.

———. *Paulus*. Wissenschaft und Bildung 48. Leipzig: Quelle und Meyer, 1909.

———. "Petrus." In *Die Religion in Geschichte und Gegenwart*, edited by Friedrich Michael Schiele et al., 4:1408–12. 5 vols. Tübingen: Mohr, 1909–13.

———. *Probleme der Paulusforschung*. Sammlung gemeinverständlicher Vorträge und Schriften 77. Tübingen: Mohr, 1913.

Knopf, Rudolf, et al. *Einführung in das Neue Testament: Bibelkunde des Neuen Testaments Geschichte und Religion des Urchristentums*. Giessen: Töpelmann, 1919.

———. *Einführung in das Neue Testament: Bibelkunde des Neuen Testaments Geschichte und Religion des Urchristentums*. 2nd rev. and exp. ed. Giessen: A. Töpelmann, 1923.

Knopf, Rudolf, et al. *Einführung in das Neue Testament: Bibelkunde des Neuen Testaments Geschichte und Religion des Urchristentums*. 3rd rev. and exp. ed. Giessen: Töpelmann, 1930.

———. *Einführung in das Neue Testament: Bibelkunde des Neuen Testaments Geschichte und Religion des Urchristentums*. 4th rev. and exp. ed. Giessen: Töpelmann, 1934.

Knöpfler, Alexander I. "Liturgische Neuerungen der Päpste Alexander I. (c. 110) und Sixtus I. (c. 120) in der römischen Messe nach dem liber pontiflcalis." In *Festgabe Alois Knöpfler zur Vollendung des 60. Lebensjahres gewidmet von A. Biglmair, S. Euringer, J. Greving, K. Holzhey, J. Hürbin, R. Jud, A. Kempfler, A.M. Königer, G. Pfeilschifter, T. Schermann, J. Schnitzer, A. Seider, J. Sickenberger, F. X. Thalhofer, H. Vogels, M. Weiss, F. Wieland*, 276–89. Leipzig: Herder, 1917.

Kock, Theodor. *Comicorum Atticorum Fragmenta*. Leipzig: Teubner, 1888.

Koetschau, Paul, ed and trans. *Origenes Werke. Buch 5–8 gegen Celsus. Die Schrift vom Gebet*. Vol. 2. Leipzig: Hinrichs, 1899.

Körte, Alfred. "Zu den eleusinischen Mysterien." *Archiv für Religionswissenschaft* 18 (1915) 116–26.

Körtner, Ulrich H. J., and Martin Leutzsch. *Die Apostolischen Väter. Eingeleitet, herausgegeben, übertragen und erläutert*. Schriften des Urchristentums. Dritter Teil. Darmstadt: Wissenschaftliche Buchgesellschaft, 1998.

Kraft, Heinrich. *Clavis Patrum Apostolicorum*. Darmstadt: Wissenschaftliche Buchgesellschaft, 1963.

Krüger, Gustav. *Geschichte der altchristlichen Literatur*. 2nd ed. Freiburg im Breisgau: Mohr, 1898.

Kühner, Raphael, and Bernhard Gerth. *Ausführliche Grammatik der griechischen Sprache*. Vol. 2. 3rd ed. Hannover: Hahn, 1904.

Kühner, Raphael, and Friedrich W. Blass. *Ausführliche Grammatik der griechischen Sprache*. Hannover: Hahn, 1890.

Kümmel, Werner Georg. *Das Neue Testament. Geschichte der Erforschung seiner Probleme*. 2nd ed. Freiburg and München: Verlag Karl Alber, 1970.

———. *Einleitung in das Neue Testament*. 17th ed. Heidelberg: Quelle und Meyer, 1973.

Leipoldt, Johannes. *Geschichte des neutestamentlichen Kanons*. Leipzig: Hinrichs, 1907–8.

Lietzmann, Hans. *Der Weltheiland: Eine Jenaer Rosenvorlesung mit Anmerkungen*. Bonn: Marcus und Weber, 1909.

———. *Die Briefe des Apostels Paulus. An die Korinther*. Handbuch zum Neuen Testament 3, 1.2. Tübingen: Mohr, 1909.

———. *Die Briefe des Apostels Paulus*. Edited by Martin Dibelius. Handbuch zum Neuen Testament 3.2. Tübingen: Mohr, 1913.

———. *Die Didache, mit kritischem Apparat*. Kleine Texte 2. 3rd ed. Bonn: Marcus und Weber, 1912.

———. *Einführung in die textgeschichte der Paulusbriefe: An die* Römer. Handbuch zum Neuen Testament 8. 2nd ed. Tübingen: Mohr, 1919.

———. *Griechische Papyri*. Kleine Texte für Vorlesungen und Übungen 14. 2nd ed. Bonn: Marcus und Weber, 1910.

———. *Liturgische Texte. I: Zur Geschichte der orientalischen Taufe und Messe im 2. und 4. Jahrhundert*. Kleine Texte für Vorlesungen und Übungen 5. Bonn: Marcus und Weber, 1904.

———. *Liturgische Text VIII. Die klementinische Liturgie aus den Constitutiones Apostolorum*. Kleine Texte für Vorlesungen und Übungen 61. Bonn: Marcus und Weber, 1910.

———. "Zur altchristlichen Verfassungsgeschichte." *Zeitschrift für wissenschaftliche Theologie* 55 (1914) 97–153.

Lightfoot, J. B. *The Apostolic Fathers, Part 1: S. Clement of Rome*. 2 vols. London: Macmillan, 1890.

———. *The Apostolic Fathers: Revised Texts with Short Introductions and English Translations*. Edited and completed by J. R. Harmer. London: Macmillan, 1891.

Lindemann, Andreas. "Apostolische Väter." In *Religion in Geschichte und Gegenwart*, 1:652–53. 4th ed. 9 vols. Tübingen: Mohr Siebeck, 1998.

————. "Der erste Clemensbrief." In *Die Apostolischen Väter. Eine Einleitung*, edited by W. Pratscher, 59–82. Uni-Taschenbücher 3272. Göttingen: Vandenhoeck & Ruprecht, 2009.

————. "Der 'Erste Clemensbrief' und die Freiheit der Kirche." In *Bestimmte Freiheit. Festschrift für Christof Landmesser zum 60. Geburtstag*, edited by Martin Bauspieß et al., 219–44. Archiv für Begriffsgeschichte 64. Leipzig: Evangelische Verlagsanstalt, 2020.

————. *Die Clemensbriefe. Die Apostolischen Väter I*. Handbuch zum Neuen Testament 17. Tübingen: Mohr Siebeck, 1992.

————. "Die Endzeitrede in Didache 16 und die Jesus-Apokalypse in Matthäus 24–25." In *Sayings of Jesus: Canonical and Non-Canonical—Essays in Honour of Tjitze Baarda*, edited by William L. Petersen et al., 155–74. Supplements to Novum Testamentum 89. Leiden: Brill, 1997.

————. "Paul in the Writings of the Apostolic Fathers." In *Paul and the Legacies of Paul*, edited by William S. Babcock, 25–45. Dallas: Southern Methodist University Press, 1990.

————. "Paulus in den Schriften der 'Apostolischen Väter.'" In *Paulus, Apostel und Lehrer der Kirche: Studien zu Paulus und zum frühen Paulusverständnis*, 252–79. Tübingen: Mohr Siebeck, 1999.

————. "Zur frühchristlichen Taufpraxis. Die Taufe in der Didache, bei Justin und in der Didaskalia." In *Ablution, Inititation, and Baptism: Waschungen, Initiation und Taufe, Late Antiquity, Early Judaism, and Early Christianity. Spätantike, Frühes Judenum und Frühes Christentum*, edited by David Hellholm et al., 767–815. Beihefte zur Zeitschrift für Religions und Geistesgeschichte 176/II. Berlin: de Gruyter, 2011.

Lindemann, Andreas, and H. Paulsen, eds. *Die Apostolischen Väter*. Newly translated and edited by Andreas Lindemann and Henning Paulsen. Tübingen: Mohr, 1992.

Lobeck, Christian August. *Eclogæ nominum et verborum Atticorum cum notis*. Leipzig: Weidmann, 1820.

Lommatzsch, Karl Heinrich Eduard. *Origenis Opera omnia quae graece vel latine tantum exstant et ejus nomine circumferuntur. Ex variis editionibus, et codicibus manu exaratis*. Berolini: Sumtibus Haude et Spener, 1831–42.

Lona, Horacio E. *Der erste Clemensbrief*. Kommentar zu den Apostolischen Vätern 2. Göttingen: Vandenhoeck & Ruprecht, 1998.

Loofs, Friedrich. *Leitfaden zum Studium der Dogmengeschichte*. 4th ed. Halle: Niemeyer, 1906.

Mangey, Thomas. *Opera omnia Graece et Latine*. Erlangae: Heyderiana, 1820.

Marquardt, Karl Joachim. *Das Privatleben der Römer*. Vol. 1. Handbuch der römischen alterthümer von Joachim Marquardt und Theodor Mommsen 7. Leipzig: Hirzel, 1886.

Marucchi, Orazio. *Handbuch der christlichen Archäologie*. Einsiedeln: Benziger, 1912.

Meineke, August, ed. *Menandri et Philemonis reliquiae*. Berolini: Myl, 1823.

Merk, Otto. "Knopf, Rudolf." In *Neue deutsche Biographie*, 12:215. 28 vols. Berlin: Duncker & Humblot, 1953–forthcoming.

Meyer, Heinrich August Wilhelm. *Kritisch exegetisches Handbuch über die Briefe Pauli an die Philipper, Kolosser und an Philemon*. Meyers kritisch-exegetischer Kommentar über das Neue Testament 9. Göttingen: Vandenhoeck & Ruprecht, 1874.

Migne, J.-P. *Patrologia Graeca*. Vol. 27. Turnholti: Brepols, 1857.

———. *Patrologia Graeca*. Vol. 36. Turnholti: Brepols, 1858.

Mikat, Paul. *Die Bedeutung der Begriffe Stasis und Aponoia für das Verständnis des 1. Clemensbriefes*. Köln: Westdeutscherverlag, 1969.

Mitteis, Ludwig. *Reichsrecht und Volksrecht in den östlichen Provinzen des römischen Kaiserreichs, mit Beiträgen zur Kenntniss des griechischen Rechts und der spätrömischen Rechtsentwicklung*. Leipzig: Teubner, 1891.

Mommsen, Theodor. *Römische Geschichte*. Vol. 5. Berlin: Weidmann, 1904.

Morin, Germain. *Anecdota Maredsolana; Seu, Monumenta Ecclesiasticae Antiquitatis en Mss. Codicibus nunc Primum Edita*. Vol. 2. Maredsoli: Monasterio S. Benedicti, 1894.

Moulton, James Hope. *Einleitung in die Sprache des Neuen Testaments*. 3rd ed. Heidelberg: Winter, 1911.

Nauck, August, ed. *Tragoediae*. Leipzig: Teubner, 1869–95.

Niederwimmer, Kurt. "Der Didachist und seine Quellen." In *The Didache in Context: Essays on Its Text, History, and Transmission*, edited by C. N. Jefford, 15–36. Supplements to Novum Testamentum 77. Leiden: Brill, 1995.

———. *Die Didache*. Kommentar zu den Apostolischen Vätern 1. Göttingen: Vandenhoeck & Ruprecht, 1989.

Norden, Eduard. *Agnostos Theos: Untersuchungen zur Formengeschichte religiöser Rede*. Leipzig: Teubner, 1913.

North, Heinrich von und Gottfried, and Stephan Braunschweig. "Das Verkehrsleben im Alterthum." *Historisches Taschenbuch* 9 (1868) 1–136.

Oldenberg, Hermann. *Buddha, seine Lehre, seine Gemeinde*. 5th ed. Berlin: Cotta, 1906.

Oxford Society of Historical Theology. *The New Testament in the Apostolic Fathers*. Oxford: Clarendon, 1905.

Passow, Franz. *W. Pape's Handwörterbuch der griechischen Sprache*. Leipzig: Vogel, 1841–57.

Peschel, Oscar. *Geschichte der Erdkunde bis auf Alexander von Humboldt und Karl Ritter*. 2nd ed. München: Oldenbourg, 1877.

Pitra, Jean-Baptiste. *Analecta sacra Spicilegio Solesmensi parata*. Vol. 4, *Patres Antenicaeni*. Paris: Jouby et Roger, 1883.

Plümacher, Eckkard. "Knopf, Rudolf." In *Biographisch-Bibliographisches Kirchenlexikon*, 4:165–66. Herzberg: Verlag Traugott Bautz, 1992.

Praechter, Karl. *Hierokles der Stoiker*. Leipzig: Dieterich, 1901.

Praetorius, Walther. "Die Bedeutung der beiden Clemensbriefe für die älteste Geschichte der kirchlichen Praxis." *Zeitschrift für Kirchengeschichte* 33 (1912) 347–63, 501–28.

Pratscher, Wilhelm. "Das Corpus der Apostolischen Väter." In *Die Apostolischen Väter. Eine Einleitung*, 11–16. Uni-Taschenbücher 3272. Göttingen: Vandenhoeck & Ruprecht, 2009.

———. "Der zweite Clemensbrief." In *Die Apostolischen Väter. Eine Einleitung*, 83–103. Uni-Taschenbücher 3272. Göttingen: Vandenhoeck & Ruprecht, 2009.

———. *Der zweite Clemensbrief*. Kommentar zu den Apostolischen Vätern 3. Göttingen: Vandenhoeck & Ruprecht, 2007.

———. "Die Rezeption des Neuen Testaments bei den Apostolischen Vätern." *Theologische Literaturzeitung* 137 (2012) 139–52.

Preuschen, Erwin. *Analecta Teil 1. Staat und Christentum bis auf Konstantin.* Vol. 1. 2nd Edition. Tübingen: Mohr, 1909.

———. *Analecta Teil 2. Zur Kanonsgeschichte.* Vol. 2. 2nd ed. Tübingen: Mohr, 1910.

———. *Antilegomena die Reste der außerkanonischen Evangelien und urchristlichen Überlieferungen.* 2nd ed. Gieszen: Töpelmann, 1905.

Probst, Ferdinand. *Liturgie der drei ersten christlichen Jahrhunderte.* Tübingen: Laupp, 1870.

Radermacher, Ludwig. *Neutestamentliche Grammatik: Das Griechisch des Neuen Testaments im Zusammenhang mit der Volkssprache.* Tübingen: Mohr, 1911.

Rahmani, Ignatius Ephraem, ed. and trans. *Testamentum Domini nostri Jesu Christi.* Moguntiae: Kirchheim, 1899.

Rauschen, Gerhard. *Florilegium Patristicum I: Monumenta aevi apostolici.* Bonn: Hanstein, 1904.

Reitzenstein, Richard. *Die hellenistischen Mysterienreligionen. Nach ihren Grundgedanken und Wirkungen.* Leipzig: Teubner, 1910.

———. *Historia Monachorum und Historia Lausiaca Eine Studie zur Geschichte des Mönchtums und der frühchristlichen Begriffe Gnostiker und Pneumatiker.* Forschungen zur Religion und Literatur des Alten und Neuen Testaments 7. Göttingen: Vandenhoeck & Ruprecht, 1916.

———. *Poimandres: Studien zur griechisch-ägyptische und frühchristlichen Literatur.* Leipzig: Teubner, 1904.

Resch, Alfred. *Agrapha: Aussercanonische Schriftfragmente.* Texte und Untersuchungen zur Geschichte der altchristlichen Literatur 30. 2nd ed. Leipzig: Hinrichs, 1906.

Resch, Gotthold. *Das Aposteldekret nach seiner ausserkanonischen Textgestalt.* Texte und Untersuchungen zur Geschichte der altchristlichen Literatur 28. Leipzig: Hinrichs, 1905.

Riedel, Wilhelm. *Die Kirchenrechtsquellen des Patriarchats Alexandrien.* Leipzig: A. Deichert, 1900.

Riehm, Eduard. "Carmesin." In *Handwörterbuch des biblischen Altertums für gebildete Bibelleser,* edited by Eduard Riehm, 260–61. Leipzig: Velhagen and Klasing, 1893–94.

Rohde, E. *Psyche.* Vol. 1. 3rd ed. Freiburg: Mohr, 1903.

———. *Psyche.* Vol. 2. 3rd ed. Freiburg: Mohr, 1903.

Rösch, Friedrich. *Bruchstücke des ersten Clemensbriefes: Nach dem Achmimischen Papyrus der Strassburger Universitäts und Landesbibliothek, mit biblischen Texten derselben Handschrift.* Straßburg: Schlesier & Schweikhardt, 1910.

Roscher, Wihelm. "Phönix." In *Ausführliches Lexikon der griechischen und römischen Mythologie,* 3.2:3450–72. Leipzig: Teubner, 1909.

Rothschild. C. K. "1 Clement as Pseudepigraphon." In *New Essays on the Apostolic Fathers,* 61–68. Wissenschaftliche Untersuchungen zum Neuen Testament 375. Tübingen: Mohr Siebeck, 2017.

———. "'Belittling' or 'Undervaluing' in 2 Clem 1:1–2?" In *New Essays on the Apostolic Fathers,* 111–23. Wissenschaftliche Untersuchungen zum Neuen Testament 375. Tübingen: Mohr Siebeck, 2017.

———. "On the Invention of the Term *Patres Apostolici.*" In *New Essays on the Apostolic Fathers,* 7–33. Wissenschaftliche Untersuchungen zum Neuen Testament 375. Tübingen: Mohr Siebeck, 2017.

———. "Reception of First Corinthians in First Clement." In *New Essays on the Apostolic Fathers*, 35–60. Wissenschaftliche Untersuchungen zum Neuen Testament 375. Tübingen: Mohr Siebeck, 2017.

Ruinart, Thierry. *Acta Martyrum P. Theodorici Ruinart opera ac studio collecta, selecta, atque illustrata.* Ratisbonae: Manz, 1859.

Rzach, Aliosius, ed. *Hesiodi Carmina.* 3rd ed. Leipzig: Teubner, 1913.

Sabatier, Paul. *La Didachè ou l'Enseignement des douze apôtres.* Paris: Fischbacher, 1885.

Schaff, Philip. *The Teaching of the Twelve Apostles.* New York: Funk and Wagnalls, 1889.

Schenkl, Henricus. *Quaestiones Epictetae.* Leipzig: Teubner, 1894.

Schermann, Theodor. *Bibliothek der Kirchenväter. Griechische Liturgien.* Vol. 5. Translated by Remigius Storf. Kempten: Kösel, 1912.

———. *Eine Elfapostelmoral oder die X-Rezension der "Beiden Wege".* München: Lentner, 1903.

———. "Eucharistievollzug und Eucharistieverständnis in der Didache." In *The Eucharist—Its Origins and Contexts: Sacred Meal, Communal Meal, Table Fellowship in Late Antiquity, Early Judaism, and Early Christianity*, edited by D. Hellholm and D. Sänger, 276–89. Wissenschaftliche Untersuchungen zum Neuen Testament 376. Tübingen: Mohr Siebeck, 2017.

———. *Griechische Zauberpapyri und das Gemeinde und Dankgebet im I. Klemensbriefe.* Texte und Untersuchungen 34.2. Leipzig: Hinrichs, 1909.

Schlecht, Joseph. *Doctrina XII Apostolorum: Die Apostellehre in der Liturgie der katholischen Kirche.* Freiburg im Breisgau: Herder, 1901.

Schmidt, Carl. *Der erste Clemensbrief in altkoptischer Übersetzung.* Texte und Untersuchungen 32.1. Leipzig: Hinrichs, 1908.

Schmidt, Moritz, ed. *Hesychii Alexandrini Lexicon.* Vol. 3. Jenae: Maukius, 1861.

Schmiedel, P. W. "Simon Peter." In *Encyclopedia Biblica*, edited by T. K. Cheyne and J. Sutherland Black, 4:4559–4627. 4 vols. London: Black, 1899–1903.

Schmitt, Tassilo. *Paroikie und Oikoumene. Sozial und mentalitätsgeschichtliche Untersuchungen zum 1.* Clemensbrief. Beihefte zur Zeitschrift für die neutestamentliche Wissenschaft 110. Berlin: de Gruyter, 2002.

Schöllgen, Georg, and Wilhelm Geerlings, eds. and trans. *Didache: Zwölf-Apostel-Lehre. Traditio Apostolica. Apostolische Überlieferung.* Fontes Christiani 1. Freiburg: Herder, 1991.

Schürer, Emil. "Die Juden im bosporanischen Reiche und die Genossenschaften der σεβόμενοι θεὸν ὕψιστον ebendaselbst." *Sitzungsberichte der Königlich Preußischen Akademie der Wissenschaften zu Berlin* (1897) 200–225.

———. *Geschichte des jüdischen Volkes im Zeitalter Jesu Christi.* Vol. 2. 3rd ed. Leipzig: Hinrichs, 1901.

———. *Geschichte des jüdischen Volkes im Zeitalter Jesu Christi.* Vol. 3. 3rd ed. Leipzig: Hinrichs, 1901.

Schüßler, Wilhelm. "Ist der zweite Clemensbrief ein einheitliches Ganzes?" *Zeitschrift für Kirchengeschichte* 28 (1907) 1–13.

Seeberg, A. *Die beiden Wege und das Aposteldekret.* Leipzig: A. Deichert, 1906.

———. *Die Didache des Judentums und der Urchristenheit.* Leipzig: A. Deichert, 1908.

———. *Das Evangelium Christi.* Leipzig: A Deichert, 1905.

———. *Der Katechismus der Urchristenheit.* Leipzig: A. Deichert, 1903.

———. *Lehrbuch der* Dogmengeschichte I. *Die Anfänge des Dogmas im nachapostolischen und altkatholischen Zeitalter.* 2nd ed. Leipzig: A. Deichert, 1908.

Sieffert, Friedrich. "Petrus, the Apostle." In *Realencyklopädie für protestantische Theologie und Kirche*, edited by Johann Jakob Herzog et al., 186–212. 3rd ed. Leipzig: Hinrichs, 1896– 1913.

Skutsch, Franz. "Ein neuer Zeuge der altchristlichen Liturgie." *Archiv für Religionswissenschaft* 13 (1910) 291–305.

Sophocles, E. A. *Greek Lexicon of the Roman and Byzantine Periods from B.C. 146 to A.D. 1100.* New York: Scribner, 1893.

Staerk, Willy, ed. *Altjüdische liturgische Gebete.* Kleine Texte für Vorlesungen und Übungen 58. Bonn: Marcus und Weber, 1910.

Stahl, Arthur. *Patristische Untersuchungen: Der erste brief des romischen Clemens; Ignatius von Antiochien; der Hirt des Hermas.* Leipzig: Deichert, 1901.

Stählin, William O., ed. *Clemens Alexandrinus III. Stromata Buch VII und VIII; Excerpta ex Theodoto; Eclogae propheticae; Quis dives salvetur; Fragmente.* Griechischen christlichen Schriftsteller der ersten drei Jahrhunderte 17. Leipzig: Hinrichs, 1910.

Steimer, Bruno. *Vertex Traditionis. Die Gattung der altchristlichen Kirchenordnungen.* Beihefte zur Zeitschrift für die neutestamentliche Wissenschaft 63. Berlin: de Gruyter, 1998.

Strack, Hermann Leberecht. *Berakhoth der Mišnatraktat "Lobsagungen."* Schriften des Institutum Judaicum in Berlin 44. Leipzig: Hinrichs, 1915.

Swainson, C. A. *The Greek Liturgies: Chiefly from Original Authorities.* Cambridge: Cambridge University Press, 1884.

Taylor, Charles. "The Homily of Pseudo-Clement." *Journal of Philology* 28 (1901) 195–208.

———. *The Teaching of the Twelve Apostles with Illustrations from the Talmud (Lectures).* Cambridge: Bell, 1886.

Tuckett, C. M., ed. *2 Clement: Introduction, Text, and Commentary.* Oxford Apostolic Fathers. Oxford: Oxford University Press, 2012.

Ukert, F. A. *Geographie der Griechen und Römer von den frühesten Zeiten bis auf Ptolemäus.* Vol. 3.1. Weimar: Weimar Verlag, 1846.

Ulrich, J. "Die Apostolichen Väter gestern und heute." In *Die Apostolischen Väter. Eine Einleitung*, edited by Wilhelm Pratscher, 254–71. Uni-Taschenbücher 3272. Göttingen: Vandenhoeck & Ruprecht, 2009.

Vielhauer, Philipp. *Geschichte der urchristlichen Literatur. Einleitung in der Neue Testament, die Apokryphen und die Apostolischen Väter.* Berlin: de Gruyter, 1975.

Völter, Daniel. "Bemerkungen zum ersten Klemensbrief." *Zeitschrift für neutestamentlichen Wissenschaft* 7 (1906) 261–64.

———. *Die apostolischen Väter neu untersucht.* Vol. 1, *Clemens, Hermas, Barnabas.* Leiden: Brill, 1904.

———. *Die apostolischen Väter neu untersucht.* Vol. 2.1, *Die älteste Predigt aus Rom (der sogenannte zweite Clemensbrief).* Leiden: Brill, 1908.

Volz, Paul. *Der Geist Gottes und die verwandten Erscheinungen im Alten Testament und im anschliessenden Judentum.* Tübingen: Mohr, 1910.

———. *Jüdische Eschatologie von Daniel bis Akiba.* Tübingen: Mohr, 1903.

Von Arnim, Hans Friedrich August. *Stoicorum veterum fragmenta.* 3 vols. Leipzig: Teubner, 1903.

Von der Goltz, Eduard. *Das Gebet in der ältesten Christenheit: Eine geschichtliche Untersuchung.* Leipzig: Hinrichs, 1901.

Von Gebhardt, Oscar. *Ausgewählte Märtyreracten und andere Urkunden aus der Verfolgungszeit der christlichen Kirche.* Berlin: Duncker, 1902.

Von Gebhardt, Oscar, et al. *Patrum apostolicorum opera ed. minor.* 5th ed. Leipzig: Hinrichs, 1906.

———. *Patrum apostolicorum opera I.* 2nd ed. Leipzig: Hinrichs, 1876.

Von Harnack, Adolf. *Apokrypha. Band 4. Die apokryphen Briefe des Paulus an die Laodicener und Korinther.* Kleine Texte für Vorlesungen und Übungen 12. Bonn: Marcus und Weber, 1905.

———. "Apostellehre." In *Realenzyklopädie,* edited by Johann Jakob Herzog et al., 1:711–30. 3rd ed. 24 vols. Leipzig: Hinrichs, 1896–1913.

———. "Der erste Klemensbrief: Eine Studie zur Bestimmung des Charakters des ältesten Heidenchristentums." *Sitzungsberichte der Preußischen Akademie der Wissenschaften: Philosophisch-historische Klasse* (1909) 38–61.

———. *Die Apostellehre und die Jüdischen beiden Wege.* 2nd ed. Leipzig: Hinrichs, 1895.

———. *Die Mission und Ausbreitung des Christentums in den ersten drei Jahrhunderten.* Volume 1. 3rd ed. Leipzig: Hinrichs, 1915.

———. *Entstehung und Entwicklung der Kirchenverfassung und des Kirchenrechts in den zwei ersten Jahrhunderten: Nebst einer Kritik der Abhandlung R. Sohm's: Wesen und Ursprung des Katholizismus und Untersuchungen über "Evangelium," "Wort Gottes" und Das trinitarische Bekenntnis: Verfassung u. Recht d. alten Kirche.* Leipzig: Hinrichs, 1910.

———. "The First Letter of Clement: A Study to Determine the Character of the Oldest Form of Gentile Christianity." In *The Letter of the Roman Church to the Corinthian Church from the Era of Domitian: 1 Clement,* edited and translated by Jacob N. Cerone, 144–68. Classic Studies on the Apostolic Fathers 1. Eugene, OR: Pickwick, 2021.

———. *Geschichte der altchristlichen Literatur bis Eusebius.* Vol. 1, *Die Ueberlieferung und der Bestand.* Leipzig: Mohr, 1893.

———. *Geschichte der altchristlichen Literatur bis Eusebius.* Vol. 2.1, *Die Chronologie.* Leipzig: Mohr, 1897.

———. *Lehrbuch der Dogmengeschichte I. Die Entstehung des kirchlichen Dogmas.* 4th ed. Tübingen: Mohr, 1909.

———. *Lehre der zwölf Apostel: Nebst Untersuchungen zur ältesten Geschichte der Kirchenverfassung und des Kirchenrechts.* Texte und Untersuchungen zur Geschichte der altchristlichen Literatur 2. Leipzig: Hinrich, 1884.

———. *Militia Christi: Die christliche Religion und der Soldatenstand in den ersten drei Jahrhunderten.* Tübingen: Mohr, 1905.

———. *Reden und Aufsätze.* Volume 1. 2nd ed. Gieszen: Töpelmann, 1906.

———. "Ueber den sogenannten zweiten Brief des Clemens an die Korinther." *Zeitschrift für Kirchengeschichte* 1 (1877) 264–83, 329–64.

———. "Zum Ursprung des sogenannte zweiten Clemensbriefes." *Zeitschrift für die Neutestamentliche Wissenschaft* 6 (1905) 67–71.

Von Humboldt, Alexander. *Kritische Untersuchungen über die historische Entwicklung der geografischen Kenntnisse von der neuen Welt.* Berlin: Nicolai'schen Buchhandlung, 1892.

Von Otto, Johann Karl Theodor. *Corpus Apologetarum Christianorum Saeculi Secundi.* Vol. 8. Lena: Mauke, 1861.

Von Schubert, Hans. "Der sogenannte 2. Clemensbrief, eine Gemeindepredigt." In *Handbuch zu den neutestamentlichen Apokryphen*, edited by Edgar Hennecke, 248–55. Tübingen: Mohr, 1904.

———. "Der sogenannte zweite Clemensbrief, eine Gemeindepredigt." In *Neutestamentliche Apokryphen*, edited by Edgar Hennecke, 172–79. Tübingen: Mohr, 1904.

Von Soden, Hans. "ΜΥΣΤΗΡΙΟΝ und sacramentum in den ersten zwei Jahrhunderten der Kirche." *Zeitschrift für die Neutestamentliche Wissenschaft* 12 (1911) 188–227.

Von Sybel, Ludwig. *Christliche Antike: Einführung in die altchristliche Kunst*. Marburg: Elwert, 1909.

Von Wilamowitz-Moellendorff, Ulrich. *Griechisches Lesebuch*. Vol. 1.2. Berlin: Weidmann, 1906.

———. *Griechisches Lesebuch*. Vol. 2. Berlin: Weidmann, 1912.

Wachsmuth, Curt, ed. *Anthologium*. Berolini: Apud Weidmannos, 1884–1912.

Wake, William. *The Genuine Epistles of the Apostolic Fathers*. Philadelphia: Davis, 1846.

Warns, Rüdiger. "Untersuchungen zum 2. Clemens-Brief." PhD diss., University of Marburg, 1989.

Weber, F. W. *Jüdische Theologie: Auf Grund des Talmud und verwandter Schriften*. 2nd ed. Leipzig: Dörffling & Franke, 1897.

Wehofer, Thomas M. "Untersuchungen zur altchristlichen Epistolographie." *Sitzungsberichte der Wiener Akademie, philosophisch-historische Klasse* 143.17 (1901) 102–37.

Weinel, Heinrich. *Die Wirkungen des Geistes und der Geister im nachapostolischen Zeitalter bis Irenäus*. Freiburg: Mohr, 1899.

Weiß, Johannes. *Das Urchristentum*. Göttingen: Vandenhoeck & Ruprecht, 1917.

———. *Der erste Korintherbrief*. Meyers kritisch-exegetischer Kommentar über das Neue Testament. 9th ed. Göttingen: Vandenhoeck & Ruprecht, 1910.

Weizsäcker, Carl. *Das apostolische Zeitalter der christlichen Kirche*. Freiburg: Mohr, 1902.

Wendland, Paul. "Beiträge zu athenischer Politik und Publicistik des vierten Jahrhunderts." *Nachrichten von der Königlichen Gesellschaft der Wissenschaften zu Göttingen, Philologisch-historische Klasse* 1 (1910) 330–34.

———. *Die hellenistisch-römische Kultur in ihren Beziehungen zum Judentum und Christentum: Die urchristlichen Literaturformen*. Handbuch zum Neuen Testament 1. 2nd ed. Tübingen: Mohr, 1912.

———. "Σωτήρ." *Zeitschrift für die Neutestamentliche Wissenschaft* 5 (1904) 335–53.

Wengst, Klaus. *Die Apostolischen Väter. Eingeleitet, herausgegeben, übertragen und erläutert*. Schriften des Urchristentums. Zweiter Teil. Darmstadt: Wissenschaftliche Buchgesellschaft, 1984.

Wessely, Carl. "Griechische Zauberpapyrus von Paris und London." *Denkschriften der Akademie der Wissenschaften in Wien, philosophisch-historische Klasse* 36 (1888) 27–208.

Wetter, Gills P. *Phōs: Eine Untersuchung über hellenistische Frömmigkeit, zugleich ein Beitrag zum Verständnis des Manichäismus*. Leipzig: Harrassowitz, 1915.

Weyman, Carl. "Analecta VI. Liturgisches aus Novatian und dem Martyrium der kappadokischen Drillinge." *Historisches Jahrbuch* 29 (1908) 575–90.

Wiedemann, Alfred. *Herodots zweites Buch mit sachlichen Erläuterungen*. Leipzig: Teubner, 1890.

Wilcken, Ulrich, and Ludwig Mitteis. *Grundzüge und Chrestomathie der Papyruskunde.* Vol. 1.2. Leipzig: Teubner, 1912.

Windisch, Hans. *Taufe und Sünde im ältesten Christentum.* Tübingen: Mohr, 1908.

Wobbermin, Georg. *Religionsgeschichtliche Studien zur Frage der Beeinflussung des Urchristentums durch das antike Mysterienwesen.* Berlin: E. Ebering, 1896.

Wohleb, Leo. *Die lateinische Uebersetzung der Didache kritisch und sprachlich untersucht mit einer Wiederherstellung der griechischen Vorlage und einem Anhang ueber das Verbum "altare" und seine Komposita.* Studien zur Geschichte und Kultur des Altertums 7.1. Paderborn: Schoeningh, 1913.

Wrede, William. *Untersuchungen zum ersten Klemensbriefe.* Göttingen: Vandenhoeck & Ruprecht, 1891.

Wünsch, Richard. *Antike Fluchtafeln.* Kleine Texte für Vorlesungen und Übungen 10. Bonn: Marcus und Weber, 1907.

———. *Aus einem griechischen Zauberpapyrus.* Kleine Texte für Vorlesungen und Übungen 84. Bonn: Marcus und Weber, 1911.

Wünsche, Aug. *Der Midrasch Wajikra Rabba Zum ersten Male ins Deutsche übertragen.* Leipzig: Schulze, 1881–85.

Zahn, T. Die. *Forschungen zur Geschichte des neutestamentlichen Kanons und der altkirchlichen Literatur: Der Evangeliencommentar des Theophilus von Antiochien.* Leipzig: Deichert, 1883.

———. *Forschungen zur Geschichte des neutestamentlichen Kanons und der altkirchlichen Literatur: Supplementum Clementinum.* Leipzig: Deichert, 1881.

———. *Forschungen zur Geschichte des neutestamentlichen Kanons und der altkirchlichen Literatur: Tatians Diatessaron.* Leipzig: Deichert, 1881.

———. *Grundriß der Geschichte des neutestamentlichen Kanons: Eine Ergänzung zu der Einleitung in das neue Testament.* 2nd ed. Leipzig: Deichert, 1904.

———. "'Lehre der zwölf Apostel' in Deutschland." *Theologische Literaturzeitung* 26 (1884) 201–4.

———. *Weltverkehr und Kirche während der drei ersten Jahrhunderte Vortrag in den evangelischen Vereinen zu Bremen und Hannover.* Hannover: Meyer, 1877.

Zeller, Eduard. *Die Philosophie der Griechen in ihrer geschichtlichen Entwicklung.* 4th ed. Leipzig: Reisland, 1909.

Zimmermann, Friedrich M. "Die Phönixsage. Ihr religionsgeschichtlicher Ursprung und ihre Verwertung in der Heiligen Schrift und im Dienste kirchenschriftstellerischer Argumentation. Ein Beitrag zur Religionsgeschichte." *Theologie und Glaube* 4 (1912) 202–23.

Index of Authors

Index of Ancient Sources

Old Testament Pseudepigrapha

1 Enoch

1:2	85
1:22	112
10f	112
12:4	85
14	112
14:1	85
21	112
22	172
40:5	202
45:3f	202
51:4	202
53:6	202

Jubilees

15:31f	130
19:9	86

Letter of Aristeas

16	106

Psalms of Solomon

4:8	236
4:10	236
4:21	236
16:4	191
27	57
43:1–3	57

Sibylline Oracles

I 125–98	85
I 127–29	81
I 150–70	81
I 195	85
II 62f	29
II 64	17
II 68f	17
II 78	26
II 79	15
II 80	26
II 88f	14
II 165f	56
II 167	56

III 6.3ff	56
III 36ff	17
III 37	17
VI 26f	57

New Testament

Matthew

1:18	196
3:8	210
3:12	224, 242
5:5	22
5:7	95
5:21f	20
5:22f	53
5:23f	51
5:25f	14
5:39–48	11
5:39–41	11, 13
5:42	11, 14
5:44	11, 196
5:46	11
6	33, 54
6:1–18	240
6:2–6	54
6:9–13	xxxiii
6:13	5
6:14	95
6:15ff	45
6:16	32
6:24	219
7:1f	25, 95
7:15	56
7:13f	7, 170
7:15	44
7:21	215
7:23	216
8:1	196
8:17	99
9:13	213
9:18	196
10:10	43, 49
10:16	218
10:22	55
10:32	214
10:33	214
10:40f	43

Matthew (*continued*)

11:7	109
11:25	137
11:28	218
11:29f	100
12:31	43
12:50	228
15	88
15:8	97, 215
16:26	219
16:27	231, 242
17:12	9
18:6f	166
18:8	178
18:15	53
18:21f	53
18:25	196
18:34	14
19:18	16
19:28	85–86
20:15	23
21:9	41
21:15	41
22:1–10	45, 238
22:11f	221
22:37	215
22:38	9
22:39	9
23:3	45
23:12	23, 190
24	55
24:10	56
24:11	56
24:12	56
24:13	55
24:15	56
24:24	56
24:29	109
24:30f	56, 241
24:30	242
24:31	39, 41
24:42	55
24:44	55
25:1–13	45, 238
25:31	242
25:32	241
25:46	219
26:24	166
27:9	143
27:39	100
27:43	100
28	31
28:19f	5, 240
28:19	6, 31, 166

Mark

2:17	213
2:19	45, 238
3:35	228
4:3	122
4:8	122
4:29	224
6:8	44
7:6	97, 215
8:36	219
9:42	166
9:43	178, 242
9:44–48	242
9:44	223
9:45	178
9:46	223
9:48	223
10:18	194
10:27	126
11:17	237
12:28–34	9
12:28	9
12:29	9
12:30	215
12:31	9
12:39	24
13:1	196
13:22	56
13:25	109
14:21	166
14:38	248
15:28	99
16:15	240

Luke

1:3	238
1:23	53

1 Corinthians (continued)

9:24–27	80, 222
9:25	223
9:26	210
10:3	40
10:6	37
10:13	125
10:16f	237
10:16	51
10:17	39
10:20	30
10:21	37
10:25	30
10:32	170
11:20	142
12	151
12:2	30
12:9	170
12:10	44
12:12–26	151
12:12f	166
12:12	150
12:17	151
12:21	151
12:22	151
12:26	151
12:27	237
12:28	44, 48
13	171
13:2	170
13:4	93
13:7	172
14:16	201
14:24f	18, 44
14:26	245
14:29f	44
14:29	44
14:34f	117
15	120, 227
15:20	121
15:23	121
15:35–38	122
15:37	122
15:52	57
16:2	51
16:3–14	99
16:5	159
16:17	203
16:22	41

2 Corinthians

1:22	220–21
2:4	135
3:11	239
3:18	147, 169
4:4	219
4:16	230
4:18	196
5:10	231
6:9	211
6:13	210
6:16	227
6:18	210
7:1	248
8:9	99
10:17	94
11:13	44
11:25	76
11:32	76
12:20	131
13:13	166

Galatians

1:4	219
2	74
2:2	183
2:6	183
2:9	183
2:20	172
3:1	67
3:7–18	73
3:14	135, 229
3:27	31
4:4	248
4:20	212
4:21	212
4:31	94
5:21	20
6:10	224
6:16	218
6:17	220